Designing Security Architecture Solutions

Designing Security Architecture Solutions

Jay Ramachandran

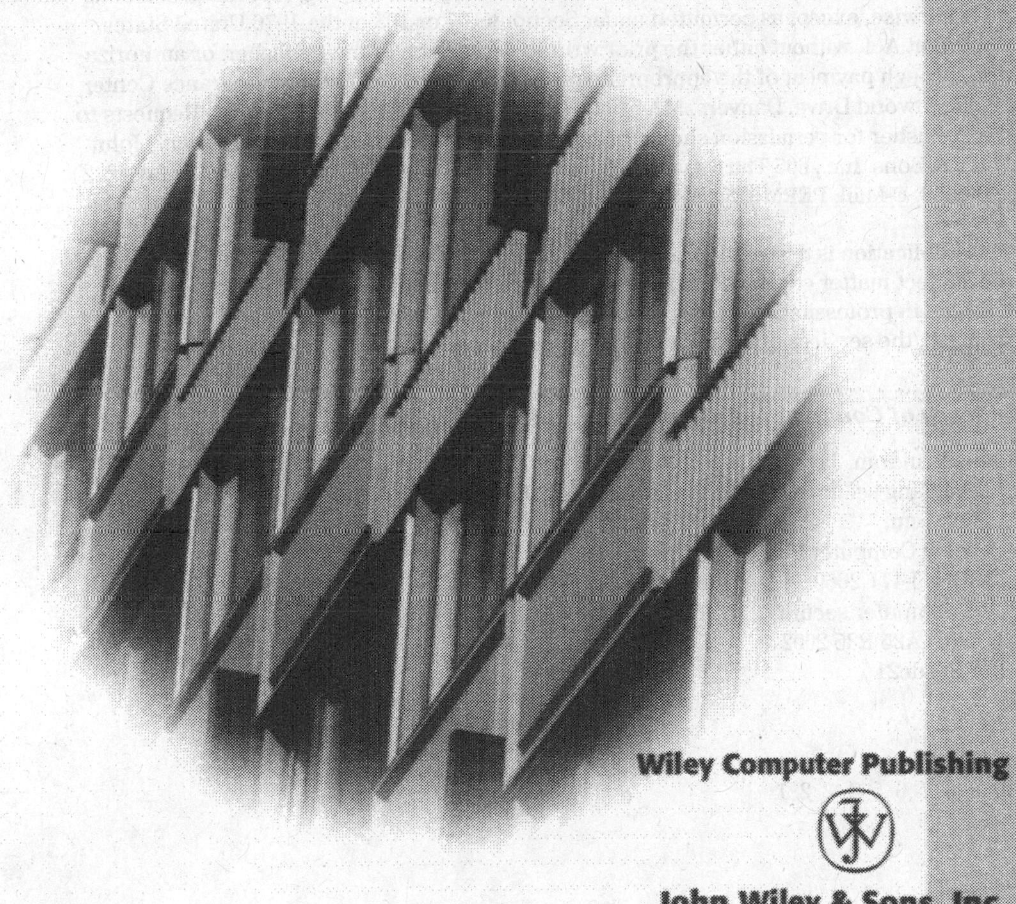

Wiley Computer Publishing

John Wiley & Sons, Inc.

Publisher: Robert Ipsen
Editor: Carol Long
Managing Editor: Micheline Frederick
Developmental Editor: Adaobi Obi
Text Design & Composition: D&G Limited, LLC

This book is printed on acid-free paper. ♾

Published by John Wiley & Sons, Inc.
Published simultaneously in Canada.

Library of Congress Cataloging-in-Publication Data:

Ramachandran, Jay
Designing security architecture solutions / Jay Ramachandran.
p. cm.
"Wiley Computer Publishing."
ISBN: 0-471-20602-4 (acid-free paper)
1. Computer security. I. Title.
QA76.9.A25 R35 2002
005.8—dc21 2001006821

10 9 8 7 6 5 4 3 2 1

For Ronak, Mallika, and Beena

There is an invisible elephant in this book: your application. And, it sits at the center of every topic we touch in each chapter we present. This book is for systems architects who are interested in building security into their applications. The book is designed to be useful to architects in three ways: as an introduction to security architecture, as a handbook on security issues for architecture review, and as a catalog of designs to look for within a security product.

Audience

This book is meant to be a practical handbook on security architecture. It aims to provide software systems architects with a contextual framework for thinking about security. This book is not for code writers directly, although we do talk about code when appropriate. It is targeted toward the growing technical community of people who call themselves systems architects. A systems architect is the technical leader on any large project with overall responsibility for architecture, design, interface definition, and implementation for the system. Architects play nontechnical roles, as well. They are often involved in the planning and feasibility stages of the project, helping its owners make a business case for the system. They must ensure that the project team follows corporate security guidelines and the software development process all the way to delivery. Architects have deep domain knowledge of the application, its function, and its evolution but often are not as experienced in security architecture.

The primary audience for this book consists of project managers, systems architects, and software engineers who need to secure their applications. It provides a conceptual architectural framework that answers the questions, "What is systems security architecture? How should I choose from a bewildering array of security product offerings? How should I then integrate my choices into my software? What common problems occur during this process? How does security affect the other goals of my system architecture? How can I justify the expense of building security into my application?"

If you are currently working on a large project or you have access to the architecture documentation of a software system you are familiar with, keep it handy and use its architecture to give yourself a frame of reference for the discussion. A good application can give additional depth to a particular recommendation or provide context for any architectural issues on security or software design.

ting your hands dirty. Although we introduce and present many security concepts, we would not recommend learning about computer security from this book, because in the interests of covering as many aspects of architecture and security as we can, we will often cheerfully commit the sin of simplification. We will always add references to more detail when we do simplify matters and hope this situation will not confuse the novice reader. We hope that by the end of the book, the systems architects among you will have gained some insights into security while the security experts wryly note our mastery of the obvious. That would mean that we have succeeded in striking the right balance!

Software Architecture

Software architecture in the past 10 years has seen growing respectability. More and more software professionals are calling themselves software *architects* in recognition that enterprise systems are increasingly complex, expensive, and distributed. Applications have raised the bar for feature requirements such as availability, scalability, robustness, and interoperability. At the same time, as a business driver, enterprise security is front and center in the minds of many managers. There is a tremendously diverse community of security professionals providing valuable but complicated services to these enterprise architects. Architects have clear mandates to implement corporate security policy, and many certainly feel a need for guidelines on how to do so. We wrote this book to provide architects with a better understanding of security.

Software development converts requirements into systems, products, and services. Software architecture has emerged as an important organizing principle, providing a framework upon which we hang the mass of the application. Companies are recognizing the value of enterprise architecture guidelines, along with support for process definition, certification of architects, and training. Software architecture promises cost savings by improving release cycle time, reducing software defects, enabling reuse of architecture and design ideas, and improving technical communication.

There are many excellent books on security and on software architecture. There is also a vast and mature collection of academic literature in both areas, many listed in our bibliography. This book targets readers in the intersection of the two fields.

When we use the term *system* or *application* in this book, we mean a collection of hardware and software components on a platform to support a business function with boundaries that demark the inside and outside of the system, along with definitions of interfaces to other systems. Systems have business roles in the company. They belong to business processes and have labels: customer Web application, benefits directory, employee payroll database, customer order provisioning, billing, network management, fulfillment, library document server, and so on.

Security can be approached from perspectives other than the viewpoint of securing a system. A project might be developing a shrink-wrapped product, such as a computer

or naming server; or be working on an infrastructure component, such as a corporate directory. Security goals change with each change in perspective. Our presentation of security principles in this book is general enough to apply to these other viewpoints, which also can benefit from secure design.

Project Objectives versus Security Experience

Companies wish to include security policy into architecture guidelines but run into difficulties trying to chart a path on implementation decisions. Unless we realize that the problem does not lie with our talented and competent development teams but instead lies in their lack of background information about security, we will run into significant resistance project after project—repeatedly going over the same security issues at the architecture review. We must be able to present security issues in an architectural context to guide the project.

As system architects, we would like to believe that all our decisions are driven by technical considerations and business goals. We would like to believe that every time our project team meets to make a decision, we would be consistent—arriving at the same decision no matter who took the day off. Human nature and personal experience inform our decisions as well, however. On a system that is under construction within the confines of budget and time, the strengths of the lead architects and developers can strongly warp the direction and priority of functional and non-functional goals.

An object-oriented methodology guru might spend a fair amount of resources developing the data model and class diagrams. A programmer with a lot of experience building concurrent code might introduce multi-threading everywhere, creating producers and consumers that juggle mutexes, locks, and condition variables in the design. A database designer with experience in one product might bring preconceived notions of how things should be to the project that uses another database. A CORBA expert might engineer interface definitions or services with all kinds of detail to anticipate evolution, just because he knows how. A Web designer on the front-end team might go crazy with the eye candy of the day on the user interface. None of these actions are inherently bad, and much of it is very valuable and clearly useful. At the end, however, if the project does not deliver what the customer wants with adequate performance and reliability, we have failed.

What if no one on your team has much experience with security? In a conflict between an area where we are somewhat lost and another where we can accomplish a significant amount of productive work, we pick the task where we will make the most progress. The problem arises with other facets of systems architecture as well, which might fall by the wayside because of a lack of experience or a lack of priority. Project teams declare that they cannot be highly available, cannot do thorough testing, or cannot do performance modeling because they do not have the time or the money to do so. This situation might often be the case, but if no one on the team has expertise building

then human nature might drive behavior away from these tasks.

Security architecture often suffers from this syndrome. Fortunately, we have a solution to our knowledge gap: Buy security and hire experts to secure our system. This point is where vendors come in to help us integrate their solutions into our applications.

Vendor Security Products

The Internet boom has also driven the growth of security standards and technologies. Software vendors provide feature-rich security solutions and components at a level of complexity and maturity beyond almost all projects. Building our own components is rarely an option, and security architecture work is primarily integration work. In today's environment, the emerging dominance of vendor products aiding software development for enterprise security cannot be ignored.

We interact with vendors on many levels, and our understanding of their product offerings depends on a combination of information from many sources: marketing, sales, customer service support, vendor architects, and other applications with experience with the product. We have to be careful when viewing the entire application from the perspective of the security vendor. Looking at the application through a fisheye lens to get a wide-angle view could give us a warped perspective, with all of the elements of the system distorted around one central component: their security product. Here are three architectural flaws in vendor products:

The product enjoys a central place in the architecture. The product places itself at the center of the universe, which might not be where you, as the architect, would place it.

The product hides assumptions. The product hides assumptions that are critical to a successful deployment or does not articulate these assumptions as clear architectural prerequisites and requirements to the project.

The context behind the product is unclear. Context describes the design philosophy behind the purpose and placement of the product in some market niche. What is the history of the company with respect to building this particular security product? The vendor might be the originator of the technology, might have diversified into the product space, acquired a smaller company with expertise in the security area, or might have a strong background in a particular competing design philosophy.

Vendors have advantages over architects.

- They tend to have comparatively greater security expertise.
- They often do not tell architects about gaps in their own product's design voluntarily. You have to ask specific questions about product features.
- They rarely present their products in terms clearly comparable with those of their competitors. Project teams have to expend effort in understanding the feature sets well enough to do so themselves.

responsibility to the user, administrator, application process, or other side of an interface, and so on.

- They rarely support the evolution path of an application over a two- to three-year timeframe.

This book is meant to swing the advantage back in the architect's court. We will describe how projects can evaluate vendor products, discover limitations and boundaries within solutions, and overcome them. Vendors are not antagonistic to the project's objectives, but miscommunication during vendor management might cause considerable friction as the application evolves and we learn more about real-world deployment issues surrounding the product. Building a good relationship between application architect and lead vendor engineers is critical and holds long-run benefits for the project and vendor alike. We hope that better information will lead to better decisions on security architecture.

Our Goals in Writing This Book

On a first level, we will present an overview of the software process behind systems architecture. We focus on the architecture review, a checkpoint within the software development cycle that gives the project an opportunity to validate the solution architecture and verify that it meets requirements. We will describe how to assess a system for security issues, how to organize the architecture to add security as a system feature, and how to provide architectural context information that will help minimize the impact of implementing one security choice over another. We emphasize including security early in the design cycle instead of waiting until the application is in production and adding security as an afterthought.

On a second level, this book will provide hands-on help in understanding common, repeating patterns of design in the vast array of security products available. This book will help describe the vocabulary used surrounding security products as applied to systems architecture. We borrow the term *patterns* from the Object Patterns design community but do not intend to use the term beyond its common-sense meaning. Specifically, something is a security pattern if we can give it a name, observe its design appearing repeatedly in many security products, and see some benefit in defining and describing the pattern.

On a third level, we describe common security architecture issues and talk about security issues for specific technologies. We use three layers of application granularity to examine security.

- Low-level issues regarding code review, cryptographic primitives, and trusting code.
- Mid-level issues regarding middleware or Web services, operating systems, hosts, and databases.
- High-level issues regarding security components, conflicts between security and other system goals, and enterprise security.

we justify the expense of securing our application?

Reading This Book

We have organized the book into five parts, and aside from the chapters in Part I, any chapter can be read on its own. We would recommend that readers with specific interests and skills try the following tracks, however:

Project and software process managers. Begin by reading Chapters 1, 2, 3, 4, and 15. These chapters present vocabulary and basic concerns surrounding security architecture.

Security assessors. Begin by reading Chapters 1, 2, 3, 4, 13, and 14. Much of the information needed to sit in a review and understand the presentation is described there.

Developers. Read Chapters 1 through 4 in order and then Chapters 5 through 12 in any order—looking for the particular platform or software component that you are responsible for developing.

Systems architects. Read the book from start to finish, one complete part at a time. The presentation order, from Process to Technology to Enterprise concerns, parallels the requirements of systems architecture for a large application. All of these topics are now considered part of the domain of software architects.

Business executives. Read Chapters 1, 2, 16, and 17 for a start and then continue as your interests guide you with anything in between.

Outline of the Book

Each chapter is a mix of the abstract and the concrete. For more detail on any technical matter, please see the list of bibliographic references at the end of the book. Each chapter will also contain questions to ask at an architecture review on a specific subject.

Part I, Architecture and Security, introduces the business processes of architecture review and security assessments. We describe the basics of security architecture and a catalog of security patterns.

Chapter 1, "Architecture Reviews," describes a key checkpoint in the software development cycle where architects can ask and answer the question, "Does the solution fit the problem?" We present a description of the review process along with its benefits.

Chapter 2, "Security Assessments," defines the process of security assessment by using the Federal Information Technology Security Assessment Framework along with other industry standards. We describe how assessments realize many of the benefits of architecture reviews within the specific context of security.

describe the concepts of authentication, authorization, access control, auditing, confidentiality, integrity, and nonrepudiation from an architectural viewpoint. We discuss other security properties and models of access control.

Chapter 4, "Architecture Patterns in Security," defines the terms architectural style and pattern and describes how each of the basic security architecture requirements in the previous chapter lead to common implementation patterns. We also present a catalog of security patterns.

Part II, Low-Level Architecture, describes common issues surrounding developing secure software at the code level. We introduce the basics of cryptography and discuss its application in trusting code and in communications security protocols.

Chapter 5, "Code Review," discusses the importance of code review from a security viewpoint. We describe buffer overflow exploits, one of the most common sources of security vulnerabilities. We discuss strategies for preventing exploits based on this attack. We also discuss security in Perl and the Java byte code verifier.

Chapter 6, "Cryptography," introduces cryptographic primitives and protocols and the difficulty an architect faces in constructing and validating the same. We present guidelines for using cryptography.

Chapter 7, "Trusted Code," discusses one consequence of the growth of the Web: the emergence of digitally delivered software. We describe the risks of downloading active content over the Internet, some responses to mitigating this risk, and why code is hard to trust.

Chapter 8, "Secure Communications," introduces two methods for securing sessions—the SSL protocol and IPSec—and discusses the infrastructure support needed to implement such protocols. We discuss security layering and describe why is there plenty of security work left to be done at the application level.

Part III, Mid-Level Architecture, introduces common issues faced by application architects building security into their systems from a component and connector viewpoint.

Chapter 9, "Middleware Security," discusses the impact of platform independence, a central goal of middleware products, on security. We describe the CORBA security specification, its service modules, and the various levels of CORBA-compliant security and administrative support. We also discuss other middleware security products at a high level.

Chapter 10, "Web Security," is a short introduction to Web security from an architecture viewpoint, including information on security for standards such as J2EE.

Chapter 11, "Application and OS Security," reviews the components that go into the design of an application, including OS security, network services, process descriptions, interface definitions, process flow diagrams, workflow maps, and administration tools. We discuss operating systems hardening and other deployment and development issues with building secure production applications. We also discuss UNIX ACLs.

architecture. We discuss the evolution of databases from a security standpoint and describe several models of securing persistent data. We also discuss the security features within Oracle, a leading commercial database product.

Part IV, High-Level Architecture, introduces common issues faced by enterprise architects charged with guiding software architecture discipline across many individual applications, all sharing some "enterprise" characteristic, such as being components of a high-level business process or domain.

Chapter 13, "Security Components," discusses the building blocks available to systems architects and some guidelines for their usage. The list includes single sign-on servers, PKI, firewalls, network intrusion detection, directories, along with audit and security management products. We discuss issues that architects should or should not worry about and components they should or should not try to use. We also discuss the impact of new technologies like mobile devices that cause unique security integration issues for architects.

Chapter 14, "Security and Other Architectural Goals," discusses the myths and realities about conflicts between security and other architectural goals. We discuss the impact of security on other goals such as performance, high availability, robustness, scalability, interoperability, maintainability, portability, ease of use, adaptability, and evolution. We conclude with guidelines for recognizing conflicts in the architecture, setting priorities, and deciding which goal wins.

Chapter 15, "Enterprise Security Architecture," discusses the question, "How do we architect security and security management across applications?" We discuss the assets stored in the enterprise and the notion of database-of-record status. We also discuss common issues with enterprise infrastructure needs for security, such as user management, corporate directories, and legacy systems. We present and defend the thesis that enterprise security architecture is above all a data-management problem and propose a resolution using XML-based standards.

Part V, Business Cases for Security, introduces common issues faced by architects making a business case for security for their applications.

Chapter 16, "Building Business Cases for Security," asks why it is hard to build business cases for security. We present the *Saved Losses Model* for justifying security business cases. We assign value to down time, loss of revenue, and reputation and assess the costs of guarding against loss. We discuss the role of an architect in incident prevention, industry information about costs, and the reconstruction of events across complex, distributed environments in a manner that holds water in a court of law. We ask whether security is insurable in the sense that we can buy hacker insurance that works like life insurance or fire insurance and discuss the properties that make something insurable.

Chapter 17, "Conclusion," reviews security architecture lessons that we learned. We present some advice and further resources for architects.

We conclude with a bibliography of resources for architects and a glossary of acronyms.

Online Information

Although we have reviewed the book and attempted to remove any technical errors, some surely remain. Readers with comments, questions, or bug fixes can email me at book@jay-ramachandran.com or visit my Web site at www.jay-ramachandran.com for Web links referred to in the text, updated vendor product information, or other information.

Conclusion

A note before we start: although it might seem that way sometimes, our intent is not to present vendors and their security offerings as in constant conflict with your application and its objectives and needs. Security vendors provide essential services, and no discussion of security will be complete without recognition of their value and the role that their products play.

Security is commonly presented as a conflict between the good and the bad, with our application on one hand and the evil hacker on the other. This dichotomy is analogous to describing the application as a medieval castle and describing its defense: "Put the moat here," "Make it yea deep," "Use more than one portcullis," "Here's where you boil the oil," "Here's how you recognize a ladder propped against the wall," and so on. This view presents security as an active conflict, and we often use the terms of war to describe details. In this case, we view ourselves as generals in the battle and our opponents as Huns (my apologies if you are a Hun, I'm just trying to make a point here).

Our basic goal is to frame the debate about systems security around a different dichotomy, one that recognizes that the castle also has a role in peacetime, as a market place for the surrounding villages, as the seat of authority in the realm, as a cantonment for troops, and as a place of residence for its inhabitants. Think of the system's architect as the mayor of the town who has hired a knight to assemble a standing army for its defense. The knight knows warfare, but the mayor has the money. Note that we said that the architect is the mayor and not the king—that would be the customer.

I thank John Wiley & Sons for the opportunity to write this book, especially my editor, Carol Long. Carol read the proposal on a plane flight back from RSA 2001 and sent me a response the day she received it. From the start, Carol shared my perspective that security as seen by a software architect presents a unique and interesting viewpoint. I thank her for her belief in the idea. I thank my assistant editor, Adaobi Obi, for her careful reviews of the first draft and her many suggestions for improving the presentation. I thank my managing editor, Micheline Frederick, for her many ideas for improving the readability of the manuscript. I would also like to thank Radia Perlman for some valuable advice on the structure of this book at an early stage.

I thank the technical review team of Arun Iyer and Jai Chhugani for their excellent and insightful remarks, their thorough and careful chapter-by-chapter review, and many suggestions that have improved the text immeasurably. I also thank Steve Bellovin and Radia Perlman for reading the final draft of the manuscript. I am solely responsible for any errors and omissions that remain. Please visit my Web site www.jay-ramachandran.com for the book for more information on security architecture, including Wiley's official links for the book, errata submissions, or permission requests.

I thank Tim Long, Don Aliberti, Alberto Avritzer, and Arun Iyer for their guidance in the past and for the many ideas and opinions that they offered me on security, architecture, and computer science. I am sure that the four of you will enjoy reading this book, because so much of it is based on stuff I learned from you in the conversations we have had.

I am heavily indebted to and thank the many security gurus, assessors, and developers I have had the pleasure of working with over the years on many systems, feasibility studies, applications, and consulting services. Their remarks and insight pepper this book: Steve Bellovin, Pete Bleznyk, Frank Carey, Juan Castillo, Dick Court, Joe DiBiase, Dave Gross, Daryl Hollar, Phil Hollembeak, Steve Meyer, Betsy Morgan, Shapour Neshatfar, Dino Perone, Bob Reed, Greg Rogers, George Schwerdtman, Gopi Shankavaram, Joyce Weekley, and Vivian Ye.

I thank Jane Bogdan, Dennis Holland, Brenda Liggs, and other members of the research staff at the Middletown Library for their assistance. I would also like to thank the staff of Woodbridge Public Library, my home away from home.

I am especially grateful to the brilliant and dedicated group of people at AT&T who call themselves certified software architects. You made my life as Architecture Review Coordinator so much easier. On my behalf and on behalf of all the projects you have helped, I

Irwin Dunietz, John Eddy, Neal Fildes, Cindy Flaspohler, Tim Frommeyer, Don Gerth, Doug Ginn, Abhay Jain, Steve Meyer, Mike Newbury, Randy Ringeisen, Hans Ros, Ray Sandfoss, George Schwerdtman, Manoucher Shahrava, Mohammed Shakir, David Simen, Anoop Singhal, David Timidaiski, Tim Velten, and Dave Williamson.

Special thanks go to many friends and their families for countless hours over two decades spent debating all things under the sun, some of which related to computing and engineering. I thank Pankaj Agarwal, Alok Baveja, Paolo Bucci, Jai and Veena Chhugani, Anil and Punam Goel, Nilendu and Urmila Gupta, Nirmala Iyer, Aarati Kanekar, Atul and Manu Khare, K. Ananth Krishnan, Asish and Anandi Law, Pushkal Pandey, Sushant and Susan Patnaik, Mahendra Ramachandran, Ming Jye-Sheu, and Manoj and Neeta Tandon for their friendship.

This book would not exist but for my family. I thank my family, Jayashree, Akhila and Madhavan, Bhaskar and Vidyut, and especially Amma, Appa, Aai, and Daiyya for their blessings. Without their confidence, support, and help in so many ways, I could not have attempted let alone completed this task. Hats off to you all. To Ronak and Mallika, for their patience and humor, and last but not least, to Beena, for all the support in the world. You steered the ship through the storm while the first mate was down in the bilge thinking this book up. This book is for you.

Architecture and Security

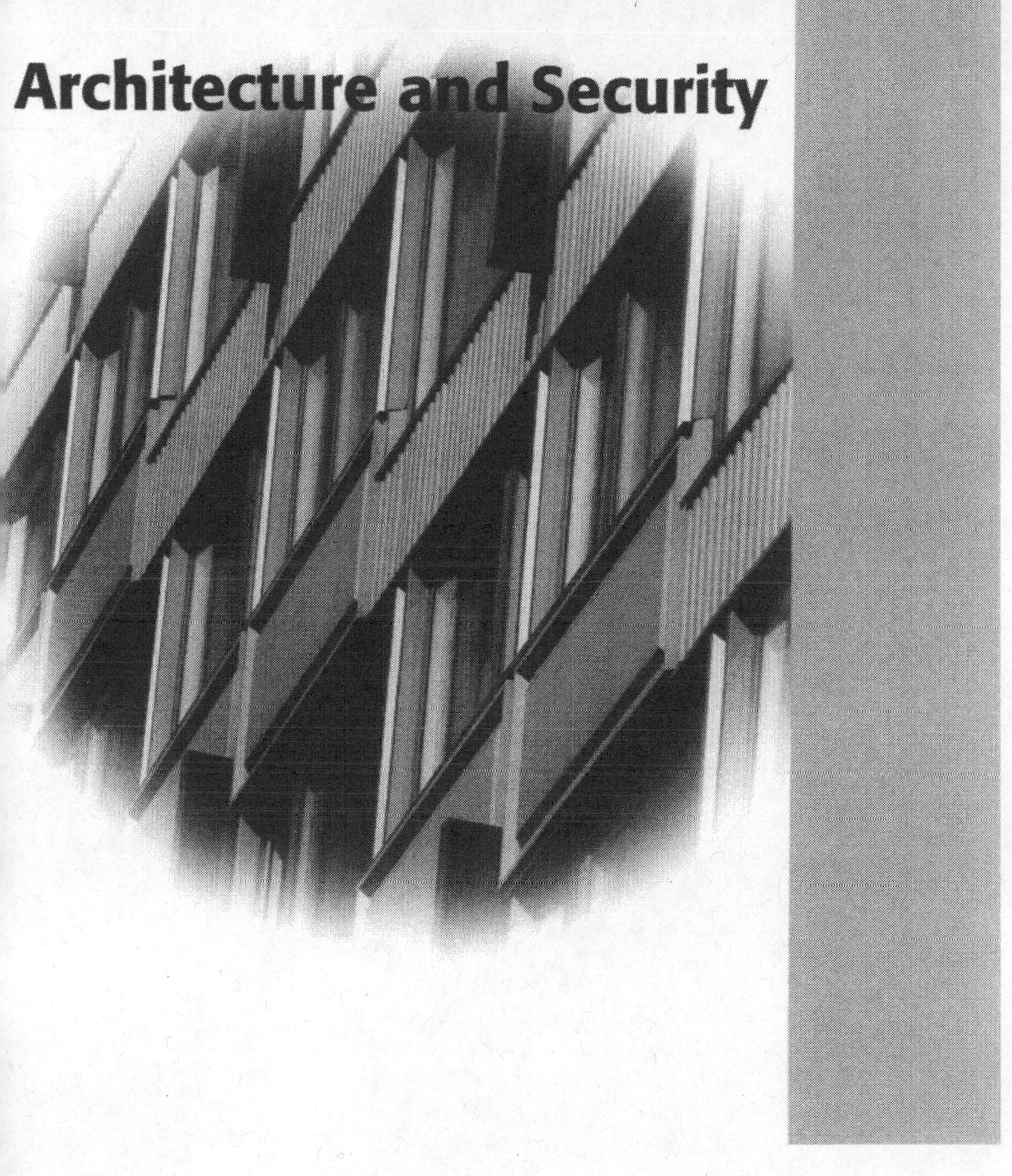

1

Architecture Reviews

Software architecture review is a key step in the software development cycle. In this chapter, we will describe the process of conducting architecture reviews. We need reviews to validate the architectural choices made by projects within our organization. Each project makes its own choices in the context of solving a specific problem, but we need a coordinated effort—a software process—across projects to make convergent choices. Software process can prevent projects from taking divergent evolutionary paths formed from conflicting or contradicting decisions.

Each project's passage from requirements definition to product delivery can be considered an instance of the implementation of some software process. The organization that owns the project and the system that it delivers might also be interested in evaluating the success of the software process itself. A successful process helps the project meet the customer's goals, within budget and on time.

Simply put, project stakeholders and external reviewers meet at an architecture review to discuss a proposed solution to a problem. The outcome of the meeting will be an answer to the question, "Does the solution fit the problem?"

Software Process

Software process codifies a set of practices that provides measurable and repeatable methods for building quality into software. As corporations struggle with the complexities of developing software systems, acquiring resources, providing services, deploying products, operating infrastructures, and managing evolution, the adoption of software processes has been seen as a key step in bringing order to chaos. In turn, standards bodies have grown conceptual frameworks around the software process definition itself. We will simplify the vast quantity of literature in this field to three reference levels.

and conformity of particular instances of software processes used within an organization. Examples include the Software Engineering Institute's *Capability Maturity Model* (CMM) and supporting standards like the *Software Process Improvement and Capability dEtermination* (SPICE) model for defining frameworks for the assessment of software processes. These frameworks guide organizations through process deployment, assessment, measurement, improvement, and certification. They can be applied to any particular choice of software process.

Software meta-processes recognize critical success factors within any software process definition and measure the project's success in achieving these factors. This function is required for the process itself to be considered successful. One critical success factor for any software system is validation of the system architecture document.

Software processes. These define methodologies for building complex software systems. Rational's Unified Process, built on the principle of use-case driven, architecture-centric, iterative, and incremental design through a four-phase evolution is an example of a software process.

Architecture Models. These model the system's architecture as a collection of components, joined by connectors, operating under constraints, and with a rationale that justifies the mapping of requirements to functionality throughout the architecture. Good architecture models presenting the system from multiple viewpoints are vital to the success of any software process. Kruchten's 4+1 View Model from Rational [Kru95]; Soni, Nord, and Hofmeister's alternative four view model from research at Siemens [HSN99]; and the *Open Systems Interconnectivity* (OSI) standard for a *Reference Model for Open Distributed Processing*, [ISO96], [MM00], are all examples of architecture models.

Reviews and the Software Development Cycle

Software development flows iteratively or incrementally through a sequence of steps: feasibility, requirements definition, architecture, analysis, design, development, testing, delivery, and maintenance. Software experience has created a wide variety of tools, processes, and methodologies to assist with each step. A formal software development process manages complexity. A software process attempts to guide the order of activities, direct development tasks, specify artifacts, and monitor and measure activities by using concrete metrics [JBR99].

There are many different software process movements, each with its own philosophical underpinnings on the essential nature of developing systems software. We will describe one approach to software process definition, the Unified Process, and its notion of modeling architecture, design, and development, but we do not state a preference for this process. The expertise of the lead architect and the experience of the project's management play a far greater role in the project's success than any software process. We can-

software practice and process implementation will help a dysfunctional project.

Independent of the software process and architectural methodology embraced within your organization, an architecture review, customized to that process and methodology, is a valuable source of feedback, advice, redirection, and risk assessment information. Some industry metrics state that as many as 80 percent of projects fail (when we define success as the delivery of a system under budget, on time, and with full customer acceptance), and methods for improving a system's architecture can only help against those odds.

Reviews call on external objective technical resources to look at the project's choices and to critique them. Reviews interrupt the process flow after architecture and design are complete and before the project has invested time and money in the implementation and coding phase. At this point, the system requirements are hopefully stable, all stakeholders have signed off on the project schedule, and prototyping efforts and experience have produced data and use-case models that break down the deliverables into well-defined artifacts. The greatest risk to the project at this stage is poor architecture, often driven by a lack of adequate communication about the assumptions behind the design. Issues that are designated as trivial or obvious by one part of the project might have hidden and expensive consequences known only to another part of the project. Reviews lay all of the technical details out in the open. They enable all stakeholders to see the system from all vantage points. Issues raised in the review can result, if correctly resolved, in significant savings in cost and time to the project.

Software Process and Architecture Models

Notwithstanding the groundbreaking work of Alexander on pattern languages and of Parnas on software architecture, the origin of the growth of software architecture as a formal academic discipline is often cited as Perry and Wolf's seminal paper [PW92], where they described software systems in abstract terms of elements, forms, and rationale. Garlan and Shaw in [GS96] extended this viewpoint, classifying software systems according to a catalog of architectural styles—each expressing the structure of the underlying system in terms of components joined by connectors, operating under constraints. Gacek et. al. [GACB95] added the condition that the architecture should also provide a rationale explaining why it satisfied the system's goals. We refer the reader to several excellent references in the bibliography, [GS96], [Kru95], [BCK98], and [JRvL98], for example, for definition and extensive detail on several conceptual technical frameworks for the description of system architecture as the composition of multiple system views. CMU's Software Engineering Institute home page, www.sei.cmu.edu/, is an excellent starting point for resources on software architecture. Its online bibliography has almost 1,000 references on the subject.

Architecture models attempt to describe a system and its architecture from multiple viewpoints, each supporting specific functional and non-functional requirements—thereby simplifying the apparent complexity of the system. Each view might require its own notation and analysis. The implementation of the system requires resolution of the

ments. Sequence diagrams, traces, process histories capturing interactions within and between views, or other timeline-based methods are necessary to show how components work together.

We will briefly discuss two architecture definition models.

- Kruchten's 4+1 View Model
- The OSI Standard Reference Model for Open Distributed Processing (RM-ODP)

We will also discuss one example of a software development process, Rational's Unified Process. The success of any architectural process depends on many factors. Again, we stress that we do not wish to recommend any particular model for architecture description, but we will use this short overview to introduce vocabulary and set the stage for the activity of conducting architecture reviews.

Kruchten's 4+1 View Model

Philippe Kruchten's 4+1 View Model, seen in Figure 1.1, from Rational Corporation describes four main views of software architecture plus a fifth view that ties the other four together.

The views are as follows:

- The *logical view* describes the objects or object models within the architecture that support behavioral requirements.
- The *process view* describes the architecture as a logical network of communicating processes. This view assigns each method of the object model to a thread of execution and captures concurrency and synchronization aspects of the design.

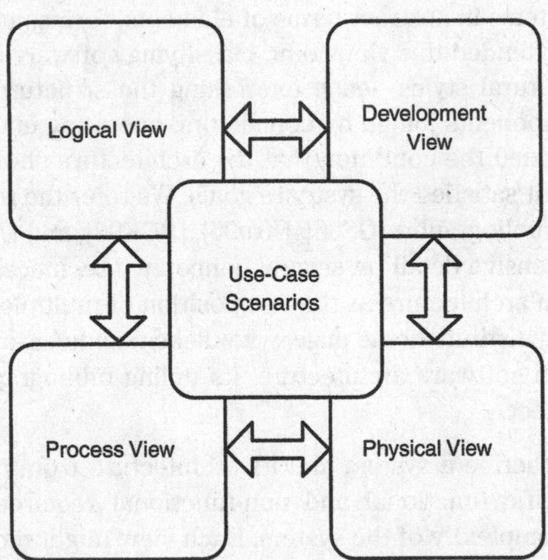

Figure 1.1 Kruchten's 4+1 View Model. (© 1995 IEEE)

reflects the distributed aspect of the architecture.

- The *development view* focuses on the static organization of the software in the development environment and deals with issues of configuration management, deployment, development assignments, responsibilities, and product construction.
- The fifth (and final) view, called the *scenario view*, is organized around all four of these views. Its definition is driven by the system's use cases.

In Kruchten's original paper, the information flow in Figure 1.1 was only from top to bottom and left to right between views. We have made the arrows bidirectional because information can flow in both directions as the system evolves. The last use-case driven aspect of this model has been a critical factor in its success in describing architectures, leading to its widespread adoption.

Rational's UML and the supporting cast of UML-based tools enable projects to define and annotate elements within each of these views by using a standard notation. There is some justification to the claim that UML is the de facto, standard notation language for architecture definition—a claim driven partly by merit and partly by the usage and growth of a shared knowledge base on how to specify elements using UML.

Once a system has been adequately described by using some well-defined notation for each viewpoint, the 4+1 Model guides the system's architects through the process of resolving view interactions. The mappings between views and the relationships between the elements described in each can be brought together to provide some concrete and measurable proof that the system meets its requirements. The separation into viewpoints enables specific architectural styles to be discussed without the cognitive dissonance of trying to have everything make sense all at once.

Conflicts are not automatically resolved by looking at the system from different views, but the ability to recognize a conflict as a clash between two specific style choices for a single component can lead to a resolution of technical problems through more productive discussions. For example, the choice of object design and definition for an element could conflict with the performance requirements for the process that executes some key method within the same element, forcing one or the other to make a compromise. Good viewpoint definition illuminates the conflicts caused by the technical choices made, which might be hidden as a result of a lack of understanding of the underlying interaction.

The Reference Model for Open Distributed Processing

The *Reference Model for Open Distributed Processing* (RM-ODP), seen in Figure 1.2, is an architectural model that also describes a system's architecture from five viewpoints. Our description is from [ISO96] and [MM00]. Malveau and Mowbray argue, in fact, that RM-ODP's more generic, domain-independent descriptions produce the 4+1 View Model as a profile-based application instance of RM-ODP. We leave it to the reader to draw analogies between the two models.

The RM-ODP viewpoints are as follows:

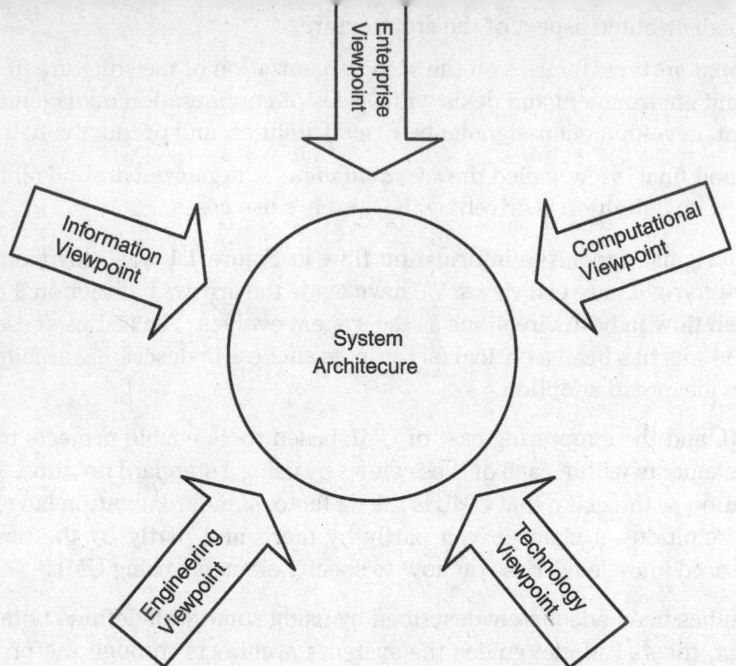

Figure 1.2 Reference Model for Open Distributed Processing. (*Software Architecture Bootcamp* by Malveau/Mowbray, © 2001. Reprinted by permission of Pearson Education, Inc., Upper Saddle River, NJ.)

The enterprise viewpoint. This viewpoint presents the system from the perspective of a business model, understandable by process owners and users within the business environment. This essentially non-technical view could support the business case for the implementation of the system and provide justification for metrics such as cost, revenue generated, return on investment, or other business values. The system's role in supporting higher-level business processes such as marketing, sales, fulfillment, provisioning, and maintenance should be clearly stated. This viewpoint states, "This system makes business sense."

The information viewpoint. This viewpoint defines information flows, representing both logical data and the processes that operate on the data. This viewpoint is an object model of the informational assets in the system and describes how they are presented, manipulated, and otherwise modified.

The computational viewpoint. This viewpoint partitions the system into component-based software elements, each of which is capable of supporting some (possibly distributed) informational structure through an *application programming interface* (API). Components and objects are not synonyms, and the last two viewpoints stress this difference.

The engineering viewpoint. This viewpoint exposes the distributed nature of the system, opening the physical resource map underlying the object and component model views discussed previously. Details of operating systems, networks, process location, and communication are all visible.

components and objects to specific technologies, products, versions, standards, and tools.

All five viewpoints are considered peers in that they are not hierarchically organized.

RM-ODP provides an additional dimension for architecture analysis, namely support for eight distribution transparencies. A transparency, overlaid on the architecture, masks from our view some critical property of the underlying distributed system. The property is guaranteed; that is, we can assume that it is correctly implemented, available, and dependable—thereby simplifying our task of validating the remaining visible portions of the architecture. The guarantee that some distributed property holds true can be used to prove that some other quality or requirement of the system, dependent on the first property, will also hold true. This principle of separation of concerns enables us to reason about the activities of the system and independently reason about the properties of the underlying distributed infrastructure. This knowledge is important because the former is often under our control at a fine-grained level, whereas the latter might be part of a vendor product that is not visible.

The eight distributed transparencies are Access, Failure, Location, Migration, Relocation, Replication, Persistence, and Transaction.

Rational's Unified Process

The genesis behind Rational's Unified Software Development Process, as described in [Jac00], lies in Ivar Jacobson's experience with use-case methodology, object-oriented design, and architectural frameworks in the design of the AXA telecommunications switch—now a two decade-old success story for Ericsson. The Unified Process takes a system from requirements definition to successful deployment through four phases:

Telecommunications Management Network

The RM-ODP standard contrasts with other ISO standards such as TMN (ISO M.3000) that specifically organize telecommunications networks into a hierarchy of functional layers supporting Business, Service, Network Management, Element Management, and Network Element layers. In TMN, each layer is assigned some component of the following five properties: performance, fault, configuration, account, and security. The TMN definition uses the domain knowledge of the designers in developing telecommunications systems. Such domain knowledge is required before a system's true hierarchical structure can be made apparent. For other domains, fitting an abstract hierarchical definition on top of an existing system supporting some current business process can be a daunting and sometimes counterproductive activity. As a result of its domain-independent nature, RM-ODP does not order the viewpoints.

tem is within a fifth Production phase. The Unified Software Development Process emphasizes the following practices for guiding the requirements, architecture, analysis, design, implementation, and testing of the system.

UP is use-case driven. UP places strong emphasis on describing all system functionality through use cases. A use case interaction describes a single activity by an actor, from process initiation to completion, along with the delivery and the receipt of some well-defined end-result or value from the system. Each such interaction, called a use case, is described by using formal notation. We can use business criteria to prioritize the system's use cases.

UP is architecture-centric. Use case prioritization guides us while making architecture choices. As we decide how to implement each use case, we make architectural decisions that can support or obstruct our ability to implement other use cases. We use this design knowledge in a feedback loop, forcing architectural evolution.

UP is iterative and incremental. The process builds the entire project through a series of incremental releases, each solving some well-defined sub-element of the project and enabling developers to discard bad choices, revisit ones that need work, and reuse good design elements until the result of the iteration is a sound element worthy of inclusion in the overall system architecture.

The life cycle of the project tracks multiple workflows and their evolution within the phases of Inception, Elaboration, Construction, and Transition. At the end of the last phase, the product delivered consists of not just a compiled and tested code base, but also all the artifacts that go into the Unified Process, such as documentation, test case methodologies, architecture prototypes, business cases, and other elements of the project's knowledge base.

There is a tremendous amount of literature on UML and the Unified Process. Jacobson's *The Road to the Unified Software Development Process* [Jac00], the reference that helped me the most in understanding the evolution of this process, is listed along with other references in the bibliography.

Software Process and Security

Why have we spent a significant amount of time discussing the software process? After all, this book is about security and architecture. We have done so because most software process definitions lump security into the same class as other non-functional system requirements, such as reliability, availability, portability, performance, and testability. Security does not belong within a system in the same manner as these other non-functional requirements, however, and cannot be treated in a uniform manner.

We believe that this situation is a fundamental cause of many of the difficulties associated with introducing security into a system's architecture. Security differs from the other system properties in the following ways:

group, not the system's business process owner. Although the costs of an nonsecure system are borne by the actual customer, that customer is not the correct source for guidelines on security requirements.

- Hacking has no use cases. Use case methodology is wonderful for describing what the system should do when users act upon it. Securing a use case can also make sense, guaranteeing that any user who wishes to modify the system is authenticated and authorized to do so. All the interactions allowed by the system that could be exploited by a malicious agent are not, however, and cannot be part of some use case scenario and cannot be captured at requirements definition. There are no *abuse cases*; there are too many variables. Including security correctly in the architecture would require of our architects too much security domain knowledge along with the corresponding and relevant expertise to respond to intrusions or incidents. No operational profile includes malicious use.
- Customer acceptance of a system can never be predicated on the absence of bugs. Edgar Dijkstra famously stated that "Testing can only prove the presence of bugs, not their absence." You cannot test for the unknown. It is impossible to guarantee the absence of security bugs, because their existence is unknown at deployment. As and when they are discovered, and resolutions are provided, the system reacts accordingly.

The literature on software process as far as we can detect is silent on how to manage security under these unique circumstances. The literature concerning security is very rich but has few recommendations for practicing software architects to guide decisions in the architecture phase of the system. Most focus on immediate production concerns on deployed systems, such as correct configuration and deployment of security components, the use of security audit tools, intrusion detection systems, firewalls, and the like. We do not have a resolution to this issue, but in the succeeding chapters, we will make this conflict the centerpiece of all our discussions. We also include a list of security references in the bibliography that can help architects.

We will now return to our discussion of architecture reviews to further elaborate on their merits and their role in software development.

Architecture Review of a System

Reviews examine the planned architecture and try to understand the problem, its proposed solution, and management expectations for success. The project has the responsibility of identifying stakeholders, choosing an architecture team, and preparing an architecture document. The document will normally grow from a draft with high-level architecture alternatives into a final form based on a single architecture on the basis of evaluating the alternatives and assigning cost versus benefits to each choice.

The review is led and conducted by a team of external experts with expertise in the domain of the application and the technologies used. The review brings together all

sion. The conversation within this session is focused on a single goal—providing a detailed rationale that the solution meets system requirements along a number of dimensions: project management, requirements, performance, scalability, reliability, high availability, disaster recovery, security, testability, hardware and software configuration needs, administration, future evolution needs, and cost.

Architecture reviews give projects feedback on a number of issues, categorize problems, assign priorities to issues, suggest remedies, and present alternatives. All of the feedback does not need to be critical or negative; an architecture review is an excellent checkpoint in the cycle to highlight the application's architectural accomplishments, such as sound object-oriented design; good performance modeling; good choices of technology; quality in documentation; project management; or clear financial modeling of the costs and benefits provided by the application.

Architecture reviews are not about enforcement of guidelines handed down from some overarching authority. They should not be conducted in a confrontational manner, nor should they focus on problems outside real technical issues. Each technical issue should be subjected to architecture problem resolution: description, examination, remedy recommendation, and solution. The quality of technical discussion can be harmed by sidebars into organizational politics, funding problems, unnecessary expansions and contractions of scope during the review, and the absence of key stakeholders. Reviews cannot be rubber-stamp procedures used more as a means to gain a checkmark on some management milestone list. The review team and the project team must forge a partnership with the common goals of validating technical architecture decisions, fostering the cross-pollination of architecture experience across the organization, learning from past real-world experiences, and forming a forum where feedback to upper management can be formulated to state risks and opportunities based solely on technical and business merits.

The Architecture Document

Before we present our outline of the structure of an architecture document, we strongly urge any systems software architect to read Strunk and White's *Elements of Style*. Another good reference is the Software Engineering Institute's Technical Report CMU/SEI-2000-SR-004 on *Software Architecture Documentation in Practice* by Bachman et al. [BBC00]. This report provides some abstract advice on writing style that I wish was available to the authors of the many architecture documents that I have had the pleasure of reading over the years.

The systems architect is responsible for preparing the documentation for the review. The architecture document and the accompanying presentation slides are all the documentation that should be allowed at the review, thus forcing all relevant issues into one single document and keeping the reviewers from being swamped with unnecessary details. The documentation need not be overly formal but must have enough information for the reviewers to gain a basic understanding of every facet of the application. Architecture documents should be held to fewer than 100 pages to prevent unnecessary bloat, but at the same time the team must ensure that the document is a true record of

investment pays off over time in many ways: the team can clearly track system modification; train new personnel about the problem domain of the application; or form a single reference for tools, technology, methodologies, and benchmarks that can be updated as the system evolves.

We will present the sections of a good architecture document as a series of answers to pertinent questions. The document must describe the high-level system details outlined in the sections that follow.

The Introduction Section

This section answers a series of questions about the project.

What Problem Are We Solving?

This section will set the agenda for the meeting. A summary of the topics under review must be available to the review coordinator early in the project management schedule so that the review team selected reflects and covers the subject matter expertise areas of all aspects of the project under review.

This section will also describe, at a high level, the motivation for funding this project along with an overview of its role within the organization and the business processes that will be supported by its implementation and delivery. The project should present background information on the system's evolution, its current state in deployment, the business forces behind the new requirements, and the software development processes, tools, and standards in place for this release.

Who Are the Stakeholders?

In this section of the document, the project team will answer the question, "Who are we solving this problem for?" By clearly defining the scope of the review and identifying the stakeholders and their roles within the project, we set the stage for a detailed discussion of all the architectural goals. If the systems architecture is presented by using one of the "multiple viewpoints" models, then the project must make sure that each viewpoint has a representative stakeholder at the review. The absence of representatives for a particular view could create an imbalance in the treatment of that view, with a corresponding risk to the project.

How Are We Solving the Problem?

This section will describe how the project plans to convert requirements into features. This point is a good place to catalog all current software processes and design methodologies used to achieve the system goals. Software engineering is a growing field with many valuable tools and methodologies for process improvement, component-based

ing. The bibliography contains references to some of the dominant theories. The choice of theory is often less important than the quality of effort made by the project to understand and implement the software process requirements in a correct manner. We again therefore will not recommend any particular process because the experience of the system architect and the specific domain engineering required by the application are critical unknowns.

Can We Define All the Terms and Technologies under Discussion?

The document should provide a glossary of terms that the review team can refer to as the review proceeds and should keep the use of *three letter acronyms* (TLAs) to a minimum. This feature is more important than it might seem at first glance. If considerable overlap exists in the definition of certain technical terms, we run the risk of "operator overloading" when those terms are used in the presentation. This confusion can create difficulties in understanding and possibly can cause the presentation to track back and forth. Issues previously considered closed might be reopened in light of the review team having an "aha!" experience about the use of a technical term.

What Do We Know from Experience about This Particular Problem?

The results of any prototyping efforts, pilots, proofs of concept, or other fact-finding missions conducted before the review should be summarized to provide some concrete data from the prototyping experiments of the team. The review team should carefully note the assumptions behind such prototyping work and revisit the assumptions to check for violations in the actual architecture of the system.

What Are the Criteria for Success for the Project as a Whole?

In this section, the team should present the criteria for success. This section could also describe abstract architectural goals and any metrics used to measure success in meeting each goal.

What Are the Project Management Details for the Project?

This section is an appendix with details on the project's schedule, budget, time frames, resources, milestones, risks, costs, benefits, and competitive advantages. The team's project management is responsible for the details within this section.

Does the Project Have Formal Requirements?

The review team should have access to a detailed list of feature requirements. Each requirement should, if possible, be associated with some architectural component of the system that identifies the logical implementation point of the requirement. Requirements should be either prioritized as high/medium/low or be pairwise comparable based on some scheme of relative weights. Without assigning values to features, it is difficult to size the feature relative to the entire release and assess whether the project's resource budget appropriately accounts for the feature's cost.

Where Are We Coming from?

If this version is not release 1.0, then the project team must specify a baseline requirements document that is being modified by the deliverables in the current release. Each requirement must be specified as an addition to the baseline, a modification of an existing baseline feature, or a deletion from the baseline. Deletions are often not described adequately in architecture documents, which tend to emphasize the new but run the risk of ignoring backward compatibility with external interfaces. Some special support might be required to support older interfaces along with a project timeline for eventual discontinuation with the agreement of the partners using the interface. This situation might represent a nasty risk at deployment.

Sections of the Architecture Document

The architecture document must describe all aspects of the application architecture.

Architecture and Design Documentation

The following section describes the heart of the architecture document: the proposed architecture and design of the system . The presentation will be very much driven by the architecture model and methodology embraced by the development team. We assume that the project will follow some viewpoint-based architectural model in the discussion that follows.

Software Architecture

This part is the most critical section of the architecture document. This section provides detailed information on the components, connectors, and constraints of the architecture. The object model, process maps, and information flows within the application must be described. The three levels of detail specified are only guides, and individual applications might choose to specify structure by any means that is complete and that

ment should specify, among other details, the following:

High-level design. This section should describe abstract business components, domain engineering constraints, and architectural style. It should also describe the architecture in terms of one of the specific "multiple viewpoints" models previously described. The application should catalog design patterns used, user interface models, multi-tiered architecture diagrams, and all interfaces to external systems. This step is dominated by "boxology" and emphasizes abstraction and information hiding. The review team must be convinced after just this step that the architecture is viable and consistent, without detailed knowledge of the internals of the components. Gross architectural errors should be caught at this level.

Mid-level design. This section should describe the middleware used along with definitions of all the service and infrastructure components that support communications within the application. The database schema definition, along with the associated mapping to the application's object model, might also be described at this level. We consider the database as a mechanism for achieving persistence of the object model and therefore assign it to this level. If the application is data intensive or directly models its informational structures relative to relational theory, then the schema is elevated to the previous design level.

Low-level design. This section should describe individual processes and entities in the system, each tied to the set of use cases where it plays an interactive role. Details of coding tools, languages, object models, interfaces, method definitions, and data persistence might be relevant. The review team must ensure that each process definition corresponds to a set of test cases that can verify correctness and completeness. The layout of process communication, synchronization, protocols, and storage can be specified.

Usability engineering. The design and definition of user interfaces should be provided. Human factors engineering can extend to system-to-system interface definitions or dependencies. Interfaces to external systems can be opened for examination, and decisions concerning protocols, direction of data flow, service commitments, and quality can also be explained.

Hardware Architecture

The project should present an overview of all hardware devices in the architecture with emphasis on ownership and relative importance of each component. Each component should have a resource associated with it—either a person or a vendor contact—to answer questions about its configuration, computational power, networking, and failure modes. Network topology and architecture, along with any underlying infrastructure components, should be described in addition to any persons or contacts capable of resolving issues on the properties of these hardware components.

Other Requirements

Our description of the technical core of the document, information about requirements, and the architecture and design of the previous sections is not enough. The remaining components of the document must cover a number of other issues; namely, some or all of the following could be part of the document.

- *External assumptions.* List critical assumptions at a high level, including dependencies on external systems and schedule risks with other projects.
- *Software process and methodology.* List the tools, technologies, methodologies, and quality metrics used in development. If the project uses a particular process-driven structure, such as component-based software engineering, include a pointer to the use case methodology used in the presentation of requirements.
- *Organizational information.* Describe project management and organizational structure and introduce personnel, roles, and other resources (such as external consultants or outsourcing components) within the application.
- *Regulatory affairs.* Briefly, point to requirements for environmental health and safety, legal issues, and so on. Describe intellectual property issues such as the use of open source along with details of submission of licenses to any corporate legal entity for review for intellectual property rights.
- *Business alignment.* Describe alignment with organizational, corporate, industry, or academic directions.
- *Non-functional requirements.* Provide concrete, model-driven data on requirements for reliability, performance, high availability, portability, serviceability, internationalization, security, and so on.
- *Functional testing.* Describe any methodologies used for regression testing along with descriptions of test suites or toolkits. Applications must demonstrate that provisions have been made to adequately test features at the unit, integration, and system level. The application does not need to have a detailed test plan at the time of the architecture review. Such a test plan can only be made concrete after developers map requirements to features, because the implementation chosen will drive the development of useful test cases. The project must provide a high-level strategy for the normal stages of testing, however: unit (developer), integration, system, and acceptance testing.
- *Performance testing.* Define the application's operational profile as a structured list of events, invocations, interactions, and transactions within the system. The operational profile represents the execution model of the application, and all use case requirements are captured by some data or control flow within the system.
- *Load and stress testing.* The architecture document should contain expected maximum load criteria in terms of data transfer rates, number of transactions per second, memory utilization, the number of concurrent users, maximum acceptable delay in response time, and so on. The application should set aside time during system testing to test these assumptions in a production-like environment.

deployment. Examples should be given of development instances, build methods and tools, the transfer of code instances between environments, the delivery of software to production, sanity checking, procedures for cutover or parallel deployment, and so on. Methods and procedures for *operations, administration, and maintenance* (OA&M) of the system after deployment should be described. OA&M is the most commonly neglected detail in systems architecture and receives almost no attention at the early design and prototyping stages.

Risks

The project should review each aspect of architecture and process for risks to successful delivery.

- Are the requirements reasonably complete? Are there any outstanding system engineering issues that might negate the assumptions behind requirements definition?
- Are the resource budgets for each aspect of the architecture complete? Are unreasonable demands being placed on hardware, software, or component ware in terms of speed, throughput, and error handling?
- Is the definition of each external systems interface acceptable to the corresponding external system? Is the external system also in the process of a software delivery cycle, and if so, will their release create impedance mismatches with the currently accepted interface?
- Are there personnel risks? Is the project adequately staffed? Has retention been a problem? How will critical resources be replaced if they leave? Does the project team have sufficient training with the tools and technologies that will be used? Does the project have access to professional consulting to cover knowledge gaps?
- Are there vendor risks? How much of the technology base is bleeding edge? How many instances have been tested and deployed within other projects within the organization? Could key personnel from these other teams be made available for knowledge transfer?
- Is there a budget risk? If the release has long cycle times, how will it respond to a fixed percentage decrease in funding? Does the project have agreement on feature priorities with the customer to gracefully degrade the delivery set of the release? Do all parties understand that the percentage of funding cut and the percentage of features dropped have no explicit relationship?
- Are there testing risks? Does the project have a process for responding to the inevitable, critical bugs that will surface on deployment even after the most extensive and exhaustive testing? Will the existence of such bugs cause contractual obligations to be violated, service level agreements to be broken, or loss of revenue or reputation? Does the system test environment have the capability of regression testing the full feature set after emergency patches are installed?

place that defines responses in the event of extreme and improbable failure?

- Does the solution have dependencies on network and physical infrastructure components that can result in unacceptable risk? These could include communications services, power, heating, ventilation, air-conditioning, and so on.
- Does the application conform to all legal, environment, health, and safety regulations of the deployment arena?

Risk depends on many other application- and domain-specific circumstances. The project should prepare a section on risk assessment within the document.

The Architecture Review Report

The Architecture Review Report is prepared by the review team to provide documented feedback to the project team. It must contain the following components:

- A list of the metrics used by the review team to measure compliance with architectural goals.
- A list of issues for each architectural goal in descending order of criticality. For each identified issue, can the review team recommend options or alternatives? The report should include, if possible, the project's preference or responses to the issue resolution strategy.
- A list of targets that the project clearly missed that require immediate action on the part of all stakeholders in order to maintain the viability of the project, documentation of the costs of such action, and the risks associated with other options.
- A list of "pull the plug" criteria. These criteria should detail scenarios where the team decides that the project would fail and accordingly cease operations. For example, if the project is developing a hard drive with certain speed and size characteristics, the ability of competitors to produce a similar product is critical. Abandoning the project might be the best option if the team loses a critical first-to-market advantage or if market conditions invalidate the assumptions stated in the architecture document. Similar issues could exist with system deliveries as described for product delivery.
- A list of action items for later review. Does the project require a retrospective to share war stories after the deployment? Is there a need to baseline the architecture for the next review cycle? Is there an opportunity to cross-pollinate the architecture experience of this project to other projects within the organization?

Conclusions

The architecture document should be the one single repository for definitive information on the software paradigm used, hardware and software configurations, interfaces profiles, security architecture, and much more. The benefits of conducting reviews early in the software cycle cannot be understated. We can avoid costly modifications to mismatched implementations, reduce project risk, communicate unpalatable technical knowledge to management in a structured and analytical mode, gain management support by identifying cost savings through reuse, reduce cycle time, and share architecture experience across the organization.

We have focused solely on one critical need for an architecture document; namely, as a platform for conducting a review. A good architecture document has many other applications. It can improve the decisions we make when allocating tasks to designers and implementers, deciding team structure as coding progresses, negotiating compromises within the team, recognizing black box components capable of replacement with other existing components built either in-house or purchased off the shelf, training new project team members, or tracking the historical evolution of the system from a library of architecture documents—each representing a snapshot of a release.

The task of creating such a versatile document from scratch for a new system is daunting, but with practice, repetition, reuse, and experience the process can be both educating and rewarding. If we cannot clearly state what we plan to do, how do we know when, or even if, we actually have done what we set out to do?

In the next chapter, we will describe the process of security assessment, which parallels that of architecture review (but with a tight focus on security).

Security Assessments

A systems security assessment is the process of matching security policy against the architecture of a system in order to measure compliance. Security assessments on systems are best conducted as early as possible in the design cycle, preferably in conjunction with architecture reviews and only after the architecture document for the system is considered stable.

Assessing risk on a system already in production is not easy. The challenge lies in knowing how to implement the recommendations that come out of the assessment, evaluating the costs of creating security controls after the fact, or creating space within the project schedule to insert a special security features release. These tasks can be very expensive; therefore, forming a security architecture baseline during the design phase of release 1.0 is a critical step in the evolution of any secure system.

In this chapter, we will define the process of security assessment by using the Federal Information Technology Security Assessment Framework championed by the *National Institute for Standards and Technology* (NIST), www.nist.gov. We will extend this abstract framework with guidelines from other industry standards. We will end the chapter with information about additional resources to help projects develop and implement their own assessment processes.

What Is a Security Assessment?

The goal of a security assessment is to evaluate threats against and vulnerabilities within the assets of the system and to certify all implemented security controls as adequate, either completely secure or meeting acceptable levels of risk.

- *Risk* is defined as the possibility of harm or loss to any resource within an information system. We can classify a wide variety of concepts, ranging from concrete components to abstract properties, as resources. Our revenue, reputation, software, hardware, data, or even personnel can all be viewed as resources that are subject to risk.
- An *asset* is any entity of value within the system. Assets within the underlying system can be defined at many levels of granularity; a secret password stored encrypted in a file, a single physical host, or a worldwide telecommunications network can all be considered assets. Assets are always owned by other entities. The owner determines the value of the asset and the maximum expense he or she is willing to incur in implementing controls to protect that value.
- Any asset whose value is less than the cost of securing that value is said to be vulnerable at an acceptable level of risk. NIST defines *acceptable risk* as a concern about a potential hazard that is acceptable to responsible management due to the cost and magnitude of implementing controls.
- A *threat* is any malicious or accidental activity that has the potential to compromise an asset within the system.
- A *vulnerability* is a flaw in the design of the system that can potentially expose assets to risk.

The security assessment process is not synonymous with any active audit tool analysis or even white hat hacking or the related activity of tiger teaming, where security experts hired by the project actively launch attacks against the system. It is a separate step in the software development cycle, aiming to improve quality. Many of the benefits of architecture review are realized within the specific context of security.

The Organizational Viewpoint

Assessments are motivated by the recognition that information is among the most valuable assets of any organization. NIST's guidelines to organizations define a way of establishing security policies by using a level-based compliance model. Organizations climb the levels within the model, from accepting policy at level 1 to having a comprehensive security infrastructure at level 5. This process has obvious parallels to software meta-processes like the five-level Capability Maturity Model (CMM) and can be similarly used to analyze systems for *critical success factors* (CSFs).

The framework charges upper levels of management with accepting responsibility for putting together a program to adequately protect information assets, implementing such a program, and providing funding to maintain security as systems evolve. The NIST guidelines establish the following management goals:

confidentiality, integrity, and availability

- Protecting information in a manner that is commensurate with the level of risk and magnitude of harm resulting from loss, misuse, unauthorized access, or modification

The Five-Level Compliance Model

The NIST Security Assessment Framework described in [NIST00] consists of five levels to guide government agencies in the assessment of their security programs. The framework assists organizations with setting priorities for improvement efforts. Although designed for government agencies, the process is equally applicable to mid- to large-size commercial organizations. The framework provides a vehicle for consistent and effective measurement of the security status of a given asset. The security status is evaluated by determining whether specific security controls are documented, implemented, tested, and reviewed; if the system owning the asset is incorporated into a cyclical review/improvement program; and whether unacceptable risks are identified and mitigated. Requirements for certification at each of the levels of the Federal IT Security Assessment Framework levels are defined as follows:

Level 1, Documented Policy. The organization must establish a documented security policy to cover all aspects of security management, operations, procedures, technology, implementation, and maintenance. The policy must be reviewed and approved by all affected parties. A security management structure must exist within the organization, from the highest executive level down to the rank-and-file. The policy must describe procedures for incident response and specify penalties for non-compliance.

Level 2, Documented Procedures. Organizations must state their position with respect to the policy, list the security controls they will use to implement policy, and describe the procedures involved. Projects are required to document applicability and assign responsibility to persons within the project for implementation. Projects must provide security contacts and document their exceptions to the policy.

Level 3, Implemented Procedures and Controls. Organizations must ensure implementation of their security procedures. Policies and procedures must be socialized, and rules of use must be documented and formally adopted. Technology to implement security must be documented along with methods and procedures for use. Certification, which is the technical evaluation that systems meet security requirements, must be formally defined. Procedures for security skills assessment and training needs must be documented.

Level 4, Tested and Reviewed Procedures and Controls. The organization must establish an effective program for evaluating the adequacy of security policy, procedures, and controls. Test methodologies with clear definitions of risk levels,

testing security in the presence of system evolution must exist. Procedures for incident response, audit trail analysis, management of maintaining up-to-date vendor security patches, intrusion detection, and configuration standards for all security equipment must be in place. Effective alarm notification methods along with procedures for escalation and response management must be created with involvement from senior management.

Level 5, Fully Integrated Procedures and Controls. Security must be fully integrated into the enterprise. Security management and compliance measurement must be proactive, cost-effective, adaptive, expert, and metric-driven.

Although these guidelines are targeted towards the entire enterprise, they are also valuable to an individual system. Within a system, compliance with a level can exist through a combination of existing implemented security controls and external security resources that enhance and protect the system architecture. The security assessment process should document these dependencies explicitly to enable regression testing of security as the system evolves.

The System Viewpoint

We will approach our description of the assessment process from a system architecture viewpoint. Assessments are often conducted from other viewpoints in situations where we wish to evaluate the risk of a service, a product, a process, or an infrastructure model. The systems-specific focus has the benefit of putting virtual boxes around the solution and around subsystems within the solution, enabling us to label components as being *inside* or *outside* a boundary, as being *trusted* according to some definition, or as having a position within a hierarchy of security levels. The assessment of a system also enables us to focus on a specific implementation instance where hardware, software, and vendor product choices are firm and therefore can be discussed in concrete terms.

Assessments will not help fundamentally dysfunctional projects. Expertise matters. Hand-waving consultants cannot match hands-on security experts guided by domain knowledge. The project designers should be committed to implementing security as a system feature, and upper management should fund security as an explicit cost item in the project funding. The assessment participants should cover all significant aspects of the project, because the absence of key participants is a sure indicator of a failed process. Vendor participation also should be carefully managed, because the goals of the vendor and the goals of the project might not coincide. Finally, no amount of good process will work in the face of organizational politics.

Judging whether a system complies with corporate guidelines for security policy is often the primary and only driver for security assessments. This situation has the unfortunate side effect of driving design to meet minimum requirements, rather than implementing best-in-class security solutions. Projects that are given little or no corporate support but are mandated to hit a target will often aim for the edge of the target instead of the bull's-eye. This situation leads, of course, to a higher chance of missing the target altogether. Aiming for the bull's-eye does not guarantee that you will hit it, but at least it

around the bull's-eye makes for a better environment for evaluating enterprise level security. Projects that are presented with an internally consistent rationale, explaining why investing in a quality security solution is cost effective, will benefit in the long term.

Another weaker alternative is to explicitly charge the project with the costs of fixing vulnerabilities once they happen. An analogy from the highway construction industry illustrates this situation. Interstate construction projects in America in the early 1960s were awarded to the lowest bidder, and any defects in construction were uninsured. The roadway bed was often built only two feet deep, and repairs were often assigned to the same company that did the original construction. The need for repairs in some cases occurred in as little as one year after completion of the roadway. This situation contrasts with many European highway construction projects, in which the builder is required to insure the roadway for 10 years. The bids were often much higher, but roadways were built on foundations six feet deep. As a result, it is common for many well-constructed stretches to require no major repairs even after 40 years. Software does not have the same shelf life, but the lesson that quality pays for itself can still be learned.

Projects often build prototypes to learn more about the design forces in the solution architecture. Security is frequently hampered by the problem of the *successful* prototype, however. Successful prototypes implement many of the features of the mature system well enough to quickly take over the design phase and form the core of the system, pushing out features like good support for administration, error recovery, scalability, and of course, security. Throwing away the actual code base of a successful prototype and starting fresh, retaining only the lessons learned, is sometimes in the long-term best interests of the project.

Project designers who wish to implement corporate security standards and policies must first understand these policies in the context of their own applications. Project designers need help understanding the threats to their system architecture and the business benefits of assessing and minimizing security risk. We will describe an assessment process known as the Security Assessment Balance Sheet as a methodology for fostering such understanding.

Assessments are essentially structured like architecture reviews (which were the topic of discussion in Chapter 1, "Architecture Reviews").

Pre-assessment preparation. The architecture review process results in the creation of a stable, acceptable architecture solution. The security assessment must examine this architecture for risks. No undocumented modifications to the architecture must be allowed between the review and the assessment.

The assessment meeting. This meeting is a one-day lockup session where the project stakeholders, identified at the architecture review process, interact with security experts and security process owners.

Post-assessment readout and assignment of responsibilities. The security assessment readout lists the consensus recommendations reached by the assessment team. This report provides upper management with technical and objective reasons to support the costs of implementing security. It provides the project with guidelines for assigning responsibility to team members for

process owners for sharing architectural experience across the organization.

Retrospective at deployment to evaluate implementation success. We are not recommending that the first time any project examines its security solution be at system deployment. This process should be continual through the entire software cycle. The security retrospective is useful in baselining security for future releases, however, or for mid-release production system assessments. The retrospective also identifies assets that have fallen off the wagon (that is, assets once thought secure that are exposed at unacceptable levels of risk, possibly due to changes in project schedules, budgets, or feature requirements).

Pre-Assessment Preparation

The project designers must conduct a series of activities before the assessment in order to ensure its success. The project designers must also make time on the schedule for the assessment, make sure that the architecture document is stable, and ensure that all key stakeholders are available. The project team needs to define the scope, clearly stating the boundaries of the assessment's applicability. The benefits of conducting the assessment as part of organizational process should be recognized by the project owners to ensure that they will accept recommendations (whether they will act upon them is another matter).

The project must identify stakeholders. These can include the business process owners, customers, users, project management, systems engineers, developers, build coordinators, testers, and trainers. Once the system is in production, the list of stakeholders will include system administrators and other maintenance personnel.

The project needs help from security policy owners and security subject matter experts to map generic corporate security policy guidelines into requirements that apply to the particular needs and peculiarities of the application. Finally, the project should review the security assessment checklist and be prepared to respond to findings from the assessment.

There are a growing number of companies that specialize in managing the assessment process, providing a coordinator, furnishing subject matter experts, and conducting the assessment. We recommend purchasing this expertise if unavailable in-house.

The Security Assessment Meeting

The agenda for the assessment has these six steps:

1. Formally, present the architecture within the context of security.
2. Identify high-level assets.
3. Identify high-level vulnerabilities and attach criticality levels to each.
4. Develop the system security balance sheet.

6. Generate assessment findings along with recommendations for threat prevention, detection, or correction.

It helps to keep the assessment to a small but complete team of essential stakeholders and assign a moderator to facilitate the meeting, thereby staying away from unproductive activities.

We will now describe a framework for defining the goal of the assessment meeting itself.

Security Assessment Balance Sheet Model

The Balance Sheet Assessment model provides a framework for the assessment process, and as its name implies, it is analogous to a corporate balance sheet in an annual report. A corporate balance sheet provides a snapshot in time of a dynamic entity with the goal of capturing all assets controlled by the company and documenting the sources of funding for these assets. It enables the company to capture the result of being in business for a period of time; say, a quarter, a year, or since the company was founded. As time passes, the dynamic within the company changes as business quickly and continually invalidates the balance sheet. In abstract terms, however, it enables us to measure the progress of the company by examining a sequence of snapshots taken at discrete intervals.

Double entry bookkeeping matches all assets to liabilities (actually, a misnomer for the sources that funded the assets). Each value appears twice in the balance sheet, first as something of tangible value held and secondly as a series of obligations (loans) and rights (shares) used to raise resources to acquire the asset.

Double Entry Bookkeeping

Balance sheets were the invention of Luca Pacioli, a 14th-century Italian monk. Frater Luca Bartolomes Pacioli, born about 1445 in Tuscany, was truly a Renaissance man, acquiring an amazing knowledge of diverse technical subjects from religion to mathematics to warfare. Modern accounting historians credit Pacioli, in his *Summa de Arithmetica, Geometria, Proportioni et Proportionalita* ("Everything About Arithmetic, Geometry, and Proportion"), with the invention of double entry bookkeeping. Pacioli himself credited Benedetto Cotrugli, and his *Delia Mercatura et del Mercante Perfetto* ("Of Trading and the Perfect Trader"), with the invention, which describes the three things that the successful merchant needs: sufficient cash or credit, good bookkeepers, and an accounting system that enables him to view his finances at a glance.

please refer to [WBB96]—or better yet, get a copy of your company's annual report to see how the financial organization captures the complex entity that is your employer into a single page of balanced data.

We will build an analogy between using a corporate balance sheet to capture a snapshot of a company and using a Security Assessment Balance Sheet to capture the state of security of the assets of a system. The analogy is imperfect because security risk has an additional dimension of uncertainty associated with the probability of compromise of an asset. How likely is it that a known vulnerability will actually be exploited? We do not know. Nevertheless, we can sometimes make an educated guess. We will return to this issue after describing the process and also make the financial aspects of risk the centerpiece of Chapter 16, "Building Business Cases for Security."

Designing a secure system is based on a similar balancing act between value and cost.

- Each asset has a value that is put at risk without security.
- Each security control minimizes or removes the risk of loss of value for one or more assets.

Security costs money. Projects have a fixed budget for implementing all security controls, typically 2 percent to 5 percent of the total cost of the current system release. Alternatively, we can buy insurance from companies that offer to secure computer security risks. Their policies can easily hit a project with an annual premium of 10 percent of the application costs, however (to say nothing of the value of such a policy in the unfortunate circumstance of a rejected claim after an intrusion). Each alternative security control has an associated time and materials cost required to implement the control within the system. Of course, no system is perfectly secure—because perfect security costs too much.

A system is *secure to acceptable levels of risk* if all the following statements hold true:

- The total value of all assets at risk without any security implementation equals the total value of assets protected by all implemented controls plus the value of all assets exposed at acceptable levels of risk.
- The budget associated with security is greater than the cost of all of the implemented security controls.
- The budget remaining after implementing all necessary security controls is less than the cost of implementing security for any individual asset that is still exposed to risk.
- There is a consensus between all stakeholders on a definition of acceptable risk (which we will elaborate on in a following section) that applies to all assets that remain exposed to risk. The stakeholders involved must include the project owner, project management, and security management. Ownership of this risk must be explicitly defined and assigned to one or more stakeholders.

The process of evaluating a system during the assessment, under these constraints, should not actually use dollar values for any of these measures. This situation could easily cause the technical nature of the discussion to be sidetracked by the essentially

have only partial information about a system that is not yet in production. Instead, we recommend the following tactics:

- *Assets.* Use labels on either a three-level scale of High, Medium, or Low or on a five-point scale of 1 to 5 to assign value to assets. Alternatively, describe the value of the asset in terms of a relative weight in comparison with the value of the whole system ("90 percent of our critical assets are in the database").
- *Security controls.* Measure the time and materials values for the cost of implementation of a security control by using person-weeks of schedule time. Use labels to measure the quality of the control by using a similar three-level or five-level value structure. Alternatively, describe the cost of the control as a percentage of the total security budget ("Integration with the corporate PKI will cost us only 5 percent of the budget, whereas building our own infrastructure will cost 50 percent of the budget").
- *Probability.* Measure the probability of compromise of an asset again by using labels; say, in a three-level High, Medium, and Low probability structure or in a five-level structure. All risks with high probability of compromise must be secured.

The closing session of the assessment will be the only time that costs and values are discussed in economic terms. During this session, the assessment team will decide whether the project, after implementing all recommendations, would have secured the system to an acceptable level of risk.

The balance sheet process is designed to drive the team during the assessment towards more goal-oriented behavior. We will now return to a more technical discussion of how the assessment process works. The remaining chapters in the book will focus on specific architectural elements that are common to most systems and will prescribe security solutions in each case in more technical detail. The assessment proceeds as follows.

Describe the Application Security Process

Describe how the application's own security process integrates with generic corporate security process.

- Does the application run security audit tools and scanners? Provide a schedule of execution of audit tools. ("We run nightly security audits during system maintenance mode.")
- How are logs collected, filtered, and offloaded to secure locations, and otherwise managed?
- How are logs analyzed to generate alarms? How are alarms collected, and how does alarm notification and analysis work?
- Is security monitoring active? Does the system take automatic steps to change configurations to a paranoid mode, or does this action require manual intervention?

administrator or developer in the event of an intrusion? Will the answer have an impact on the published high availability of the application?

Identify Assets

Assets include all of the entities and resources in the system. Entities are active agents (also called subjects) that access and perform actions on system elements (called objects) as part of the system's normal operational profile. Subjects include users, customers, administrators, processes, external systems, or hosts. Objects include code, files, directories, devices, disks, and data. Not only must hardware, software, networking, and data components of the system be cataloged, but the software development process that surrounds the application, such as the development environment, the software configuration, versioning and build management tools, technical documentation, backup plans, disaster recovery plans, and other operational plans of record must also be cataloged.

Assets can include interfaces to external systems along with constraints (such as the class of service or quality of service expected by the peer system on the other side of the interface). Assets can include any form of data; for example, a customer list that must be kept private for legal reasons or for competitive advantage.

Identify Vulnerabilities and Threats

Next, we must perform the following tasks:

- Systematically work through the architecture document, identifying assets at risk.
- Examine each asset for vulnerabilities against a schedule of known threats.
- Catalog the existing security controls and assign costs of maintenance of these controls in the current release.
- Catalog new proposed security controls and assign costs of development of these controls in the current release.
- Catalog controls that will be retired or removed from the architecture due to architectural evolution. There is an associated cost with these controls, especially if interfaces to external systems require retooling or if users require new training.
- Proceed to examine each control and its strength in thwarting attacks from an up-to-date schedule of exploits and attacks. The analysis will result in a detailed list of assets protected by the control's implementation and the extent to which the asset's value is protected from harm.

Identify Potential Risks

Identifying applicable security vulnerabilities on an existing or future application is a complex task. The flood of security vulnerability sources that are available today further complicates this task. Moreover, the information overload is growing worse daily.

vulnerability database, which started as a mailing list in the early 1990s and has evolved into a forum to discuss security exploits, how they work, where are they applicable, and how to fix them.

- Many other public and proprietary vulnerability databases exist, sometimes requiring specialized tools and techniques wherever the problem domain grows too large.
- Security organizations such as SANS (www.sans.org) and Security Focus (http://securityfocus.org) carry up-to-date bulletins of vulnerabilities required by hardware platforms or software products.
- Vendor sites for major hardware platforms list security vulnerabilities and patches on their homepages. Many vendors also provide tools for automating patch downloads and installations, which can be risky. The patch process itself might break your application, so it is best to test automated patches in a development environment first.
- UNIX audit tools contain several hundred checks against common *operating system* (OS) file and service configuration problems.
- Virus scanners contain databases of tens of thousands of viruses.
- Intrusion detection tools maintain signatures for thousands of exploits and detect intrusions by matching these signatures to network traffic.

Keeping up with this flood of information is beyond most projects. From an application standpoint, we need help. The application must match its inventory of assets against the catalog of exploits, extract all applicable hardware and software exploits, prioritize the vulnerabilities in terms of the application environment, and then map resolution schemes to security policy and extract recommendations to be implemented. The general theme is as follows (but the difficulty lies in the details).

- Identify existing security management schemes.
- Baseline the current level of security as a reference point as the architecture evolves.
- Translate generic corporate security requirements into application-specific security scenarios to identify gaps between security requirements and current implementation.
- Freeze the architecture, then analyze it in a hands-off mode to assure that the compendium of security recommendations does not introduce new vulnerabilities through incremental implementation.
- Examine object models, database schemas, workflow maps, process flow diagrams, and data flow for security scenarios. How do we authenticate and authorize principals or validate the source or destination of a communication? The basic security principles, discussed in the next chapter, are reviewed here.
- Identify boundaries around entities to provide clear inside versus outside divisions within the architecture.

- Model risk by asking, "Who poses risk to the system?" "Are employees disgruntled?" "What practices create the potential for risk?" "Is logical inference a relevant risk?" "What systems external to this system's boundary are compromised by its exposure to a hacker?"
- Can we roll back to a safe state in case of system compromise? Backups are critical to secure systems design.

Examples of Threats and Countermeasures

Every application has its own unique notion of acceptable risk. Any threat that is considered highly unlikely or that cannot be protected against but can be recovered from in a timely fashion or that will not cause any degradation in service could be considered acceptable. Unfortunately, the definition of acceptable risk changes with time, and we must always re-examine and re-evaluate the holes in our architecture as the system evolves.

Some examples (and these are just examples from a single architecture) of vulnerability identification and resolution that might appear in an assessment findings document are as shown in Table 2.1.

Post-Assessment Activities

The assessment should result in a findings document with detailed recommendations for improving the systems security. If the report is acceptable to the project team, the assessment team should also provide metrics that enable a comparison to other projects within the organization or to other companies within the industry profile that could help in ranking the project's success in complying with security policy. Specifically, the assessment findings should do the following:

- List measures of success
- Rate the system within the organization on security compliance
- Provide guidelines on how to assign responsibilities
- Document vulnerabilities left open after all recommendations are implemented
- Document the entire process and copy to project management

Why Are Assessments So Hard?

The hardest part about conducting an assessment is getting an answer to the question, "Did I get my money's worth out of the security solution?" We blame our inability to answer the question on imperfect information. How much does an asset really cost? How likely is a vulnerability to be exploited? How successful is a control in protecting

are faced with a difficult problem. Our lack of confidence in the soundness of a security solution is due in part to imperfect information but also in part to making optimal choices. This situation is an instance of the law: "All interesting problems are hard."

We have focused on the balance sheet approach to conducting assessments to bring this question to the forefront. There is a good reason why answering this question in the general case is hard: this situation is equivalent to answering an intractable theoretical question called the *knapsack* problem. The problem of optimizing the security of a system, defined in terms of choosing the best set of security controls that provide the maximum value under given budget constraints, is difficult from a concrete viewpoint. Picking the best security solution is hard because in the general case, it is an instance of a provably hard problem.

The knapsack problem asks, given a knapsack of a certain size and a target value up to which we must fill the knapsack and a set of objects each with a value and a size attribute, how can we decide which objects to put into the knapsack to reach the target size? Is it even possible to reach the target? The knapsack problem, as stated previously, is a decision problem and has an optimization analog that asks the question, "What subset of objects will give us the best value?"

$$s(u) \in Z^+ \; v(u) \in Z^+ \; u \in U \; B \in Z^+ \; K \in Z^+ U' \in U \sum_{u \in U'} s(u) \leq B \sum_{u \in U'} v(u) \geq K$$

In the general case, our problem of deciding which assets to protect by using which controls in order to maximize value protected is an optimization version of this decision problem (which is NP-complete). Well, actually, the situation is both simpler and more complicated than saying that conducting security assessments is akin to solving a hard problem. The larger point is that assessments are hard because of imperfect knowledge and because we must choose a solution from a large set of alternatives. Mathematician Ron Graham, widely considered as the father of Worst Case Analysis Theory, proposed a simple alternative to solving hard problems such as Knapsack: Pick a fast strategy that arrives at a suboptimal answer and then prove that the answer we have is no worse than some fixed percentage of the optimal although infeasible-to-compute answer. For example, a simple prioritization scheme imposed over the objects may consistently yield an answer no less than half the value of the optimal solution. In many cases, this may be good enough.

Matching Cost Against Value

From an abstract viewpoint, security assessments and the process of cost-benefit analysis involve making a series of decisions. Each decision secures an asset with a certain value by implementing a security control with a certain cost. This basic cost-value block is shown in Figure 2.1(a).

In reality, securing an asset might require implementing several controls (see Figure 2.1[b]). Alternatively, several assets can all be protected by a single control, as seen in Figure 2.1(c). In addition, there might be several valid alternative security solutions for securing any particular asset.

Table 2.1 Examples of Vulnerability Identification and Resolution

	FINDING	ASSET VALUE	PROBABILITY	RESOLUTION	CONTRO COST
1	Version of rlogin daemon on legacy system is vulnerable to buffer overflow attack.	H	L	Apply OS vendor's current security patch to the rlogin daemon.	L
2	Internet-facing Web server outside corporate firewall might be compromised.	H	H	Install corporate intrusion detection sensor on Web server. Install latest security patches. Run Tripwire on a clean document tree, and run nightly sanity checks to see whether files are compromised.	M
3	CORBA connection from application server to legacy database server is over an untrusted WAN.	H	M	Implement point-to-point IIOP over SSL connection between the two servers. Provision certificates from corporate PKI. Add performance test cases to test plan. Add certificate expiry notification as an event. Comply with corporate guidelines on cipher suites.	H
4	Administrator's Telnet session to application server might be compromised.	H	H	Require all administrators to install and use secure shell programs such as ssh and disable standard Telnet daemon.	L
5	Database allows ad hoc query access that can be compromised.	H	M	Examine application functionality to replace ad hoc query access with access to canned, stored procedures with controlled execution privileges. Parse the user query string for malicious characters.	H

contin

Table 2.1 continued

	FINDING	ASSET VALUE	PROBABILITY	RESOLUTION	CONTRO COST
6	Web server uses cgi-bin scripts that might be compromised.	H	H	Apply command line argument validation rules to scripts and configure the scripts to run securely with limited privileges.	
7	Users on UNIX file system indiscriminately share files.	M	H	Implement a file permissions policy. Extend policy using UNIX access control lists to securely enable all valid user file sharing according to access permission bits.	L
8	Passwords might be weak.	H	H	Run password crackers, age passwords, prevent users from reusing past three old passwords, and check passwords for strength whenever changed.	L
9	Users download applets from partner's Web site.	M	L	Require partner to sign up for software publisher status with VeriSign and to only serve signed applets.	M
10	Solaris system might be susceptible to buffer overflow attacks.	H	L	Set `noexec_user_stack=1` and `noexec_user_stack_log=1` in `/etc/system`. The first prevents stack execution in user programs; the second turns off logging to reduce noise.	L

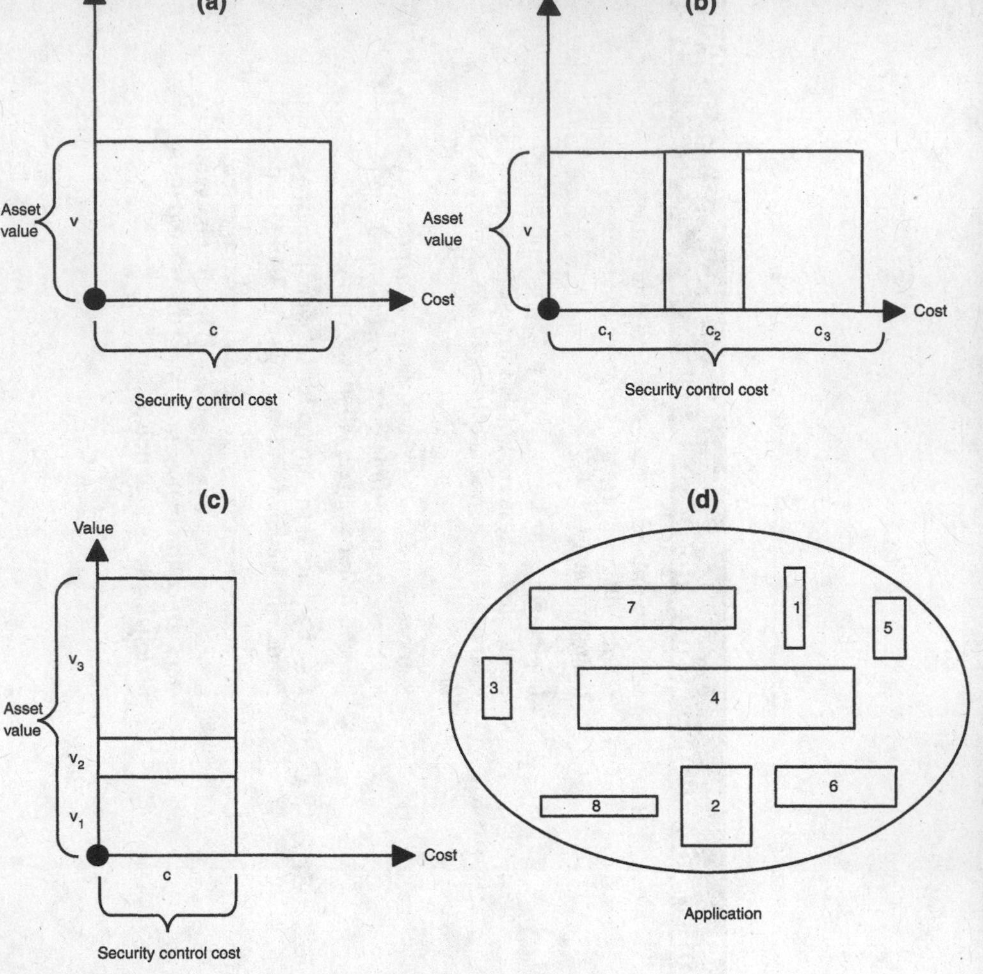

Figure 2.1(a-d) Cost versus value blocks in an application.

A cost-value block represents each control-asset combination. An application's *security solution space* consists of a collection of cost-value blocks, including alternative solutions to securing the same asset (as shown in Figure 2.1[d]).

Why Assessments Are Like the Knapsack Problem

Securing the application can be seen as selecting a subset of cost-value blocks from all such possible basic components so as to maximize the value of the assets protected, given the constraints of our budget. In actual applications, the blocks might not be perfect, disjoint rectangles. The controls might overlap in multiple blocks, as might the

revisit this topic and other complications at the end of our discussion.

This act of choosing an optimal subset is an instance of the knapsack problem. Consider Figure 2.2, where we have collected the application's cost-value blocks in a stack to the left and mapped a potential security solution on the right. The solution secures the assets of blocks 2, 7, and 3. Securing 6 results in a budget overrun.

This solution might not be optimal. In general, finding an optimal solution is as hard as the knapsack problem. Consider, however, the case of a project team that sets clear priorities for the assets to be protected.

In Figure 2.3, we have ordered the stack of cost-value blocks in decreasing order of asset value. Ordering the assets greatly simplifies the decision process, and the problem is easily (although perhaps not optimally) solved. We proceed to implement controls from bottom to top, in increasing order of value, without regard to cost. When we encounter an asset that cannot be protected with the budget remaining, we pass it over and proceed to the next. The risk to the list of assets left unprotected at the end of this process are either deemed as acceptable or the list can be reviewed by the project stakeholders to find additional resources. In Figure 2.3, we implement security controls to protect assets 1, 2, 3, 5, and 6.

This solution is not necessarily optimal. In fact, it is easy to create counterexamples where this strategy is not optimal. Nevertheless, prioritizing work is a useful way of managing complexity.

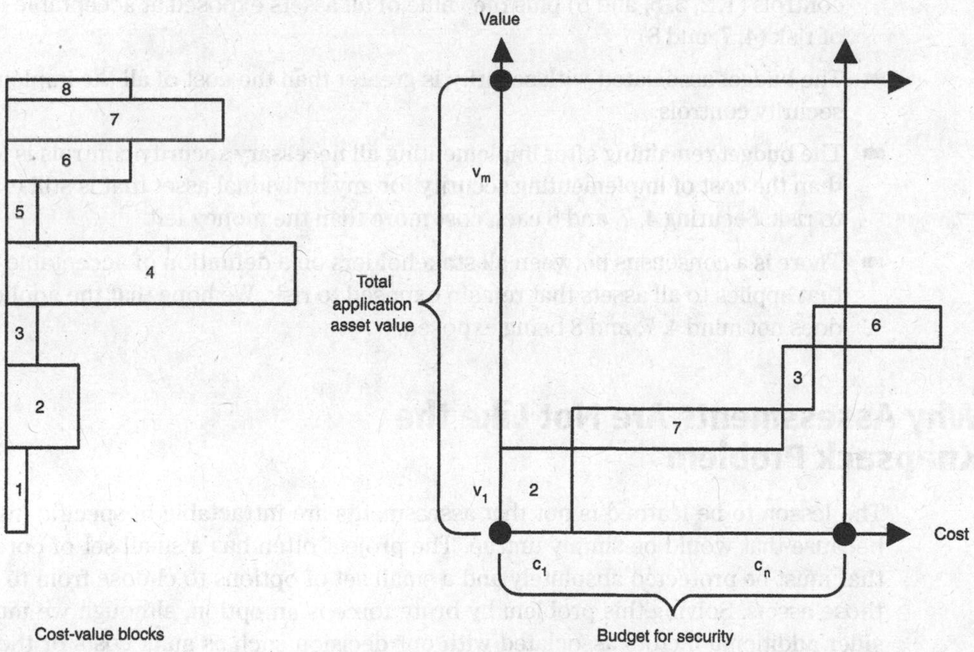

Figure 2.2 Choosing cost-value blocks requires compromises.

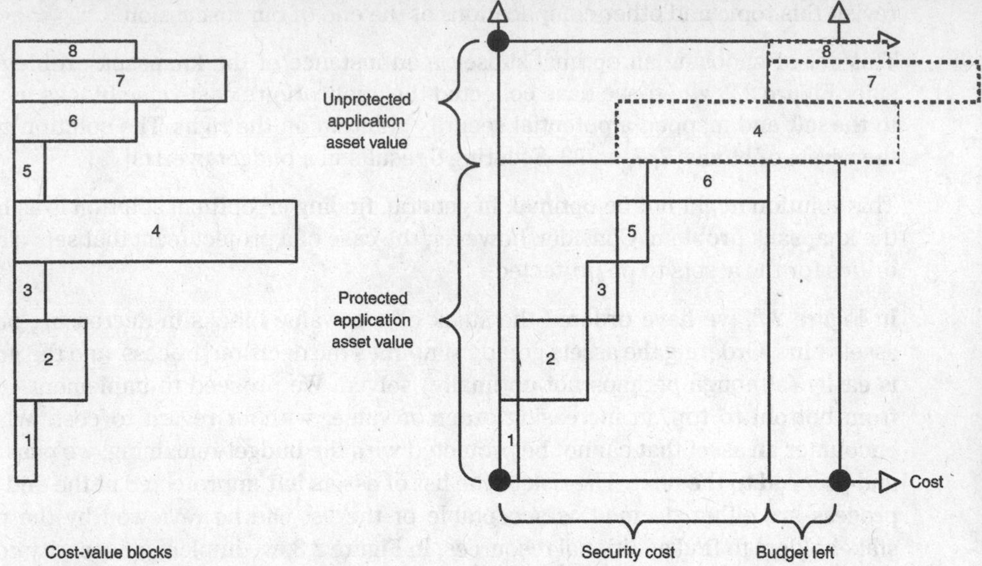

Figure 2.3 Prioritizing values makes decisions easier.

In security balance sheet terms,

- The total value of all assets at risk (1 through 8), without any security implementation, equals the total value of assets protected by all implemented controls (1, 2, 3, 5, and 6) plus the value of all assets exposed at acceptable levels of risk (4, 7, and 8).
- The budget associated with security is greater than the cost of all the implemented security controls.
- The budget remaining after implementing all necessary security controls is less than the cost of implementing security for any individual asset that is still exposed to risk. Securing 4, 7, and 8 each cost more than the money left.
- There is a consensus between all stakeholders on a definition of acceptable risk that applies to all assets that remain exposed to risk. We hope that the application does not mind 4, 7, and 8 being exposed.

Why Assessments Are Not Like the Knapsack Problem

The lesson to be learned is not that assessments are intractable in specific instances, because that would be simply untrue. The project often has a small set of core assets that must be protected absolutely and a small set of options to choose from to protect those assets. Solving this problem by brute force is an option, although we must consider additional factors associated with our decision such as sunk costs or the probability of compromise. But even in a world where we divide our threats into ones we will

threats have a probability of 1 while the latter have a probability of 0. Only time can tell whether we were right.

Consider the picture from an enterprise level, with hundreds of projects and a limited security budget. Even when allowing for the fact that we have large error bars on our security goals, it might be impossible to make an optimal (or even a reasonable) assignment of resources. Although an optimal choice might be feasible at the application level through brute force, the intractable nature of decision-making has moved to a higher level, manifested in the complexity of cost-benefit analysis across multiple projects and across many organizations. Unlike the knapsack problem, the true cost-benefit analysis of security implementation in an organization is distributed across all the projects in the company. Each project is assigned a piece of the pie, its security budget, and can only make local decisions. This situation does not guarantee optimal allocation of resources at the corporate level as an aggregation of all these low-level decisions. What appears feasible at the project level ("Decide an optimal allocation of security resources in project XYZ") in aggregate might be far from optimal when viewed at the enterprise level. It might not even be feasible to compute an optimal allocation.

Even in simple systems, the interactions between the various security components are as critical a factor as the cost-value blocks themselves. The abstract problem does not correspond to reality. As we mentioned earlier, there are always overlaps between cost-value blocks because controls provide security support to multiple assets and assets require multiple controls to comply with security policy.

Our purpose of going into this much detail is to describe an inherent complexity in the assessment process. Matching threats to vulnerabilities is hard enough, but deciding what to protect and how does not get enough attention at the review. Domain knowledge can also be critical to resolving conflicts between options. We know more about the application than can be captured in a simple cost-value block. We can use that knowledge to prioritize our options.

Note that these differences do not make assessments uniformly easier or harder. They represent classic architectural forces that pull and push us in different directions as we try to pick the best path through the woods. The technical content of the chapters that follow will describe patterns of security architecture, along with context information, to strengthen our ability to decide.

Enterprise Security and Low Amortized Cost Security Controls

In our section on security balance sheets, we recommended applying three levels of cost labels to security controls: High, Medium, and Low. There is a fourth label, however, that is architecturally the most important: Low Amortized cost.

Security controls with low amortized cost are too expensive for any individual project to embrace but are quite affordable if the costs are shared among many applications. Amortization spreads costs over many projects. Enterprise security is all about the

prise security products that promise reusability but actually are quite re-useless. In this case, the benefits of sharing the deployment cost are not realized. Therefore, successful enterprise security requires corporations to adopt several measures. For example, organizations must perform the following tasks:

- Organizations must centralize corporate security policy and standards.
- Corporate security groups must educate projects on corporate-wide security guidelines.
- Organizations must pick high value, low amortized cost security solutions and invest in enterprise-wide implementations.
- Project teams might need to call in expert outside consultants to manage key security processes.

Examples of enterprise security products include *Public-Key Infrastructure* (PKI), security management through COTS policy servers, corporate-wide intrusion detection infrastructures, the use of standardized virus scanning tools, enterprise security audit tools, and corporate X.500 directories with *Lightweight Directory Access Protocol* (LDAP) support. Each of these would be impossible for any individual project to deploy in a good way, but sharing these resources makes sense. Suddenly, with the addition of many high-value/low-cost blocks within the applications security architecture space, a project's available security options increase. Although this information is obvious, it does bear stating in the context of our discussion of security assessments and balance sheets. These benefits of amortization are over *space*, where many applications share security components and services. Cost can also be amortized over time, where we can justify the expense of a security component over several application releases if its features match the evolutionary path of the application. We must convince the project's owner of the investment value that the choice represents over cheaper alternatives that might need to be replaced as the application grows.

Conclusion

Security assessments applied to the systems architecture rather than after delivery to production can be of value. We have less information about implementation, but security assessments are still an important yet often neglected part of the software development cycle. Assessments target the benefits to be gained from identifying and closing potential security problems within the system under design. The project team can match the costs of the proposed preventive or corrective measures against the estimated value of the assets protected or against the business risk associated with leaving these vulnerabilities open. The process of choosing alternatives for implementing customer requirements and needs within the solution can be guided by the cost-benefit analysis produced as an output of the security assessment.

The Security Assessment Balance Sheet is a useful model for creating a process for conducting assessments. The analogy with corporate balance sheets and the notion that we are capturing a snapshot of a system at an instance in time by using the framework is

costs. It is more in line with developing *Generally Accepted Security Principles* (GASP), much like the *generally accepted accounting principles* (GAAP) of the accounting world. As with all analogies, this situation does not bear stretching too far. If someone suggests a Security Assessment Income Statement or a Security Assessment Cash Flow Statement, they are just being weird. In the next chapter, we will present basic security architecture principles and the system properties that are supported by secure design. The security assessment must validate all the security properties of the application.

Security Architecture Basics

The benefits of security are difficult to quantify. We often can estimate security development costs within a small margin of error around a fixed dollar figure, but the benefits of spending those dollars are more elusive. These are often described in qualitative rather than quantitative terms. The cultural images regarding computer security do not really help. The news media is full of vague references to hackers and the dire consequences of succumbing to their inexorable and continual assaults on systems, without explanation as to why such attacks might happen and without regard to the probability or feasibility of such attacks. This situation causes confusion, for want of a better word, amongst project managers and customers. We can reduce some of this confusion if we understand computer risks better, but we must first understand the principles and goals of security architecture and decide which ones apply to any system at hand. Similar systems often adopt similar security solutions. The grain of the underlying application guides the patterns of implementation.

A *pattern* is a common and repeating idiom of solution design and architecture. A pattern is defined as a solution to a problem in the context of an application. Security components tend to focus on hardening the system against threat to the exclusion of other goals. Patterns bring balance to the definition of security architecture because they place equal emphasis on good architecture and strong security. Our choices of security properties, authentication mechanisms, and access control models can either drive our architecture towards some well-understood pattern of design or turn us towards some ad hoc solution with considerable architectural tensions. Without a model for security architecture, if we take the latter path we might discover flaws or risks in the solution's construction only at deployment. That might be too late.

In this chapter, we will define security architecture, outline the goals of security architecture, and describe the properties of well-behaved, secure systems. We will also discuss the architectural implications of our security principles. We will present a synopsis

design. In the chapters that follow, we will introduce patterns and describe how they can be used to achieve the principles of security. Before we can discuss security architecture patterns in Chapter 4, however, we must first describe the goals of security.

Security As an Architectural Goal

Software architects are often charged with the goal of making future-proof architecture design decisions. A future-proof system has the flexibility to accommodate change of any nature: technology, feature creep, data volume growth, or the introduction of new interfaces. This goal adds some level of complexity to the system. One solution to managing this complexity lies in defining the software architecture at multiple levels of abstraction. We can then create interface definitions between subsystems that minimize, or at the least manage, the impacts of changes within subcomponents on the system architecture as a whole. This separation into architectural levels parallels a separation in concerns and enables us to hide design decisions within one component from other areas of the system. Each component is focused on one aspect of functionality that defines its purpose and is based on a subset of the overall solution's assumptions. So far so good, but here comes the hard part.

Adding security to the architecture often has the negative impact of collapsing the levels of abstraction in the architecture and elevating low-level design decisions to a higher and often wrong level, to be re-evaluated and perhaps changed. Integrating vendor products that do not acknowledge this phenomenon is very difficult.

Vendor products favor flexibility to capture a wider market share—and despite claims of seamless interoperability often require careful and specific configuration at a low level. We make architecture decisions that damage the future-proof quality of the system due to time constraints or our inability to set priorities. The vendors identify the cause of insecure design as a lack of sophistication on the part of the architect in understanding security principles; the project architect, on the other hand, lays the blame on the vendor, citing its lack of domain knowledge required for understanding the system.

Security implemented as a system feature without clear security architecture guidelines will cause tension in design. We must follow corporate security policy, but the requirements of that policy are often orthogonal to the functional goals of the system. Meeting corporate security requirements, especially as an afterthought imposed upon existing production systems, is not an activity for the weak of resolve. Poor architecture has caused many of these partial myths to crop up.

- Security causes huge performance problems.
- Security increases system management complexity.
- Security features can complicate the implementation of other common enterprise architecture features, such as high availability or disaster recovery.
- Security products are immature.
- Security for legacy systems is too costly.

is more than a small amount of truth to each charge in specific system instances. In most cases, however, there is room for improvement. We can perform the following actions:

- Adopt processes for improving system quality or security, such as architecture reviews and security assessments. These processes can create significant improvements in the correct, robust, scalable, and extensible implementation of security within a system.
- Incorporate security artifacts early into the design cycle to increase awareness of the constraints imposed by security.
- Articulate security options in concrete, measurable, and comparable terms, describing costs, coverage, and compromises.
- Gather hard data on the performance costs by using prototyping or modeling before making unwise investments in hardware and software.
- Minimize interoperability woes through clear interface definitions.
- Give vendors feedback on the impact their products have on other system goals. Take performance as an example. Performance is a project-critical goal, but some vendors, when told of their product's rather dismal performance, reply, "What performance issue?" They believe that security always carries a performance penalty. This situation is generally true as a principle, but closer examination might yield opportunities for optimization with little or no reduction in security (see Chapter 14, "Security and Other Architectural Goals," for other examples).

Any amount of planning will never help a dysfunctional development organization, and no amount of software process around the system implementation will replace good teamwork, design knowledge, experience, and quality management. Nevertheless, even with all of these latter virtues, the lack of expertise in security among the members of the project team often creates poor decisions within the architecture.

Corporate Security Policy and Architecture

Some project teams view the ownership of the security of their system as external to their organization. "If Bob is vice-president of security, well, then its Bob's problem, not mine." This theory is, of course, flawed. Security is everyone's business, and the project team cannot navigate this path alone. We cannot overemphasize the value of an internal organization devoted to defining policy around security issues, forming standard practice statements, evaluating tools for deployment, and performing the roles of assessor, auditor, and defender in the event of an intrusion.

Information must flow in the other direction too, however, where policy is guided through the explicit, active, and continual participation of all the domain specific architects within the company. These people build the systems that make money for the company. Securing these assets cannot be accomplished by writing down cookie-cutter rules.

ment organizations with very tight deadlines and small budgets are wary of any process that could cost time or money. Project teams need assistance beyond the threat of punishment for not implementing security policy. Rather than operating out of some nameless fear of all the hackers out there, project teams should integrate security into their architectures because it makes good business sense.

At this point, we would like to make two statements. First, we cannot help you build a concrete dollar figure cost-benefit analysis for your system (although in Chapter 16, "Building Business Cases for Security," we try), but we will try to explain our experiences from evaluating vendor products, opening legacy systems, implementing magic bullet technologies, and building systems from scratch. Much of secure design belongs where all software design principles belong: right at the beginning alongside feature coverage, performance, usability, scalability, and so on.

Second, the technical security community does a tremendous job of discovering, explaining, demystifying, and fixing security holes. What they do not do as often is as follows:

- Describe in terms familiar to the development community at large how to think as they do.
- Describe how to recognize common patterns in the design of complex systems.
- Describe how to prevent security holes as a design principle.
- Describe how to view security solutions as black boxes with well-defined and usable properties.

Let's face it: most security gurus find the rest of us a bit thick.

Our primary emphasis is on becoming a better architect, not becoming a security expert. To do so, we have to start asking some of the questions that security experts ask when confronted with some new vendor product, security standard, protocol, or black box with magic properties. The experts ask these questions from many years of experience with security solutions: from common problems emerge common patterns of implementation. A vendor presents a seemingly perfect security solution, and no chink appears to exist in the armor. Then, an experienced security guru starts asking hard questions that do not seem to have good answers, and suddenly the solution appears suspect.

We will address security design from the viewpoint of the practicing software architect, a label we use for the technical leader on any software project with broad oversight over systems architecture and design and who provides guidance on interface definition and design to all external components. We hope that our presentation will make for better systems architecture through improving security.

Vendor Bashing for Fun and Profit

As a practical matter, the same issues with identification, access control, authorization, auditing, logging, and so on crop up repeatedly. Software architects can learn some of these patterns and ask the same questions. Access to context creates a level of under-

as common sense. This thinking is a core principle behind the success of the pattern community. Discovering security architecture patterns is about developing such common sense.

Security vendors in today's environment, because of their growing sophistication and maturity, can design and develop products at a production quality level above the reach of most applications. Buying off the shelf is more attractive than attempting an in-house, homegrown solution. Vendor maturity also reduces costs as successful products reach economies of scale and competition keeps margins in check. This situation leads to the common problem of security architecture work being primarily integration work, where existing legacy systems have commercial security solutions grafted onto (or, if you prefer, finely crafted onto) existing insecure architectures. We will address the issue of security as an afterthought in detail.

In the preface, we described some of the advantages that vendors had over projects, including better knowledge of security, biased feature presentation with emphasis on the good while hiding the bad, and deflection of valid product criticisms as external flaws in the application. On the other side, vendors of security products often share common flaws. We will introduce three in the following discussion and expand on their resolution in the chapters to follow.

- *Central placement in the architecture.* The first and foremost flaw is the view that the vendor security solution is somehow THE central component of your software solution or system. Customers who have difficulty implementing the vendor's so-called *enterprise* security solutions have the same complaint: the vendor's product is technically well designed and works as advertised, but only under its own design assumption of being the center of the universe. The reality is often dramatically different. User communities are fragmented and under different organizations, business processes are not uniform and cannot be applied across the board to all participants, users have vastly differing operational profiles and skill and experience sets, and "seamlessly integrated" software (well, to put it bluntly) isn't. This situation leads us to the second-largest problem with vendor security solutions.
- *Hidden assumptions.* The assumptions implicit in the vendor solution are not articulated clearly as architectural requirements of the project. These assumptions are critical to understanding why the solution will or will not work. Hidden assumptions that do not map to the solution architecture might introduce design forces that tear apart the application. The tensions between these assumptions and those of your own architectural design choices are what make integration hard. This discussion, of course, leads us to the third problem that security architects face.
- *Unclear context.* The context in which the security solution works might not be clear. Context is larger than a list of assumptions. Context describes the design philosophy behind the assumptions, explaining the tensions with development realities. All security products have built-in assumptions of use. Few products have a well-thought out philosophy that includes the purpose and placement of the product in some market niche. The reason why some security products port so

hardware, operating system, or software technology. One size rarely fits all, especially if context mismatch is great. For instance, porting security products from UNIX to NT or vice versa is difficult because of fundamental differences in OS support for security. Another common example of context mismatch is impedance on application interfaces because of differences in the granularity of the objects protected.

Architectural design is about placing system design choices, whether they are about object design, database design, module creation, interface definition, or choices of tools and technologies, within the context of a specific feature requirement. Applications rarely have clear security requirements over and above the vague injunction to follow all corporate security policies. The architect is left groping in the dark when confronted with the question, "Does this product support the context in which security appears within my application?"

This problem often manifests itself in the principle of ping-pong responsibility. If there is a problem, then the responsibility is never the vendor's centrally placed product. It's a user problem, it's a deployment issue, it's an application problem, or it's a problem that is best addressed by methods and procedures, to be put in place by person or persons unknown and implemented by means unknown, at some indeterminate time in the future (most likely after the customer's check clears at the bank).

The common response is to implement security solutions partially or not at all and to abandon any security requirements that get in the way of the deployment trinity of Time, Budget, and Features. The resolution to this conflict is to make security an architectural goal instead of a system property.

Security and Software Architecture

The discipline of Software Architecture has only recently started to integrate security as a design principle into its methodologies, giving it the weight normally accorded to the better-understood principles of performance, portability, scalability, reliability, maintainability, profiling, and testability. In the past, unlike these established principles of software development, security has been presented as an independent property of a system rather than as a fundamental system feature to be specified, designed, and developed.

System Security Architecture Definitions

There are many definitions of software architecture, and all share a common emphasis. They describe a system's software architecture as a sum of cooperating and interacting parts. Here are several definitions, each followed by our attempt to define security architecture in a derivative manner.

The architecture of a system can be captured as a collection of computational components, together with a description of the interactions between these components. Software architects must choose from a catalog of architectural styles, each defining a system in terms of a pattern of structural organization.

Choosing an architectural style gives a system designer access to the style's vocabulary and specific constraints. Each style presents a framework within which common patterns of system development appear. Garlan and Shaw call this feature *design reuse.*

Within this definition, an architect building a secure system must perform the following actions:

- Decompose the system into subsystems, where each subsystem is an exemplar of a specific architectural style.
- For each subsystem, choose a security component that matches its style and that implements its required security properties.
- Add the security constraints imposed by implementing this security component to the system's constraint set.
- Examine the connectors between subsystems, and choose communication security components that enforce the security properties required on each interface.

Thus, the choice of architectural style drives the selection of security components and their integration with all other system components under additional security constraints. Complex systems often use multiple styles. This process must therefore occur on several levels in order to resolve conflicts between security constraints driven by conflicting styles. For example, using different vendor products on either side of an interface can cause security on the interface to fail.

Our second software architecture definition is as follows:

GACEK, ABD-ALLAH, CLARK, AND BOEHM, 1995:

A software system architecture comprises of a collection of software and system components, connections, and constraints; a collection of system stakeholders' need statements; and a rationale which demonstrates that the components, connections, and constraints define a system that, if implemented, would satisfy the collection of system stakeholders' need statements.

The security architecture of a software system, paraphrasing this text, consists of the following:

- A collection of security software and security components along with their position and relationships to the system's components, connections, and constraints.
- A collection of security requirements from system stakeholders.

system's own components, connections, and constraints would satisfy the requirements of corporate security policy.

This definition adds the requirement that the application have an argument, a *rationale*, to support the assertion that the system is compliant with security policy.

Our third definition is similar but in addition emphasizes visibility.

BASS, CLEMENTS, AND KAZMAN, 1998:

> *The software architecture of a computing system is the structure or structures of the system, which comprise software components, the externally visible properties of those components, and the relationships between them.*

The authors define a component's externally visible properties as those assumptions that other components can make of a component, such as its provided services, performance characteristics, shared resource usage, and so on.

In the context of security, externally visible properties would include proof of identity, enforcement of access control by a user of the component, privacy, defense against denial of service, and so on. The security architecture for the system must enforce the visible security properties of components and the relationships between components.

Security and Software Process

As mentioned in the previous two chapters, adding security to a system requires rethinking the software development process surrounding the system. We can create a process for building a secure architecture by extending existing architecture models for building software.

Consider, for example, ISO's Reference Model for Open Distributed Processing, introduced in Chapter 1, "Architecture Reviews." RM-ODP defines a five-viewpoint reference model for a system. The model defines architecture features for information systems from the following five perspectives: the business viewpoint, the informational viewpoint, the computational viewpoint, the engineering viewpoint, and the technology viewpoint.

Implementing security within this framework requires examining the problem of security from each of the five viewpoints.

- *Business.* Business processes that own the assets within the system are ultimately responsible for security. A compromise of the system could entail loss of revenue and reputation.
- *Information.* Security orders information within the system according to some notion of value. The greater the value, the greater the loss to the business if the information is lost or stolen.

latter being of particular interest to a systems architect.

- *Engineering.* Security architecture is hardest to implement in a distributed environment. Many security products and protocols assume the existence of some centralized component, knowledge base, directory, or security service. These assumptions must be subject to careful analysis before implementation into a specific distributed environment.
- *Technology.* Security is presented and described in terms of its technologies and specific standards. Vendor products that claim interoperability based on compliance with today's popular standard and the technological choices of today might be the security maintenance headaches of tomorrow.

We can thus examine each system security property from multiple viewpoints to ask, "Which entities are protected?" "Which entities are subordinate to others?" "How are authenticating credentials distributed, validated, aged, replaced, or subject to expiry?" "What computational resources do we require to correctly implement security at each entity within the environment?" For example, the emergence of mobile technology has created new issues for security. The physical constraints of handheld devices, in terms of memory and CPU, the requirement of quick response times, and the need to secure proprietary data on the devices when not linked to the network, all constitute challenges to the distributed systems architect.

Security Design Forces against Other Goals

Once we pick a style or identify a subsystem within the system that can be secured by using a particular approach, we are confronted with the possibility that our choices to secure one subsystem cause violations in the constraints in other subsystems. We could violate other architectural goals for other system features superficially unrelated to security.

For example, using products that prevent buffer overflows used by stack-smashing exploits could cause valid legacy code to fail. Implementing SSL to encrypt transport between two systems might degrade performance requirements. Requiring entities to possess X.509v3 certificates without a proper operational PKI to support their use might cause violations of down time requirements. Implementing complex revocation or expiry notification processes might disrupt the operations, administration, and management of the system.

Conversely, achieving other architectural goals could have an adverse effect on security goals. Implementing a middleware communications bus by using multiple vendor products could violate security management goals. We might lose interoperability. For example, consider a system that uses CORBA technology to support access to multiple distributed objects. Subsystems can implement each object by using a different ORB vendor. The vendors can all claim to be certified as meeting the OMG standards for interoperability, but because the OMG Security Service Specification is not specific

rity management), each vendor can choose to support different cipher suites or implement standard algorithms by using proprietary libraries. For more information about this topic, please see Chapter 9, "Middleware Security."

It is possible that aiming for two goals at the same time causes us to miss both. Wrapping a business object within a security wrapper could break interface agreements and security management. If the wrapper adds authentication and access control mechanisms in a vendor-specific manner, we might have enhanced the interface definitions—but at a cost. Our solution for secure method invocation might create conflicts, causing working interfaces to fail. Simultaneously, even if the authentication and access control mechanism interoperate, we might need separate security management for each subsystem on its own vendor-constrained path. The goal of integrated security administration will not be met under these circumstances.

We will return to this topic in Chapter 14, "Security and Other Architectural Goals," to expand upon these conflicts and their resolution.

Security Principles

The following seven security principles are generally accepted as the foundation of a good security solution.

- *Authentication.* The process of establishing the validity of a claimed identity. The originator of a request for access to a secured component, or initiator of a secured session or transaction, must present credentials that prove his or her identity.
- *Authorization.* The process of determining whether a validated entity is allowed access to a secured resource based on attributes, predicates, or context. Attributes are name-value pairs. We use attributes to describe details about the entity. Predicates are conditions based on the environment of the secured asset that must hold true in order to access the resource. Context places the requested transaction within a frame of reference associated with the system. This frame of reference can be based on time, a history of actions, or on the position of a rule within a rule-base.
- *Integrity.* The prevention of modification or destruction of an asset by an unauthorized user or entity; often used synonymously with data integrity, which asserts that data has not been exposed to malicious or accidental alteration or destruction.
- *Availability.* The protection of assets from denial-of-service threats that might impact system availability. Availability is also a critical system property from a non-security standpoint, where the source of system down time is due to faults rather than malicious attacks. Strategies based on software reliability theory for designing fault prevention, detection, tolerance, forecasting, and recovery, however, are often not very useful in protecting systems against active and intentional attacks. Modeling availability under malicious conditions is distinct

probabilistic models do not hold.

- *Confidentiality.* The property of non-disclosure of information to unauthorized users, entities, or processes.
- *Auditing.* The property of logging all system activities at levels sufficient for reconstruction of events. Auditing is often combined with alarming, which is the process of linking triggers to events. A trigger is any process that, based on system state, raises an exception to the administrative interface of the system. The action associated with the trigger defines the system's response to this exception. We say that the system has raised an alarm.
- *Nonrepudiation.* The prevention of any participant in a communication or transaction denying his or her role in the interaction once it is completed.

In addition to these seven key security principles, systems architects should provide support for other principles that improve the ease-of-use, maintainability, serviceability, and security administration of the system. These properties are generally at a higher level of abstraction and overlap with other architectural goals.

Additional Security-Related Properties

The seven principles of the last section are the most commonly cited, but good architecture choices also encourage other properties.

- *Secure Single Sign-On.* This capability allows an authenticated user access to all permitted assets and resources without reauthentication. The validity of the user's session can be limited by factors such as the time connected, the time of day, the expiry of credentials, or any other system-wide property. Once the system has terminated the user's session, all components within the system must deny the user access until he or she reauthenticates. Single sign-on is primarily a usability feature, but systems that require this functionality must be capable of doing so securely. We must guard against variations of password attacks in SSO environments, such as the theft of session credentials, replay attacks, masquerades, or denial-of-service attacks through lockouts.
- *Merged audit logs and log analysis.* This property requires all components to log events for analysis. Auditing should enable log integration, analysis, alarming, and system-wide incidence response. This situation is often a sticking point with architects, because auditing can cause performance and integration issues. Architects can optionally perform log analysis offline rather than in real time. This procedure might not prevent intrusions but only detect them after the fact. At the enterprise level, if we are able to standardize logging formats and consolidate audit information, we can enable higher functions, such as possibly using sophisticated analysis tools for knowledge extraction or case-based reasoning to understand alarms and network traffic. Merged audit logs are also useful for other goals such as performance testing and construction of operational profiles.

system and the associated data must be secure. In addition, security administration must not place unreasonable restrictions on system architecture or design. This property is often in conflict with other architectural goals, such as portability (because the administrative interface might not extend to a new platform) or scalability (because although the system itself can handle growth, the administrative component of the security solution cannot handle larger volumes of users, hosts, alarms, and so on).

- *Session protection.* This property ensures that unauthorized users cannot take over sessions or transactions of authenticated and authorized users.
- *Uniform security granularity.* This property ensures that the various components and subsystems of the architecture share similar definitions and granularities of assets and define access control rules in a similar manner. It is difficult to define security policy in an architecture in which one subsystem defines row-level, labeled security within its database and another subsystem recognizes only two levels of users; say, admin with root privileges and customers without root privileges.

Most vendors have standard responses to questions about the implementation of the first seven security principles. Our ability to differentiate between products is often at the level of the second list of properties described in this section.

Other Abstract or Hard-to-Provide Properties

The literature concerning security has an enormous amount of information about other properties of secure systems. Unfortunately, many are sometimes too abstract or difficult to implement in commercial software systems. These definitions have value because they support reasoning about system properties and formal proofs of correctness.

These properties require human intervention for analysis, and their implementation can restrict the feature set of the application in critical ways. Many of these properties cannot be asserted as true at the architecture phase of the application but must instead be deferred until the production system is available for a complete analysis. This issue is not so much about complexity as it is about ignorance. We lack the knowledge of implementation details. Unless we build the system, proving the existence or absence of one of these properties is difficult.

Inference

Mandatory access control, discussed next, uses hierarchies of security levels. Inference is defined as the ability to examine knowledge at one level of classification to acquire knowledge at a higher level of classification. Inference is a subtle property to prove because of the many ways in which systems can leak information. A user can view a process list, dig through files in a temporary directory, scan ports on a machine to see which ones do not respond, or launch carefully crafted attacks against a host to learn about the host without its knowledge.

inference, an attacker who is permitted to query a large database of information to extract a small set of permitted reports manipulates the query mechanism to infer privileged information whose access is forbidden by policy. The attacker generates a pattern of queries such that the responses all consist of permitted information when considered individually but can be combined in novel manners to leak secrets. Other examples include network mapping tools such as nmap (www.insecure.org/nmap/) which can be used for TCP fingerprinting, the process of sending specially crafted packets to a host to infer its model and operating system from the response. Nmap ("Network Mapper") is a high-performance, open-source utility for network exploration or security auditing. It is designed to scan large networks by using raw IP packets to determine dozens of characteristics of the hosts available on the network, including advertised services, operating systems, or firewall and packet filter properties. The packets have bogus source and destination IP addresses, target specific ports, and often have flags set incorrectly to generate error messages. An attacker could also examine memory by using raw disk read tools to reveal information, because running programs leave file fragments on disk or in memory that can be examined by other processes. Rogue Web sites can spoof legitimate sites, steal browser cookies, run ActiveX controls that leak information due to poor implementation, or surreptitiously download files to a host.

Aggregation

Aggregation is defined as the ability to examine a collection of data classified at one level and to learn about information at a higher level from the sum of these parts. Aggregation is more than a special case of inference because the ability to test the system for the absence of this property requires examining an exponentially larger number of scenarios. The most common example of aggregation at work is attacks designed against cryptographic protocols, such as linear and differential cryptanalysis, where the collection of enough plaintext-to-ciphertext pairs can lead to knowledge of a secret key. For example, the information leaked can be extracted through statistical analysis or through plaintext attacks using multiple agents.

The best defense against aggregation is building partitions in the architecture that implement information hiding. By examining data, implementing a need-to-know scheme of disseminating information, and by maintaining access thresholds, we can throttle the flow of information into and out of our application. If a password-guessing attack requires the capability to run several thousand passwords against a login on a host, a simple strategy can prevent it: lock out a user on three bad login attempts. If a database provides statistical averages of information but desires to hide the information itself, then users could be restricted to viewing small data sets within a smaller subtree of the data hierarchy by using only canned queries, instead of providing ad hoc query access to the entire database. Cryptography has formal theoretical models and solutions to prevent inference and aggregation; for example, protocols for zero-knowledge proofs.

Designing against all forms of aggregation is impossible. Security through obscurity works as well as any strategy to support this property, however.

Least Privilege

Least privilege requires that subjects be presented with the minimal amount of information needed to do their jobs. Least privilege is related to inference and aggregation, because violations of least privilege could lead to information leakage. Least privilege controls information flow. Architectures that desire to implement this principle need to protect against denial-of-service attacks, where the methods designed to restrict the flow of control are used to choke off legitimate access as well.

Self-Promotion

Self-promotion refers to the capability of a subject to arbitrarily, without supervision, assign itself additional privileges. Self-promotion differs from conventional self-granting of privileges because the subject that illegally grants itself access to an object is not the object's owner. Self-promotion can also involve, in addition to theft of authorization, the theft of ownership.

UNIX's infamous SUID attacks are a classic example of self-promotion. Unix SUID and SGID programs are a simplified (and patented) version of multi-level security models from the MULTICS operating system. Programs normally run with the privileges of the user who invokes them. A SUID program switches identity during execution to that of the owner of the program, however, rather than to the invoker of the program. A SUID program owned by root will run as root, for example.

Exploits on SUID programs can give the user a shell prompt on the machine. Audit tools can scan file systems for the existence of SUID programs and raise alarms on unexpected ones, such as a root-owned SUID shell interpreter in a user directory. They form the basis of rootkits, which we will discuss in our chapter on operating systems and which are used to attack systems in order to gain superuser privileges. Users who have limited privileges that need access to privileged resources such as print spoolers, protected memory, special kernel functions, or other protected resources can invoke SUID programs to do so.

Self-promotion also happens through the abuse of complex access policy mechanisms, where subjects grant privileges to other subjects and then allow recipients to pass on these privileges. Transitive grants of access muddy the picture by extending privileges without the owner's knowledge. Revoking privileges in this scenario can be difficult or can create paradoxes. We will revisit this issue in our discussion of access control.

Graceful Failure

Security exists in order to enable valid communication. This statement raises a point of contention between architects and security experts on the response of a system to the failure of a security component. The failure in this case can be accidental or can be due to compromise by a hacker through a successful exploit.

A component that fails is said to fail *closed* if all communication that depended on the component functioning correctly is now denied. A component is said to fail *open* if all communication, including invalid communication that would otherwise have been

not be compromised by a security component that fails closed. The equally obvious opinion of security experts is that a failed component should not expose the system to a new vulnerability and should therefore fail closed.

If we lived in a world where security components never failed due to non-malicious reasons, this situation would not be an issue. Note that failing open does not guarantee the success of any attack that would have previously been blocked. The system knows about the component failure and is most likely actively working on restoration while at the same time putting in place alternative measures to block invalid communication. The system might even have a means of identifying all invalid traffic at another choke point in the system and controlling it. The component that fails closed does not allow any communication, however.

This situation can have serious consequences. The system might have quality of service guarantees in its service-level agreement with customers that could cause considerable hardship, loss of revenue, or reputation. The problem arises when the component is a choke point, where the only means of continued service is through the component. The common architecture guideline used in this circumstance is as follows:

- All security components fail closed.
- No security component is a single point of failure.

The former is almost universally true, exceptions being normally the result of buggy software rather than intentional design. The latter is very hard to enforce and requires that security components such as packet-filtering routers, firewalls, or VPN gateways, secure DNS servers, and all security servers must always be built in highly available configurations. All systems must have failover networking, dual power supplies, and battery power to remain available all of the time. Systems that cannot ensure this function often give up instead and fail open.

Safety

Reasoning about security in an abstract fashion requires a definition of the system and its behavior in terms of entities operating on objects, along with a definition of the events and actions that transform the system in operation. The safety property asks, "Given a system in a certain initial state, can we reach some other state in the future where a particular subject has a specific privilege on a particular object?"

Reasoning about safety is valuable from an academic viewpoint because it requires rigorous definition of the system's states and transitions and the flow of ownership and privileges between entities. From a practical standpoint, however, we have never seen it applied in the field. Complex, real-world applications cannot be captured accurately through abstractions that are quickly invalidated by simple operational details of the system. The safety problem is not even decidable in some security models, and in general can be used only to demonstrate or present a sequence of steps that lead to a compromise of some asset.

and a security architect; one is focused on writing requirements to capture required features and the other is trying to determine whether satisfying those requirements could lead to insecure design. In interactions with projects at reviews, we have often noticed that the description of some implementation detail immediately raises security concerns. These concerns are best described in turn as a violation of some safety property: "Here is a sequence of actions that will lead to a compromise of a secured asset."

Safety analysis is also useful in weeding out false positives from audit tool reports. Ghosh and O'Connor in [GO98] analyze a popular open-source FTP server, wu-ftpd 2.4. Their analysis identified three potential code segments susceptible to buffer overflow attacks, but on further examination they decided that the FTP daemon was safe because there was no execution path to the code segments that would preserve the (carefully crafted) overflow-generating buffer up to that code segment. In each case, the buffer was either split up into multiple buffers (breaking apart the exploit) or forced to pass a "valid pathname" test that would detect an exploit.

Authentication

User authentication is the first step in many end-to-end use cases in an application. Authentication is the process of establishing the validity of a claimed identity. There are many authentication schemes, and here are a few.

User IDs and Passwords

User ID/password schemes are also called one-factor authentication schemes. They authenticate a user based on something the user knows. The application assigns users or other entities a unique identifier. This identifier alone is not sufficient for authentication but must be accompanied by some proof of identity. UNIX logins use a password scheme based on the security of the Data Encryption Standard (DES) algorithm. The user supplies a password that is then used, along with a two-byte "salt" subfield in the user's /etc/passwd entry, to encrypt a block of eight null bytes using the UNIX crypt( ) function. If the resulting value matches the remaining password hash stored in the password field of the entry, the user is authenticated and granted access to the system based on his or her user ID.

Passwords have had a very long and successful run, but the DES algorithm is showing its age as password crackers become more successful in exposing weak passwords. Applications can enhance the strength of user ID and password schemes by aging passwords, requiring minimum password strength, or enforcing lockouts based on too many bad login attempts.

Alternatively, an application can use one-time password schemes. Some one-time password schemes are software based; others use hardware tokens. For example, Bellcore's S/KEY, described in [Hal94], is based on Leslie Lamport's [Lam78] hash chaining one-time password scheme. S/Key extends the UNIX password mechanism to protect against passive password sniffing attacks. Although it improves the default UNIX pass-

[BS01]. S/Key does not protect against man-in-the-middle attacks, and because it does not use encryption, it also does not prevent network sniffing attacks that attempt to crack the root password on the hash chain from any one-time password seen from the sequence of passwords. IETF RFC 1938 defines a standard for one-time password schemes such as S/Key. This scheme is interesting from an architectural viewpoint because it takes the constrained environment of UNIX password authentication and enhances it in a clever way to support one-time passwords. There is an additional performance cost on the client side.

The more common one-time password schemes involve tokens.

Tokens

Authentication schemes based on tokens are also called two-factor authentication schemes. They authenticate a user based on something the user knows (a password) and something the user owns (a token). The two most popular token-based schemes are SecurID tokens and Smartcards.

- RSA Data Security Inc.'s SecurID token uses a proprietary algorithm running on both the user's token and a corporate token authentication server that uses the same set of inputs (a secret card-specific seed, the time of day, and other inputs) to generate a pass-code on the user's token that can be verified by the server. The display on the token changes once every minute (and, on some versions, requires the user to enter a *personal identification number* [PIN]).
- Smartcards are credit-card-sized computers based on the ISO 78xx standards series and other standards. Smartcards generally have cryptographic co-processors to support strong cryptography that would otherwise be impossible on their rather slow mid-80s processors (most often Motorola 6805 or Intel 8051). Smartcards have three memory segments: public (accessible to anyone), private (accessible to authenticated users), and secret (accessible only to the processor and administrative personnel). Smartcards support one-way symmetric authentication, mutual symmetric authentication, and static or dynamic asymmetric authentication. Asymmetric authentication schemes are challenge-response protocols based on RSA or on other asymmetric cryptography protocols. Smartcards are susceptible to *Power Differential Analysis* (PDA), an exploit invented by Paul Kocher. PDA uses the card's power usage to extract the secret keys stored on the card.

Biometric Schemes

Biometric schemes are also called three-factor authentication schemes and authenticate users based on something they know (a password), something they have (a token), and something they are (a retinal scan, thumbprint, or thermal scan). These schemes are very strong but are expensive and therefore inapplicable in many scenarios. Standards for using biometrics are still being worked on, and although they represent the future of authentication, we are nowhere near that future today. We refer the reader

www.securityfocus.com/, and www.digitalpersona.com/, for more information.

Authentication Infrastructures

Applications can implement security infrastructures such as Kerberos, DCE, or PKI to provide authentication services. We will describe application configuration issues for authentication infrastructures in the context of specific application domains and vendor products in Chapter 13, "Security Components."

Authorization

Authorization is also sometimes referred to as access control. Over the past three decades, a tremendous amount of academic and government research on access control has been completed alongside work on commercial implementations in products ranging from operating systems and databases to military command and control systems and banking networks. Each model of access control management is based on specific assumptions about the nature of the problem domain and the policy we desire to enforce. For example, theoretical models emphasize our ability to prove properties such as safety, whereas commercial implementations desire ease of administration and configuration.

At the heart of an access control model is the ability to make access decisions. An access decision must be made whenever a subject requests access to an object. Any decision requires two components: *data attributes* describing the subject and the object and a *decision procedure* that combines this information to arrive at an "allow" or "deny" answer. Some access control models even allow negotiation, in which the subject can provide additional information, change roles, or request a different access mode on the object. The model must enforce policy at all times. Consider, for example, the process of electing the President of the United States, which consists of data in the form of the votes cast and a decision process embodied by the Electoral College. If the result is in dispute, both parties can question either the data or the decision process. This results in the need for other important properties within a good access control model: the ability to administer the model and the ability to review aspects of the data.

In general, access controls are responsible for ensuring that all requests are handled according to security policy. Security policy defines rules of engagement and modes of operation permitted within the system. Normally, anything not explicitly permitted by the policy is denied. The system security policy represents the system's defined guidelines for management of security to attain the security principles mandated by the corporate security policy.

At times, there is an overlap between the needs of the application in controlling access according to the security policy and its needs in controlling access as part of the application business logic. In the following discussion, we will focus only on a security policy-

robust framework for defining permissions are willing to exploit it to embed business logic into the security framework). This choice has many risks; it is best not to muddle business rules with security policy. We will return to this issue in later chapters when we describe specific technologies.

Models for Access Control

Access control models provide high-level, domain-independent, and implementation-independent reference models for the architecture and design of access mechanisms. Models are built on certain assumptions that the underlying application must make concrete. In turn, models can guarantee security properties by using rigorous analysis (under the generic assumption of error-free implementation and configuration).

Historically, access control models are classified in two broad categories: mandatory and discretionary. We will describe each model in the next section and highlight their characteristics and differences for access management, but we will reserve the major part of our presentation for a description of the most popular model of access control: role-based access control (RBAC).

Mandatory Access Control

Mandatory access control governs the access of objects by subjects by using a classification hierarchy of labels. Every subject and object is assigned a label. All access is based on comparisons of these labels and, in general, is statically enforced. We say that access control is mandatory because the system centrally enforces all decisions to permit a subject's activities based on labels alone. Entities have no say in the matter.

Exceptions to static enforcement occur in models that support dynamic labeling at run time or in systems that assign multiple labels to subjects or objects and use an arbitrator to make an allow/deny decision. This situation can complicate management significantly and make analysis of properties such as safety difficult. Other models extend the label hierarchy horizontally at each label level by adding compartments, which represent categories of information at that level.

Mandatory access control centralizes the knowledge base used to make decisions, although subjects and objects can negotiate access based on local information. Entities are allowed to read objects with lower classifications and can write to objects only with the same classification level.

Discretionary Access Control

Discretionary access models are all descendants of Lampson's access matrix [Lam73], which organizes the security of a system into a two-dimensional matrix of authorizations in which each subject-object pair corresponds to a set of allowed access modes.

must satisfy consistency rules.

Discretionary access control governs the access of objects by subjects based on ownership or delegation credentials provided by the subject. These models are implicitly dynamic in that they allow users to grant and revoke privileges to other users or entities. Once access is granted, it can be transitively passed onto other entities either with or without the knowledge of the owner or originator of the permissions. Discretionary access control models enable subjects to transfer access rights for the objects they own or inherit, or for which they have received "grantor" privileges.

Consider they are a simplified model restricted to having only two kinds of entities, namely subjects and objects (setting aside roles for a moment). A subject can have system-wide privileges tied to whom they own (identity-based rights) and object-ownership privileges tied to the objects they own (ownership rights). In such a model, users can grant rights in three manners: A subject that owns an object can permit another subject to access it; a subject that owns an object can transfer ownership to another subject; or a subject can transfer all or part of its identity-based rights to another subject thereby granting all its modes of access to the receiver. The relationships are described in Figure 3.1.

Discretionary access control is flexible, but the propagation of rights through the system can be complex to track and can create paradoxes. If A grants B the "grant" right (effectively sharing ownership) to an object, and B in turn grants C "read" permission, what happens when A revokes the "grant" privilege from B? Does C still have "read" access to the object, or does the original revocation cascade through the system, generating additional revocations? Alternatively, does the security model reject A's revocation request, requiring that B first revoke C's rights? Reasoning about properties such as safety is also complex in DAC models.

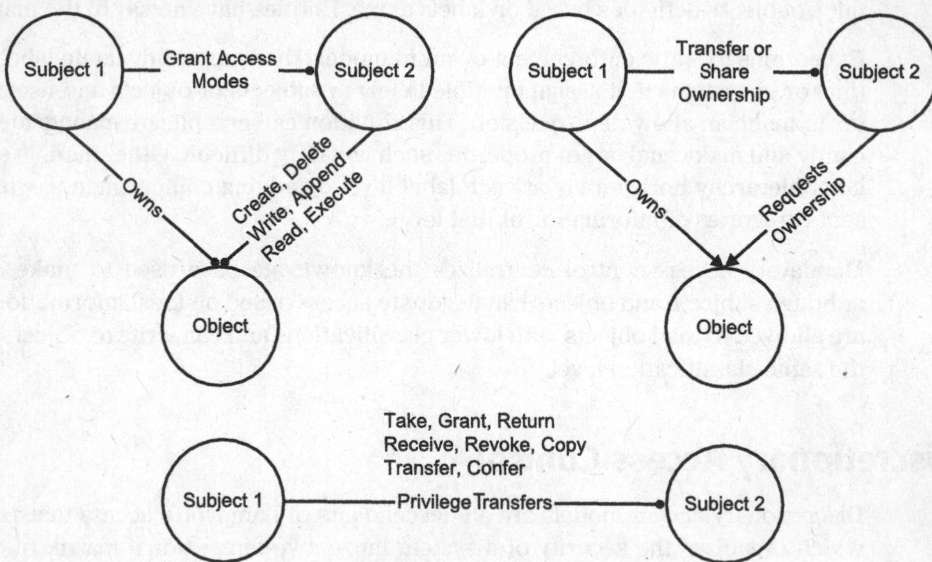

Figure 3.1 Ownership and access permission grants.

The adjectives mandatory and discretionary referring to a user's ability to modify access rights are no longer considered the most critical defining property of an access model. Current presentations (for an excellent survey please see [And01]) express the access model structurally as multi-level layers or multi-lateral smokestacks defined to accomplish some objective goal.

- Military multi-level models such as Bell-LaPadula protect the confidentiality of information.
- The multi-level Biba model protects data integrity.
- The multi-lateral Chinese Wall model of Brewer and Nash protects against conflicts of interest.
- The multi-lateral BMA model described in [And01] protects patient privacy.

The dominant access control model in academic research and commercial products is role-based access control (RBAC). RBAC has seen widespread acceptance because its objectives are architectural. RBAC simplifies security administration, includes role inheritance semantics to enable rich policy definition, and permits easy review of subject-to-role as well as role-to-permission assignments. RBAC is ideal for security architecture because of its alignment with our other architectural goals of simplicity, reliability, adaptability, and serviceability.

Although implicit role-based schemes have existed for more than 25 years in the form of models that use grouping, the first formal model for role-based access control was introduced in [FK92]. That same year, ANSI released the SQL92 standard for database management systems, which introduced data manipulation statements for defining roles, granting and revoking permissions, and managing role-based security policy. Ferraiolo and Kuhn in [FK92] insist that RBAC is a mandatory access control policy in contrast to Castano et al. in [CFMS94] who are just as insistent that RBAC is discretionary. In reality, there is a wide spectrum of RBAC-like security models with no standard reference model to describe subject and object groupings, role definition semantics, operations to access and modify policy, or resolutions to the complex transaction-based dynamics of role-based access. A recent innovative proposal from NIST (csrc.nist.gov/rbac) seeks to present a standard RBAC model that unifies key concepts from many implementations into a feature definition document supported by a reference implementation of the model and its management software. The advantages of such a reference model include common vocabulary, compliance tests, reuse of policy definition across products, and easier pairwise comparison of vendor products. Please refer to [SFK00] for a description of the standard or visit the NIST RBAC site for more information.

In this book, after describing RBAC, we will present several commercial access control models in terms of the vocabulary and concepts of this chapter. Some implementations are very feature-rich, while others barely qualify to be called RBAC. Because of the many advantages of a role-based security policy definition, we will make the reasonable assumption that most applications will build their security solutions around this model. Viewing vendor products in this light starkly contrasts the gap between policy and

own take on what role-based access control is and, therefore, configuration is not easy.

RBAC Concepts and Terminology

Role-based access control attempts to simplify the number of access definitions required between a large pool of subjects and a large pool of objects. This simplification is critical for achieving security in conjunction with other architectural goals, such as scalability, ease of administration, and performance. Adding users might not require additional user groups, and adding objects might not require additional object-access groups.

RBAC introduces roles to associate a use case of the system with a label that describes all the functions that are permitted and forbidden during the execution of the use case. Users execute transactions, which are higher abstractions corresponding to business actions, on the system. Within a single transaction, a user may assume multiple roles, either concurrently or serially, to access and modify objects. Separating users into domains and determining policy at the domain level insulates us from the churn in the underlying user population. Similarly, creating object groups adds simplicity to the classification of access modes to objects. Consider a database in which the basic object accessed could be of very fine granularity—for example, a single row or field of a table. Handling access labels at this fine level of granularity can add a huge performance cost, because every query against the table is now interrupted to check row-level access permissions. To avoid this performance hit we can grant the role access to the entire table instead of individual rows.

RBAC works as follows. Users are assigned to roles; objects are assigned to groups based on the access modes required; roles are associated with permissions; and users acquire access permissions on objects or object groups through roles by virtue of their membership in a role with the associated permissions. Roles can be organized into hierarchies with implicit inheritance of permissions or explicit denial of some subset of access permissions owned by the parent role. RBAC solutions define the following:

- *Object-access groups.* Objects can be organized into groups based on some attribute such as location (files in the same directory, rows in the same table) or by access modes (all objects readable in a context, all URLs in a document tree that are readable by a user, all valid SUID files executable by a user).
- *Access permissions.* Access permissions define the operations needed to legitimately access elements of an object group (access modes are also sometimes called operations). Any user that requests access to the object group must do so from a role that has been assigned the correct access permissions.
- *Roles.* Roles are use-case driven definitions extracted from the application's operational profile describing patterns of interaction within the application. We organize users into roles based on some *functional* attribute, such as affiliation (all users in the Sales organization; all administrators of the application; all managers requiring read-only, ad hoc query access to the database), by *access modes* (all users permitted to execute commands, all Web sites trusted to serve safe applets,

(manager, foreman, or shop worker). Static non-functional attributes of a user do not define roles (such as location, years of service, or annual income). The user must *do* something to belong to a role.

- *Role assignment.* We assign users or user groups to roles. Users can be assigned to multiple roles and must have a default role for any specific access decision. Users can dynamically change roles during a session. Transitions between roles may be password protected, and the application might even maintain a history of past roles for a user over the life of a session.

Figure 3.2 is a common pattern. In this diagram, we organize users into roles, organize objects and the modes of operation upon them into groups, and assign permissions to roles to enable specific access operations to any object within an object-access group.

In addition, the policy may place restrictions (either statically or dynamically) on how many roles can be simultaneously assumed by a subject or explicitly forbid a subject to be in two conflicting roles at the same time. In addition, the policy should specify default role assignments for users and group and ownership assignments for objects, respectively.

A critical innovation described in [SFK00] and pioneered by many models and implementations is the ability to define role hierarchies. Borrowing from the inheritance models of the object-oriented world, we may define hierarchies of roles and define the semantics of transfer of privileges between a parent role and its children to either empower or restrict the subordinate role in some key fashion. Permissions can be inherited, or users can be automatically added to a newly created instance of a role within the hierarchy. The role inherits the permissions of its subordinate roles and the users of its parent roles automatically.

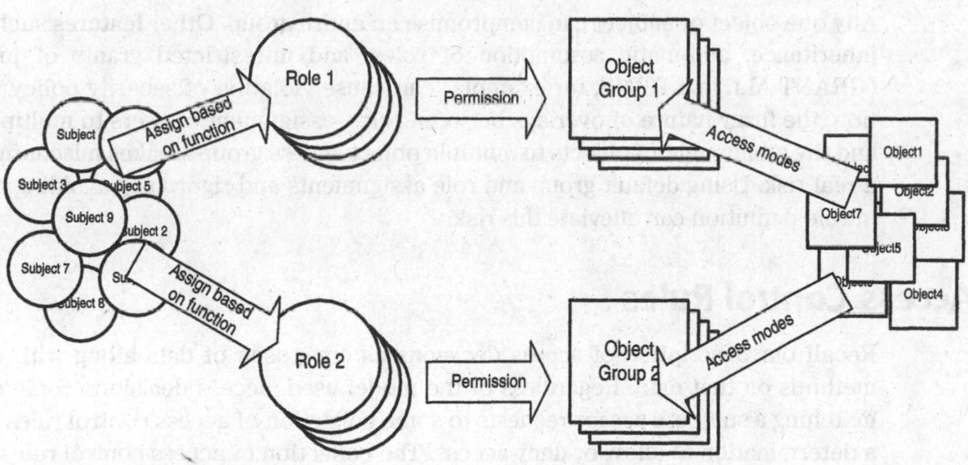

Figure 3.2 Role-based access control.

trol feature described in the following chapters into this basic mold. The variations can:

- Collapse the structure to make it even simpler, or conversely, introduce new context-based elements that make access definition more rich and complex.
- Make roles object-centric, in which a role defines a list of allowed access operations on all objects assigned to that role.
- Make roles user-centric, in which a role defines a list of capabilities shared by all the users assigned to that role.
- Apply an access definition transparency or mask to a role, which specifies maximum permissions allowed on the object regardless of any modifications to the access definitions on the role. Masks prevent accidental misconfiguration from exposing an object.
- Store evaluations of access decisions in a cache or ticket that can be saved or transported over the network.
- Allow subjects access to administrative roles that allow roles to be created, transferred, granted, revoked, or otherwise manipulated dynamically at run time. This can significantly complicate analysis but can present powerful tools for implementing the principle of least privilege in your application.
- Add extensive support for administrative operations, role and object definition review, guard against misconfiguration and paranoid modes for roles that redefine policy dynamically.

Why is role-based access control so popular? The answer is simplicity. The complexity of access control implementation is contained in the initial configuration of the application. After this point, making access decisions is made easier because the dynamic nature of the subject-object endpoints of the access decision is largely hidden.

What is bad about role-based access control? RBAC reduces identity theft to role theft. Any one object or subject can compromise an entire group. Other features such as role inheritance, automatic assumption of roles, and unrestricted grants of privileges (GRANT ALL in a DBMS, for example) can cause violation of security policy. In addition, the fuzzy nature of overlaps between roles, assignment of users to multiple roles, and the assignment of objects to multiple object-access groups makes misconfiguration a real risk. Using default group and role assignments and rigorously avoiding overlaps in role definition can alleviate this risk.

Access Control Rules

Recall our description of access decisions as composed of data along with decision methods on that data. Regardless of the model used, access decisions come down to matching a subject's access requests to some collection of access control rules to make a determination to allow or deny access. The collection of access control rules embodies an instance of the security policy at work.

Access control models aim to fulfill two performance goals. The first seeks to represent all the data required for access decisions as compactly as possible. The second seeks to

conflict with others such as speed of access definition review or administration. Any particular vendor solution will represent a unique set of compromises. For example, a model may store access rules for a subject in a set-theoretic manner: User X is ALLOWED access to {A,B,C,D,E} via one rule, but DENIED access to {C,D} via another. We have to compute the set difference between these two rules to arrive at a decision on a specific access request ("Can X read B?" "Yes"). We can view each access decision as combining all available data to arrive at a list of access control rules and applying a decision process to the set of rules.

In general, when multiple rules apply to an access decision on whether a given subject in a given context can access an object, the policy must resolve the multiple directives into an acceptable decision. The resolution strategy should have the following properties:

- *Consistency.* The outcome of an access decision should be the same whenever all the parameters to the decision, and any external factors used in resolution, are repeated.
- *Completeness.* Every form of allowed access should correspond to an expected application of the security policy.

The resolution algorithm must, of course, correctly implement policy. The modes of resolving multiple rules fall into one of three options.

- *First fit.* The access control rules are ordered in a linear fashion, and rules are applied in order until one rule either explicitly allows or denies access. No further examination is conducted. If all rules have been found inapplicable, access is denied by a "fall-through exception" rule of least privilege.
- *Worst fit.* All applicable rules are extracted from the rule base and examined against the parameters of the access decision. Access is allowed only if all rules allow access. If no applicable rules are found, or if any rule denies access, then the subject is refused access to the object.
- *Best fit.* All applicable rules are extracted from the rule base and passed to an arbitrator. The arbitrator uses an algorithm based on all parameters and possibly on information external to the parameters of the access decision and priorities between applicable rules to make the best possible decision (which is, of course, application specific). The arbitrator must be consistent.

Choosing the right strategy is dependent on application domain knowledge. We recommend defining access control rules that satisfy the disjoint property: For any access decision, at most one rule applies. Network appliances that filter packets use this strategy. Often, although the access control rules within the appliance work on the first-fit strategy, the architect can ensure that in the design of the policy no further rules will apply. Thus, the configuration of rules on the appliance reflects a uniqueness property.

In the following description, we will ignore the dynamic nature of access decision making, in which either the data or the access control rules can change as we apply our access decision algorithm. In general, access control rules use the following parameters to define an access control rule-base as a function mapping a 4-tuple to the set {ALLOW, DENY}. The fields of the 4-tuple are as follows:

resource. The subject is assumed to have passed some identity and authentication test before requesting service.

- *Object.* The passive target of the access, possibly providing a service, accepting a message, returning a value, or changing state. The object is assumed to have passed some validation test before being made available for access.
- *Privileged Operation.* The type of access requested. For a data object, access could include create, update, delete, insert, append, read, or write modes.
- *Context.* A predicate about the environment that must hold true. Context can catch many environment attributes, such as the following:
  - *Ownership.* Did the subject create the object?
  - *History.* What sequence of events led to this access request?
  - *Time.* Is the time of day relevant?
  - *Quality of service.* Has the subject subscribed to some stated level of quality of service that would prevent an otherwise allowed access due to a competing request from higher levels? QoS for business reasons sometimes appears in security solutions.
  - *Rights.* Has the subject been granted or revoked certain rights by the system?
  - *Delegation.* Does the subject possess credentials from a secondary subject on whose behalf access is being requested? This situation might require a loop back to the beginning to refer to a different rule with all other parameters remaining the same.
  - *Inference.* Will permitting access result in a breach in the security policies guidelines for preventing logical inference of information by unauthorized entities?

Thus, an access control rule-base defines a function as follows:

$$ACRB : \langle s,o,p,c \rangle \rightarrow \{ALLOW, DENY\}$$

This function gives us the ability to organize the rules according to different viewpoints.

- An *access control list* is a collection of all access-allowing rules that apply to a single object. For example, an ACL for a file describes all the users who are allowed access and their associated permissions to read, write, or execute the file.
- A *capability list* is a collection of all access-allowing rules that apply to a single subject. For example, based on the security policy, a signed Java applet might be granted access to a collection of system resources normally otherwise blocked by the Java sandbox.
- An *access mode list* is a collection of all access-allowing rules that specify the same mode of access. For example, a corporate directory could specify a permissive security policy with respect to reads, but restrict writes to strongly authenticated administrators only.

context. For example, an application could distinguish between access control definitions during normal operations and those in situations in which the application is responding to a disaster or to a work stoppage by a large pool of users.

Applications sometimes abuse the ability to organize by context by exhibiting the inadvisable habit of including business logic into security policy definitions. For example, an application could specify access control rules that restrict, during peak usage, some resource-intensive activities or require all funds transfers to be done before 3 p.m. Monday through Friday because that is when the banks are open. This overlap of functionality tends to muddy the distinction between corporate security policy and the operational profile of the system.

Understanding the Application's Access Needs

To design a robust model of access control from an architecture perspective, we must first ask ourselves questions about the application domain. RBAC has both flexibility and architectural support for evolution.

Creation and Ownership

Questions on object creation and ownership include the following:

- Do subjects create objects? If so, do we maintain knowledge of an object's creator within the application?
- Do subjects own objects? If so, do we maintain knowledge of an object's (possibly multiple) owners? Is there a default owner for each object?
- Do objects have fine-grained structure? Does access to the object imply access to all parts of the object?
- Are objects organized in a hierarchical fashion according to a labeling scheme that honors some security principle? The principle could be:
  - *Secrecy.* A subject must have a certain level of clearance to access the object (the Bell-LaPadula model).
  - *Integrity.* A subject must have a certain level of trustworthiness to access the object (the Biba model).
  - *Non-repudiation.* A subject's access to an object at one level must be undeniable by a higher standard of proof compared to access to an object at a lower level (this situation does not correspond to a formal model, but non-repudiation protocols consider this factor).
- Do objects have non-hierarchical labels that could also be used as context information to make access decisions?

Questions on roles and access modes include the following:

- Does the application divide its user community into classes of users based on the grouping of user activities into roles in the application's operational profile?
- What access modes do subjects need? Can they create, delete, update, insert, read, write, alter, append, or otherwise modify objects? Does the object need to be protected during each mode of access? Do we audit all object access for forensics?
- Does the application assign distinguished status to one member of each role as the member responsible for the integrity of the object? This could be necessary if another user in the role corrupts an object by accident or malice.
- Do the access modes of objects within the application have dramatically different structures? This situation occurs if the application has a corporate directory function with wide read access but very restricted write access. If performance requirements are different for different access modes, this might impact the choice of security around each mode (for example, no security for reads to the directory, but writers must be authenticated).

Application Structure

Questions about structure include the following:

- Does the application partition the object space according to some well-defined method? Are objects within each partition invisible to objects in other partitions? Are users aware of the existence of the partitions, or does the application give them the virtual feeling of full access while invisibly implementing access control?
- Are any objects contained within a critical section? Will access control to resources in a critical section cause undesirable properties in the system? A critical section within an application is accessible by only using specific atomic requests, which are carefully managed. Critical sections protect resources from corruption or race conditions but can result in deadlock if incorrectly designed and implemented.
- Can objects present polyinstantiated interfaces? Polyinstantiation is the ability to create multiple virtual instances of an object based on the credentials of the subject. Access to the actual data, to perform reads or writes, is carefully monitored by coordinating reads and writes to the virtual objects. Users are unaware that they are interacting with polyinstantiated objects.
- Does the application contain multiple access control decision points? Is access control implemented at each of the points, and if so, does the chained sequence of decisions comply with the intended security policy? Are all decisions made under a single security policy, or do different information flow points reference different masters for access control decisions?

Discretionary Rules

Questions about discretionary access control include the following:

- Can users grant privileges to other users? Can users assume the identity of other users legitimately, through delegation?
- Can users revoke privileges previously granted to other users? Revocation can cause paradoxes if users are allowed to transitively grant access to other users after they have acquired access themselves. Is revocation implemented in a manner that avoids or detects and corrects paradoxes?
- Can objects assume the identity of other objects?
- Is delegation allowed? Do we inform the original owner of the object when a downstream delegate accesses it?

Obviously, resolving these issues is difficult. We believe, however, that understanding the implications of the architect's responses to these questions is critical to the design of a correct, consistent, complete, and usable access control solution. The exercise of examining these questions should be accomplished before choosing any vendor product from several alternatives.

Other Core Security Properties

We will revisit the other core security properties, such as integrity, availability, confidentiality, auditing, and non-repudiation, in the following chapters. Unlike access control, which has a long and rich history of theoretical models, these properties are best discussed with reference to a problem at hand. It is easier to recommend strategies for ensuring these properties within the context of specific application components and technologies.

Analyzing a Generic System

A generic system or application solves some well-defined problem within a context. The project must build the application around corporate standards and must conform to security policy. Figure 3.3 shows some of the design tensions faced by an architect from an engineering and technology viewpoint.

Our example application consists of a Web front end to an application server. The application server can access legacy applications for data and wrapped business functions and can query a corporate directory for user, group, organization, and system profiles. Infrastructure components for providing services like mail, DNS, time, news, messaging, or backup might also need security.

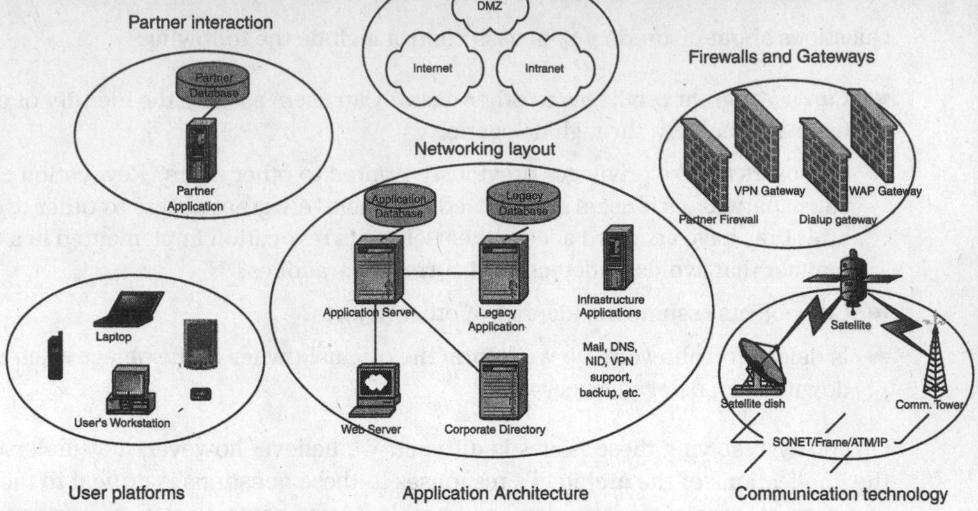

Figure 3.3 Architectural tensions surrounding an application.

Around the application, shown in Figure 3.3, are constellations of components that the architect must depend upon, over which he or she might have very little control or choice.

- *User platforms.* Users can access data and services by using a variety of devices including desktops, laptops, pagers, cellular phones, and handheld devices. Each device can support a thin client such as a browser, or a custom-embedded client that must be developed in-house or purchased. The user can communicate with the application with a wide variety of protocols.
- *Partner applications.* The application might have a tight coupling to business partners and require connectivity to a demilitarized zone for secure access to partner data and services.
- *Networks.* A wide variety of logical networks, at varying levels of trust, can carry application traffic.
- *Firewalls and gateways.* Connectivity to the application from each user platform and over each network might require authentication and session validation at one or more gateways. Intermediate firewalls and routers on communications paths might need special configuration.
- *Communications technology.* The application can use several different communications technologies, each supporting security by using a unique paradigm.

Other architectural viewpoints also reveal similar collections of artifacts all jostling for attention. Consider a process viewpoint that reorganizes engineering or technology issues on a component basis. Figure 3.4 shows the same example application as it would appear with connections to partners and backend systems, in a generic enterprise.

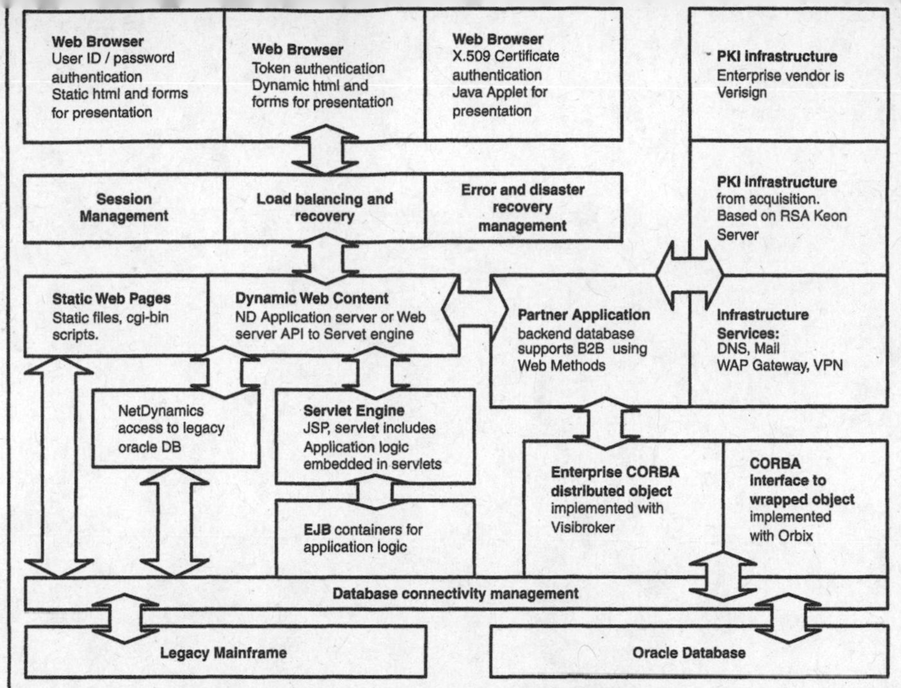

Figure 3.4 An enterprise application with many components.

Thinking about security for the application in the above environment is very difficult, and measuring compliance to policy is even harder. Examine the diagram to see parallels or departures from your own application architecture.

The remainder of our presentation will explore specific concerns such as writing safe code; trusting downloaded code; securing operating systems, Web servers, and databases; and using middleware products securely. We will end by returning to enterprise security as a rallying point for building consensus among systems architects across the corporation.

Conclusion

The bibliography contains several references for more information about security principles, properties, authentication mechanisms, and access control. We recommend reading about the history of access control models to better understand the evolution of authorization principles, and the background behind the adoption, by commercial products of several common mechanisms.

In the next chapter, we now proceed to our next task: building a catalog of security architecture patterns.

Architecture Patterns in Security

The purpose of security is to enable valid communication, preferably in as transparent a manner as possible. At the same moment, all invalid communication—whether unauthorized, unauthenticated, unexpected, uninvited, or unwanted—should be blocked. The only way of accomplishing these goals is through authentication of all principals within the application and through inspection of all communication. There are many technologies—each a collection of tools, protocols, and components—all available for designing security solutions to accomplish these two goals. Despite this variety, when we look at the system we can see patterns of implementation emerge at the architecture level as a network of components interacting based on the logical relationships imposed by the problem domain.

Pattern Goals

Our choice of the word *patterns* might cause some misconceptions because of the considerable baggage that the term carries. We thought about alternative terms, such as styles or profiles, but in the end stayed with patterns because, simply, the good outweighed the bad. Our collection of security patterns shares some of the same goals as the pattern community at large. Specifically, something is a security pattern if:

- We can give it a name.
- We have observed its design repeated over and over in many security products.
- There is a benefit to defining some standard vocabulary dictated by common usage rules to describe the pattern.
- There is a good security product that exemplifies the pattern.

complex portions of an architecture diagram more intelligible. The pattern might make the evaluation of a product easier by highlighting departures from a standard way of approaching a problem. It might also raise a core set of issues against these departures.

We would like to note several important distinctions because of the differences between our pattern descriptions and those of the object-oriented pattern community.

- The patterns we describe are not object-oriented in any manner.
- We will not use the presentation style commonly used for pattern description. Issues of context, forces, variation, and so on will be described informally when we reach our discussion of specific security scenarios in later chapters.
- These patterns do not generate architectural decisions, nor do they provide guidance on how to structure other portions of the system architecture.
- They do not codify best practices. Using one of these patterns will not necessarily make your product or system safer.

We have a lot of respect for the wonderful contributions of the pattern community and strongly believe in the measurable and quantifiable merits of patterns, both for object reuse and for architecture analysis purposes. We do not want to present the material in the chapter as having virtues beyond that of enabling us to think about security architectures more easily, however.

We abstract and present these only so that architects can easily recognize them in designs and then ask good questions about their implementation. We do not intend to start a cottage industry in security pattern definition.

Common Terminology

There are some terms used by vendors and application developers alike that often reoccur in security architecture descriptions. In the following sections, we will describe certain patterns of interaction and label them with a name. This procedure is not an attempt to enforce some abstract nomenclature on an existing and diverse collection of

Pattern Origins

Many of the security patterns that follow have been introduced and discussed in the pattern literature before, albeit not in a security context. We believe all of these concepts are, by their very nature, too well known for any one source to claim original definition. Patterns are, by definition, codified common-sense recognition of solutions to problems within contexts. We will, however, cite references with each pattern when we are aware of a prior description.

words and terminology of their creators, but we will use the patterns described in this chapter as the starting point for a taxonomy for describing security options available in particular parts of the systems architecture: within code, within the OS, within the Web server, within the database, or within middleware.

When there are subtle differences in the way the same concept is defined from two different and equally authoritative sources, we are often left with a confusing choice. Is the distinction critical, revealing a fundamental gap in functionality? Or, as is more often the case, are we looking at a distinction with no real difference? We will try to avoid such confusion. We will define any security terms used in support of the pattern within the pattern description itself. Again, the purpose is to guide the reader by providing a single point of reference for vocabulary.

We refer the reader to the previous chapter for the definition of security principles and some common terms required for the following descriptions.

Architecture Principles and Patterns

Implementation of the seven security principles, discussed in Chapter 3, "Security Architecture Basics," within any system architecture occurs through a process of decomposition and examination of the components of the system. The architect must perform the following jobs.

Identify entities. These might be subjects, objects, hosts, users, applications, processes, databases, code, or in general any entity that requests and requires resources within the application.

Map entities to context attributes. The context attributes of an entity add to our knowledge of the entity. These are values, possibly used in authentication or access decisions involving the entity, that are external to the collection of identifying credentials carried by the entity itself. Context attributes are made available by the environment of the entity or by service providers. When an entity requests a resource, its identity and context are necessary for making access decisions about the request.

Identify security service providers. Security service providers are most often third-party products, located locally or remotely, that perform some security function. A security service provider could perform cryptographic operations, perform lookups on behalf of a client to trusted third-party components such as a directory or an OCSP server, manage secure access to data stores, provide network time service, or enable token authentication.

Identify communication channels between entities. This identification could be through a description of common interactions where security is needed, such as on the wire, between the user and the Web server, during object-to-object invocation, from an application to the database, across firewalls, and so on. Depending on the architectural viewpoint model used, such as the object view, the process view, the network view, or the workflow view, each channel might require security from one of two perspectives:

protection is accomplished by using a *channel element* to control communication on the channel.

- Protection against external malicious agents. The communication channel itself must be confidential and tamperproof, and connectivity must be guaranteed.

Identify platform components. Platform components create structure in the architecture. They divide the proposed architecture into horizontal or vertical layers, create messaging or software bus components, identify clustering or grouping, and enable us to identify *inside* and *outside* dimensions on boundary layers. Platform components can be defined at any level: machine, network, protocol, object, service, or process.

Identify a source for policy. This source is a single, abstract point of reference within the architecture that serves as an authority and an arbitrator for any security policy implementation issues. All entities load their local policies from this source.

At this point, due to the very general nature of the discussion, there is really not much to debate about this process. Before we can meaningfully apply these concepts, we must first describe patterns of use in their application.

The Security Pattern Catalog

Here is our catalog of security patterns, shown in Figure 4.1, organized into five categories—each corresponding to one of the steps listed in the previous section.

We will now proceed to describe each pattern, give examples of its use within a system's architecture, and discuss some issues with its use.

Entity

Entities are actors in our application use cases. Entities can be users, administrators, or customers. Entities can also be inanimate objects, such as hosts or other systems that can send messages to our application. Entities can be internal to the application (for example, a system process) or can be external to the application (for example, a user at a terminal).

Principal

A *principal* is any entity within the application that must be authenticated in some manner. A principal is an active agent and has a profile of system use. An access request by a principal initiates a security policy decision on authorized use. A principal can engage in a transaction or communication that requires the presentation and validation of an identifying credential. An identifying credential has attributes that describe the

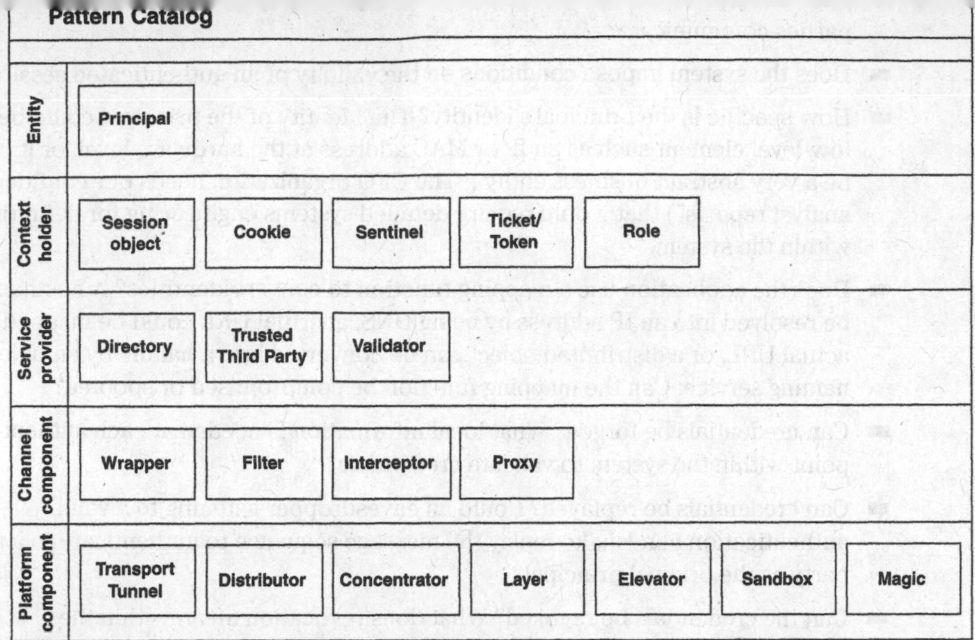

Figure 4.1 The security patterns catalog.

entity, along with authentication information. The principal's identity is bound to the authentication information somewhere in the architecture.

There are many methods of authenticating a principal, based on how many pieces or factors of information are required.

- One factor, or "something you know" (for example, user IDs and passwords). A UNIX login has a corresponding password hash entry in /etc/passwd used for password validation. An X.509v3 certificate binds the owner's distinguished name to the public half of a key pair. The system authenticates the principal through a challenge-response protocol requiring knowledge of the corresponding private key.
- Two factors, or "something you know and something you have" (for example, tokens and smartcards that use challenge-response protocols)
- Three factors, or "something you know, something you have, and something you are" (for example, systems that use biometric devices to test physical attributes)

Applications can use the principle of transitive trust, where A authenticates to system B which then invokes C on A's behalf. C only authenticates B and not A. Transitive trust is an important simplifying element in security architectures that could result in system compromise if a multi-hop trusted relationship is violated.

Several common issues must be raised at the architecture review about the method of authentication of a principal within an application.

parties communicate?

- Does the system impose conditions on the validity of an authenticated session?
- How specific is the principal's identity? The identity of the principal could be a low-level element such as an IP or MAC address at the hardware level, or it could be a very abstract business entity ("The CFO organization needs our confidential analyst reports") that would require detailed systems engineering for definition within the system.
- Does the application use a mapping function to convert identities? A hostname can be resolved into an IP address by using DNS, a virtual URL could be mapped to an actual URL, or a distributed object can be converted into a handle by an object naming service. Can the mapping function be compromised or spoofed?
- Can credentials be forged? What local information is needed at each authentication point within the system to validate credentials?
- Can credentials be replayed? Could an eavesdropper listening to a valid authentication handshake replay the message sequence to authenticate to a third party as the original principal?
- Can the credentials be revoked? What does revocation mean within the application? Revocation of an X.509v3 certificate could imply the addition of the certificate's serial number to a published Certificate Revocation List or the addition of the serial number to the *Online Certificate Status Protocol* (OCSP) server. In another case, within a database, a revocation request could be restricted or even not honored if there are implicit grants of privileges made by the principal that would result in logical inconsistencies in the privilege model. Alternatively, the database could choose to cascade revocations, using additional logic to force additional privileges that were once granted by this principal, to be revoked. Thus, once a principal is revoked, additional revocations are generated that cascade through the system.
- Can the credentials be delegated? A delegate is a principal who presents credentials authorizing access to a resource as another principal. In a UNIX environment, SUID programs allow a user to assume the identity of the program's owner in order to access resources such as a print queue or a file that would normally be hidden from the user.
- Does the application use the principle of transitive trust? If so, do we log the claimed identity of the subject?
- Can the principal assume the identity of another principal? This process is possibly different from delegation, in which the principal is not a delegate for an upstream entity but merely wishes to masquerade as another entity for the duration of a transaction.
- Can credentials be lost? Can they be replaced in a timely fashion?

The first step in any security architecture is the identification and classification of all participating principals.

Context Holders

Context holders contain context attributes that add to our knowledge of the principal during a security access decision, within a session, on a resource request.

Session Objects and Cookies

Context attributes on sessions add to our knowledge of the principal or the session under consideration during a security access decision. Context information can be stored on the server, often called a *session object*, or on the client, often referred to as a *cookie*.

Context attributes in session objects and cookies are lists of name-value pairs attached to a principal or to an object that the principal wishes to access. Client-side attributes are often established at the server (or in general, the destination entity) and transported to the client (or in general, the source of the request). This process enables the server to add integrity checks to the values, format the contents of the cookie, maintain uniqueness across all the cookies issued, and maintain some level of trust. If the context was manufactured only by the source, then other means of validation of the attributes, involving third parties, must be used before the session can be established.

Context attributes can qualify properties of the session from a security perspective. They can add to our ability to make an access decision by describing the source, the destination, the role of the principal, the access requested, the privileges available at the destination, and the time of the conversation. Session objects and cookies can also store security state information.

The use of context attributes within secure sessions in the application raises several issues at the architecture review.

- Does the session have an expiration time?
- Can it be re-established without reauthentication based on information within session objects and cookies?
- Is the session shared? Can several servers support a client, and if so, is this connectivity transparent?
- Can the context attributes be modified, deleted, enhanced, appended to, or forged in any manner? Can sessions be stolen as a result?
- Are context attributes automatically invalidated on a session termination request, either by the client or the server or when certain session conditions ("Time is up," "Too many messages," "Too much data transferred," or "Name value pair is invalid") occur?
- Do context attributes protect against session hijacks? A hijack gives control of a valid and authenticated session to an untrusted party. The party might not have the

impersonated.

- Are context attributes long-lived? Are they reused? Can they be added to logs? Can they be delegated to other sessions in an inheritance model? Is it possible to audit their use?
- Do attributes use cryptographic primitives, such as encryption or message authentication codes? In this case, do we save the key material used for validating attributes at any point, perhaps for key recovery or nonrepudiation?

Ticket/Token

A *ticket* or *token* is a mobile context holder given to a previously authenticated principal. The details of the transaction that authenticated the principal might not be available to a ticket or token server or a third party, but the fact that the principal successfully passed authentication can be verified by examining the ticket or token.

Tickets support requests for service, where the identity of the principal may or may not be integral to a response. Tickets and tokens appear in security tools in a number of ways.

- Web browsers send portions of cookies back to the servers that originally generated the cookie in order to re-establish a disconnected session.
- Kerberos contains two services—an authentication server and a ticket-granting server—to separate the concerns of authenticating principals and making access decisions.
- Some applications use tokens to perform operations on critical sections. A process that requests access from the critical section must first wait in a queue to acquire a token from a token-granting service. This bakery line model appears in atomic primitives such as semaphores, which can be useful for resolving synchronization issues within operating systems. Tickets also appear in many security products that implement resource locking.

Because tickets or tokens are issued in response to a request for service, their use enables a separation of authentication and access decision concerns. A third party that has access to specialized information that can be bundled into the ticket can generate the ticket, thereby simplifying access decisions. Tickets also help applications build transaction traces.

Tokens encapsulate privileges and as a result often carry timestamps to force expiry (to manage the life of the privilege granted). The principal's permission to perform an action can be limited. Tokens sometimes are used in delegation of credentials, where principal B, acting on behalf of principal A, upon server C, can present a token proving that B has authority to do so. Access decisions, once made and approved, can be recorded to tokens, and circulated to other components in the architecture. This process can simplify decision making when complex arbitration, involving the history of the principal's actions, is required.

ing possession of a token. The token is a prerequisite for action, and exchanges of tokens are predicated on correct state transitions.

Sentinel

A *sentinel* is a data item within a transaction or communication that is invisible during normal execution but can be used to detect malicious use that damages the sentinel or some property of the sentinel.

A sentinel guards against improper use that would otherwise go undetected. The sentinel does not perform error correction, error prevention, or error avoidance. It only falls over when the system is abused. Other monitoring entities must detect the sentinel's failure and raise alarms appropriately.

Examples of sentinels include the following:

- StackGuard protects programs from buffer overflows by inserting an additional word, called a *canary*, onto the user stack within the stack frame below the return address location. A buffer overflow exploit in the stack frame will overrun the canary. The canary can be checked upon exit to detect the exploit.
- Tripwire creates a database of cryptographic checksums of all the files in a file system. Any modification to a file can be detected when its checksum is recomputed and compared to the sentinel value in the Tripwire database.
- IP datagrams carry a checksum to ensure the integrity of the transmitted packet. This checksum is not as strong as the cryptographic checksums used by Tripwire, but it can guard against noise.

Sentinels protect the boundaries of the system space in a passive manner. They are useful in situations where prevention or correction creates prohibitive performance penalties.

Roles

Roles define use-case driven functional patterns of behavior within the application. The role is often stored as part of the session object describing the current transaction within which the principal is involved. The transmission of the role to a participating entity is equivalent to transmitting an entire list of attributes describing the role, its permissions, and the objects a user can access from the role. A user may dynamically switch roles within a single user session and may be forced to authenticate to assume the new role.

Roles are abstract notions created primarily to simplify authorization. Roles organize potentially thousands of users into user groups and assign permissions to the groups rather than to individual users. Roles are normally stored in some central policy database within the application, and authenticated users can choose one of the many roles they can be assigned within a specific session.

example,

- The role can be part of the attribute extensions available within an X509v3 certificate. In this case, the role is static, and the user cannot change roles easily. The certificate must be reissued if the role field is modified.
- In UNIX, the role might be captured in the user's group ID. A principal can access files belonging to other users that share a group with the principal.
- In UNIX, a program switches execution roles between User mode and Kernel mode as execution proceeds, whenever the user program requests access to system resources through the well-defined interface of allowed system calls.
- Programs that use the SUID and SGID feature in UNIX to access privileged resources change their user or group ID, effectively changing their role on the system.

Users can be denied privileges by deleting them from roles. In general, it is advisable to assign users to disjoint roles, in which membership in multiple roles does not create conflicts in privilege definition. A user who has multiple roles can pick a default active role for all decisions within a particular session. The default role assignment will determine authorizations. Please refer to the discussion in Chapter 3 on issues relating to access control rules and mandatory, discretionary, and role-based models of access control.

Service Providers

Security service providers perform some well-defined, possibly complex, and distinguished action on behalf of any entity involved in a secure communication. We will separate service providers into three classes: *directories*, *trusted third parties*, and *validators* (the third being a catch-all category to cover the huge variety in security services possible).

Directory

Directories are databases that are read often but written to infrequently. Directories have seen a tremendous growth in recent years. The widespread acceptance has been fueled in part by improvements in directory standards and the availability of good commercial directories and directory-enabled products. Deployment has been helped by the development of common schemas and access protocols for many standard problems, such as the definition of user communities, organizational hierarchies, user profiles, and application profiles.

The original X.500 directory definition had a complex access method supporting combinations of scoping and filtering predicates on a query accessing objects in the directory, called the X.500 Directory Access Protocol. The X.500 standard has been stable since 1993, although compliant products have only been a recent phenomenon.

factor in the widespread acceptance of directories today. The de facto directory standard on the Internet today is the *Lightweight Directory Access Protocol* (LDAP), developed at the University of Michigan. For additional details, please refer to Chapter 13, "Security Components." In the mid 1980s, networking exploded with the introduction of TCP/IP, which simplified the seven-layer ISO network stack definition into a four-layer stack implementation. This feature enabled rapid product development on a functional but immature protocol. On the downside many of the complexities of securing TCP/IP stem from the lack of security architecture in its original simple design.

Directories are following the same evolution path. The original LDAP protocol shortens message lengths, removes rarely used components of the DAP protocol, while still supporting reasonable powerful access to a wide array of schemas. However, as more features and functionality are added to LDAP to support enterprise directory-enabled networking, its complexity is growing to match and exceed DAP.

Directories are an important security component because they allow enterprises to partition and manage user communities. Corporations need directions on how to allow access to several user groups:

Customers, in very large numbers. We have a limited amount of information on each customer who in turn has limited access to resources.

Employees and contractors, in medium to large numbers. This community has very extensive, complex access to many systems, in many roles. This user community should consume the lion's share of our security resources.

Partners, in small numbers. Partners have very specific access requirements, possibly restricted to a DMZ, but support mission critical business needs. Other architectural goals such as reliability, availability, and safety apply to partner access.

Upper management, such as officers of the company. This is a very small community that requires access to the critical and high value information in the systems. Upper management may also have access to external documents such as legal contracts or analyst reports. The theft or exposure of this information could result in enormous costs and risks to the company, not to mention the creation of legal liabilities. This community also requires access to analysis reports generated by many systems within the company, whose access might be restricted to the majority of users.

We, therefore, have to deal with diverse user communities, multiple hierarchies of information, and legacy directories that compete with one another for database-of-record status—in addition to directory data integration across the enterprise.

How should we resolve conflicts in directory deployment? Data architects implement the following common architectural paradigm:

- Build outward facing directories supporting customers and partners.
- Build inward facing directories supporting employees.

- Place all these diverse data repositories under the umbrella of a federated directory structure, controlled by one or more meta directories.

Directories are also key security components because they are repositories of security policy. Directories are considered the database of record for user profile information and also support additional user attributes, such as application specific roles, lists of services permitted, relationship hierarchies to other employees through organizational structure, and user group information. Commercial directory products come with default schemas for defining labels for the fields in a user's distinguished name. The distinguished name is a collection of name-value pairs for attributes such as the organization, organizational unit, location, address, e-mail, phone, fax, and cellular phone details. Directories also support a large collection of standard queries with very fast access implemented through the extensive use of index tables. They support secure administration and bulk uploads of data to enable rapid deployment and management.

The read-often property of directories is supported by the index table definitions, which enable data to be binary-searched in many dimensions. On directory modifications, every insertion either has to be managed in a separate transaction list with look-aside functionality, or all index tables have to be rebuilt. The community of writers to a directory must be controlled and securely administered, which contrasts with the usage model for relational databases (which balance the needs of readers and writers and do not optimize for one usage over another).

Here are some issues surrounding directory use in security architectures:

- Does the directory store all principals that can access the system? How are external system access, root access, backup system access, disaster recovery access, or maintenance access managed?
- Does the directory store the corporate security policy definitions for this application? How are roles defined and stored? How are users mapped to roles? Is the mapping from roles to object access classes stored locally within the application (which simplifies administration and the directory structure), or is application-specific resource information uploaded to the directory?
- How is corporate security policy mapped to the directory schema? How is this abstract definition simultaneously extracted and then applied to a particular application's policy needs?
- Are user profiles stored in the directory? Does the application require anti-profiles (in other words, the definition of profiles of intrusion rather than normal use for detecting illegal access)?
- Do all access decisions require a reference to the directory, or are decisions cached? Is there a caching policy more complicated than Least Recently Used (LRU)? How soon does a cache entry expire?
- How does the application manage security policy changes? How do we add users, groups, roles, policy decisions, or directory entries?

the application level. Raising these issues at the architecture review can be helpful, however. Once documented, the need for their resolution can be escalated to the proper level of management. Directories are often sold to applications as the ultimate low-amortized cost resource in an enterprise, but if not deployed correctly, they can be of limited use.

Trusted Third Party

A *trusted third party* is a security authority or its agent that is trusted by all other entities engaged in secure transactions. All participants, in an initialization or preprocessing phase, agree to trust the third party. This trust extends to any information received, decisions brokered, references given, or validations provided by the trusted third party.

Zhou in [Zho01] defines three modes of operation for a *trusted third party* (TTP). An inline TTP sits in the middle of all conversations and acts as a proxy to all the entities. An online TTP is available for real time interaction, but entities can also communicate directly with one another. An offline TTP is not available at all times. Message requests can be dropped off to the offline TTP request queue, and the TTP will batch process all requests during the next available cycle and send responses to the requestors.

There are many examples of trusted third parties in products and service descriptions. Some trusted third parties provide message delivery, notary services, time service, or can adjudicate disputes. Many cryptographic protocols refer to an entity, often called Sam, as a trusted party brokering a transaction between the two most famous cryptographers in history, Alice and Bob. Sam can broker authentication, key management, or access requests.

PKIs introduce several trusted third parties. The *Certificate Authority* (CA) is the trusted entity that signs documents. The CA certificate, if self-signed, needs to be provisioned at all communication end-points; otherwise, we have to provision a chain of CA certificates along a certification path ending in a trusted CA, along with the credentials of all intermediary CAs. PKIs use *Registration Authority* (RA), which manages proof of identity procedures for certificate requests. The *Certificate Revocation List* (CRL) server stores and serves a list of revoked certificates. The CRL stored is digitally signed by the CA and is updated frequently. The *Online Certificate Status Protocol* (OCSP) service to verify that certificates used in transactions are not revoked in real time.

The ability to pinpoint an entity external to the communication, but trusted by all entities engaged in communication, can be critical in the successful definition of a secure architecture. Such an entity can support authentication, authorization, context definition, and nonrepudiation. A trusted third party can support services like man-in-the-middle auctioning (where the parties agree on price and then exchange goods and cash through escrow accounts). Trusted third parties are also valuable in post intrusion scenarios, such as legally valid event reconstruction, re-establishment of service after a failure, or incident response management.

Once an assumption of trust is made and the architecture is validated, we can return to the assumption and ensure that it holds. No one should be able to spoof the trusted

TTP to provide.

Validator

Our third category of service provider is the *validator*. Validators take information, match it against a validation process, and then report either success or failure. Unlike trusted third parties, who are known to all entities in the application, validators are point service providers possibly tied to unique hosts or flow points in the architecture. In some cases, validators can attempt to clean up invalid information based on internal knowledge. Validators perform one of three functions based on the structure of this internal knowledge: syntax validation, threat validation, or vulnerability validation.

Syntax Validators

Syntax validators clean up argument lists to executables. They specifically target the detection and removal of deliberate, malicious syntax. Examples include the cleaning up of strings presented to cgi-bin scripts as arguments, strings presented to the UNIX system( ) command within programs, shell scripts that contain dangerous characters (such as ";", "|", or ">"), or strings presented as SQL statement definitions to be inserted into placeholders within ad hoc query definitions. Syntax validators are baby language parsers possessing a grammar defining the structure of all valid inputs, a list of keywords, an alphabet of allowed symbols, and an anti-alphabet of disallowed symbols. The syntax validator allows only correctly formatted conversations with any executable.

Security experts differ on how argument validators should respond to errors in the input. A validator can parse the input, and if the input is discovered to be bad, it will perform one of the following actions:

- Accept with no modification (not much of a validation, but it might be required in some cases based on the input string)
- Try to make partial sense of the input by using only information within the input string to clean it up
- Use external information, and possible replacement, to actually clean up the input to a guaranteed meaningful form (but perhaps not exactly what the user desired)
- Reject the input based on strict rules that will brook no deviation

Threat Validators

Threat validators verify the absence of any one of a known list of threats within a message or packet. Examples include virus scanning software, e-mail attachment scanners, and components on firewalls that enable the screening of active content such as ActiveX or Java applets. This capability to screen information depends on the accessibility of content, along with the resources to perform application-level, database-intensive searches. If the information is encrypted or if the performance cost is severe, applica-

also clean up information but in a simpler manner than syntax validators by either making no modification to the input data stream or by removing logically consistent pieces of information entirely. For example, an e-mail scanner might remove attachments that end in .exe automatically and send an e-mail notification to the recipient.

Vulnerability Validators

Vulnerability validators verify the absence of any of a known list of vulnerabilities within a host or a service offering. War dialers, host vulnerability scanners, and network IP and port scanning products fall in this category. They serve the function of a home security inspection expert visiting your house to verify the quality of the doors, windows, latches, and alarm system. They do not support defense against active attacks, like a watchdog or the alarm system itself could or as would be the case with an intrusion detection system.

Although only one entity requests the service, a validator might notify either the source or destination, or both entities, of invalid content in the communication. The internal knowledge base within a validator might be enhanced. This situation might require, as is the case with virus scanners, a robust service management process to keep all users up to date on their virus definitions.

Sometimes the knowledge base is unique to each source-destination entity pair, which adds an additional specialization step to the deployment of validators in the systems architecture. For example, the audit checks for NT differ from those used on Solaris. This additional data management is an architectural burden, complicated by the multiple vendors that provide validators (each with its own management tools).

Channel Elements

Channel elements sit on the wire between the client and the server. Management of a channel element is associated with one endpoint of communication (normally, the server). Channel elements inspect, augment, modify, or otherwise add value to the communication. All channel elements carry a performance cost that must be weighed against the security benefit provided.

Wrapper

The *wrapper* pattern was first introduced as the *adaptor* pattern in the Gang of Four book on Design Patterns [GHJV95]. As a security component, the wrapper shown in Figure 4.2 enhances an interface presented by a server by adding information or by augmenting the incoming message and the outgoing response. Thus, wrappers impact all requests, even those not modified in any manner by the wrapper. The client must conform to the wrapper's interface instead of the interface of the underlying object. The use of a single security wrapper around a collection of diverse objects can potentially

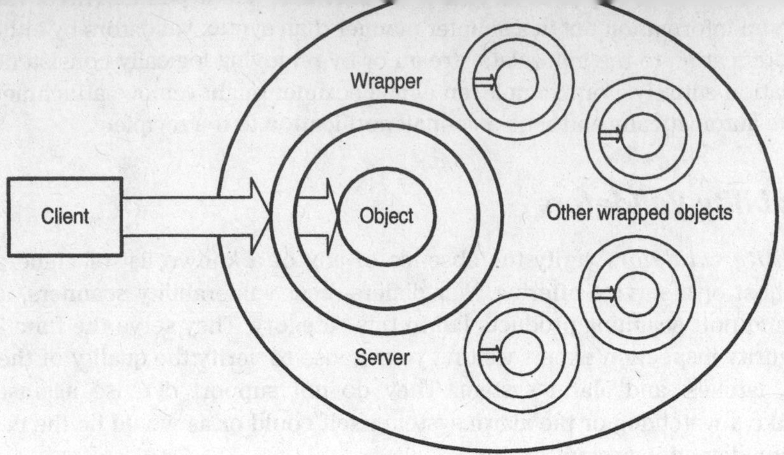

Figure 4.2 Wrapper.

cause architecture mismatches. We recommend defining a wrapper to have a one-to-one relationship with the resource being wrapped.

Wrappers are visible entities. They replace the interface of the object on the server with a new interface with which clients must comply. If the wrapper adds additional arguments to a call in order to check client information before allowing the call to proceed, the client must conform to the new interface definition and must add the correct arguments to all calls. The wrapper strips off the additional arguments after validation and presents the object with a request conforming to the original interface. Although the wrapper could theoretically modify the object's response, this situation is rarely the case. Wrappers do not protect the client from the server.

Wrappers can support some level of abstraction by hiding variations in the members of a class of objects on a server. The wrapper can also perform a look-aside call to a service provider to validate an argument. As the wrapper brokers all conversations with the object, this situation might result in a performance penalty. To avoid this penalty, we normally restrict the look-aside functionality to third-party providers that reside on the server. The wrapper represents a bottleneck as well and must be designed to have reasonable performance.

Multiple wrapped objects are sometimes a source of implementation and performance problems. Multiple wrappers complicate the one-to-one relationship between wrapper and object. In general, multiple interfaces wrapping a single object should be examined for redefinition to see whether they can be replaced with a single wrapper. For an overview of security wrappers, please see [GS96a].

Filter

Filters are the first of three man-in-the-middle security components of the channel elements section—the others being interceptors and proxies. Filters were also defined in the Gang of Four book [GHJV95] under the label Bridge and in [POSA1] as a software architecture pattern called Pipes and Filters.

Filters are channel elements that are invisible to the endpoints of the communication. The filter, shown in Figure 4.3, sits on the wire between the client and the server and moderates all messages from either endpoint and filters the set of all messages, passing along some messages and blocking others. The filter uses a local store to assist with decision-making. Look-aside queries to a third party are uncommon due to the performance penalty incurred.

Filters can have the following characteristics:

- *Auditing.* The filter can record the list of actions taken to an audit log and send blocked message notification to either the source or the destination, based on some definition of direction. Information notifications normally go to both entities, in contrast to warnings and alarms (which are sent only to the server). Configuring an endpoint to handle these messages makes the filter visible in the architecture. If this feature is undesirable, then notifications must be sent to a log file or a third party.
- *Multiple interfaces.* Filters can support multiple interfaces and can broker several point-to-point conversations simultaneously.
- *Stateful inspection.* Filters can maintain application, circuit, or network-level state about a session and can use this information to make access decisions.
- *Level granularity.* Filters can operate on packet information at any level of the protocol stack: physical, network, transport, or application.

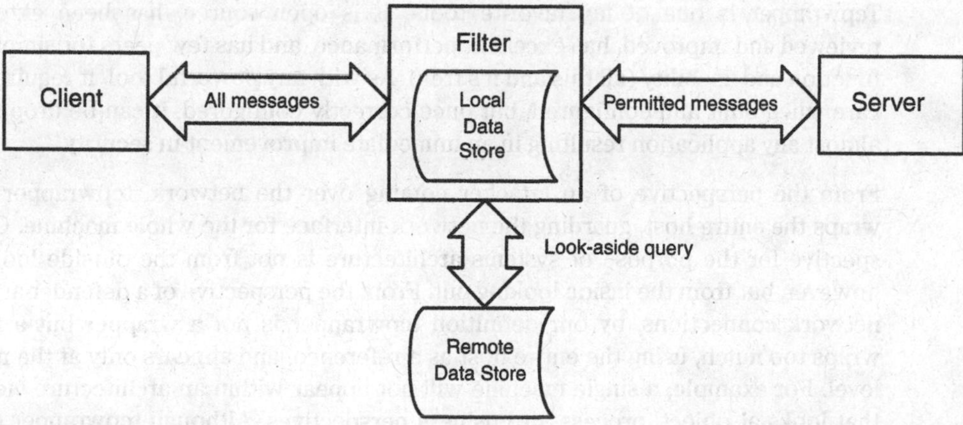

Figure 4.3 A filter.

they only permit or deny passage. This absence of message modification or enhancement differentiates filters from interceptors or proxies.

- *Directionality.* Filters have knowledge of incoming versus outgoing traffic and can recognize attempts to spoof traffic, such as the arrival of packets with interior source IP addresses on external incoming interfaces.
- *Local data store.* It is uncommon for a filter to reference a remote server to make an access decision. The rule base configuration on a filter is stable for the most part and does not support dynamic configuration on the basis of content.
- *Remote management.* Rule base configuration is always from a remote intelligent management point.
- *Clean up role.* Filters are often used in a clean-up role. A filter that does not implement the principal of least privilege is called a *permissive* filter. It assumes that upstream validation has happened on messages or that downstream validation will catch bad data streams. This lack of knowledge does not lead to permissive or insecure architecture if the principle of least privilege is maintained at another point in the architecture, at the application level. A filter in front of a firewall will block a significant volume of bad traffic that should not reach the firewall where inspection at a higher level could possibly result in a performance hit.
- *Safety.* Filters are sometimes used as a means of guarding against misconfiguration. A filter that strictly enforces the principal of least privilege is called a *restrictive* filter. Such a filter interprets security policy in the most Draconian manner: Any access decision that is not explicitly permitted will be denied.

We would like to make a short point about nomenclature and discuss one of the reasons why the pattern community comes under fire. Consider tcpwrapper, Wietse Venema's excellent security tool, which rides behind the inetd daemon on a UNIX box and references a local database of ALLOW and DENY rules to transparently manage network access to the host machine based on the source IP address of the incoming request. Tcpwrapper is one of my favorite tools. It is open source, has been extensively reviewed and improved, has excellent performance, and has few peers for simplicity of function and usability (all this and it's free). As with any powerful tool, it requires some care when built and configured, but once correctly configured, it can be dropped into almost any application resulting in an immediate improvement in security.

From the perspective of an attacker coming over the network, tcpwrapper indeed wraps the entire host, guarding the network interface for the whole machine. Our perspective for the purpose of systems architecture is not from the outside looking in, however, but from the inside looking out. From the perspective of a defender accepting network connections, by our definition tcpwrapper is not a wrapper but a filter. It wraps too much, using the entire host as a reference, and appears only at the network level. For example, a single machine will not appear within an architecture viewpoint that looks at object, process, or business perspectives. Although tcpwrapper does an excellent job of securing network access to a single host, a security architect has additional concerns. What if hosts are clustered, objects are distributed over the network,

tecture point or from host to host? You can add tcpwrapper to a boxology diagram that describes the physical architecture, but how and where do you add this security component to a use case? How do we describe interface mapping or enhancement in an object diagram?

Renaming a tool does not solve any problems, but recognizing that filters are invisible on valid communications from most viewpoints allows the architect to restrict the visibility of any instances of tcpwrapper to the hardware, engineering, or networking viewpoints of the architecture. We do not recommend renaming a popular and valuable tool. In fact, the practice within the pattern community of sometimes redefining recognizable, common usage terms invariably causes irritation among practicing architects and developers. We apologize for adding to this nomenclature confusion and recommend keeping our definitions in mind only as architectural artifacts for the discussions in this chapter. Do not put too much thought into this distinction or hire a language lawyer to examine this definition.

Interceptor

Interceptors also sit on the wire between the client and server but provide functionality that is more general over filters. Interceptors can still be invisible to the communicating client and server. In contrast to wrappers, which are visible and require clients to obey the wrapped interface definition, interceptors are often paired to provide this functionality transparently.

Interceptors are seen in technologies that provide their own run-time environment and embedded event loop. Middleware products and messaging software are good candidates for interceptor-based security. The run time environment already brokers all communication, and the event loop provides a structured sequence of blocks that performs specific atomic actions. The event loop uses event-triggered transitions to jump from one block to the next. Breaking open one of the atomic blocks is hard as the blocks are best treated as black boxes. The transition points can be used to introduce interceptors as new blocks within the event loop, however. This strategy makes it easy to *chain* or *pair* interceptors.

Interceptors can modify the conversation between a client and a server. They can add, delete, or in any manner augment a message or a packet. Command-line arguments can be augmented with additional arguments specifying context or details of the local environment of the process, which might be unavailable to the client or the server. Interceptors often reference third parties such as a status server and authentication server or a directory. The capability to refer to remote storage for decision-making is a critical component of the interceptor definition.

Interceptors differ from filters in two significant ways.

- *They can be chained.* A series of interceptors blocks the client from connecting to the server.
- *They can be paired.* A client-side interceptor is matched to a server-side interceptor.

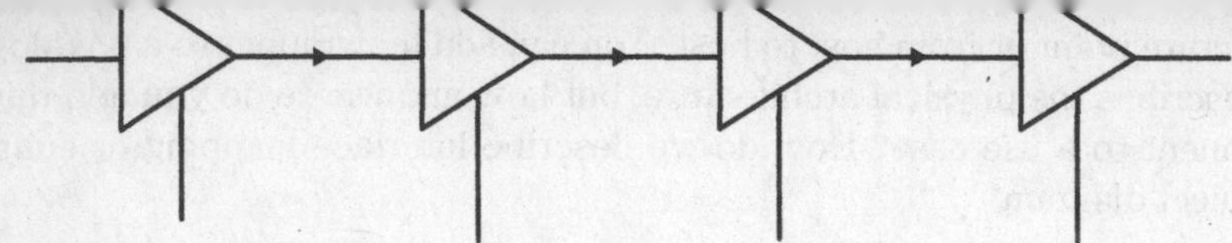

Figure 4.4 Chained interceptors.

An interceptor chain, as shown in Figure 4.4, can provide complex access decision support where each element can operate at a different level of granularity of access and reference different local or remote data stores. Access is only permitted if all interceptors allow the message through.

An interceptor pair, shown in Figure 4.5, can add complex security support to an existing communication channel by modifying low-level run-time environments on the client and the server so that the modification of messages, their receipt, and validation are all transparent to the parties involved. The interceptors on either endpoint can reference remote data or service providers to build a secure communication path.

Many software products use interceptor-based security solutions.

- CORBA vendors support the definition of interceptors that can be added at any of four points on the client to server message path: client-side pre-marshalling, client-side post-marshalling, server-side pre-marshalling, and server-side post marshalling. Each point can have multiple interceptors chained together. In addition, client-side and server-side interceptors can communicate without the knowledge of either the client or the server.
- Web servers use a standard event loop to handle HTTP requests. The event loop on the Apache Web server can be enhanced with authentication or authorization

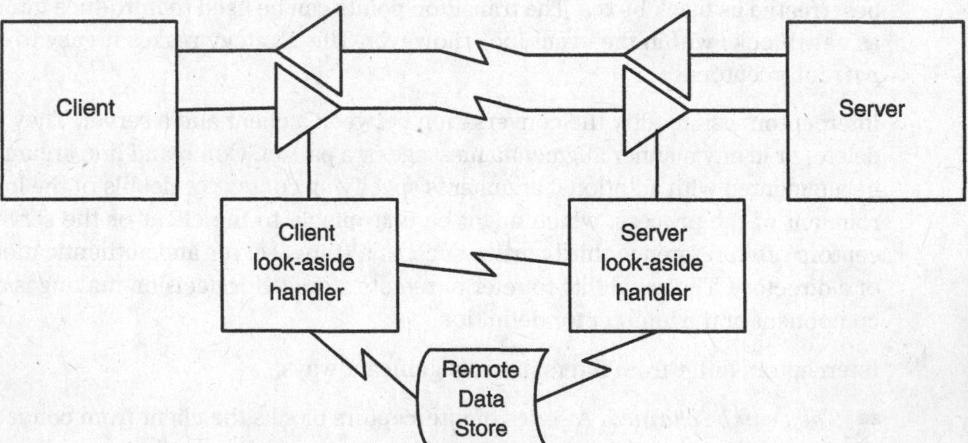

Figure 4.5 Paired interceptors.

intercept messages on the transitions on the event loop.

- Some software products for hardening the UNIX operating system from any executing application on the host do so by intercepting all system calls to privileged resources, permitting access only after an authorization check is passed.

Proxy

The *proxy* pattern was also introduced in [GHJV95]. Unlike filters or interceptors, proxies are visible to all parties—and as a direct result, the parties themselves are invisible to each other. All communication is directed to the proxy, shown in Figure 4.6, which maintains separate open sessions to the client and the server. Proxies might need to maintain state information to make access decisions. For an overview of security proxies, please see [GS96a].

If the proxy is used in conjunction with a firewall, the proxy becomes the only communication pathway for the client to reach the server. Otherwise, the client and server might be able to bypass the proxy. Therefore, proxies are deployed at choke points in the network, behind or in front of firewalls. The failure or removal of a proxy can cause a loss in connectivity because proxies cannot be bypassed. As a result security proxies must be designed to be highly available to meet the standards of the overall application.

Maintaining a session when a proxy fails can be difficult, and most vendors just recommend re-establishing a new session. Chokepoints cause performance problems. In some cases, proxies are chained for protocol separation. In this circumstance, it is common for only one proxy to make an access decision. Proxies can also operate in parallel for load balancing, in which case all proxies should support identical access rules.

Proxies are primarily useful for information hiding and can perform many security functions. Examples include the following:

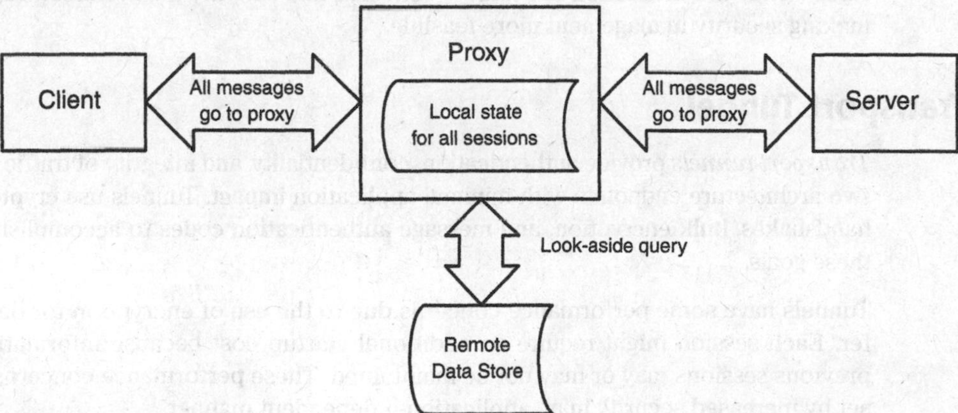

Figure 4.6 A proxy.

mobile devices to regular Web sites perform protocol conversion. Because the mobile device is very resource constrained, it cannot support the same cryptographic protocols that a regular PC or Web server can. This situation creates the so-called *wireless air gap problem,* where the WAP gateway acts as a proxy between two different physical networking architectures—a wireless protocol to the mobile device (such as CDPD) and regular TCP/IP to the Web server. In addition to protocol conversion, the gateway must also perform cryptographic conversions. The gateway maintains two cryptographic key stores, decrypting traffic from the mobile device and re-encrypting it before sending it to the Web server. If your application supports mobile devices, be mindful of the security of the gateway itself. One solution, rather than trusting a commercial gateway, is to purchase your own gateway and deploy it on an internal, secure network.

- *Network address translation (NAT).* NAT on a router enables internal client networks to be concealed from the open Internet. NAT hides IP addresses and also enables the reuse of IP addresses because it lifts the requirement that all hosts be assigned a unique IP.
- *Web proxies.* Proxies can hide internal Web servers from external Web clients or vice versa.
- *CORBA proxies.* A CORBA proxy can hide the actual IOR of an internal distributed object from an external CORBA client.
- *Firewall proxies.* These support all TCP/IP protocols across a firewall in a stateful manner. Clients can use protocols such as Telnet or FTP after authentication to the firewall.

Platforms

Our last collection of security patterns deals with more abstract architectural structures. These are often used to separate concerns and simplify the architecture, thereby making security management more feasible.

Transport Tunnel

Transport tunnels provide authentication, confidentiality, and integrity of traffic between two architecture endpoints with minimal application impact. Tunnels use cryptographic handshakes, bulk encryption, and message authentication codes to accomplish each of these goals.

Tunnels have some performance concerns due to the use of encryption for data transfer. Each session might require an additional startup cost because information from previous sessions may or may not be maintained. These performance concerns are offset by increased security in an application-independent manner.

Trust enabled by the creation of a secure tunnel can be illusory, because the identity of the principals authenticated to engage in communication might not necessarily be tied

Virtual private networking solutions often build tunnels by using IP addresses or MAC addresses along with host-specific key information. This situation gives very little information about the actual user on the host. VPN solutions for applications such as remote access services always implement a user authentication check at the client endpoint. Tunnels between systems cannot perform user authentication, and the security model falls back on to using transitive trust.

Tunnels are not subject to eavesdropping and do not protect against denial-of-service attacks. If a tunnel is improperly implemented, the architecture might be vulnerable to replay attacks or session stealing.

The tunnel is oblivious to the protocol of the traffic within it and the encryption makes content inspection impossible. So many security concerns can be addressed by using tunnels, however, that we will devote an entire chapter to the architecture of data transport security and secure communication channels (Chapter 8, "Secure Communications").

Distributor

The *distributor* pattern takes a communication stream and separates it into multiple streams based on some locally stored criteria. Distributors do not use third-party lookups to make decisions, and data transmission is not slowed down because the distributor used raw CPU power and pipelining to process messages rapidly—maintaining throughput at bandwidth speeds.

- Distributors can be symmetric, where all outgoing streams are identical. Any incoming message or packet can be routed to any outgoing channel. Symmetric distributors are sometimes called *demultiplexers*.
- Distributors can be asymmetric, separating the traffic on the basis of some property internal to each packet or message—for example, on the basis of protocol, priority flag, QoS rules, or destination address. Asymmetric distributors are sometimes called *directors*.

Distributors in the second mode, as directors, often appear in security architectures at network choke points (such as firewalls). The ability to separate traffic based on destination, protocol, or QoS attributes are critical to managing traffic. Distributors are not very intelligent devices, however, and cannot be relied upon to make sound security decisions. Consider exploits that tunnel a restricted protocol through a firewall by embedding it in a permitted protocol. A director that separates incoming traffic for load balancing purposes might compound this problem if the architecture, in an attempt to optimize performance, partitions the security policy by protocol: "This is what we check for HTTP, this is what we check for SMTP, this is what we check for IIOP, and so on." This configuration could result in an inadvertent hole by routing such tunneled traffic away from a network device that could detect and possibly block it. When distributors are used for load balancing purposes, the recommended security architecture strategy is to use identical access control mechanisms on all incoming streams. The Distributor pattern is shown in Figure 4.7.

A recent penetration of a large software manufacturer, along with the theft of source code, was accomplished by tunneling through the corporate firewall over a legally

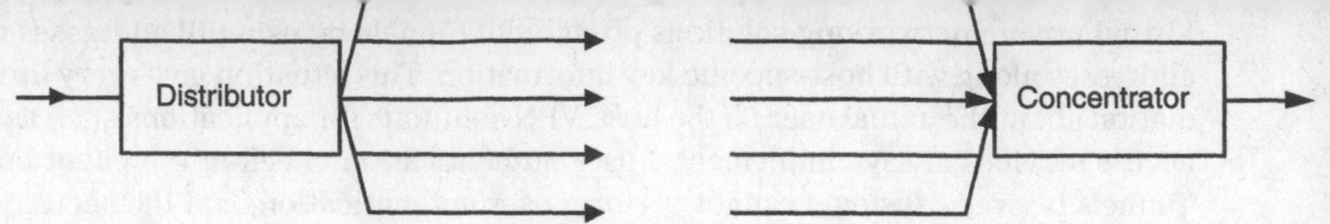

Figure 4.7 Distributors and concentrators.

established VPN connection. The conflicts between encrypting traffic to achieve confidentiality and the need to view traffic to perform content-based access management will continue to plague architects for a while. Distributors add to this problem by now creating multiple paths from source to destination, each path being a possible source of vulnerability waiting to be exploited.

Concentrator

The *concentrator* pattern reverses the effects of distributors and is commonly used to multiplex several communication streams and create a choke point. This situation is good for security but has obvious implications for other goals, such as high availability and performance. In addition, exploits that cause the concentrator to fail can result in denial of service.

Concentrators occur in software architectures at shared resources and critical sections. Multithreaded applications must use synchronization strategies such as mutexes, conditional variables, semaphores, and locks to protect shared resources or perform atomic operations. They must use thread-safe libraries to ensure that the library can handle re-entrant threads. If access to the shared resource is privileged, then we must perform security checks against resource requests. This procedure requires some care. If a client locks a resource and then fails to pass an authorization test, it might successfully launch a denial-of-service attack by refusing to unlock the resource.

Deadlocks are also possible when locks and security checks are mixed. Two clients who wish to access a resource might have to first authenticate to a security service provider. If one client locks the service provider and the other locks the resource, neither can gain access. Security service providers must enforce the principle that they must not lock on reads.

Concentrators have started appearing in security products such as hardware multiplexers for VPN traffic, supplied by backbone ISPs to manage the heavy use of virtual pipes by corporations. Performing security checks at a concentrator can cause performance problems.

Layer

The *layer* pattern has been described in many places in computer science literature, most notably in the definition of the ISO seven-layer network protocol stack. Other references exist within the pattern community (see [POSA1]) and within the software

as well. A system's *Trusted Computing Base* (TCB), defined as a subset of resources that are guaranteed to be safe and can be trusted to execute correctly, is an example of a security layer.

The layer pattern, shown in Figure 4.8, is one of the most popular architecture artifacts and has been used in many applications for a diverse collection of needs. We will focus on security architecture by using layers. A layer separates two levels of a protocol or interaction by creating two clearly defined interfaces: one defining interaction with the lower service provider level, and the other defining interaction with the higher service requestor level. This additional abstraction enables us to hide implementation changes within one level from the other. It supports modifiability and portability by hiding changes in hardware details from below and changes in functional requirements from above. The internal structure of any intermediate layer in multilayer stack architecture can be modified without affecting either the layer above or the layer below. Neither will know about the modification.

Layers provide contracts. The contract between two layers enables the integration of like features and functionality across several vertical smokestacks into a single, abstract, horizontal layer that guarantees communication across the layer to the upper protocol and that requires similar guarantees from the lower protocol. The separation of concerns enables problems to be handled at an appropriate level of detail with the confidence that each protocol level will work as desired.

Security architectures use layers to separate security functionality. Examples include mechanisms for secure transport such as SSL, mechanisms for secure infrastructure such as PKI, and security services such as virus scanning within e-mail applications.

Layered architectures are often strict; layered *security* architectures are even more so. Strict layering forbids any interaction of a higher layer with anything other than the immediate lower layer. Strict layering in an application, for example, enables us to replace SSL links with hardware encryption units providing IPSec tunnels and still expect secure data delivery to the application. Layers introduce performance costs, sometimes through excessive packing and unpacking of intermediate messages or through unnecessary decomposition and recomposition of high-level data artifacts.

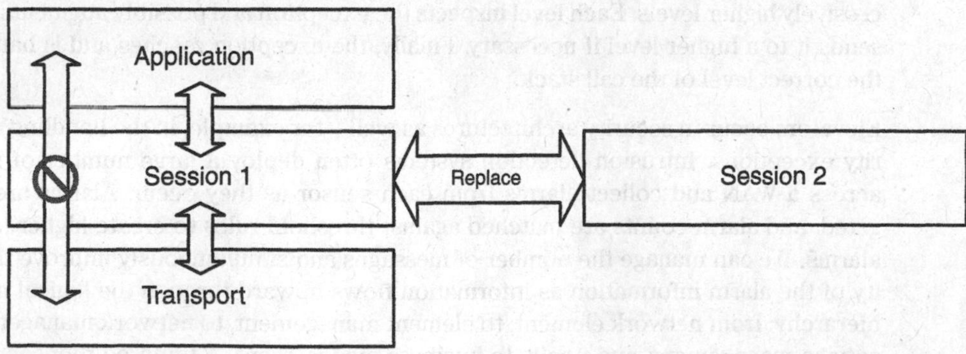

Figure 4.8 Layer.

we will defer discussion of the JVM in this security pattern because we will devote an entire pattern called the Sandbox to discussing such functionality.

Layers also appear in API definitions, separating the implementation of library calls from their usage. This feature enables a developer to swap in and out cryptographic primitives, enabling different levels of encryption strength, integrity, and performance—all with no effect on the application code.

If we review any commonly occurring security service, we will see a layered definition. The layer definition depends on the level targeted. For example, VPN technology, secure Web hosting, PKI, secure e-mail, secure software distribution, and security auditing tools all exhibit layering. The focus for adding security ranges from the network layer to the business process layer.

The most important property of a layer is modifiability. As long as a layer implements and supports its interfaces, it can be modified at will. This feature provides us with the best chance for adding security to an existing application without affecting application code.

It has often been said that TCP/IP's popularity was due to its simplification of the seven-layer ISO network protocol stack into only four layers: Application, Transport, Network, and Data Link. This functionality enabled the rapid development of networking solutions. Security architects would have liked to retain a well-defined and modifiable session layer within the TCP/IP stack, however. Many efforts to secure network communication are essentially efforts to add an additional session layer into the protocol. For example, CORBA security solutions secure IIOP over TCP/IP, adding an application level security layer by running IIOP over SSL over TCP/IP. Alternatively, hardware encryption units that implement encrypted Ethernet LANs add communications security at the other extreme.

Elevator

The *elevator* pattern is commonly seen in layered architectures, where strict layering is desired, but some interaction across all layers is required. For example, in a common nonsecurity related example, the design of exception handlers often uses the Elevator pattern. The handlers trap an exception thrown at one level and carry it up through successively higher levels. Each level inspects the exception and possibly augments it, then sends it to a higher level if necessary. Finally, the exception reaches and is handled at the correct level of the call stack.

Elevators occur in security architectures as well—for example, in the handling of security exceptions. Intrusion detection systems often deploy a large number of sensors across a WAN and collect alarms from each sensor as they occur. Alarms are aggregated, and alarm counts are matched against threshold rules to create higher levels of alarms. We can manage the number of messages and simultaneously improve the quality of the alarm information as information flows upward through the logical network hierarchy: from network element, to element management, to network management, to service management, and finally to business management. A hundred thousand e-mail viruses could result in a statement from the company's CEO to analysts on the business

ucts that perform audit management for enterprise security. A single manager receives analysis reports from thousands of clients that run security audits on hosts to generate and escalate alarms or alerts.

Elevators are rarely built completely inside a single application. It would be prudent to support the ability to detect troubles, however, and escalate them in sufficient but not excessive detail to the next higher level. This feature is critical for security management services.

Sandbox

The *sandbox* pattern is an instance of the layered pattern with an important additional quality. The layered architecture does not enforce explicitly the separation of a higher-layer protocol from lower levels other than the immediate level below.

The sandbox, shown in Figure 4.9, not only enforces complete compliance with this rule but also extends enforcement as follows:

- *Inspection of entities at the higher level.* For example, the JVM runs a byte code verifier on any downloaded applet before it can be executed. The JVM within the browser can also verify the digital signature on any downloaded applet.
- *Management of policy.* The sandbox has a well-defined default security policy with hooks for enhancements that can describe content-specific subpolicies.
- *Management of underlying system resources.* The sandbox can monitor the use of allowed resources, and on the basis of thresholds, can block access. Methods to protect against distributed denial-of-service attacks on Web sites attempt this strategy by subjecting incoming requests to threshold criteria. A host can terminate old, incomplete connection setups if too many new connections have been requested, thus preventing a flood attack on a daemon before it escalates.

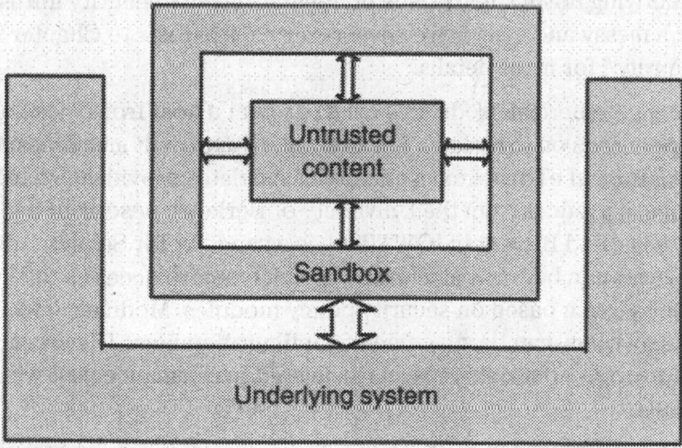

Figure 4.9 Sandbox.

packet queues for half-open and ongoing open communication links, which enables them to throttle denial-of-service attacks on one queue while still accepting packets for open connections on the other to some extent (flooding and packet loss is still a likelihood). Other solutions to block SYN floods modify the TCP/IP handshake to minimize state information for half open connections to prevent resource overload.

- *Audit management.* The sandbox can log activity at fine levels of granularity for later analysis.

The sandbox creates a secure operating environment where entities are authenticated when they request to join, and all interaction within the environment is controlled. All authenticated entities within the sandbox can freely interact without any concern about the security architecture principles. The principles are guaranteed to hold.

Many products describe their environments as a sandbox with varying degrees of success.

- The Java sandbox has a well thought-out but complex security architecture. Initial implementations of the sandbox were found to have security holes, which have been patched. We will defer our discussion of security policy management, the security manager, the access controller, and applet validation to Chapter 7, "Trusted Code."
- VPNs make poor sandboxes, although they support secure communication. Superficially, communication might seem secure, but if any host is compromised, then all hosts on the VPN might be vulnerable to attack.
- CORBA security solutions aim at protecting all clients and distributed objects interacting on a secure software bus. Messages carry authentication and authorization information, and all IIOP traffic can be encrypted. All vendors allow servers and daemons to be configured to accept insecure connections for backward compatibility, however. Although application clients and servers can be configured to accept secure connections only, not all daemons can be secured using the currently available security solutions. The security holes in the underlying hosts and the lack of integration with security infrastructures all make for a messy and insecure environment. Please refer to Chapter 9, "Middleware Security," for more details.
- Many commercial products exist to protect a host from (possibly untrusted) applications on the host. For example, Virtual Vault and Praesidium from Hewlett-Packard and eTrust from Computer Associates provide OS hardening as a feature. Janus, a product from the University of Berkeley described by Goldberg, Wagner, Thomas, and Brewer in [GWTB96], is a sandbox for Solaris. Any untrusted program can be run inside Janus, which controls access to all system calls made by that program based on security policy modules. Modules, which are sets of access control rules, can be specified in configuration files. There is no modification to the program, but there is an associated performance cost with intercepting all calls.
- Globally distributed applications. There are some products that allow distributed applications to tap the resources of idle, networked workstations. Each

only when available. Such a client must have minimal privileges, because outside of CPU cycles the application has no access privileges on the host. The solution is to create a distributed sandbox that controls the resource requests and communications of all participating clients. Distributed sandboxes have been used for a diverse collection of problems: discovering large primes, brute force password cracking, protein structural analysis, massively parallel computing, and distributed analysis of radio wave data for signs of extraterrestrial signals. Many important problems can be solved if every networked host provided a secure distributed sandbox that can tap the idle potential of the computer with no detrimental affect on the user. This function requires OS support from all vendors.

Sandboxes do not always protect entities within the sandbox from each other or from the sandbox itself. Entities must agree to obey the rules of the sandbox and not implement attacks in their own functionality that cannot violate the sandbox but that can adversely affect other participants. There is an assumption of fair play among good citizens. An uninvited guest or an intruder might have no qualms about damaging the contents of the sandbox without being able to affect the underlying host. This situation might still result in the violation of some security policy.

Magic

Our last pattern, *magic*, gives us a means to simplify an architecture diagram. According to Arthur C. Clarke, "Any technology, sufficiently advanced, is indistinguishable from magic." The *Magic* pattern is the simplest security artifact because it labels elements that must be treated as a black box in the architecture. Architecture reasoning is simplified by identifying components that are part of the solution but whose internal details are not subject to review. A magic component is monolithic, deterministic, well-defined, deep, and not subject to review. We define each of these terms as follows:

Monolithic. A magic component does not have a complex internal structure and is restricted to a single process on a single machine. There are no architecture concerns within the component. Performance concerns such as its speed of execution are considered external.

Deterministic. It has a single path of execution and is often implemented as a library function.

Well-defined. It implements a short, well-defined property that can be guaranteed correct through a (possibly mathematical) proof.

Deep. The property provided by the component is based on knowledge uncommon in an average development team.

Not subject to review. The actual algorithm implemented by the component is not subject to review for correctness, improvement, or performance enhancement. Its implementation—in other words, the matching of its specification to a code base—is of course subject to review. Magic components represent optimum solutions in some sense. This restriction applies to the project team of course; the original creators of the component can modify and improve it.

peachable credentials, but most successful projects do not depend on the existence of a single extraordinary individual capable of critically acclaimed breakthroughs. Some depend on heroic programming, but the results of heroic programming are never magic, resulting more often in spaghetti code and poor architecture design rather than in producing a truly landmark solution.

A magic component often represents a paradigm shift in a broader area or field of technology. Thomas Kuhn, in his 1962 treatise "The Structure of Scientific Revolution," defined a paradigm shift as a revolutionary event that divides a field into those who adapt and thrive and those who are left behind. The discovery of public-key technology is such an event in cryptography. Magic is the product of the uncommon intellects, and we should not expect our architecture problems to be solved by similar insights from our architects. You have to buy or lease magic.

Conclusion

We suggest that the reader revisit this chapter as and when necessary to understand our motivations in picking these patterns for our catalog. This list is by no means comprehensive. We encourage the user to think of additional examples for each pattern category. There is also considerable room for argument about the names of the patterns themselves and the properties that I have ascribed to each.

In the following chapters, we will examine application security from the viewpoint of components and connectors operating under constraints. This topic is, after all, the basis for software architecture. We will use our catalog of security patterns to draw parallels across solutions in different domains. Our goals are to provide evidence that each of these patterns is indeed the solution to some problem in some context with the potential for reuse.

Low-Level Architecture

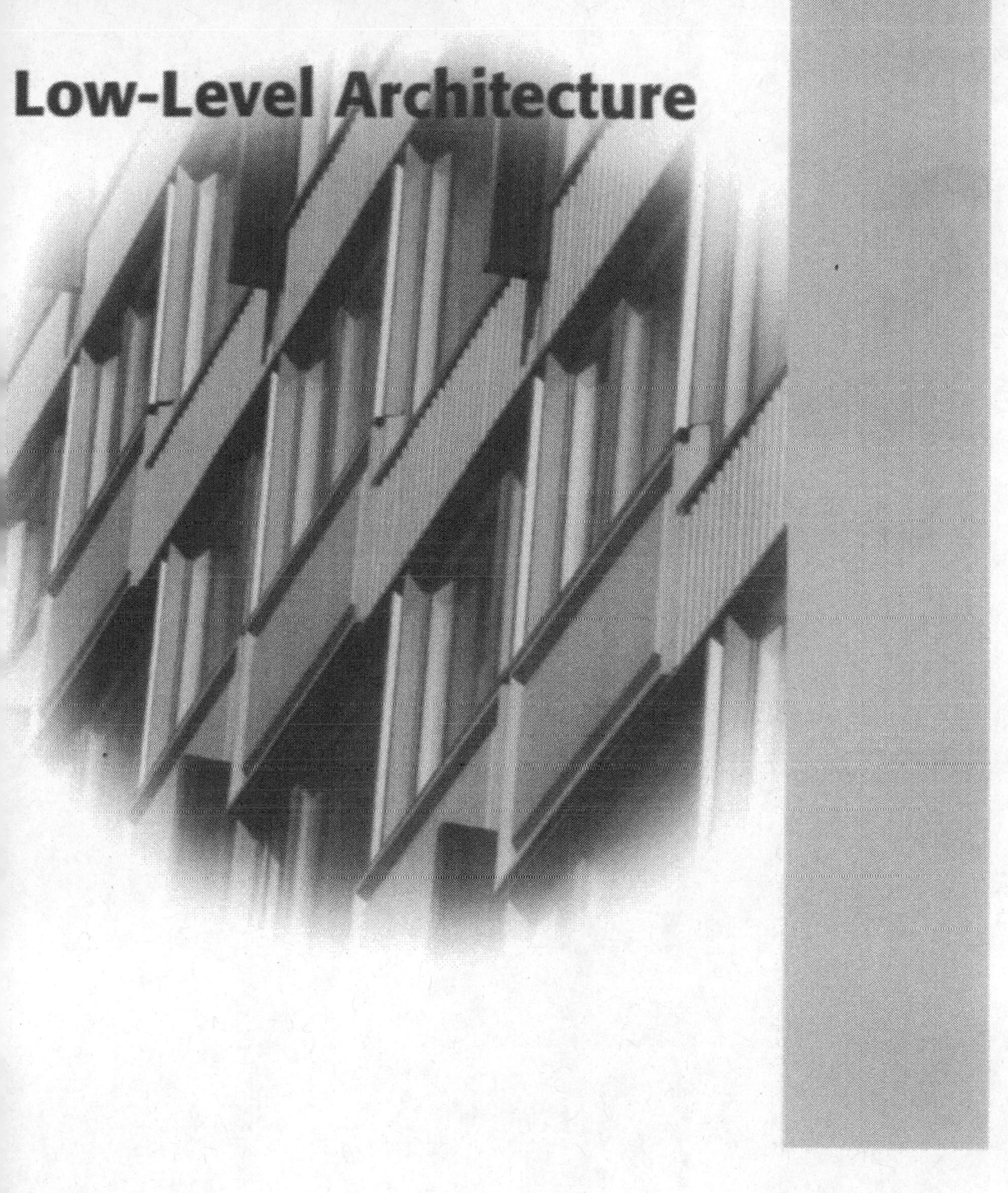

Code Review

Our focus in this chapter is code review. We will examine why code review is a critical step in the software development cycle. Code review is often not conducted on the entire code base but instead is restricted to critical segments of code that represent serious performance bottlenecks or that have complex bugs. Code review for the purpose of security is less common but no less important. Exploits against processes can occur in infrequently executed code, for example, within code that performs partial input validation and that fails to account for extreme or malicious inputs. Code that passes testing with standard test suites might have vulnerabilities that exploit built-in assumptions of normal behavior made by the test team. Understanding the code through review mitigates some of this risk.

In this chapter, we will describe buffer overflow exploits, the most common of all Bugtraq exploit notices, and classify the countermeasures by using some of the pattern terminology of the last chapter. We will discuss the Perl interpreter and security. We will also describe Java's byte code validation scheme, a form of code review on the fly that safeguards a system from many exploits (including those based on overflows).

We will end with some remarks on programming style. We believe that the true basis for writing secure code is writing good code, period.

Why Code Review Is Important

Security expert Steve Bellovin blames buggy software for most of our security problems. He targets poor coding practices as the number one reason why, despite all our advances in security, many systems continue to be hacked.

ing bases to access control models. We have made practical advances from security components like firewalls through security protocols like IPSec to infrastructure products like Kerberos or PKI. We must face the reality that all our security advances have not helped us as much as they should, however, because buggy code is the downfall of them all.

Code often fails because it does not anticipate all possible inputs. The *Garbage In, Garbage Out* (GIGO) principle is firmly entrenched in coding practice, which has had the unfortunate side effect of leaving behavior on bad input unspecified. The code fails, but with what consequences? Miller et al., in [Mill00], provide some empirical evidence on the input validation issue. They use a fuzz generator to throw randomly generated values at system utilities on several flavors of Unix. Many utilities fail because they mishandle one of several input validation tests, causing the majority of crashed, hung, or otherwise failed end results. The problems identified include pointer handling without NULL tests, array bounds checks, the use of bad input functions, the use of char to represent symbolic and numeric data, division by zero checks, and end-of-file checks. These activities can also lead to security bugs and therefore are targets for code review.

One outcome of the Miller survey is the discovery that open source is often best in class for speed and security: quality drives security. This common viewpoint is also expressed in [KP00], [COP97], and [VFTOSM99]. These authors note the curious paradox of why open source is of such high quality despite being developed with very little software process by a diverse group of programmers distributed over time and space. This situation is true, perhaps, because the popular open-source projects tend to be more visible and better understood. Open source code is often written by expert programmers, reviewed and debugged by a wide and vocal group of testers, and ported to many platforms—weeding out OS and hardware-specific design quirks. Ownership and pride in craftsmanship are also cited as drivers of quality in open source. Although open source might not be an option for your application, external code review can help improve quality.

Buffer Overflow Exploits

Consider the layout of the process-addressable space in a running program. After a program is compiled and linked, the loader maps the process's linked module into memory beginning at a lower address and ending at a higher address (this process might not be true of all hardware architectures; we are simplifying here). The stack segment within the process, on which function calls are handled, grows from higher addresses to lower addresses. The stack segment consists of multiple stack frames. Each stack frame represents the state of a single function call and contains the parameters, the return address after the call completes, a stack frame pointer for computing frame addresses easily, and local variables such as character arrays declared within the function code. Figure 5.1 shows the layout of a generic UNIX process loaded into memory.

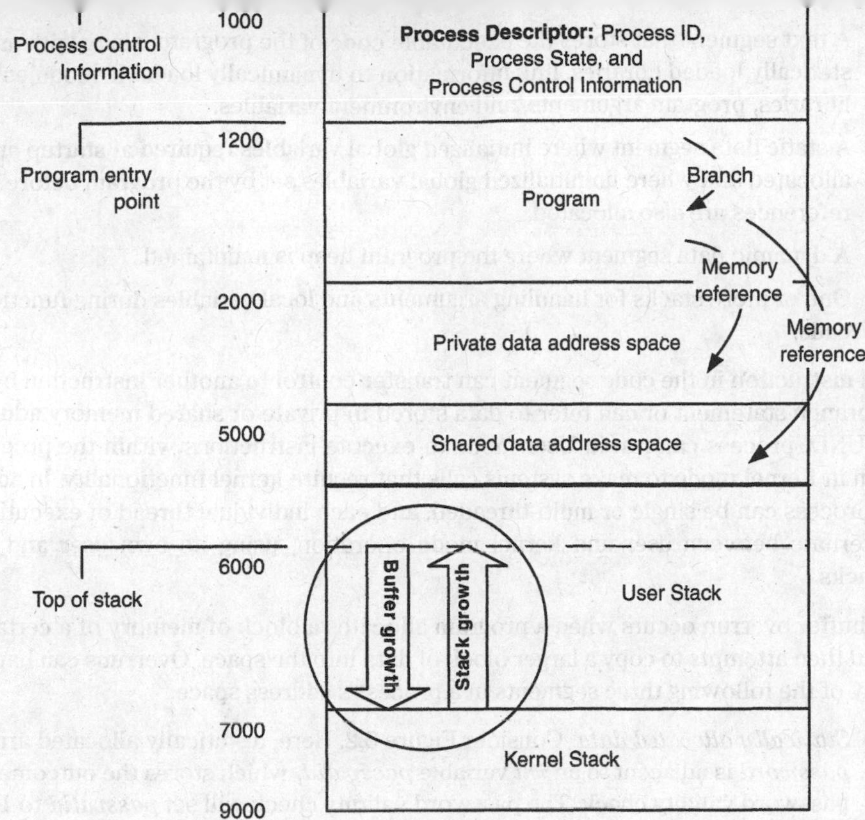

Figure 5.1 Process address space.

Buffer overflow exploits use two characteristics to gain access to a system.

- The first characteristic is the layout of the addressable space in a running process. A buffer stored on the stack is allocated space below the return address on the stack frame for a function call and grows toward this return address. Any data that overruns the buffer can write over the return address.
- The second characteristic is the lack of bounds checking within implementations of both the standard C and C++ libraries and within user code.

These two elements give rise to a class of attacks based on constructing special inputs to programs running in privileged mode that overrun internal buffers in the program in a manner that transfers control to the hacker. The hacker might explicitly provide malicious code to be executed or transfer execution to other general-purpose programs, such as a shell program or Perl interpreter.

The process address space has the following elements:

- A text segment that stores the executable code of the program, along with any statically loaded libraries, link information to dynamically loadable modules or libraries, program arguments, and environment variables.
- A static data segment where initialized global variables required at startup are allocated and where uninitialized global variables set by the program before any references are also allocated.
- A dynamic data segment where the program heap is maintained.
- One or more stacks for handling arguments and local variables during function calls.

An instruction in the code segment can transfer control to another instruction by using a branch statement or can refer to data stored in private or shared memory addresses. A UNIX process can run in User mode to execute instructions within the program or run in Kernel mode to make systems calls that require kernel functionality. In addition, a process can be single or multi-threaded, and each individual thread of execution can alternate between user and kernel mode operation, using its own user and kernel stacks.

A buffer overrun occurs when a program allocates a block of memory of a certain size and then attempts to copy a larger block of data into the space. Overruns can happen in any of the following three segments in a process's address space.

- *Statically allocated data.* Consider Figure 5.2. Here, a statically allocated array *password* is adjacent to an *int* variable *passvalid,* which stores the outcome of a password validity check. The password validity check will set *passvalid* to 1 (TRUE) if the user password is correct and will leave the field untouched otherwise. The user input to the field *password* can be carefully chosen to overwrite *passvalid* with a 1 even though the password validity check fails. If the program does not check for overflows on reading input into the password field, a hacker may be allowed access.
- *Dynamically allocated data.* The program heap allocates and de-allocates dynamic memory through system calls (such as *malloc*() and *free*() in C). Overwriting dynamic memory has fewer negative consequences because dynamic memory is not used for execution, i.e. the instruction pointer of the program is never set from the contents of dynamic memory. We also, in general, cannot guarantee an exact relative location of two dynamically allocated segments. In this situation, overrunning the first segment cannot precisely target the second. However,

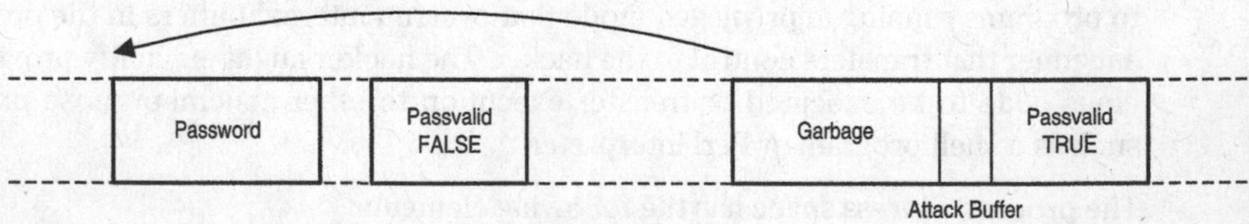

Figure 5.2 Static data attack.

denial-of-service attacks, for example within a daemon that does not have automatic restarts.

- *The program stack.* Unlike the first two options, which are sometimes called data or variable attacks, the stack contains data (and references to data) and return addresses for setting instruction pointers after a call completes. A buffer overflow in a local variable can overwrite the return address, which is used to set the instruction pointer—thereby transferring control to a memory location of the hacker's choice.

Stack smashing buffer overflow exploits are the most common variety. We must first describe how an executing program transfers control to another program before we can describe how these exploits work.

Switching Execution Contexts in UNIX

UNIX provides programmers with system functions that can replace the execution context of a program with a new context. Alternatively, a program can transfer control to another arbitrary program by using the standard C library call to system( ).

The exec family of functions is built by wrapping the basic system call to execve() and includes execl( ), execlp( ), execle( ), execv( ), and execvp( ). The new execution context is described by three values, a path to an executable file (found through a fully qualified path or by searching the PATH variable), command-line arguments, and the process's inherited environment (including the process owner's ID). For example, under Linux [BC00], the execve( ) system call takes three arguments: a pathname of the file to be executed (hence the "exec" prefix in the function name), a pointer to an array of command-line argument strings ("v" for vector), and a pointer to an array of environment strings ("e" for environment). Each of the arrays must be NULL terminated. This call is handled by the sys_execve( ) service routine that receives three address reference parameters that point to the respective execve( ) parameters.

Building a Buffer Overflow Exploit

Building a buffer overflow exploit requires a target, a payload, and a prefix to place the payload within the stack frame.

The *target* is a privileged program or daemon that overflows on bad user input data, normally character strings. Access to source code makes building the exploit easier, but it is not necessary.

The *payload* is used to switch execution context to code of our choice (for example, shell codes that use the execve( ) pattern of behavior to change execution context to a shell program). Shell codes are sequences of assembly language instructions that give the user shell access by calling execve(p, NULL, NULL), where p is a pointer to the string "/bin/sh/". Shell codes for all platforms and operating systems, including NT and all flavors of the UNIX operating system, are available on the Internet. For example, see

NT buffer overruns" at www.atstake.com.

The *prefix* pads the payload (in our example, a shell code) to give us the final value for the input string. Once we have a shell code (or any other executable payload) for a program with a known buffer overflow problem, we must figure out the prefix to pad the payload with to correctly overflow the buffer, overwriting the return address on the stack. In many attacks, the return address points back into the buffer string containing the shell code. Aleph One describes why prefix construction requires less precision than you would expect, because most hardware architectures support a NOP instruction that does nothing. This NOP instruction can be repeated many times in the prefix before the shell code. Transferring control anywhere within the NOP prefix will result in the shell code executing, albeit after a short delay.

Components of a Stack Frame

Active countermeasures against buffer overflow exploits attempt to preserve the integrity of the stack frame. Consider the image of a stack frame in Figure 5.3.

The stack frame for a function call is built on top of the stack frame of the calling program. Function parameters are pushed onto the stack and are followed by a copy of the instruction pointer, stored in the return address, so that control can be returned to the correct

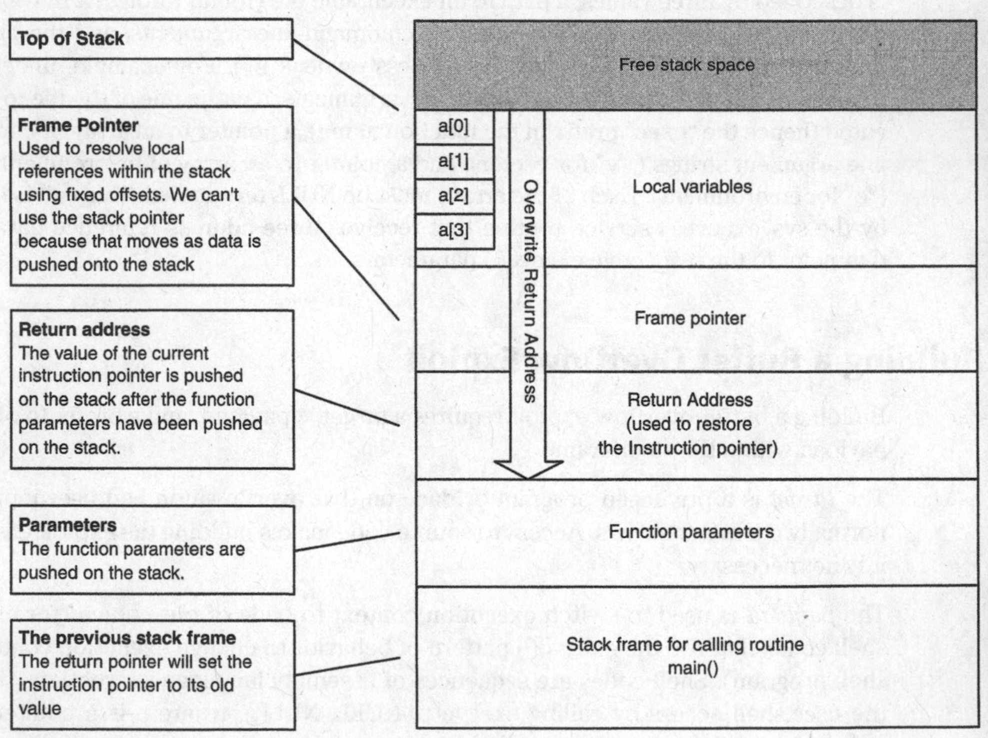

Figure 5.3 Stack frame components.

ences the stack frame pointer within the previous frame, onto the stack. The address of the stack frame pointer is at a fixed location within the current stack frame. The stack frame pointer is useful for resolving local references that would otherwise require some book-keeping and arithmetic on the stack pointer. The stackpointer moves, as the stack can grow and shrink during execution, whereas the frame pointer does not.

Once a return address is overwritten, exploits can compromise the system in many ways.

- The return address can be incremented to jump past critical security-related code blocks in the calling routine, bypassing checks within the program.
- The return code can transfer control into the local (automatic) variable buffer itself, where the hacker has placed instructions to exit the program in a privileged mode.
- The return code can transfer control to a system call at a known address, already in a library loaded into process memory, by using arguments from the user stack. The control is transferred to the system() function call, which invokes another general-purpose program that executes with the process executable owner's identity, not the hacker's. Linus Torvalds describes an overflow exploit that runs the "system()" call with argument "/bin/sh." This exploit will work even if the stack is designated as non-executable, because no instructions are loaded from the user stack.

Why Buffer Overflow Exploits Enjoy Most-Favored Status

Stack overflow exploits are popular because of many reasons.

- *Self-promotion of privileges.* Rather than modifying the flow of control through the program (which might be difficult to exploit without source code), they can replace the execution context of the process with another program or execute instructions of their own choice.
- *Location independence.* Buffer overflows can be launched locally or over the network.
- *Privileged targets.* Many operations on a system enable a user who has limited privileges to invoke an SUID daemon or program owned by root. A user might need to initiate a Telnet or FTP session, start a remote access connection, or run an SUID root utility to access shared resources. In each case, the process must use inputs provided by the untrusted user. System daemons and utilities are usually written in C because of performance requirements and an existing robust code base. If these processes use unsafe system calls, they might be susceptible.
- *Testing and instrumentation.* As is often the case with common utilities and popular platforms, hackers can create an identical configuration for testing the exploit. Shared libraries are stored in common locations, dynamically loaded modules have common size and positions in the loaded module, and strings like "/bin/sh" or registry entry values appear at guessable locations. The target program

caused a core dump on failure.

- *Standing on the shoulders of others.* The source for many buffer overflow exploits is available on the Internet, and many of the harder parts (such as building a shell code for a particular OS or program) can be readily copied. Design reuse helps the hacker in this case.

Countermeasures Against Buffer Overflow Attacks

There are many countermeasures against buffer overflows. We will present each in the context of the patterns described in Chapter 4, "Architecture Patterns in Security."

Avoidance

At a fundamental level, buffer overflows can be avoided by not using the tools that make them feasible. This situation means writing in languages other than C or C++. Languages such as Java have built in bounds checking on all arrays, especially on strings, where the String object is an abstract data type rather than collection of contiguous memory locations with a pointer to the first element. Switching languages might be infeasible for a number of reasons, however.

- *Poor performance.* Languages that perform bounds checking slow down execution.
- *Existing embedded code base.* The application environment might have a considerable legacy C code base.
- *The project has no choice.* The application might include vendor software coded in C, or the vendor software might require root-owned SUID privileges.
- *Philosophical differences.* It is possible to write bad code in any language, and conversely, it is possible to write safe code in C. Brian Kernighan called C, "A fine scalpel, fit for a surgeon, although, in the hands of the incompetent, it can create a bloody mess." This statement also applies to coding securely.

Prevention by Using Validators

Validation is the best option if source code is available. We can detect and remove all potentially unsafe system calls, such as calls to *gets*(), *strcpy*, *strcat*(), *printf*(), and others. Alternatively, we can mitigate some overflow exploits by using code validators that perform static bounds checks on code before compilation. Rational Corp.'s Purify tools can detect most common sources of memory leaks and can perform static bounds checking on C and C++ code.

We can replace unsafe libraries entirely. Alexandre Snarskii has reimplemented the FreeBSD standard C library to add bounds checking on all unsafe function calls. This

FreeBSD is the core for the new Mac X OS kernel, which also comes with open-source versions of secure shell (using OpenSSH) and SSL support (using OpenSSL). This situation might mean that Apple's new OS represents a leap in PC security and reliability (or maybe not).

Sentinel

There are several compile-time solutions to stack overflow problems. StackGuard implements a Sentinel-based overflow protection solution. StackGuard uses a compiler extension that adds stack-bounds checks to the generated code. Function calls, in code compiled with StackGuard, are modified to first insert a *sentinel* word called a *canary* onto the stack before the return address. All exploits that use sequential writing of bytes to write down the user stack until the return address is overrun must first cross the canary value. The canary is chosen at random to prevent attacks that guess the canary. Before the function returns, the canary is checked—and if modified, the program terminates. StackGuard will not protect against attacks that can skip over the canary word. Such exploits are believed to be very difficult to construct.

Layer

Layers are used to separate concerns. The user stack is essentially a collection of vertically layered stack frames, each containing two kinds of elements.

- Local variables and parameters that will change during the stack frame's life.
- The frame pointers and return addresses, which should not change.

Layers can be implemented at a fine level, separating data elements within the stack frame. Separating the data elements within the stack frame based on this division creates a fine-level separation of concerns. Consider Figure 5.4, which shows this layered solution to buffer overflows.

One solution is to reserve the stack for return addresses only and force all variables to be dynamically allocated. This solution has performance problems and is infeasible in cases where the source is unavailable.

Another solution to buffer overflows is to use multiple stacks. This solution creates a data stack and an address stack, then separates the horizontal layers within each stack frame and moves the elements to the appropriate stack. The address stack is not modifiable by data overflows and cannot be set programmatically. The return address cannot be modified by the program through overruns and is controlled by the kernel. This solution requires significant re-architecture of the OS and compilation tools (and is inapplicable in most circumstances).

Multiple stacks are possible within tools that execute as a single process on the host and provide their own run-time environment. Perl's run-time environment uses multiple stacks. There are separate stacks for function call parameters, local variables, temporary variables created during execution, return addresses (which are pointers to the next opcode), and scope-related current block execution information (execution jumps

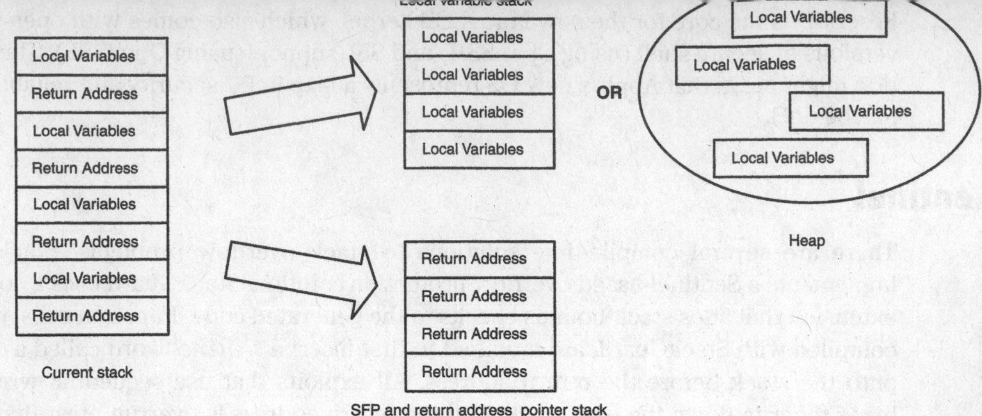

Figure 5.4 Splitting the stack.

after a *next*, *last*, or *redo* statement in a block). Perl also performs memory expansion by automatically resizing arrays. The underlying C libraries have been scrubbed of all known unsafe calls that might cause buffer overflows. If an application uses embedded Perl, however, where the interpreter is incorporated into a wrapper written in C code that uses unsafe library calls, it might still have buffer overflows caused by long strings returned by the Perl interpreter. The references contain links to more information about embedded Perl.

Sandbox

Layers can be implemented at a coarse level of granularity by isolating the entire application from the underlying machine. Recall the Sandbox pattern, a special case of the Layer pattern, used for abstraction. The sandbox separates the program from its execution environment. Using this pattern, another solution to the buffer overflow exploit works by dropping the entire program into a sandbox.

Goldberg, Wagner, Thomas, and Brewer, in [GWTB96], present a sandbox for Solaris called Janus. When a program is run inside the sandbox, Janus controls access to all system calls made by that program based on security policy modules. Modules, which are sets of access control rules, can be specified in configuration files. There is no modification to the program, but there is an associated performance cost with intercepting all calls (Figure 5.5). The sandbox restricts access privileges absolutely; therefore, it might not be feasible to run certain daemons within Janus. Buffer overflows are contained because the sandbox, under the correct policy module, can prevent an execution context switch from succeeding.

Wrapper

If modification of the program is not an option, we can place the entire executable within a wrapper. Rogers in [Rog98] suggests fixing a buffer overflow problem in some

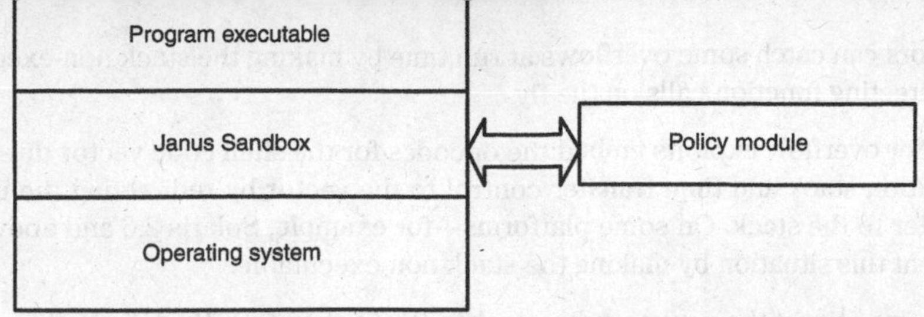

Figure 5.5 The sandbox.

versions of rlogin by placing the executable within a wrapper. The overflow occurs in the TERM variable, used to set the user's remote terminal description from the local terminal description. The wrapper either truncates the input string to the correct length or replaces a malformed input string with a correct default value. The wrapper then invokes rlogin with safe arguments (Figure 5.6.[a]).

Libverify is a solution based on the wrapper pattern developed by Baratloo, Singh, and Tsai [BST00] and is provided as a dynamically loaded library (Figure 5.6[b]). Libverify does not require source code, unlike StackGuard, and can prevent overflows in compiled executables. The solution is somewhat unusual, however, because it rewrites and relocates the instructions of the original program. The libverify library, at link time, rewrites the entire program so that each function call is preceded with a *wrapper_entry* call and succeeded by a *wrapper_exit* call within the library. In their implementation, each function is relocated to the heap because the Intel architecture does not allow enough space within the text segment of the process. The entry function stores the correct return address on a canary stack. The exit function verifies the return address of the function against the stored *canary* value (Figure 5.6[b]). The canary value is stored on a canary stack, also allocated on the heap. If the canary is modified, the wrapper_exit procedure terminates the program.

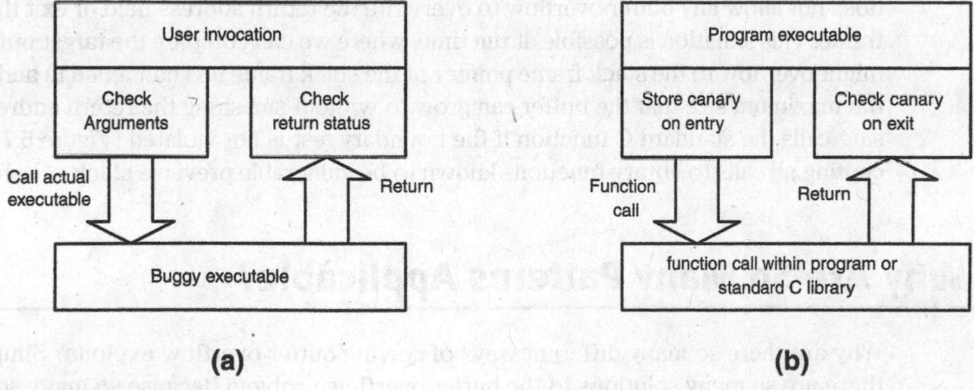

Figure 5.6 Wrapper.

Interceptors

Interceptors can catch some overflows at run time by making the stack non-executable or by redirecting function calls on the fly.

Many buffer overflow exploits embed the opcodes for the shell code vector directly on the execution stack and then transfer control to the vector by redirecting the instruction pointer to the stack. On some platforms—for example, Solaris 2.6 and above—we can prevent this situation by making the stack non-executable.

In Solaris, we can set the *noexec_user_stack* in /etc/system to 1. By default, this value is set to 0 to be compliant with the Sparc Application Binary Interface (ABI) and Intel ABI. Any program that attempts to execute code on the stack will receive a SIGSEGV signal and will most likely core dump. A message will be logged by *syslogd* to the console and to */var/adm/messages*. Setting the *noexec_user_stack_log* variable to 0 turns this logging behavior off.

Intel chips do not provide hardware support for making stack segments non-executable. By default, it is not possible to designate the user stack non-executable on Linux, but there is a kernel patch that is not part of the standard Linux kernel from Solar Designer (www.openwall.com) that enables the administrator to make the user stack non-executable. Linus Torvalds resists including non-executable stacks as a kernel option on Linux because other overflow attacks do not depend on executing code on the stack. Intel chips permit the transfer of control to system calls at addresses not on the stack segment, using only arguments from the stack. Making the stack non-executable does nothing to prevent such an overflow exploit from succeeding and adds a performance penalty to the kernel.

Some applications require an executable stack. For example, the Linux kernel makes legitimate use of an executable stack for handling trampolines. Although some UNIX systems make legitimate use of an executable stack, most programs do not need this feature.

Another alternative, developed again by Baratloo, Singh, and Tsai [BST00] from Bell Labs, works in situations where we do not have access to source code. Their solution for Linux, provided through a dynamically loaded library called *libsafe*, intercepts all unsafe function calls and reroutes them to a version that implements the original functionality but does not allow any buffer overflow to overwrite the return address field or exit the stack frame. This situation is possible at run time, where we can compare the target buffer that might overflow to the stack frame pointer of the stack frame it is contained in and decide the maximum size that the buffer can grow to without smashing the return address. Libsafe calls the standard C function if the boundary test is not violated (Figure 5.7). Intercepting all calls to library functions known to be vulnerable prevents stack smashing.

Why Are So Many Patterns Applicable?

Why are there so many different ways of solving buffer overflow exploits? Simply put, there are so many solutions to the buffer overflow problem because so many solutions

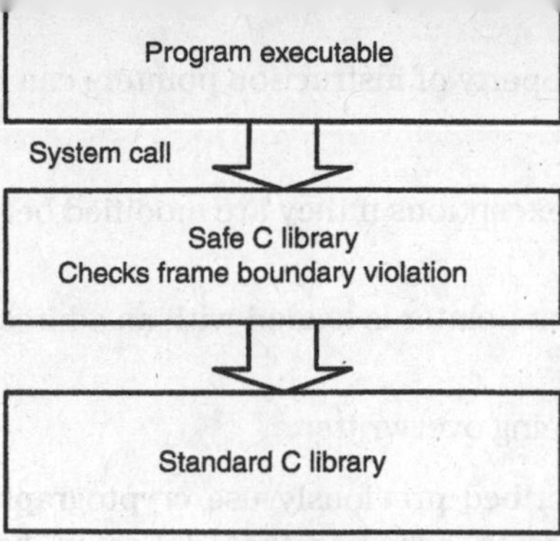

Figure 5.7 Interceptor.

work. Every point in program evolution, from static source to running executable, presents its own opportunity to add overflow checks.

Overflow attacks work at a fundamental level, exploiting the stored-program concept that allows us to treat data and instructions alike. We mix instruction executions ("Branch here," "Load from there," "Use this value to set the instruction pointer," and so on) with program data ("Store this array of characters."). We allow location proximity between data and instructions because we need speed within a processor. This proximity has led to an assumed safety property: if we compile and debug our programs correctly, the flow of control in the assembly code generated will follow the flow of control of the source code. We assume that we will always load the instruction pointer from a trusted location in the address space, and we assume that return addresses on the stack will be written once on entry and read once on exit. Buffer overflow exploits violate this desired safety property.

Stack Growth Redirection

Changing the direction that the stack grows in so that buffers grow away from the return address on a stack frame and not toward it will prevent all currently known buffer overflow attacks. This action is infeasible, however, because the stack growth feature of the process segment is built into too many operating systems, hardware platforms, and tools.

Buffer overflows are still feasible even if the stack growth is reversed; they are just harder to build. The exploits work by overflowing a buffer in the calling routine's stack frame, not the current stack frame, by using a stolen reference to a buffer within the parent stack frame. If we can overflow this buffer, writing upward until the return address on the current stack frame is reached, we can overwrite the return value. No known exploits work this way, but the mechanism has been documented. Most solutions for buffer flow attacks with no or small changes can prevent this variation.

Hardware Support

Hardware support for ensuring the safety property of instruction pointers can help.

- We can trap overflows in hardware.
- We can flag return addresses and throw exceptions if they are modified before the call returns.
- We can throw exceptions if the instruction pointer is loaded with an address that is out of some allowed set.
- We can protect frame boundaries from being overwritten.

Indeed, although none of the patterns described previously use cryptographic techniques to block overflows, we could envision schemes that do so in hardware. Programs can have cryptographic keys that describe allowed context switches to block attempts to run */bin/sh/*. Hardware modifications are unlikely to happen in the near future. Until we have hardware support, we must actively pursue the other alternatives that we have described in the preceding sections.

Security and Perl

Larry Wall's Perl programming language has been called the "duct tape of the Internet." It provides a powerful and flexible environment for prototyping, systems administration, maintenance, and data manipulation and is excellent for building one-time solutions for complicated problems that would otherwise require too much effort when using C. There are several million Perl programmers and many excellent references on Perl usage (for example, [SC97], [WCO00], and [Sri98]).

The Perl interpreter consists of a *translator* and an *opcode executor*. The translator converts a Perl script into a syntax tree of abstract opcodes. Each opcode corresponds to a call to a carefully optimized C function. The current stable version of Perl, release 5.6.1, has more than 350 opcodes. The Perl opcode generator then scans through the completed syntax tree, performing local optimizations to collapse subtrees or to precompute values known at compile time. Each opcode stores the next opcode to be potentially executed, imposing an execution sequence on the syntax tree. At run time, the executor follows a path through the syntax tree, running opcodes as it goes. Each opcode returns the next opcode to be run, which can be identical to the *op_next* links within each node (except in cases where branch statements and indirect function calls redirect traversal of the syntax tree).

Perl is a full-fledged programming language, and the user can implement any security mechanism desired in code. There are several reasons for Perl's undeserved reputation as a security risk.

Perl and CGI. Perl powers many of the cgi-bin scripts used on Web servers. Poor argument validation, along with root-owned SUID Perl scripts, allowed many exploits based on carefully constructed URLs to succeed. Some exploits confused the issue, blaming the Perl language because of Perl code that implemented security

visible in the source html), values in the HTTP header (which can be spoofed), or code that contained nonPerl-related Web security problems.

Perl and system calls. SUID Perl scripts that do not validate command-line arguments or check environment variables and yet invoke a shell are susceptible (this statement applies to any program). Malicious users could insert *input field separator* (IFS) characters, such as pipes or semicolons, into arguments or could modify the PATH variable or change the current working directory in ways that give them a root shell.

Bugs in old versions of Perl. Many of the exploits that worked on bugs in earlier versions have been fixed in current stable releases.

Home-grown libraries. Perl provides support for almost all Internet protocols. Users who rolled their own, with all the attendant risks, blamed Perl for security holes.

Poor coding practices. Almost anything goes in Perl (that includes almost anything dangerous).

Execution of untrusted scripts. Once a host has been compromised, the presence of a powerful interpreter such as Perl makes automated attacks easier. This situation is not a fault of Perl's but does highlight the risks of putting a powerful tool on a production box, where it can be exploited. HP machines configured in trusted computing mode forbid the use of compilers. This feature is useful for protecting production machines, because you should not be building software on a production box anyway. Unlike compiled code, which no longer needs the compiler, the Perl interpreter must be present for Perl scripts to execute.

We will describe three patterns that Perl uses for supporting secure programming.

Syntax Validation

Perl has few rivals for manipulating text for complex pattern matching through regular expressions. You can write a lexical analyzer for most simple applications in one line. Command-line argument validation in Perl uses regular expressions whose syntax, for example, supports the following items:

- *Single character matches.* /[aeiouAEIOU]/ matches the vowels.
- *Predefined character matches.* \d matches a single digit, \w matches a single legal Perl name, \W matches any input that is not a legal Perl name, and so on.
- *Sequencing.* /tom/ matches tom exactly.
- *Multipliers.* /A+/ matches a string of one or more As. /A*/ matches a string of zero or more As.
- *Alternation.* /(a|b|c)/ matches any one of a, b, or c.

Perl also has many other features for pattern matching, such as memory placeholders, anchors, substitutions, and pattern redirection.

All of these features make it easy to check the syntax of inputs. We can create an alphabet of characters, along with a syntax tree for all valid inputs defined by an application.

to valid syntax checks before we use the input string as a username, a file to be opened, a command to be executed, or a URL to be visited.

Sentinel

Perl uses the sentinel pattern to mark any data value within the program as *trusted*, by virtue of being created inside the program, or *untrusted*, by virtue of being input into the program from the outside world. The *tainted* property is a *sentinel*. Marking data as tainted prevents the interpreter from using the data in an unsafe manner by detecting some actions that attempt to affect the external environment of the Perl script and making them illegal at run time.

By default, any *SUID* or *SGID* Perl script is executed in *taint mode*. Alternatively, Perl allows *taint* checking on any script by invoking the Perl script with the -T switch, which marks all data input from outside the program as tainted. Perl marks variables that derive their values from tainted variables as also tainted. Examples of possibly tainted external values include data from a POST form to a cgi-bin script, command-line arguments, environment variables not set internally but inherited from the script's parent, and file handles.

Maintaining these markers on the flow of data through the program has a performance cost. This situation, however, enables the interpreter (which assumes that the code is trusted but the data is not) to forbid execution of dangerous actions that use the tainted data. When a Perl script running with the -T switch invokes any action that can impact the external host, such as launching a child process, opening a file, or calling *exec* with a single string argument, that action will be blocked. Although it is possible to test whether a variable is tainted, we normally already know which variables contain data from external sources. We must clean the data, *untainting* it before we can use it. The only way to extract untainted data from a tainted string is through regular expression match variables, using Perl's pattern matching memory trick using parenthesis placeholders.

Wall, Christiansen, and Schwartz in [WCS96] note that "The tainting mechanism is intended to prevent stupid mistakes, not to remove the need for thought." The taint mechanism will not prevent bad programming practices, such as marking tainted data as untainted without cleaning the data first.

Sandbox

Malcolm Beattie's *Safe module*, part of the standard Perl release, implements the Sandbox pattern. The safe module creates a compartment with well-defined access privileges.

A compartment has the following elements:

- *A name.* Each compartment in a Perl program is an instance of a Safe object, initialized with its own capability list. This feature enables a form of multi-level security. We can create several instances of Safe variables and run functions with different access privileges within each one. The Java sandbox, which we will

creation of multiple policy managers that can be dynamically loaded on the basis of the identity of the applet's digital signatory or the host from which it was downloaded.

- *A namespace.* The namespace of a safe is restricted. By default, any function executing within the safe can share only a few variables with the externally compiled code that invoked the function within the Safe object. These include the underscore variables $_, @_, and file handles. The code that invokes the safe can add variables to the namespace.
- *An opcode mask.* Each compartment has an associated operator mask. The mask represents a capability list (please refer to Chapter 3, "Security Architecture Basics") initialized to a default minimal access configuration. The mask is an array of length *MAXO( )* bytes, one for each opcode in Perl (of which there are 351 opcodes listed in opcode.h, as of release 5.6.1). A byte is set to 0x00 if execution of the corresponding opcode is allowed or 0x01 if disallowed.

Safes can evaluate functions that handled tainted data. The class Safe provides methods for handling namespaces and masks, sharing variables, trapping and permitting opcodes, cleanly setting variables inside the safe, and evaluating strings as Perl code inside the safe.

Recall our description of Perl's run-time mechanism; in particular, the execution phase. When we traverse the syntax tree created from an untrusted script executing within a Safe compartment, we can check the value of the current opcode against the opcode mask very quickly before execution. We can raise an exception if the opcode is not allowed, which helps performance but makes capability list management harder. The Safe class provides methods for opcode mask management, such as conversion of opcode names to mask settings and masking or unmasking all opcodes. It is not obvious how to map corporate security policy to an opcode mask, however. We recommend enforcing the principle of least privilege by turning off all opcodes except the minimal set required.

From another viewpoint, the opcode masks correspond to security policies enforced by a Safe object rather than capability lists assigned to code. The opcode mask in the Safe class is bound to the Safe object instance, not to the actual code that is executed within the safe. The two viewpoints are equivalent in most cases; because all functions that can be evaluated within a safe are known at compile time, only the tainted user data to the function changes. This situation contrasts with the Java sandbox, where arbitrary applets can be downloaded and where security policy enforced by the JVM is chosen based on higher-level abstractions, such as the applet's digital signatory or the host from which it was downloaded.

Bytecode Verification in Java

We described how Perl's powerful pattern matching features make input validation easier. At the other extreme, from one-line syntax validation in Perl, is the infinite variety

Theorem provers seek to establish formal and constructive proofs for abstract properties of specific programs. In general, this proof is known to be undecidable, but we can establish constraints on generality to make the problem feasible.

The creators of the Java programming language have included security in its design from the start. Comprehensive security has lead to the following situations, however:

- Complex specifications that are sometimes open to interpretation.
- Implementations of the Java virtual machine and Java libraries that have had bugs.

We will discuss some of the security mechanisms of the Java virtual machine in Chapter 7, but we will focus on byte code verification in this section.

Java is a complicated, full-fledged language including objects with single inheritance, class hierarchies of objects, interfaces with multiple inheritance, strong typing, strict rules for type conversion, visibility or extensibility properties for object fields and methods (*public*, *private*, *protected*, *abstract*, *final*), and run-time constraints on the operand stack and array bounds. Just running through the list should give you some idea of the complexity of proving a claim about some property of a given Java class. Java 1.2 adds cryptographic extensions and access control mechanisms for granting code permission to execute actions based on rights and performs run-time permissions checking (just in case you thought, after learning about byte code verification, that the hard part was behind us).

Java was designed to be portable. Java programs are compiled into bytecodes that are executed on a JVM. The JVM does not trust the compiler to correctly enforce Java language rules because the bytecodes themselves can be produced using any means, independent of the Java compiler. Other languages can be compiled into bytecodes, but the JVM must ensure that the resulting bytecodes must be forced to follow Java's language rules. There are compilers for many languages, including C, C++, Scheme, python, Perl, and Ada95, that produce bytecodes. Nevertheless, the primary language overwhelmingly used to produce class files is Java.

The initial JVM specification and reference implementation provided by Sun have been extensively studied. Java's object type model and its attempt at proving properties ("theorems") about objects have led to considerable research on formal methods for capturing the behavior of the bytecode verifier. In particular, researchers have noted differences between the prose specification and the behavior of the reference implementation. Researchers have used formal methods from type theory to reason about bytecode validity. They have analyzed the verifier's capabilities as a theorem prover on restricted subsets of the language that remove some complicated language feature in order to apply powerful methods from type theory to understand how to improve and optimize the behavior of bytecode verifiers.

The JVM relies on the bytecode verifier to perform static checks to prevent dynamic access violations. Some checks can be implemented immediately while others must be deferred until run time. For example, the bytecode verifier must perform the following actions:

specification and has the correct preamble, length, and structure.

- Prevent illegal data conversions between primitive types.
- Prevent illegal casts of objects that do not have an inheritance relationship. This action might have to be deferred until run time because we might not know which superclass an object pointer refers to in a cast.
- Maintain array bounds by ensuring that indexes into arrays do not result in overflows and underflows. These checks must also be deferred until run time because we might not know the value of an index into an array.
- Confirm constraints that remove type errors, such as dereferencing an integer.
- Enforce language rules, such as single inheritance for objects or restrictions on classes or methods defined as final.
- Ensure that the visibility properties of object fields and methods are maintained; for example, by blocking access violations such as access of a private method from outside its class.
- Prevent other dynamic errors, such as accessing a new object before its constructor has been called.

Bytecode verification is a critical component in Java's security architecture. By default, the JVM trusts only the core Java API. All other class files, whether loaded from the local host or over the network, must be verified. The other components, including the class loader, the security manager, access controller, cryptographic extensions, and security policies, all depend on the verifier's ability to vet the code.

The Java security model suffers from one fundamental flaw: complexity. The consensus in security architecture is that simplicity is the best route to security. Simplicity in design leads to simplicity in implementation and makes reasoning about security possible. The goal of Sun in introducing Java as a write once, run anywhere solution to many software problems is a complex one, however, and simplification that results in flawed implementations would be to err in the other direction. We do keep in mind Einstein's admonition that "everything should be made as simple as possible, but not simpler," but the theoretical advances in bytecode verification promise room for improvement. We recommend Scott Oaks's *Java Security, (2nd Edition)* ([Oaks01]), as an excellent book on Java's security architecture.

Good Coding Practices Lead to Secure Code

The purpose of code review is to gain confidence in the quality of code. Although there is no guarantee that well-written code is automatically safe, there is considerable anecdotal evidence that good programmers write secure code.

Don Knuth invented and has written extensively about *literate programming* [Knuth92]. Knuth defines literate programming as, "a methodology that combines a programming language with a documentation language, thereby making programs more

programs that are written only in a high-level language." The main idea is to treat a program as a piece of literature addressed to human beings rather than to a computer. One could argue that anything that improves readability also improves understanding (and therefore improves security).

C++ and patterns guru James Coplien has written about the importance of writing understandable code. He champions the "humanistic coding patterns" of Richard Gabriel in [Cop95], which include simple guidelines to writing understandable, manageable code with the goal of reducing stress and increasing confidence for code maintainers who are unfamiliar with the source. The guidelines are elementary but powerful, including simple advice to define local variables on one page, assign variables once if possible, and make loops apparent by wrapping them in functions.

Kernighan and Pike in *The Practice of Programming* ([KP99]) describe the three guiding principles of program design: simplicity, clarity, and generality. They discuss a wide range of topics on programming style, including variable naming conventions, coding style, common C and C++ coding errors, simple data structures, algorithms, testing, portability, debugging, and performance. Although not a book on security, it is not hard to imagine that common sense and better programming style leads to faster and easily maintainable code. That makes for understandability, which leads to quicker bug detection and correction.

The study by Miller et al. [Mill00] reveals that open-source utilities are best in class for security. Eric Raymond has described why he believes this statement to be true in his essay *The Cathedral and the Bazaar* and also in *Open Sources: Voices from the Open Source Revolution* ([Ray95], [VFTOSM99]).

Matt Bishop wrote an influential note about how to write SUID and SGID programs ([Bish87]), describing coding guidelines. He recommends minimizing exposure by performing the following actions:

- Using the effective user ID rather than the owner's ID as much as possible.
- Checking the environment and PATH inherited from the parent process.
- Cleaning up the environment before invoking child processes.
- Making sure that SUID programs are vetted for buffer overflow problems.
- Using a user ID other than root, with minimal privileges needed.
- Validating all user inputs before using them.
- His best guideline: Do not write SUID and SGID programs, if possible.

All this advice leads us to the belief that the ability to write secure code is not magical but can be accomplished by competent programmers following common-sense rules of programming style, with assistance and review by security experts when necessary.

Conclusion

Code review is architecture work, but at a very fundamental level. Its major virtue is that it adds simplicity to the architecture. The more we understand and trust our code,

in our architecture.

Any architect can tell you the consequences of building the prettiest of buildings over the poorest of foundations. Good code leads to good foundations. All the topics that we will target in the chapters to follow will depend on this foundation: operating systems, Web servers, databases, middleware, secure communication, and cryptography.

Code review is not perfect but gives confidence to our pledge to build secure systems. If we give equal service to the other elements of the security architecture as well, the time comes when we shall redeem our pledge, not wholly or in full measure, but very substantially.

Cryptography

Cryptography, the art of secret writing, enables two or more parties to communicate and exchange information securely. Rulers throughout history have depended on *classical cryptography* for secure communication over insecure channels. A classical cryptographic cipher scrambles a message by using encryption rules along with a secret key. The cipher substitutes each symbol or group of symbols in the original message with a sequence of one or more cipher text symbols. The encryption rules are not secret, but only a recipient who knows the secret key will be able to decrypt the message.

The success of many operations critically depends on our ability to create confidential channels of communications. Financial institutions must conduct business negotiations securely, safe from the eyes of prying competitors. Generals require military command and control systems to relay orders down the chain of command without the fear of enemy interception. Customers must be able to buy merchandise without the risk of theft or fraud. Secrecy is essential for success.

In each of these scenarios, in addition to confidentiality we also need other security principles such as authentication, integrity, and non-repudiation. We must be able to establish with a reasonable degree of confidence that the party we are in communication with is indeed whom they claim they are. We must prevent message modification or tampering in transit. In addition, we must protect ourselves from those who deny transacting business with us if today's friend becomes tomorrow's foe. The success of the Internet as a marketplace for services and information depends on the strength of our cryptographic protocols and algorithms.

Our claims that we have accomplished some security principle are only as good as our ability to prove that our assumptions hold true. For example, cryptography assumes

sary who steals the key can now decrypt all traffic. Although this statement seems tautological, the difficulty lies in the details. We must examine implementation and procedural details to ensure that we do not attach secret information in the clear to messages in transit, leave keys in memory, append keys to files, or allow backup procedures to capture the keys. These details can break our assumptions.

Our purpose in this chapter is to support the references to cryptography in the chapters ahead. We will not consider the legal and ethical dimensions of cryptography—the battlefield between privacy and civil rights advocates who desire unbreakable security for the individual and law enforcement or national security advocates who warn against the dangers of allowing terrorists or criminals access to strong cryptography. [Sch95], [Sch00], [Den99], and [And01] are excellent resources for the social impacts of cryptographic use.

The History of Cryptography

Cryptography has a fascinating history. The story of the evolution of ever-stronger ciphers, forced by the interplay between code makers seeking to protect communications and code breakers attacking the schemes invented by the code makers, is told eloquently in [Kahn96] (and, in a shorter version, [Sin99]). Kahn and Singh describe a succession of ciphers invented for hiding military secrets through the ages, from the *Caesar Cipher* to *Lucifer* (Horst Feistel's precursor to the Data Encryption Standard) down to modern advances in both symmetric and asymmetric cryptography.

Encryption converts the original form of a message, also called the plaintext, into a cryptographically scrambled form called the ciphertext. Decryption reverses this operation, converting ciphertext into plaintext. Each step requires a key and the corresponding algorithm.

All cryptography was secret-key cryptography until 1969, when James Ellis invented non-secret encryption. In 1973, Clifford Cocks invented what we now call the RSA algorithm, and with Malcolm Williamson invented a Diffie-Hellman-like key exchange protocol [Sin99, And01]. Because their research was classified and kept secret by the British Government for decades, however, the birth of the modern era of public-key cryptography had to wait until 1976, when Whit Diffie and Martin Hellman invented their key exchange protocol and proposed the existence of asymmetric encryption schemes. In 1977, the first open public-key encryption algorithm was invented and patented by Ron Rivest, Adi Shamir, and Len Adleman. Fortunately, their independent discovery of asymmetric cryptographic algorithms occurred only a few years after the classified work of Ellis, Cocks, and Williamson and rightly forms the origin of modern cryptography.

The current state of the art has expanded the scope of cryptography far beyond secure communication between two parties. Oded Goldreich defines modern cryptography as the science of construction of secure systems that are robust against malicious attacks to make these systems deviate from their prescribed behavior [Gol01]. This definition

Secrecy and Progress

Perhaps asymmetric cryptography was an idea whose time had come given the increasing levels of military importance, commercial interest, and computing power ahead, and a public rediscovery was inevitable. The landscape of security today would be very different without the invention of public-key cryptography, however. History shows us another example of 2,000 years of conventional wisdom overturned by a radical insight. The great mathematician Gauss greeted the independent discovery of non-Euclidean geometry by Janos Bolyai in 1832 and Nicolai Lobachevsky in 1829 with the surprising revelation that he had discovered the field 30 years earlier. It is believed that his claim, and his elegant proofs of some of Bolyai's results, caused Bolyai to abandon the field entirely. Gauss had been reluctant to publish, fearing that the mathematical community would be unable to accept such a revolutionary idea. Similarly, it is possible (though highly improbable) that some government agency is sitting on a fast algorithm for factorization or discrete logs right now.

can been seen as an architectural one, using the familiar notions of components, constraints, and connectors from Chapter 3, "Security Architecture Basics."

Modern cryptography is concerned with systems composed of collections of entities (called parties) with well-defined identities and properties. Entities interact over communication channels. Each cryptographic system has a purpose: a functional goal accomplished by exchanging messages between participants. Entities share relationships and accomplish their functional goals through cryptographic protocols. The system must accomplish this goal efficiently, according to some agreed-upon notion of efficiency. Defining a secure cryptographic protocol is not an easy task. The communications channel between any two or more parties can be secure or insecure, synchronous or asynchronous, or broadcast or point-to-point. Entities can be trusted or untrusted; and their behavior can be honest, malicious, or both at various times in an interaction. Participants might desire to hide or reveal specific information in a controlled manner. Any of the security goals from Chapter 3 might also be desired.

Adversaries are limited by computational power alone, rather than artificial constraints formed by our beliefs about their behavior. Adversaries must be unable to thwart us from accomplishing the system's functional goal. If this statement is true, we say that it is *computationally infeasible* for the enemy to break the system.

Many deterministic cryptographic algorithms and protocols have randomized (and even more secure) counterparts. Probability and randomness not only play a central role in the definition of secure algorithms, pseudo-random generators, and one-way functions, but also help us define the notions of efficiency and feasibility themselves. We might not be able to guarantee absolutely that an algorithm is secure, that a number is prime, or that a system cannot be defeated, but we can prove that it is exceedingly

properties hold true.

Modern cryptographers use tools that are defined in abstract terms to separate the properties of the cryptographic primitives from our knowledge of their implementation. We only require that our implementations be indistinguishable from the abstract definitions in some formal way. Proofs of correctness, soundness, completeness, and so on should not depend on our intuitions about implementation details, hardware, software, computational limits, the environment of the system, the time needed for a reasonable communication, the order of events, or any assumptions of strategy on the part of any adversary.

Although the rarified world of cryptographic research is quite far from most of the concerns of practical, applied cryptography (and which, in turn, is mostly outside the domain of most software architects), the gaps are indeed narrowing. The Internet and all the intensive multi-party interaction that it promises will increasingly require modern cryptographic protocols for accomplishing any number of real and practical system goals. We refer the interested reader [Kob94] and [Sal96] for primers on the mathematics behind cryptography; [Den82], [KPS95], [MOV96], and [Sch95] for excellent references on applied cryptography; [Gol01] for the foundations of modern cryptography; and [And01] for the security engineering principles behind robust cryptographic protocols.

Cryptographic Toolkits

The *National Institute of Standards and Technology* (NIST) is a U.S. government body controlling standards relating to cryptographic algorithms and protocols. NIST publishes the *Federal Information Processing Standards* (FIPS) and coordinates the work of other standards (ANSI, for example) and volunteer committees (such as IETF working groups) to provide cryptographic algorithms approved for U.S. government use. NIST reviews the standards every five years and launches efforts to build replacements for algorithms that have defects or that are showing their age in the face of exploding computational power. For example, the *Advanced Encryption Standard* (AES) algorithm, selected to replace the venerable DES algorithm, was selected through an open multi-year review and testing process in a competition among 15 round-one submissions. Vincent Rijmen and Joan Daemen's Rijndael cipher was selected over four other finalists (csrc.nist.gov/encryption/aes/). We expect to see AES as an encryption option in products everywhere.

NIST has collected some basic cryptographic building blocks into the NIST Cryptographic Toolkit to provide government agencies, corporations, and others who choose to use it with a comprehensive toolkit of standardized cryptographic algorithms, protocols, and security applications. NIST reviews algorithms for the strength of security, benchmarks the speed of execution in software and hardware, and tests implementations on multiple platforms and in many languages. The rigorous validation tests can give us some confidence in these ciphers over other (proprietary, vendor invented, possibly insecure, and certainly not peer-reviewed) choices. Open standards are essential to cryptography.

- Encryption for confidentiality in several encryption modes
- Authentication
- Hash functions for integrity and authentication
- Digital signatures for integrity and authentication
- Key management
- Random number generation
- Prime number generation

NIST maintains a list of cryptographic standards and requirements for cryptographic modules at www.nist.gov/fipspubs. RSA Labs at the RSA Data Security Inc.'s Web site, www.rsa.com/rsalabs/index.html, is also an excellent starting point for information on crypto standards and algorithms.

In the following sections, we will present an overview of cryptographic building blocks.

One-Way Functions

One-way functions are easy to compute but are hard to invert (in almost all cases). A function *f* from domain *X* to range *Y* is called one-way if for all values of x, $f(x)$ is easy to compute, but for most values of y, it is computationally infeasible to compute $f^{-1}(y)$. For example, multiplying two prime numbers p and q to get the product n is easy, but factoring n is believed to be very hard.

Trapdoor one-way functions are one-way, but invertible if we have additional information called the trapdoor key. A function *f* from domain *X* to range *Y* is called trapdoor one-way if *f* is one-way and for all values of y, it is computationally feasible to compute $f^{-1}(y)$ given an additional trapdoor key.

It is not known if any function is truly one-way, and a proof of existence would have deep consequences for the foundations of computing. One-way and trapdoor one-way functions are central to asymmetric cryptography and are used as a basic building block in many cryptographic protocols. We will describe one-way *hash* functions, also called cryptographic checksums, in a section ahead.

Encryption

Cryptography broadly divides encryption algorithms into two classes.

- *Symmetric key encryption*, which uses shared secrets between the two parties.
- *Asymmetric key encryption*, which uses separate but related keys for encryption and decryption; one public, the other private.

tography to use the best features of both.

Auguste Kerckhoff first stated the fundamental principle that encryption schemes should not depend upon the secrecy of the algorithm; rather, that security should depend upon secrecy of the key alone. All encryption algorithms can be cracked by brute force by trying all possible decryption keys. The size of the key space, the set of all possible keys, should be too large for brute force attacks to be feasible.

Symmetric Encryption

Symmetric cryptography depends on both parties sharing a secret key. This key is used for both encryption and decryption. Because the security of the scheme depends on protecting this shared secret, we must establish a secure channel of communication to transmit the shared secret itself. We can accomplish this task through many out-of-band procedures, by making a phone call, by sending the secret by trusted courier, or by using a private line of communication (such as a private leased line).

Claude Shannon, in his seminal article [Sha49], proved that that we can accomplish perfect secrecy in any encryption scheme by using randomly generated keys where there are as many keys as possible plaintexts. Encryption with a one-time pad, a randomly generated key that is the same length as the message and that is used once and thrown away, is perfectly secure because all keys are equally likely implying that the ciphertext leaks no information about the plaintext. One-time pads are impractical for most applications, however.

Practical symmetric encryption schemes differ from one-time pads in two ways.

- They use short, fixed-length keys (for example, DES keys are 56 bits long) for messages of any length. In other words, the ciphertext will contain information about the plaintext message that might be extractable.
- These keys are either chosen by people (the key might not really be random), are generated by using physical processes like radioactive decay (in which case we can make some assumption of randomness), or are generated by using *pseudo-random number* (PRN) generators. PRN generators are deterministic programs that use a small seed to generate a pseudo-random sequence that is computationally indistinguishable from a true, random sequence. Implementations might use weak PRN generators with nonrandom properties exploitable by a cryptanalyst, however.

Symmetric encryption is generally very fast, uses short keys, and can be implemented in hardware. We can therefore perform bulk encryption on a communications data stream at almost line speeds or with only a small performance hit if we use the right pipelining design and architecture. We must, however, be able to negotiate a cipher algorithm with acceptable parameters for key and block size and exchange a secret key over a trusted channel of communication. Key distribution to a large user base is the single largest challenge in symmetric encryption. This task is often accomplished by

Hellman, which we will discuss later).

The earliest encryption ciphers used simple alphabetical substitution or transposition rules to map plaintext to ciphertext. These ciphers depended upon both parties sharing a secret key for encryption and decryption. Later improvements enhanced the encryption rules to strengthen the cipher. The two types of symmetric key ciphers are as follows.

Block ciphers. Block ciphers break the input into contiguous and fixed-length blocks of symbols and apply the same encryption rules to each plaintext block to produce the corresponding ciphertext block.

Stream ciphers. Stream ciphers convert the input stream of plaintext symbols into a stream of ciphertext symbols. The encryption rule used on any plaintext symbol or group of contiguous symbols depends on the relative position of that portion of the input from the beginning of the stream.

Encryption Modes

Encryption algorithms can be composed in many ways, mixing details of the plaintext or ciphertext of preceding or succeeding blocks with the plaintext or ciphertext of the current block undergoing encryption. Composition strengthens the cipher by removing patterns in the ciphertext. Identical plaintext sequences can map to completely different ciphertext blocks by using context information from blocks ahead or behind the current block. Encryption modes often represent tradeoffs between speed, security, or error recoverability.

Block Ciphers

Encryption modes for block ciphers include the following:

- *Electronic codebook mode.* We encrypt each succeeding block of plaintext with the block cipher to get cipher text. Identical plaintext blocks map to identical ciphertext blocks and might leak information if the message has structure resulting in predictable plaintext blocks or through frequency analysis to find NULL plaintext blocks.
- *Cipher block chaining.* The previous block of ciphertext is exclusive ORed with the next block of plaintext before encryption. This action removes the patterns seen in ECB. The first block requires an initialization vector to kick-start the process.
- *Cipher feedback mode.* Data is encrypted in smaller blocks than the block size, and as in CBC, a plaintext error will affect all succeeding ciphertext blocks. Ciphertext errors can be recovered from with only the loss of a few mini-blocks, however. CFB links the ciphertext for each smaller block to the outcome of the preceding mini-block's ciphertext.

Other modes include output feedback mode, counter mode, and many more.

Stream Ciphers

Simple stream ciphers use the shared secret as an input to a key stream generator that outputs a pseudo-random sequence of bits that is XOR-ed with the plaintext to produce the ciphertext. Ron Rivest's RC4, which appears in SSL and in the *Wired Equivalent Privacy* (WEP) algorithm from the IEEE 802.11b standard, is one such stream cipher. Two encryption modes, among others, for stream ciphers are as follows:

- *Output feedback mode.* Stream ciphers in OFB use the key to repeatedly encrypt an initialization vector to produce successive blocks of the key stream.
- *Counter mode.* Stream ciphers in counter mode use a counter and the key to generate each key stream block. We do not need all predecessors of a particular block of bits from the key stream in order to generate the block.

We refer the interested reader to [Sch95] and [MOV96] for more details.

Asymmetric Encryption

Asymmetric encryption uses two keys for each participant. The key pair consists of a public key, which can be viewed or copied by any person (whether trusted or untrusted) and a private key (which must be known only to its owner). Asymmetric encryption is mainly used for signatures, authentication, and key establishment.

Asymmetric algorithms do not require a trusted communications path. Authenticating the sender of a message is easy because a recipient can use the sender's public key to verify that the sender has knowledge of the private key. The keys themselves can be of variable length, allowing us to strengthen the protocol with no changes to the underlying algorithm. Finally, once public keys are bound to identities securely, key management can be centralized on an insecure host—say, a directory—because only public keys need to be published. Private keys never travel over the network.

Although public-key cryptography protocols can accomplish things that seem downright magical, they do depend on the assumption that certain mathematical problems are infeasible. Popular public-key cryptosystems depend upon the computational infeasibility of three classes of hard problems.

Integer factorization. RSA depends on the infeasibility of factoring composite numbers.

Discrete logarithms. Diffie-Hellman (DH) key exchange, the Digital Signature Algorithm (DSA), and El Gamal encryption all depend on the infeasibility of computing discrete logs over finite fields.

Elliptic curve discrete logarithms. Elliptic Curve DH, Elliptic Curve DSA, and other *Elliptic Curve Cryptographic* (ECC) variants all depend on the infeasibility of computing discrete logs on elliptic curves over finite fields. The choice of the finite field, either GF(2^n) (called EC over an even field) or GF(p) for a prime p (called EC over a prime field), results in differences in the implementation. ECC, under certain

time using shorter keys to provide comparable security. ECC crypto libraries are popular for embedded or mobile devices.

Algorithms based on other assumptions of hardness, such as the knapsack problem or the composition of polynomials over a finite field, have been defined—but for practical purposes, after many were broken soon after they were published, the three choices above are the best and only ones we have.

Asymmetric algorithms are mathematically elegant. The invention of fast algorithms for factoring large numbers or computing discrete logs will break these public-key algorithms, however. In contrast, symmetric ciphers do not depend on the belief that some mathematical property is hard to compute in subexponential time but are harder to reason about formally.

Public-key algorithms do come with some costs.

- Public-key operations are CPU-intensive. Public-key algorithms contain numerical manipulations of very large numbers, and even with optimized implementations, these operations are expensive.
- Public-key algorithms depend on some other mechanism to create a relationship between an entity and its public key. We must do additional work to authenticate this relationship and bind identifying credentials to cryptographic credentials before we can use the public key as a proxy for an identity.
- Revocation of credentials is an issue. For example, some schemes for digital signatures do not support non-repudiation well or use timestamps for freshness but allow a window of attack between the moment the private key is compromised and the time it is successfully revoked.

Number Generation

Cryptographic algorithms and protocols need to generate random numbers and prime numbers. Pseudo-random sequences must be statistically indistinguishable from a true random source, and public and private keys are derived from large (512, 1024, or 2048-bit) prime numbers.

Random Number Generation. All pseudorandom number generators are periodic, but solutions can ensure that any short sequence of pseudorandom bits is indistinguishable from a true random sequence by any computationally feasible procedure.

Prime Number Generation. Asymmetric algorithms depend on our ability to generate large primes. Deterministic primality testing would take too long, but random primality testing can show that a number is prime with very high probability. Some prime number generators also avoid primes that might have undesirable properties that would make factoring any composite number that depended on the prime easier to accomplish.

Cryptographic Hash Functions

Hash functions map inputs of arbitrary size to outputs of fixed size. Because of the pigeonhole principle, many inputs will collide and map to the same output string. Cryptographic hash functions map large input files into short bit strings that we can use to *represent* the input file. This situation is possible if the likelihood of collisions, where two different inputs hash to the same output, is extremely small and if given one input and its corresponding hash, it is computationally infeasible to find another input that collides with the first. The output of a hash is only a few bytes long. For example, SHA1 produces 20 bytes of output on any given input, and MD5 produces 16 bytes. Hash functions such as SHA1 and MD5 are also called cryptographic checksums or message digests.

Hash functions used in conjunction with other primitives give us data integrity, origin authentication, and digital signatures. Hash functions do not use keys in any manner, yet can help us guard against malicious downloads or help us maintain the integrity of the system environment if some malicious action has damaged the system.

Cryptographic hashes are useful for matching two data files quickly to detect tampering. Commercial data integrity tools can be used for a wide variety of purposes.

- Detect changes to Web server files by intruders.
- Verify that files are copied correctly from one location to another.
- Detect intrusions that modify system files, such as rootkit attacks.
- Detect modifications in firewall or router rule sets through misconfiguration or malicious tampering.
- Detect any differences between backups and restored file systems.
- Verify that installation tapes for new software are not tampered with.

Keyed Hash Functions

We can create *message authentication codes* (MACs) by combining hashes with symmetric encryption. If Bob wishes to send Alice an authenticated message, he can:

- Concatenate the message and a shared secret key, then compute the hash.
- Send the message and the resulting hash value (called the MAC) to Alice.

When Alice receives a message with an attached MAC from Bob, she can:

- Concatenate the message and a shared secret key, then compute the hash.
- Verify that the received hash matches the computed hash.

Keyed hash functions convert any hash function into a MAC generator. A special kind of keyed hash, called the HMAC, invented by Bellare, Canetti, and Krawcyk [BCK96] (and described in RFC2104), can be used with MD5 (creating HMAC-MD5) or SHA1 (creating

underlying hash function. For example, a collision attack demonstrated against MD5 failed against HMAC-MD5.

HMAC is a keyed hash within a keyed hash. It uses an inner and an outer pad value and adds only a few more simple operations to compute the hash.

$$HMAC(K,M) = H((K \oplus opad) \bullet H((K \oplus ipad) \bullet M))$$

In this equation, *opad* is a 64-byte array of the value 0x36; *ipad* is a 64-byte array of the value Ox5c; $\oplus$ is exclusive OR; and $x \bullet y$ is the concatenation of x and y. The IPSec protocols, discussed in Chapter 8 ("Secure Communications"), use HMACs for message authentication.

Authentication and Digital Certificates

Because the security of asymmetric schemes depends on each principal's private key remaining secret, no private key should travel over the network. Allowing everyone to generate their own public and private key pairs, attach their identities to their public keys, and publish them in a public repository (such as an X.500 directory or a database), however, creates a dilemma. How can we trust the binding between the identity and the public key? Can a third party replace Alice's name in the binding with his or her own? How can we ensure that the person we are communicating with is actually who they claim to be?

PKIs solve the problem of trust by introducing a trusted third party called a *Certificate Authority* (CA) that implements and enables trust. The CA creates certificates, which are digital documents that cryptographically bind identifying credentials to a public key.

If Alice needs a certificate, she must prove her identity to yet another third party called a *Registration Authority* (RA) to acquire short-lived credentials required for a certificate request. The CA verifies the authenticity of the credentials and then signs the combination of Alice's identity and her public key. If Bob trusts the CA, then Bob can acquire the CA's certificate (through a secure channel) to verify the signature on Alice's certificate. The CA's certificate can be self-signed or can be part of a certification chain that leads to a CA that Bob trusts.

We will discuss PKIs in more detail in Chapter 13, "Security Components."

Digital Signatures

Diffie and Hellman also invented digital signatures. Digital signatures, like handwritten signatures on a piece of paper, bind the identity of a principal to a message. The message is signed by using the principal's private key, and the signature can be verified by using the principal's public key. It is computationally infeasible for anyone without the principal's private key to generate the signature.

Signed Messages

Alice can send Bob a digitally signed message by using an asymmetric encryption algorithm (such as RSA) and a cryptographic hash function (such as MD5). Alice creates the signature as follows:

- She computes the hash of the message.
- She encrypts the hash with her private key.
- She transmits both the message and the encrypted hash to Bob.

Bob verifies Alice's digital signature as follows:

- He computes the hash of the message received.
- He decrypts the encrypted hash received by using Alice's public key.
- He compares the computed hash with the decrypted hash and verifies that they match.

Note that we do not need to distribute keys in this exchange. Note also that the exchange is not confidential.

Digital signatures are universally verifiable because the verification algorithm uses public information. This situation is in contrast with MACs, where the encrypted one-way hash can only be computed by anyone with the secret key. Because both parties possess this secret key, a third party adjudicating a dispute would be unable to determine whether a MAC code on a message originated from the sender was generated by the (possibly malicious) recipient. Unlike MACs, digital signatures do provide non-repudiation because only the sender knows the private key.

Digital Envelopes

Digital envelopes can ensure secrecy and integrity. Digital envelopes combine the strengths of symmetric and asymmetric cryptography to ensure the integrity and confidentiality of a message.

Alice creates a digital envelope containing a message for Bob as follows:

- She generates a random symmetric key.
- She encrypts the message with the symmetric key.
- She then encrypts the symmetric key with Bob's public key.
- She finally sends the encrypted message and the encrypted symmetric key to Bob.

Bob can open Alice's digital envelope as follows:

- He decrypts the symmetric key by using his private key.
- He decrypts the message with the symmetric key.

Only Bob can accomplish this task, ensuring confidentiality. Note that we do not need to distribute keys in this exchange. Note also that we have not authenticated Alice to Bob.

Key Management

Key management is an operational challenge. How do we generate, secure, distribute, revoke, renew, or replace keys for all the parties in our architecture? Can we recover from key loss? How many keys must we create? Where are these keys stored? Is control distributed or centralized? What assumptions of security are we making about individual hosts and the central key repository?

The key management problem describes the processes and mechanisms required to support the establishment of keys and the maintenance of ongoing relationships based on secret keys. The cryptographic primitives and protocols used affect key life cycle management, as do the number of participants and the rate of key renewal required for a desired level of security.

Key management using symmetric key techniques sometimes uses a *trusted third party* (TTP) to broker pairwise key agreement between all the parties. Key establishment is the process by which a shared secret key becomes available to two or more communicating parties. Key generation, agreement, transport, and validation are all steps in the key establishment process. The parties must agree before hand on the ground rules for accomplishing this task. In a preprocessing step, the trusted third party agrees to a separate shared secret with each of the participants. When Alice wants to communicate with Bob, she initiates a key establishment protocol with the TTP that results in a shared secret session key that might have a freshness parameter attached to prevent later replay. Kerberos (discussed in Chapter 13) uses this mediated authentication model.

Key management using public key techniques is greatly simplified not only because of a smaller number of keys that need to be managed (that is, one public key per participant) but also because all public key information is non-secret. Digital certificates introduce a TTP in the CA to bind identity and key information in a tamperproof manner.

Whit Diffie and Martin Hellman invented the first key exchange protocol, along with public-key encryption, that enables parties to exchange a shared secret on an untrusted channel where all messages can be seen by an adversary. *Diffie-Hellman* (DH) key exchange is based on the complexity of computing discrete logarithms in a finite field.

DH key exchange solves the key distribution problem in symmetric encryption. Earlier schemes for distributing shared secrets involved a risky, expensive, and labor-intensive process of generating huge numbers of symmetric keys and transporting them to each party through a secure channel (such as a courier service). DH enables two parties with a trust relationship to establish a shared secret. DH also depends on binding identities to public keys in some manner.

Hybrid systems use asymmetric techniques to establish secure channels for communicating the shared secret, which is then used for symmetric operations for authentication or encryption. In key exchange protocols such as Diffie-Hellman, all messages are open for inspection with no loss in secrecy.

heart of any cryptographic algorithm or protocol. All bets are off if the secret key is visible in a message, attached to a file on an insecure disk, copied unencrypted to a backup tape, stored on a floppy that could be lost, or sent to a user in the clear via e-mail.

Cryptanalysis

Adversaries can break a code if the choice of key is poor or if the algorithm for encryption is weak. Poor keys restrict the actual key space that an adversary must search to a tiny fraction of the possible key space, allowing brute force attacks to succeed. Poor algorithms can be broken through cryptanalysis, the science of code breaking through ciphertext analysis. Attacks on the algorithm itself look for patterns of behavior in the mapping of input bits to output bits, examining the effect of flipping bits or showing linear relationships between inputs and outputs, to drive a wedge between a perfect randomization of the input and the actual output of the encryption algorithm.

Cryptanalysis comes in many forms, depending on the resources given to the cryptanalyst. An adversary might have no information beyond a large collection of ciphertext acquired through network sniffing. The adversary might know the plaintext for the collection of ciphertext messages and seek to decrypt new messages encrypted with the same key. Alternatively, the adversary might be able to choose plaintext messages to encrypt and examine the corresponding ciphertext or choose ciphertext messages to decrypt and examine the corresponding plaintext.

Symmetric algorithms can be analyzed by using two techniques. Both techniques of cryptanalysis are very hard. We say that a cipher is secure against cryptanalysis if it is faster to use a brute force key search instead of one of these techniques.

Differential Cryptanalysis

In 1990, Eli Biham and Adi Shamir invented differential cryptanalysis and found a chosen plaintext attack against DES that was more efficient than brute force search. Differential cryptanalysis looks for characteristics, which are patterns of differences between two chosen plaintext messages that result in specific differences in the corresponding ciphertext messages, with a high or low probability of occurrence. The analysis is specific to a particular algorithm, its key length, the number of rounds, and the diffusion principles for the substitution boxes within each round. If we collect enough plain and ciphertext pairs, we can use the characteristics of a specific symmetric key algorithm to predict bits in the secret key by comparing the outputs of the algorithm to the outputs expected by the characteristics.

Linear Cryptanalysis

In 1993, Mitsuru Matsui invented linear cryptanalysis, and along with Atsuhiro Yamagishi, presented the technique to create a known plaintext attack to break the FEAL cipher [MY93]. In 1994, Matsui presented a similar attack on DES. Linear crypt-

round and combines them to form a linear approximation that shows a maximal bias in probability from the value 1/2, allowing us to distinguish the cipher from a random permutation. Linear cryptanalysts can amplify this bias, given a known plaintext collection large enough, to break the cipher through predicting key bits.

There are other forms of cryptanalysis by using truncated differentials, interpolation of polynomials, mod-*n* relationships, and other mathematical tools.

Cryptography and Systems Architecture

Every practicing software architect needs to know about standards for cryptography, choosing algorithms for various purposes, and development requirements. Judging the strength or correctness of a cryptographic protocol is very difficult, however. Protocols that have been public for years have been broken; algorithms that were once thought secure have been shown to have fatal flaws; and new techniques of parallelizing attacks make brute force solutions feasible.

If the team has any questions about cryptography at the architecture review, you must call in an expert or farm out the work before the review and present the results of protocol analysis. The most common issues are implementation and interoperability. Is the implementation correct, and can we interoperate with another system through a secure protocol? Questions that might come up in the review include the following:

- How do we compare the relative performance of algorithms?
- What primitives do vendors offer in their crypto libraries, what parameters are configurable, what key and block sizes are supported, and how hard is it to change primitives?
- Have we chosen an open-source implementation that has undergone code review?
- Can we isolate elements so that they can be replaced?
- What constitutes overkill? Does the architecture use layer upon layer of encryption, thereby wasting bandwidth? Do we compress plaintext before encryption whenever possible?

Should we, as architects, worry too much about cryptographic algorithms being broken? Probably not, if we confine ourselves to mainstream choices and focus our energies on implementation details rather than holes in the underlying mathematics. If the mathematics breaks, we all will be part of a much larger problem and will defer fixes ("Switch to a symmetric algorithm," "Change protocols," "Use bigger keys," "Change the algorithm primitives," and so on) to the experts.

Innovation and Acceptance

Cryptography is unique compared to most other areas of research. Cryptographic research for many decades was classified, and any advances made were known only to

ligence agencies. In the past 30-some years, the veil of secrecy has largely been blown away and the flood of articles, books, and software is so great that cryptographic research in the public domain is almost certainly ahead of most classified research. Sunlight is the best disinfectant; in other words, open work on theoretical cryptography, with the give and take of peer review, new cryptanalysis, and the prestige associated with discovering flaws, drives a powerful engine of innovation. Algorithms are subjected to serious cryptanalysis; protocols are analyzed formally and matched against familiar design principles; there are huge advances in the mathematical foundations of cryptography; and new and almost magical protocols are invented.

Very little of this work sees early adoption in commercial applications. Although innovation and invention are encouraged, and although we have seen dramatic advances in our knowledge of cipher building and breaking, consumers of cryptography are rarely adventurous. Many of the most commonly used cryptographic algorithms and protocols have been around for years (if not decades), and it is unlikely that an upstart will knock an established algorithm out of use unless an actual flaw is discovered in the older solution or if computing power rises to the level where brute force attacks begin to succeed.

We would not accept 20-year-old medical advances, computers, cars, or cell phones. What drives our affection for the old over the new in cryptography? In a word: dependability. The older a cryptographic solution is, the more it is subject to public review and cryptanalysis. Using primitives that have been around for a while gives us confidence in the solution. A few years of careful scrutiny by diverse experts from many areas of computer science can never hurt.

This gap between innovation and acceptance is based on a very real risk of using an immature product or protocol in real-world applications before we have reviewed the solution with due diligence. If security gurus and cryptographers have had sufficient time to examine the mathematics behind the algorithm, to analyze the interactions or properties of the protocol itself, to build reference implementations, or to make estimates of lower bounds on the strength of the solution against cryptanalysis, we can certify the solution as reliable with some degree of confidence. Otherwise, the solution could fail in the field with unexpected consequences. At best, the flaw is discovered and patched by the good guys; at worst, we learn of the problem after we have been compromised.

Cryptographic Flaws

Any enterprise security policy should consider referencing a comprehensive cryptographic toolkit that provides strong security properties, uses open standards, and provides published test results for assuring validity, performance, and strength. When it comes to cryptography, rolling your own solution is a bad idea. This action only creates security through obscurity, maintenance problems, and compatibility issues on system interfaces.

will describe some examples of flaws and end with a description of the Wired Equivalent Privacy encryption algorithm used by the IEEE 802.11b wireless LAN standard as an example of the risks of rushing to market without proper review.

Algorithmic Flaws

Early versions of many cryptographic algorithms do break in ways that are easily or quickly fixed. Other problems are more difficult to fix, and once the cryptographic community declares a vote of no confidence, the problems might not be worth fixing. Poor choices of random number generators, large portions of the key space consisting of weak keys, successful attacks using differential or linear cryptanalysis, holes in the key schedule generator, partial success in breaking versions with fewer rounds, attacks that cause collisions, or fixes to attacks that break performance characteristics are all possible show stoppers.

From an architecture perspective, there is nothing an application can do except replace a cryptographic algorithm that is deemed insecure.

Protocol Misconstruction

Protocols use well-defined and rigorously analyzed patterns of message construction and communication to establish a security objective. Protocols that use primitives in a generic way (a stream cipher, a block cipher, a hash, and so on) can replace flawed elements if any are found. Flaws in the actual logic of the protocol are not so easily fixed, however. The literature on cryptography has many examples of attacks using replayed messages, deconstructed and maliciously reconstructed messages, source or destination spoofing, timestamp attacks exploiting a window of opportunity, or man-in-the-middle attacks.

The first rule of cryptographic protocol design for application architects is, "Don't do it." It is better to get some expert help in protocol design and review or work from existing open protocols. Because protocols (especially ad hoc or proprietary protocols) break more often than algorithms do, robust protocol design is critical. Abadi, Needham, and Anderson present security principles for robust cryptographic design in [AN96], [NA95a], [NA95b], and [And01]. They describe simple guidelines for architects and engineers for setting security goals, articulating assumptions, and defining and ensuring that events occur in the correct order. They also recommend extensions to messages to capture freshness, source or destination addresses, or the identity of the principals involved. We strongly recommend these articles to anyone who is interested in rolling their own protocols.

Implementation Errors

Implementation errors are the most common of all. Because most vendor implementations are not open source, the first indications of errors are often failures caused by

graphic protocol implementation is again probably outside the domain of the majority of projects, but open standards, open source, published bug fixes, applying security patches, and ensuring that our assumptions about the environment of the protocol are safe all help to ensure a level of confidence in the implementation.

Wired Equivalent Privacy

The IEEE 802.11b standard describes a high-speed communication protocol for wireless LANs. The standard also defines the *Wired Equivalent Privacy* (WEP) algorithm to provide authenticated, encrypted, and tamperproof wireless communication between wireless network hosts and a network access point.

The Network Access Point is a gateway between the wired and wireless worlds and shares a secret session identifier with all hosts on the network. WEP feeds the shared secret and an initialization vector to the RC4 stream cipher to produce a key stream, which is XOR-ed with the plaintext payload of each datagram. Each packet also has an integrity value to prevent tampering.

The 802.11b standard is very popular, widely available, and many commercial vendors have thrown their hat into the ring to build cheap products that enable any enterprise to create and manage small wireless LANs. WEP, however, is badly broken—and until a replacement is proposed and implemented, the security community and the 802.11b standards body is recommending the use of higher-level security protocols instead of WEP.

The cast of characters responsible for discovering many WEP flaws is quite large (www.isaac.cs.berkeley.edu/isaac/wep-faq.html is a good link to online resources), and much of the research is circulating in the form of unpublished manuscripts. Intel's Jesse Walker, one of the first people to report WEP vulnerabilities, has an overview at http://grouper.ieee.org/groups/802/11/Documents/DocumentHolder/0-362.zip.

Here are three results describing WEP flaws from the many discovered.

Implementation error. WEP uses CRC-32 instead of a stronger cryptographic hash like SHA1 for the integrity check. Borisov, Goldberg, and Wagner [BGW01] showed that encrypted messages could be altered at will while preserving a valid integrity check value.

Protocol misconstruction. Borisov, Goldberg, and Wagner also showed that the protocol is vulnerable to passive attacks based on statistical analysis, active known plaintext attacks to add unauthorized traffic to a link, and active attacks to spoof hosts to the network access point.

Algorithmic flaw. Fluhrer, Mantin, and Shamir published a paper [FMS01] describing several weaknesses in the key-scheduling algorithm of RC4. They proposed attacks against WEP vulnerabilities, exploiting those weaknesses. Stubblefield, Ioannidis, and Rubin [SIR01] actually implemented one of the attacks to demonstrate that it is practical to do so. Ron Rivest proposed a fix for the problem, along with a

(www.rsa.com/rsalabs).

Other researchers also reported attacks allowing the decryption of all traffic, dictionary attacks, and key generation attacks. Some proposals for fixing WEP have been made, including the use of AES, longer initialization vectors, or other stronger stream ciphers instead of RC4.

The flaws in the Wired Equivalent Privacy algorithm in IEEE 802.11 highlight the importance of open standards, peer review, and robust design principles.

Performance

Symmetric algorithms are much faster than asymmetric algorithms for comparable levels of security based on known attacks. The level of security depends on the length of the key, the block size, and the parameters of the algorithm. Symmetric algorithm speeds of encryption and decryption are comparable, as are the speeds of generating or verifying a MAC or an HMAC.

Head-to-head comparisons of symmetric algorithms for the AES challenge sponsored by NIST matched simplicity of design, speed of execution for different combinations of key and block size, implementation details such as memory versus CPU tradeoffs, performance in hardware, software, or a combination of the two, and cryptographic strength.

It is harder to define comparable levels of security for asymmetric algorithms. What primitives are we using? What operations will we invoke? What algorithm have we chosen? The speed of execution, of course, depends on all of these choices. Benchmarks of cryptographic performance for various platforms, processors, programming languages, and key sizes have been published (for example, [Con99] using the RSA BSAFE cryptographic toolkit or [WD00] using an open source crypto C++ toolkit). The following statements about a few of the many crypto algorithms available are gross generalizations, because we must consider implementation details, but some patterns emerge.

- *Generating and verifying digital signatures.* ECDSA signing is faster than DSA, which is faster than RSA. DSA signing and verification have comparable speeds, both helped by preprocessing. RSA signature verification is much faster than ECDSA, which is faster than DSA. El Gamal signatures are about twice as fast as El Gamal verifications.
- *Asymmetric encryption and decryption.* RSA encryption is much faster than RSA decryption (for long keys, over an order or two of magnitude). El Gamal encryption is twice as slow as El Gamal decryption, but with preprocessing, it reaches comparable speeds.

To create a true benchmark, test your choice of crypto primitives in your environment.

One common performance problem is degraded performance through layered interactions of multiple protocols. This situation is common in architectures that use layers for

the solutions are turned on simultaneously. For example, consider the IP data services protocol of a major wireless data services vendor aimed at providing Internet access on mobile devices. The protocol uses RC4 stream cipher encryption to encrypt a low-level link-layer protocol called *Cellular Digital Packet Data* (CDPD). The Wireless Application Protocol (WAP) on top of CDPD uses RC5 block cipher encryption at the application and transport level. Finally, a proprietary Web browser for the PDA used the *Wireless Transport Layer Security* (WTLS) protocol between the mobile browser and the Web server to avoid insecurity at the wireless gateway, where the protocol translation from WAP to HTTP left data in the clear on the gateway. The actual bandwidth was a fraction of CDPD's advertised bandwidth of 19.2 Kbps, and the PDA's underpowered CPU was brought to its knees. The connection, although unusable, was quite secure.

Protocol layering is unavoidable in many circumstances; for example, while initializing an SSL connection from a remote laptop that is connected to the corporate intranet over a VPN. In other circumstances, it might be possible to turn off one layer of encryption if a higher layer is strong enough. This strategy could backfire if other applications that depended on the lower layer for security did not implement the higher layer at all, however.

Comparing Cryptographic Protocols

The research, development, and deployment of commercial security products have created tremendous awareness of cryptography among the general public in the past few years.

For the most part, cryptographic protocols are magic to the majority of architects and developers. Architects comparing cryptographic protocols can examine the fundamental differences in number theoretic assumptions, the specific algorithms, key sizes, block sizes, and hardware versus software solutions. Sometimes algorithmic or implementation details obscure the higher questions, however. How much time does it take to crack one scheme versus another? What computational resources do we need? How much space do we need? What intellectual resources must we marshal to use these products correctly? What are the configuration options, and what cipher suites are available? Here is an analogy to highlight the bottom line.

The March 13, 2001 issue of *The New York Times* carried an interesting article by Randy Kennedy in the Metro Section about commuting from Washington, D.C. to New York City. Three intrepid reporters embarked on the journey by using three modes of transportation. All left at 6:15 a.m. from a common starting point in front of the White House. All had the same destination, City Hall Park in New York City. One traveled by air, catching a flight from Dulles to La Guardia. One traveled by the new Acela Express, a high-speed service from Amtrak between the two cities. The third took the slow and dusty route up the New Jersey Turnpike in a 1973 Checker Cab.

Here, we have three modes of transport. We wish to compare them and could spend endless amounts of time, energy, and effort describing the structure of a Boeing airplane, the

high-speed train that can operate at 150 mph on standard railway tracks. These details obscure the only key result that any reader would like to see, however. Who got to New York first? How much time did it take? How much did each journey cost?

Comparisons of cryptographic protocols offer similar parallels. It is certainly important to get into the details of how each technology works, what bottlenecks exist in the design, and what assumptions about the underlying transport mechanism are being made. For every question we could think of, there is probably a system architecture equivalent: the environment ("How was the weather?"), network congestion ("How busy were the roads?"), team expertise ("How knowledgeable were the travelers about the route?"), planning for the unexpected ("Why did fast food at McDonald's take so long, adding 20 minutes to the car trip?"), usability ("How comfortable were the passengers in transit?"), or compliance with corporate security policy ("Did anyone get a ticket?").

It is essential to document answers to these questions in the architecture description.

- What primitives are used, along with implementation details? Are there any known vulnerabilities in these primitives?
- What standards are referenced?
- List the parameters for the algorithms and cryptographic primitives.
- How fast do these primitives run? Is encryption fast? Is decryption slow? Is information often signed and rarely verified or signed once and verified often?
- What cryptanalytic schemes have the algorithms been subjected to?
- How well did they work in terms of resource usage, in terms of CPU cycles and memory? Did they use a random source? How strong is the pseudo-random number generated?

By the way, for the curious, here are the results of *The New York Times* comparison. The plane ride took about three hours and $217 dollars, the train another 15 minutes but only $150 dollars, and the car ride an hour more than that but even cheaper, costing only $30.

We recommend against paralysis through analysis. At the end, any comparison of cryptographic protocols reduces to a tradeoff that is probably as simple as the one described earlier.

Conclusion

At the heart of any popular methodology or philosophy of software design is a kernel based on a scientifically sound notion, some good idea that defines a building block. Cryptographic protocols are at the heart of many security components, solutions, or architectures. They form the basic building blocks of larger technologies and for the most part should be considered examples of the *magic* pattern. The advantage of viewing these primitives as atomic, neither viewable nor modifiable by the project, is that

graphic concepts, design their own proprietary algorithms, and claim that they are equivalent to other well-established ones or add proprietary extensions to standard protocols in a manner that breaks interoperability.

Cryptography forms the foundation of the subjects that we will discuss under the umbrella of security architecture. In the chapters ahead, we will use cryptography in many ways. We recommend that the reader who is in need of more information follow our links to the many excellent resources cited.

Trusted Code

One consequence of the growth of the Web is the emergence of digitally delivered software. The popularity of digitally delivered active content skyrocketed with the invention of technologies such as Java and browser extensions, which changed Web browsers from display devices for static HTML to containers for a bewildering number of forms of active content. Browsers now support audio and video, Java applets, ActiveX controls, JavaScript, VBScript, and much more. Third-party vendors have created many other plug-ins that are capable of displaying anything from dynamic images of chemical molecules to 3-D wire frames for computer-aided design to virtual reality worlds.

Access to active content opens access to the local resources on the client machine, however. Files can be read, written, deleted, or otherwise modified. Network connections from other hosts can be accepted or new connections initiated. System resources such as CPU, memory, and network bandwidth can be stolen, and devices can be damaged through malicious system calls or modifications in configuration files.

Downloading software packages also has risks. The software could have been modified at the source or in transit and could harbor viruses or Trojan horses that, once installed, could harm the local machine. This risk can be compounded if the machine has network access and can spread a computer contagion within the enterprise. If the malicious software is part of a software development kit that will be used to build code that will be widely deployed by legitimate means, we might indirectly release a software time-bomb from a source that we assumed to be trustworthy.

increasingly attaching MD5 cryptographic hashes to their software packages, especially if the release is prebuilt for a particular platform and contains binaries that can be modified. Recipients of the package can verify the integrity of the package, assuming the hash value has not also been replaced with the hash of the tampered file. This technique ensures some level of trust that the software has not been tampered with.

Within any infrastructure for enabling trust, we will see many patterns. We will see layers that separate concerns, service providers that validate data, cryptographic providers that provide encryption or digital signatures, sandboxes that contain activities, and interceptors that enforce security policy before allowing access to local resources.

In this chapter, we will discuss options available for enabling trust of code within an enterprise. We will describe some common patterns in implementing trust, using the Java sandbox, applet signing, Authenticode, and secure software distribution as examples. We will invert the problem and talk about digital rights management, where the code represents digital intellectual property and the recipient of the software is untrusted. We will end with a description of Ken Thompson's Trojan compiler and some implications for trusting software.

Adding Trust Infrastructures to Systems

Infrastructures for trusting downloaded content may or may not use cryptography. Solutions that do not use cryptography rely on the *sandbox* pattern along with extensive static and dynamic checking to ensure that downloaded content does not violate security policy. Solutions that use cryptography place their trust in the validity of downloaded content based on the identity of the sender and the integrity of the package. We confirm this identity through strong authentication and confirm the integrity of the package through cryptographic checksums to verify that the code has not been tampered with at the source or in transit. Consider the generic infrastructure in Figure 7.1.

Vendor solutions to the problem of enabling downloads of active content over the network use some or all of the following elements. The solution:

- Requires some local infrastructure
- Requires some global infrastructure
- Defines local security policy
- Defines global security policy
- Creates structure on the resources within the local machine
- Creates global structure on the world outside the local machine
- Identifies a trusted third party
- Distributes credentials of the trusted third party to all participants

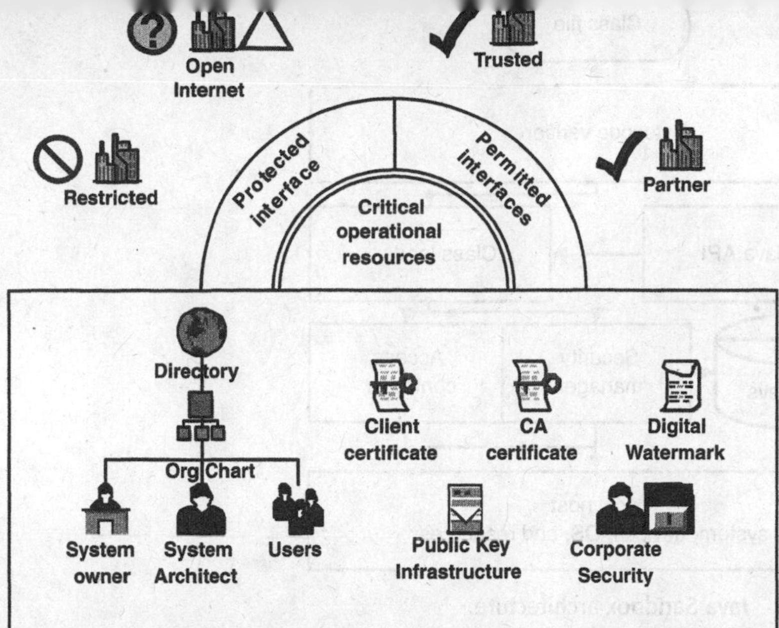

Figure 7.1 Trust infrastructures.

The Java Sandbox

The Java sandbox (shown in Figure 7.2) is an integral part of the JVM and is the product of considerable thought about how to prevent malicious Java code from harming the local machine or gaining access to private data. The original release of the sandbox implementation did not support cryptographic techniques but has been extended to include applet signing for additional trust management. Java's security design has created two consequences. The first is implementation complexity, resulting in an early slew of security bugs (see, for example, [McF97]). The second is definitional. Your notion of security might differ in a significant conceptual manner from those of the designers of Java. It might be difficult or sometimes impossible to reconcile the two viewpoints.

Neither consequence is necessarily negative. The early security holes have all been closed, although new ones no doubt exist. Complex problems require solutions with complicated design details, which often implies lots of code to support a rich feature set. The second problem has been partially addressed, if you are willing to make the development investment, through the addition of access controller and security policy extensions that enable fine-grained security configuration. The Java security model is still evolving. We expect the architecture goals of flexibility, simplicity in configuration, and performance to continue to improve.

The following is a simplified discussion of Java security. We refer the interested reader to [Oaks98], [Oaks01], [McF97], and the resources at http://java.sun.com/security for the latest developments, including resources on J2EE and security.

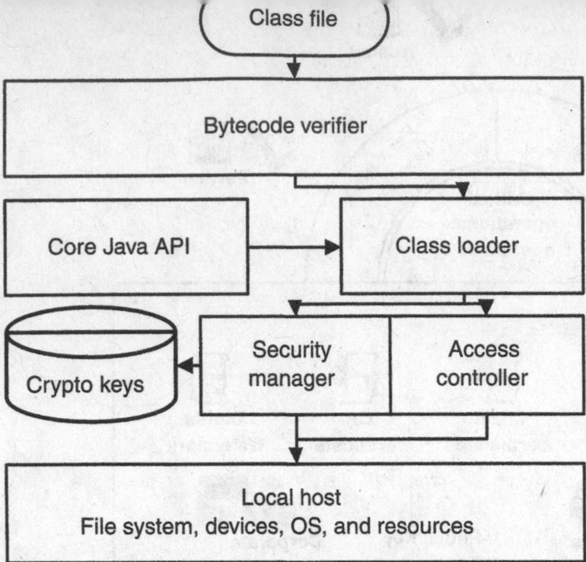

Figure 7.2 Java Sandbox architecture.

Running Applets in a Browser

We will discuss Java security from the standpoint of running Java applets within Web browsers. The Java Sandbox controls applet access to the resources of the underlying machine. Security within the sandbox is provided by four interacting components. We have already introduced the bytecode verifier in the last chapter. The other components are the class loader, the security manager, and the access controller.

The class loader ensures that classes are loaded in the correct order and from the correct location. Multiple class loaders can exist within the sandbox, and applications can create their own class loaders. The default internal class loader loads classes from the core APIs and from the user's CLASSPATH and cannot be preempted. Unlike applications, applets cannot start their own class loaders but must instead use the class loader of the browser. The browser organizes the hosts that are the source of the applets by domain name through the class loader, which partitions its name space by using domains. The class loader assists with domain handling and domain-specific access control by the other security components.

The other two security components of the JVM, the security manager and the access controller, control all core API calls made by a downloaded Java applet. The distinction is primarily a result of the evolution of Java, because existing security mechanisms for securing applets have been extended to Java applications to enable domain definition and domain-specific policy management.

This example shows the *layer* pattern at work. The security manager intercepts all interactions between an applet and the Java API. As these interactions became more complex, the designers saw a need for the separation of concerns within the original

nent and the class loader. The access controller enables the security manager to externalize policy, which is good for the ease of configuration and for implementing enterprise security policy. We will simplify the following discussion by referring only to the security manager as the single component ultimately responsible for controlling all access to system resources requested by the applet.

Local Infrastructure

Web browsers have interfaces for configuring Java security policy. This policy is used by the security components to control activities within the sandbox.

The Class Loader component in the Java security model enforces the namespace separation between classes that are loaded from different sites. This feature enables the security manager to apply the correct policy on a request based on context: Is it from a class within the applet, or is it from a trusted part of the local application (for example, if the browser itself was written in Java)? The class loader correctly enforces security policy, looking at the source of the class and not at its name. This method is better than other alternatives, such as requiring the downloaded class to present a digital signature as a means of matching its name to its source. This procedure would require all downloaded classes to be signed, which might be infeasible.

The Security Manager is invoked on all requests to the core Java API. The CLASSPATH variable points to the location of the core Java API and other local extensions. The core API throws an exception back to the caller if the security manager denies the invocation. Otherwise, the Java API completes the request normally. The security manager provides a library of methods to check the following access operations.

- File operations, such as reads, writes, and deletes.
- Network operations, such as opening a connection to, or accepting a connection from, a remote host or changing the default socket implementation.
- Run-time operations, such as dynamically linking a library, spawning a subprocess, or halting.
- Resource operations, such as opening windows or printing to a local printer.

If your application creates extensions to the JVM, it is important to make sure that the extensions invoke the security manager on all requests.

Local Security Policy Definition

The default security policies enforced by the security manager are quite simple. If the source is local, it is trusted; otherwise, it is untrusted. The design of the security manager looks at the origin of the class that makes the request. The class loader ensures that this origin is valid. The Security Manager trusts all classes loaded from the local machine and does not trust any class loaded from a remote site. Untrusted code has no access to the resources of the underlying machine and can only make network connections back to the remote host from which the code was originally downloaded.

rity manager. An application can create its own policy to override the default policy to create additional structure on the underlying resources. If your application develops its own security manager, its access decisions can be enhanced to allow a wide variety of privilege levels based on context.

Applet signing, which we will discuss in the next section, gives us a means of extending the capabilities of downloaded content.

Local and Global Infrastructure

Applet signing (and Netscape's more general object signing) is the process of attaching a digital signature to a class file by using Sun's *javakey* utility (or an equivalent tool). We must set up some infrastructure to check signatures on active content. The security manager has access to a key database, a persistent store of cryptographic key material that contains the certificate of a third party trusted by both the source of the applet and the host machine. The security manager also has access to the *java.security* package of cryptographic primitives. The security manager uses the key database to verify the digital signature accompanying any signed class file.

The basic Java sandbox does not require a complex global infrastructure for its support, aside from access to a simple PKI in terms of a local database of trusted CAs and the assurance that you have downloaded the implementation of the JVM from a trusted source. The key database contains a list of all trusted CAs, along with key material and credentials for specific users of the local machine.

Java places a simple global structure on the world outside the local machine; namely, there is the remote machine that the code originated from and then there is the rest of the world. It is possible to go much further by using security extensions to the basic Java security policy, however.

Security Extensions in Java

Java's security packages provide many ways of enhancing security. Java is very flexible and provides extensive access to cryptographic primitives and PKI integration. Three (previously optional) security extension packages are now part of the J2SDK.

- The *Java Authentication and Authorization Service* (JAAS). This package enables administrators to integrate with standard authentication frameworks and implement user, group, and role-based access control.
- The *Java Cryptography Extension* (JCE). This package provides cryptographic primitives and key management, along with primitives for encryption and digital signatures.
- The *Java Secure Socket Extension* (JSSE). This package provides primitives for secure communication.

The design of the Java security package is quite complex, caused in part by a desire to solve all problems from the ground up and in part by a desire to make the JVM and its

The goal of embedding Java on arbitrary appliances requires the design to contain no dependencies to the external system. This kitchen sink approach has its detractors, however, who point out that now security exploits might be portable, too.

Systems Architecture

An existing application that wishes to take advantage of Java might have to make some complicated architectural decisions. The application might have an architectural viewpoint or an existing security context that would be too expensive to build from scratch in Java. Some applications might have extensive controls at the operating system level to support authentication and access control or might use existing security infrastructure components such as Kerberos, DCE, or a mature but non-interoperable PKI. Writing policy managers that interface with legacy security components is hard. We would estimate that most applications use a very small portion of the complex Java security specification and use transitive trust between the application server and the backend database server within the architecture. This alternative also has its risks (as described in Chapter 3, "Security Architecture Basics").

Microsoft Authenticode

Microsoft introduced Authenticode in 1996 as a means of trusting code downloaded over the Internet. Authenticode attaches digital signatures as proof of authenticity and accountability to a wide variety of downloaded content: Java applets, ActiveX controls, and other software packages. Authenticode does nothing beyond checking the validity of the digital signature. Once an ActiveX control passes this test, it encounters no run-time checks or access restrictions.

Internet Explorer provides explicit support for partitioning the world outside the client machine into security zones. Zone-specific security policy is applied to any content downloaded from each zone.

Global Infrastructure

Authenticode requires some global infrastructure and security policy to be in place. Authenticode requires a PKI and an existing infrastructure of software publishing policy definition and management. The PKI is rooted at a CA that authorizes software publishers to sign code. The PKI registers publishers, authenticates their identity, establishes commitment to a standard of software practice that ensures the absence of malicious code through code review, and performs key life-cycle management. Software publishers can apply for certification to various levels of code quality, and once they have their certificates, they can sign their own code. Any signed code has a digital signature based on the publisher's private key. The code is packaged with the publisher's certificate containing their public key. No further restrictions are placed on the software publishers except the threat of revocation of the certificate if it is misused.

must distribute the credentials of the trusted third party to all participants. Many CA certificates are already embedded into Internet Explorer, and if you choose one of these CAs (for example, VeriSign), no further configuration is needed.

Microsoft provides tools to sign the code and create the Authenticode package. Once signed, the code cannot be modified in any manner. Any modifications will require a new signature.

Local Infrastructure

Recipients verify the authenticity of the CA certificate by looking up a local database of trusted CAs or looking for a certification path from the publisher's CA to any CA that they trust, by using the services of a directory. Once the CA certificate is verified, the certificate presented by the signer is checked. Finally, the public key in the software publisher's certificate is used to verify the digital signature on the downloaded content.

It is critical that the software publisher's private key be stored securely. Obviously, this task cannot be done in an insecure manner on the development system, but at some point the code developed must meet up with the signing tool (which needs the private key). The application must define a process that describes how and when the code is signed. Normally, the code would only be signed after all test phases are complete.

This process has the architectural impact of adding a step to the software delivery process. If we use Authenticode to ensure trust, we must make sure that all components on the installation tape are correctly signed. Development environments tend to be much less secure than production environments, and the application must trust that the software has not been tampered with in development or in transit. In the absence of any requirement by the CA that code review proving the absence of malicious content must be completed, the users are left with no option but to trust the code.

Adding more testing requirements can be expensive for the project, and most development organizations will rubber stamp the release tape with a signature once the system test is complete. Malicious modifications between system test completion and signing might not be caught. Code produced in such a manner could possibly damage the production system, and the software publisher could lose its license from the CA for violating policy. In addition, full system testing is rare when an application makes mid-release patches to a production system for post-delivery production bug fixes. Patches can be signed with little or no testing for Trojan horses.

Structure within the Local Machine

Internet Explorer can be configured to handle signed code in several ways.

- Discarding unsigned code
- Prompting the user for guidance when running unsigned code
- Running signed code from a trusted source automatically

Authenticode and Safety

Microsoft has been criticized for poor security controls on downloaded content. The fact that something is digitally signed provides no assurance against accidental disruptive behavior or against a poor software development process that allows malicious code to be signed. The failure is at the human interface, when someone clicks the "Sign content now?" dialog without considering the consequences. We perform this action all the time at our Web browsers as we download files, open attachments, visit Web sites with unrecognized certificates, or type passwords into any dialog that pops up and asks for one.

There is also the real possibility that the signer's interface is compromised and additional malicious content is signed transparently, without the user's knowledge, along with the certified safe code. There's many a slip between the cup and the lip. Every hand-off point in development represents an opportunity for the hacker. The additional safeguards for downloaded applets provided by the Java sandbox are critical, because resources should be protected at the host where they are located—not at a distance.

We will now proceed to describe zones and IE's mechanisms for security policy configuration.

Internet Explorer Zones

Internet Explorer places global structure on the world outside the local machine. IE enables a user to configure security on the browser through the Security and Content tabs under the Internet Options settings window. Internet Explorer divides the world outside the client machine into four categories called security zones. Security within each zone can be configured to be one of four default levels: High, Medium, Medium-Low, and Low. Security zones provide a coarse-grained grouping of external sites into one of four categories.

- *The Local Intranet Zone.* All content from this source is assumed to be trusted. The default security level is Medium-Low.
- *The Trusted Sites Zone.* Content from these public sites is considered trusted. The default security level is Low.
- *The Restricted Zone.* Content from these public sites is considered untrusted and will never be executed. The default security level is High.
- *The Internet Zone.* This catchall group requires the user to guide the browser whenever content is downloaded. The default security level is Medium.

Customizing Security within a Zone

We can customize security on active content requesting permission to execute an action within a Zone. We can choose to enable the content, allowing the action; we can disable the content, forbidding the action; or we can prompt the user for guidance. Some settings have additional options. Administrators can allow some pre-identified

up finer-grained Java permissions for signed and unsigned content for several actions. The control can access files, contact network addresses, execute commands, pop up dialogs, get system properties, or access print services to local or network printers.

Role-Based Access Control

Internet Explorer secures Web access by using a form of role-based access control.

- The *subjects* are Web sites that wish to serve active content. The content performs actions on the local host; hence, we can consider the Web sites as actors although we initiated the download.
- The *roles* are the four trusted zones, along with an additional Local Machine zone. This fifth zone, whose settings are in the Windows registry under HKEY_LOCAL_MACHINE\Software\Microsoft\Windows\CurrentVersion\Internet Settings\SOIEAK, cannot be configured through the user interface but can be managed by using the IE Administration Kit.
- The *objects* are the resources of the local machine, which can be accessed in many modes.
- The *object-access groups* are contained within the security levels of High, Medium, Medium-Low, and Low. Each level is a bundle of actions and associated permissions that apply to ActiveX controls, Java applets, scripting, file downloads, or cookies.
- The *role assignments* are captured by the assignment of security levels to each zone. Customization of the bundle of actions in each Zone enables us to tighten the definition of each access control rule mapping a specific security level to a specific zone.

The actual bundles within each level of security can be customized, as well. Table 7.1 shows all the configuration options available within IE. Two options have been shown to be the source of dangerous exploits: controls marked *safe for scripting* and sites that are allowed to download files.

In addition to the setting options in Table 7.1, IE enables administrators to set user authentication defaults for logons in each zone.

Accepting Directives from Downloaded Content

ActiveX controls that have been marked *safe for scripting* bypass Authenticode's signature validation entirely. This feature highlights one difference between the Java sandbox and Microsoft's security policy manager. Java does not permit downloaded content to access any part of the local file system by default and lifts the restriction only if the content is digitally signed by a signatory that is allowed by policy to access the local file system.

Table [illegible] IE Security Zone Access Control Defaults

	HIGH	MEDIUM	MED-LOW	LOW
ActiveX plug-ins				
Download signed ActiveX controls	D	P	P	E
Download unsigned ActiveX controls	D	D	D	P
Initialize and Script ActiveX controls not marked as safe	D	D	D	P
Run ActiveX controls and plug-ins	D	E	E	E
Script ActiveX controls marked safe for scripting	E	E	E	E
Cookies				
Allow cookies that are stored on your computer	D	E	E	E
Allow per-session cookies. Not stored.	D	E	E	E
Downloads				
File Download	D	E	E	E
Font download	P	E	E	E
Microsoft VM				
Java permissions (or use custom settings)	HS	HS	MS	LS
Miscellaneous				
Access Data sources across domains	D	D	P	E
Drag and drop or copy and paste files	P	E	E	E
Installation of desktop items	D	P	P	E
Launching programs and files in an IFRAME	D	P	P	E
Navigate sub-frames across different domains	D	E	E	E
Software channel permissions				
Submit non-encrypted form data	P	P	E	E
User data persistence	D	E	E	E
Scripting				
Active scripting	E	E	E	E
Allow paste operations via script	D	E	E	E
Scripting of java applets	D	E	E	E

Code: High: Restricted Zone, Medium: Internet Zone, Medium-Low: Local Intranet Zone, Low: Trusted Zone
D: Disable, P: Prompt, E: Enable, HS: High safety, MS: Medium Safety, LS: Low safety

access and execute ActiveX controls on the user's hard drive. If these controls had been adequately tested and were free of vulnerabilities, this situation would not be an issue. But of course, some controls marked "safe for scripting" were anything but safe. Scambray, McClure, and Kurtz in [SMK00] describe in detail how to exploit vulnerabilities in IE, listing vulnerabilities discovered by George Guninski and Richard Smith to create and then launch executable files on the local file system. They also describe another safe-for-scripting control that could be used to silently turn off macro virus protection within Microsoft Office. For these and many other detailed exploits, please refer to [SMK00] or visit www.microsoft.com/technet for security issues related to Internet Explorer.

Netscape Object Signing

Netscape introduced object signing as a response to Authenticode to verify digitally signed content and to enhance the capabilities of downloaded applets. Netscape object signing is very similar in structure, but the two schemes are largely not interoperable. Some commercial vendors are reportedly working to bring the two standards closer, but for now, your application should preferably pick one on its merits and stick with it. Object signing also can apply to arbitrary content, such as multimedia files. Signed objects are automatically updated by the browser, which conducts automated version checks.

Users can configure all their security options on Netscape's Security Info panel, which is accessible from the Communicator → Tools menus. Netscape stores a list of *signers*, which are CAs that are trusted to digitally sign content. These CAs are permitted to issue object-signing certificates to entities that wish to sign any content. The user is prompted for guidance if a CA other than those on the signer's list signs a downloaded file.

Downloaded content can reach out of the Java sandbox if signed by a trustworthy source. Software publishers that sign Java and JavaScript files can have more fine-grained levels of access control applied to their content upon execution. Applets request access to resources, and the user is prompted to allow or deny the requested access forever or allow the access for the duration of the user's session. Netscape also enhanced the Java API, introducing the Java Capabilities API to provide additional granularity for access control decisions—allowing subjects to access objects when privileges are granted. This functionality has been absorbed into the current Java API, which has extensive support for authentication and access control and includes the cryptographic extensions required to support object signing.

In the object-signing model,

- The sources are called *principals* and are synonymous with the identity in the software publisher's signing certificate.
- *Objects* are system resources, such as files.
- *Privileges* specify the mode of access. Applets carry capability lists, specifying all allowed access operations, and can modify their active privileges during execution by turning capabilities on and off.

signing solution: software publishing policy and management, PKI and all the attendant services, and key distribution and life-cycle management.

Signed, Self-Decrypting, and Self-Extracting Packages

The last mechanism for trusting downloaded content is a catch-all clause to support distributed software delivery through any means, not just through Web browsers. The content can be any arbitrary collection of bits and can be used for any arbitrary purpose. We need the ability to securely download software packages in many circumstances.

- We can purchase application software online and have it digitally delivered.
- We can download operating system patches that require high privileges to execute correctly.
- We might need authoritative and trusted data files containing information such as authoritative DNS mappings, stock quotes, legal contracts, configuration changes, or firmware patches for Internet appliances.

Digitally delivered software can be dangerous. How should we ensure the integrity of a download? Using digital downloads requires some level of trust. We must be sure of the source and integrity of a file before we install a patch, update a DNS server, sign a legal document, or install a new firmware release.

The same methods of using public-key technology apply here. Software must be digitally signed but might also require encryption, because we do not want unauthorized personnel to have access to valuable code. Secure software delivery solutions use public and symmetric-key cryptography to digitally sign and encrypt packages in transit.

The order of signing and encrypting is important. Anderson and Needham note in [AN95] that a digital signature on an encrypted file proves nothing about the signer's knowledge of the contents of the file. If the signer is not the entity that encrypts the package, the signer could be fooled into validating and certifying one input and digitally signing another encrypted blob that might not match the input. As a result, non-repudiation is lost. Data should always be signed first and then encrypted.

Implementing Trust within the Enterprise

Systems architects face considerable challenges in implementing models of trust in applications. Before implementing any of the mechanisms of the previous sections, we must ensure that we have satisfied the preconditions required by each solution. Ask these abstract questions, with appropriate concrete qualifications, at the architecture review.

- Has the application created the required global infrastructure?
- Has the application defined local security policy?
- Has the application defined global security policy?
- Did the architect create structure within the resources of the local machine?
- Did the architect create the global structure required of the world outside the local machine?
- Who are the required, trusted third parties?
- Has the application distributed credentials of all trusted third parties to all participants?

These steps seem obvious, but many implementations fail because of the simple and primary reason that the project executes one of these steps in an ad-hoc manner, without proper attention to details. Projects protest that they have addressed all of these issues but might not have thought the whole process through.

- "We have security because we sign our applets." How do you verify and test an applet's safety?
- "We have security because we have a configuration policy for the Java security manager." Do you have a custom implementation of the security manager? If you are using the default manager, have you configured policy correctly? How do you distribute, configure, and verify this policy on all target machines?
- "We use VeriSign as our CA." Can anyone with a valid VeriSign certificate spoof your enterprise?
- "We sign all our software before we ship it." Well, how hard is it to sign malicious code through the same process? What level of code review does the software signer institute? Has all the code that is certified as trustworthy been correctly signed? Will legitimate code ever be discarded as unsafe? Do you verify the source, destination, contents, integrity, and timestamp on a signed package?
- "We use strong cryptography." How well do you protect the private key?

Ask these questions and many more at the security assessment to define acceptable risk as clearly as possible. These are not simple issues, and often—upon close examination—the solution reveals dependencies on security by obscurity or on undocumented or unverified assumptions.

Validating the assumptions is a general problem, because as the system state evolves, conditions we believed true might no longer hold. Active monitoring or auditing should include *sanity scripts*, which are examples of the service provider pattern. Sanity scripts encode tests of the project's assumptions and when launched in the development and production environment test the assumptions for validity. Sanity scripts are useful aids to compliance. Databases sometimes use table triggers for similar purposes.

We now turn our attention to the exact inversion of the implicit trust relationship assumed in all the previous sections: the local host belongs to the good guys, and the downloaded content could be from the bad guys.

Protecting Digital Intellectual Property

All the notions of trust that we have discussed so far make an assumption about the direction of validation: the host machine is trusted, and the downloaded content is not trusted. The host must verify and validate the content before executing the code or granting the code permission to access system resources.

What if these roles were reversed? What if the asset to be secured *was* the digital content? What if the source that served the content is trusted and the recipient who downloaded it is not trusted? Consider a JVM embedded in a Web browser executing a downloaded applet. The security manager does nothing to protect the applet from the host. In fact, because the Java bytecodes are interpreted, it is possible to build a JVM that gives us full access to the execution environment of the applet. If the applet contains licensed software and enforced the license based on some local lookup, our subverted JVM can bypass this check to essentially steal the use of the applet. If the applet was a game, we could instantly give ourselves the high score. In general, active content uses the execution environment of the host. How can we guarantee good behavior from a host?

We will discuss this scenario under the general topic of digital rights, which encompass issues such as the following:

- Protecting software against piracy by enforcing software licenses. Users must pay for software.
- Protecting audio or video content from piracy by requiring a purchaser to use a license key to unlock the content before playing it.
- Protecting critical data such as financial reports or competitive analysis so that only trusted recipients can download, decrypt, and use the information.
- Controlling the use of digitally delivered information by preventing valid users who have some access to the information ("I can print myself a copy") from engaging in other activities ("I want to forward this to a competitor because I am a spy").
- Enforcing complex business rules.

The last system goal covers many new opportunities. Employees and managers might need to send messages along approval chains, gathering multiple signatures without centralized management. Managers might need to contract the services of external companies to test and debug software while assuring that the software will not be pirated. Businesses might prefer to keep critical data encrypted and decentralized and implement a complex, need-to-know permission infrastructure to gain access to encrypted data. Companies can avoid centralization of many interactions that actually correspond to independent threads of communication between participants. Removing a central bottleneck application that exists to securely manage the multiple independent threads could lead to significant cost savings, improved processing speed, and a reduction in message traffic.

Only recently have the issues surrounding the protection of digital intellectual property exploded, with all the considerable media attention focused on software and music piracy. The spectrum of discussion ranges from critical technical challenges to new business

been extensively covered in the media, but the protection of music from piracy or other associated violations desired by copyright owners is a small portion of the space of problems that need resolution.

The ability to securely deliver content and then continue to manage, monitor, and support its use at a remote location, with a minimal use of trusted third parties, can be critical to the success of many e-business models. Encryption is the most widely seen method of protecting content today—but once the content is decrypted, it is open to abuse. Indeed, the problem of delivering content to untrustworthy recipients requires building the ability to reach out and retain control of content even after it is physically not in our possession. This persistent command of usage requires two basic components to be feasible.

- *A trust infrastructure.* We need some basis for creating trust between participants and providing secure communication and credential management. PKIs are often chosen as the trust-enabling component of commercial solutions for enabling the protection of digital rights.
- *Client-side digital rights policy manager.* This client-side component can enforce the security policy desired by the content owner. Creating a policy manager that prevents abuse but at the same time allows valid use in a non-intrusive way is critical.

Security expert Bruce Schneier in [Sch00] explains why all efforts to enforce digital rights management of content on a general-purpose computer are doomed to failure. Any rights management strategy of moderate complexity will defeat the average user's ability to subvert security controls. The persistence, inventiveness, and creativity of the dedicated hacker, however, is another matter altogether. Many attempts to protect software or music from piracy have failed. Proposals for preventing DVD piracy, satellite broadcast theft, and software and music piracy have been broken and the exploits published. The basic problem is that once a security mechanism is broken and the intellectual property payload is extracted, a new and unprotected version of the payload can be built without any security controls and then distributed. This process defeats the entire premise of digital rights management.

At the heart of the matter, any scheme to protect digital information must also allow legal use. However carefully the scheme is engineered, the legal avenues can be re-engineered and subverted to gain access. The scheme can be modified to perform the following functions:

- To prevent calls to security controls
- To halt re-encryption of decrypted information
- To block calls to physically attached hardware devices (sometimes called *dongles*)
- To block interaction with a "mother-ship" component over the network
- To spoof a third party in some manner if the contact to a third party is essential

standpoint, but because our book has hewn to the viewpoint of the systems architect, we cannot dig into the details of how to accomplish the goals of digital property protection. Suffice it to say, as systems architects we are consumers of digital rights management solutions and will implement and conform to the usage guidelines of the vendor—because, after all, we have paid for the software. For the purposes of this book, we are neither vendor nor hacker but are playing the role of the honest consumer. For us, at least, digital rights management creates different systems goals.

From a systems perspective, we can assume the existence of a trust management infrastructure (say, a PKI) that conforms to the requirements of the digital rights protection software and are left with the issue of integrating a vendor's policy manager into our system. This situation normally involves the use of components such as the following:

- *Cryptographic protocols.* Delivered content is often encrypted and must be decrypted before use. Content is also digitally signed to guarantee authenticity and accountability.
- *Trusted third parties.* Certificates are key components in these protocols to identify all participants: content vendor, client, certificate authority, status servers, and (possibly untrustworthy) hosts. We need hooks to interact with corporate PKI components.
- *License servers.* The possession of software does not imply the permission to use it. Digital rights managers require clients to first download license keys that describe the modes of use, the time of use allowed, and the permissions for the sharing of content. The client must pay for these privileges and receive a token or ticket that attests to such payment.
- *Local decision arbitrators.* Whenever the client uses the content—say, to execute a program, print a report, approve a purchase, forward a quote, and so on—the local policy manager must decide whether the request is permitted or not. In essence, this situation is the JVM problem turned on its head, where now the digital content is trusted and carries its own Security Manager embedded in its own trusted virtual machine (and the underlying host is untrustworthy).

We can list, from an architect's viewpoint, the desirable features of any digital rights policy management solution.

- *Non-intrusive rights management.* The verification of access rights should be transparent to the user after the first successful validation, and rights checks should have minimal performance impacts. The solution must avoid unnecessary third-party lookups.
- *Robust rights verification methods.* The method used by the vendor to verify usage permission must be highly available and protected from network faults. The user must not lose credentials on a system failover or should experience minimal rights validation after the switch happens.

checks. This situation corresponds in spirit with single sign-on as a desirable authentication property.

- *Delegation support.* Users must be permitted to transfer their rights to delegates. The vendor can establish rules of delegation but in no circumstance should require that delegates separately purchase licenses for digital assets that are already paid for.
- *Sandbox support.* Given that DRM conflicts with several of our existing architectural goals, such as high availability, robustness, error recovery, and delegation of authority, there must be a mechanism for a legitimate user to turn it off. In this case, we do not require the vendor to relinquish his or her rights but only to provide a sandbox for authenticated content users to access the information without further checks.
- *Unusual legal restrictions.* The vendors of digital rights protection solutions often claim that their solutions can be used to prove piracy in a court of law. Under no circumstance should a legitimate user be characterized as a pirate.
- *Flexible policy features.* The solution should permit reasonable levels of access configuration.
- *No mission-impossible architecture guidelines.* There are some forms of theft of digital rights that are not preventable, purely because they occur at a level where a systems component cannot distinguish between a valid user and a thief. The solution should not add burdensome restrictions on legitimate users (such as "Buy expensive hardware," "Discard legacy software," "Throw out current hardware," and so on).

For instance, regardless of what a music protection scheme does, audio output from the speakers of a computer could be captured. No DRM solution can prevent this situation (barring the vendors coming to our homes and putting chips in our ears). A solution might protect a document from being printed more than once, but it cannot prevent photocopying as a theft mechanism. A solution can protect an e-mail message from being forwarded to unauthorized recipients, but it cannot protect against a user printing the e-mail and faxing it to an unauthorized party. Chasing after these essentially impossible-to-close holes can sometimes make the software so complex and unusable that clients might forgo the solutions. They might choose to handle valuable content insecurely rather than struggle with a secure but unwieldy solution.

Protecting digital content causes tension with other architectural goals. One critical difference between cryptography in this instance and cryptography for secure communication is in the persistence of data in encrypted form. Digital rights protection is an application-level property and requires long-term key management of bulk encryption keys or session keys. The application might not be equipped to do so. Another difference is in the conflict between firewalls and intrusion detection components that seek to protect the intranet by inspecting content and digital rights protection solutions that seek to protect the exterior content provider's asset by encrypting and selectively permitting access to content. You cannot run a virus scanner on an encrypted file or e-mail

sion detection sensors failing on encrypted traffic). If vendor content infects the application through a virus masked by encryption, is the vendor liable?

Digital rights management is based on an inversion of a common security assumption: the valid and legal possessor of an asset is also its owner. The assumption leads to the false belief that the possessor can modify the contents because the owner has full access to the asset. This statement is not true if the owner and possessor are not the same entity.

The use of smart cards for banking gives us an example of where this assumption fails. The possessor of the card owns the assets inside the bank account encrypted on the card, but the bank owns the account itself. The bank will allow only certain operations on the account. For example, the bank might require that the state on the Smartcard and the state on the bank servers are synchronized and that the card itself is tamperproof from abuse. The customer must be unable to make withdrawals larger than the balance or register deposits that do not correspond to actual cash receipts.

Consider a solution implemented by several banks in Europe by using strong cryptography and Smartcards. New Smartcards include cryptographic accelerators to enable the use of computationally expensive algorithms, such as RSA. The Smartcard is an actual computer with protected, private, and public memory areas, a small but adequate CPU, and a simple and standard card reader interface. The user's account is stored on the card, and the card can be inserted into a kiosk that allows the user to access an application that manages all transactions on the account. The strength of the solution depends entirely on the user being unable to access a private key stored in the Smartcard's private storage, accessible only to the card itself and to the bank's system administrators. The card does not have a built-in battery, however, and must therefore use an external power source. This situation led to an unusual inference attack.

Paul Kocher of Cryptography Research, Inc. invented an unusual series of attacks against Smartcards. The attacks, called Differential Power Analysis, used the power consumption patterns of the card as it executed the application to infer the individual bits in the supposedly secure private key on the cards. The cost of implementing the method was only a few hundred dollars, using commonly available electronic hardware, and the method was successful against an alarmingly large number of card vendors. This situation caused a scramble in the Smartcard industry to find fixes. The attack was notable because of its orthogonal nature. Who would have ever thought that this technique would be a way to leak information? Inference attacks come in many guises. This example captures the risks of allowing the digital content to also carry the responsibilities of managing security policy.

Finally, some have suggested security in open source. If we can read the source code for the active content and can build the content ourselves, surely we can trust the code as safe? Astonishingly, Ken Thompson (in his speech accepting the Turing Award for the creation of UNIX) showed that this assumption is not true. In the next section, we will describe Ken Thompson's Trojan horse compiler and describe the implications of his construction for trusted code today.

Thompson's Trojan Horse Compiler

In this section, we will describe the Trojan Horse compiler construction from Ken Thompson's classic 1983 ACM Turing Award speech "Reflections on Trusting Trust," which explains why you cannot trust code that you did not totally create yourself. The basic principle of the paper is valid more than ever today, in the context provided by our discussions so far. Thompson concluded that the ability to view source code is no guarantee of trust. Inspection as a means of validation can only work if the tools used to examine code are themselves trustworthy.

The first action taken by Rootkit attacks, an entire class of exploits aimed at obtaining superuser privileges, is the replacement of common system commands and utilities with Trojans that prevent detection. Commands such as su, login, telnet, ftp, ls, ps, find, du, reboot, halt, shutdown, and so on are replaced by hacked binaries that report that they have the same size and timestamp as the original executable. The most common countermeasure to detect rootkit intrusions is the deployment of a cryptographic checksum package like *Tripwire*, which can build a database of signatures for all system files and can periodically compare the stored signatures with the cryptographic checksum of the current file. Obviously, the baseline checksums must be computed before the attack and stored securely for this validity check to hold. Even so, the only recourse to cleaning a hacked system is to rebuild the system from scratch by using only data from clean backups to restore state.

Solutions such as Tripwire need both the original executable and the executable file that claims to be login or su to match its checksum against the stored and trusted value.

Thompson considered the case where we do not have access to the source file or possess cryptographic hashes of non-Trojan versions of the code. We are only able to interact with the executable by running it on some input. In this case, our only clues lie in the behavior of the Trojan program and the inputs on which it deviates from the correct code.

In this section, we present Thompson's Trojan for two programs, login and cc. On UNIX systems, `login` validates a username and password combination. The Trojanized login accepts an additional invalid username with a blank password, enabling back door access to the system. Thompson's paper describing the details of the construction of a Trojan horse compiler is available at www.acm.org/classics/sep95/. This paper is not all academic; there is a well-known story of a hacked version of the UNIX login program that was accidentally released from Ken Thompson's development group and found its way into several external UNIX environments. This Trojan version of login accepted a default magic password to give anyone in the know full access to the system.

Our presentation is only at the abstract level and is meant to highlight the difference in behavior between the Trojan horse compiler and a standard, correct C compiler. Identifying such differences, called behavioral signatures, is a common strategy for detecting intrusions or malicious data modification. Signatures enable us to distinguish the good from the bad. Behavioral signatures are common weapons in the

ware model or operating system of a target host based on responses to badly formatted TCP/IP packets.

A related purpose of this section is to describe the difficulty that programmers face in converting "meta-code" to code. We use the phrase "meta-code" to describe code that is about code, much like the specification of the Trojan compiler not as a program, but as a specification in a higher-level language (in this case, English) for constructing such a compiler. Many security specifications are not formal, creating differences in implementation that lead to signatures for attacks.

Some Notation for Compilers and Programs

We will use some obvious notation to describe a program's behavior. A program taking inputfile as input and producing outputfile as output is represented as such:

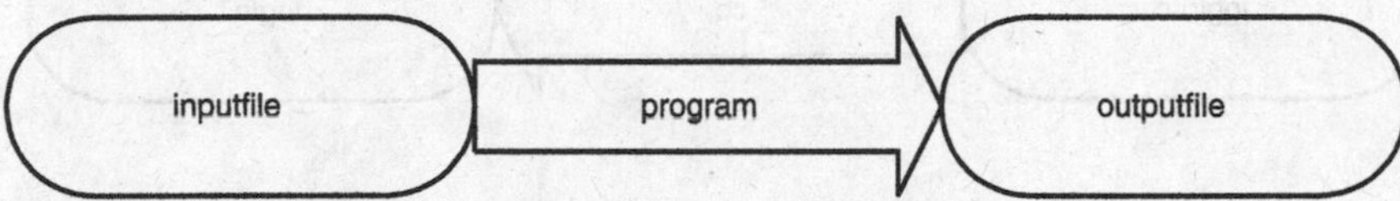

We will represent an empty input file with the text NULL. Programs that do not read their input at all will be considered as having the input file NULL. A program's source will have a .c extension, and its binary will have no extension. For example, the C compiler source will be called cc.c and the compiler itself will be called cc. The compiler's behavior can be represented as follows:

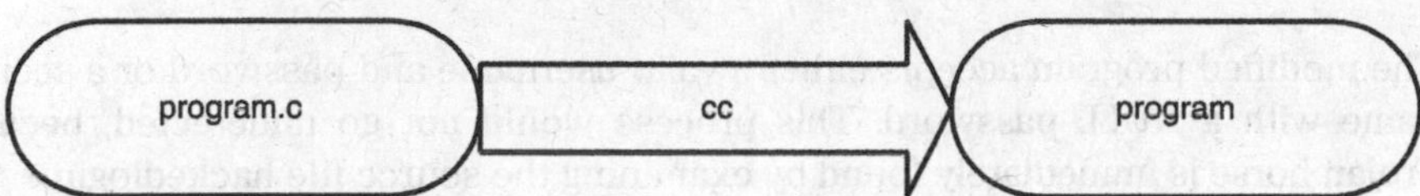

Note that a compiler is also a compilation *fixed point*, producing its own binary from its source.

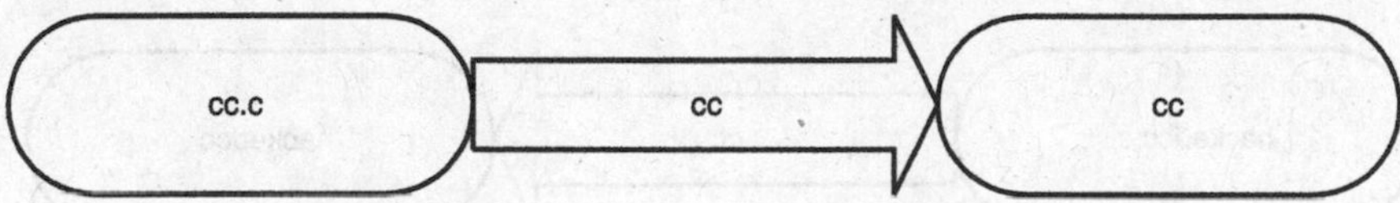

Self-Reproducing Programs

Thompson's construction uses self-reproducing programs. A self-reproducing program selfrep.c, when once compiled, performs the following actions:

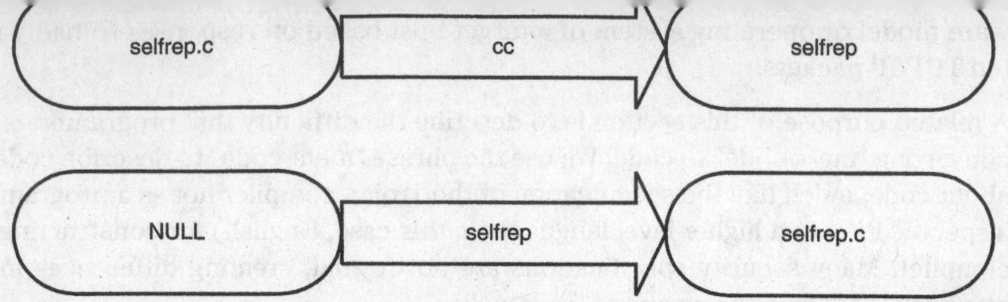

Ken Thompson, through an elegant three-stage construction, produces a hacked C compiler that will replicate the behavior of a correct C compiler on all programs except two: login.c, the UNIX login program; and cc.c, the UNIX C compiler itself.

A correct version of login is built as follows:

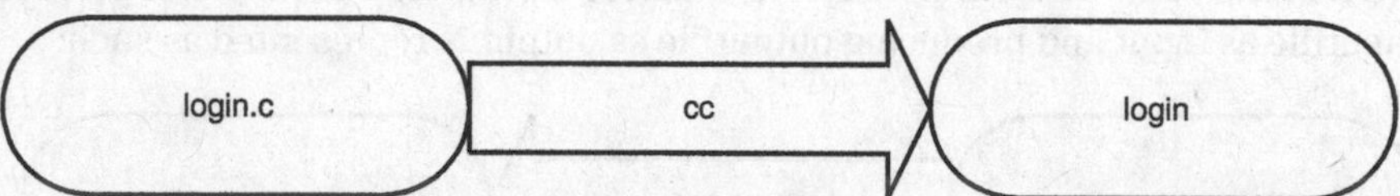

Assume that you wish to create a Trojan version of the UNIX login program, as follows:

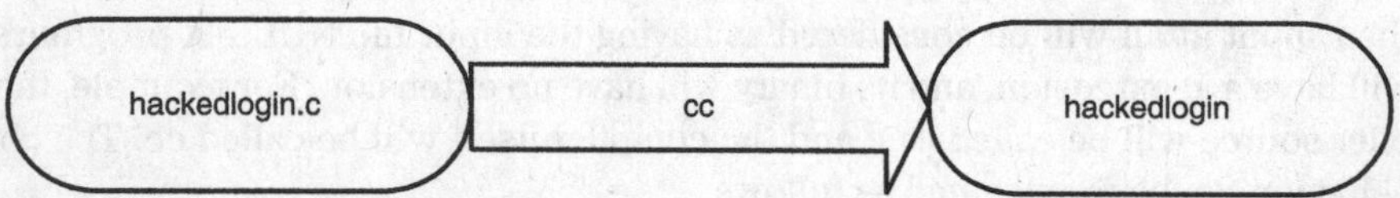

The modified program accepts either a valid username and password or a secret username with a NULL password. This process would not go undetected, because the Trojan horse is immediately found by examining the source file hackedlogin.c. Thompson gets around this situation by inserting a Trojan horse generator into the C compiler source cc.c instead, then recompiling the compiler and replacing the correct C compiler with a hacked compiler.

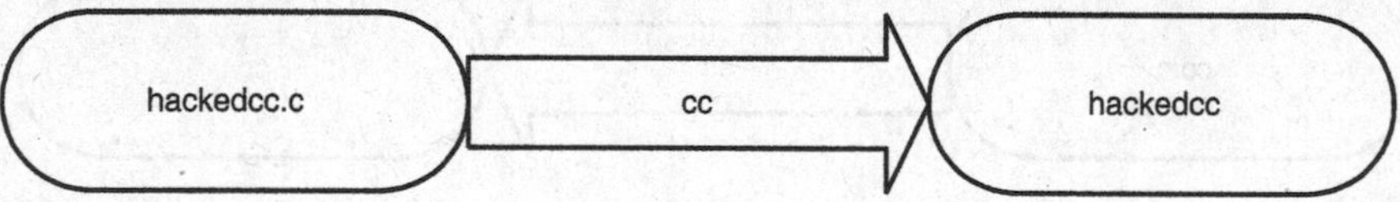

Now we can use the hacked compiler to miscompile the correct source to produce a Trojan binary.

diately give the game away. Thompson hides the modifications to the C compiler in a two-stage process that he describes as *program learning.* The process produces another compilation fixed point. At the end of the construction, the hacked compiler produces its own hacked version binary from clean C compiler source code.

How does this situation happen? In his construction, Thompson creates a self-reproducing version of the hacked compiler that can produce a copy of its own hacked source on demand. This bootstrapping behavior is possible because the sample self-reproducing program that he describes can be modified to include arbitrary code, including that of an entire compiler.

On the input string cc.c, hackedcc discards the input and instead self-reproduces its own hacked source. It then compiles the hacked source, presenting the resulting binary as the output of compiling the original input cc.c.

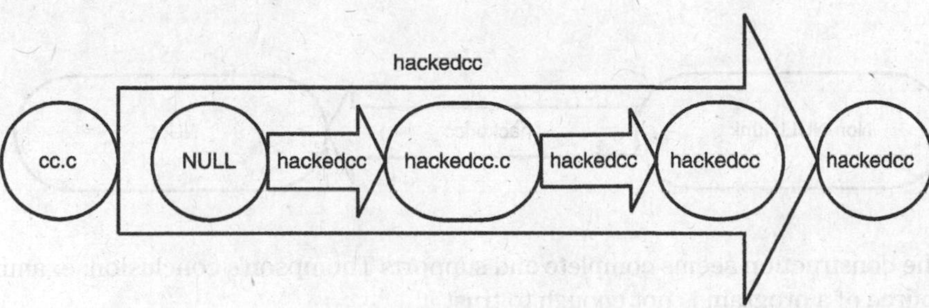

Thompson concludes that if we cannot trust our development tools and we are unable to examine binary code for tampering, as is often the case, then examination of the source alone leaves us with no clue that our binaries are actually Trojan Horses.

Looking for Signatures

Can the two programs cc and hackedcc be distinguished from one another based on behavior alone, without viewing source in any way? With the understanding that two correct but different compilers can compile the same source to produce correct but possibly different binaries, the two programs seem to have identical behavior.

The hackedcc compiler's behavior is identical to that of the cc compiler on all C programs other than login.c and cc.c (in fact it invokes an internal copy of cc to ensure that on all other programs, including its own source code, hackedcc mimics cc).

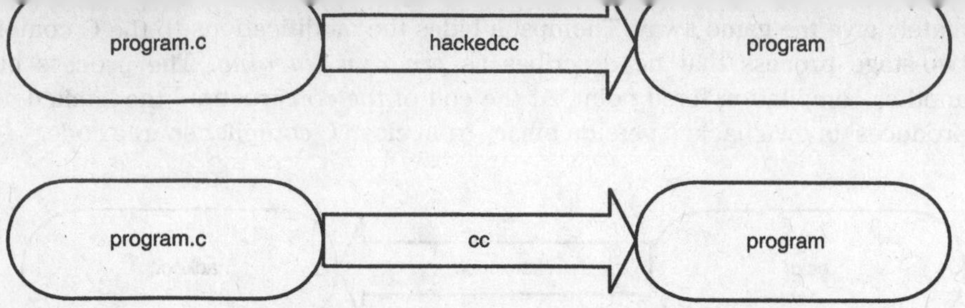

If the hackedcc compiler's behavior was also identical to that of the cc compiler on all other strings that are not syntactically correct C programs, we would have no means of detecting it other than by examining the behavior of one of its outputs, the hackedlogin program, and that, too, on the input of a special username-password combination.

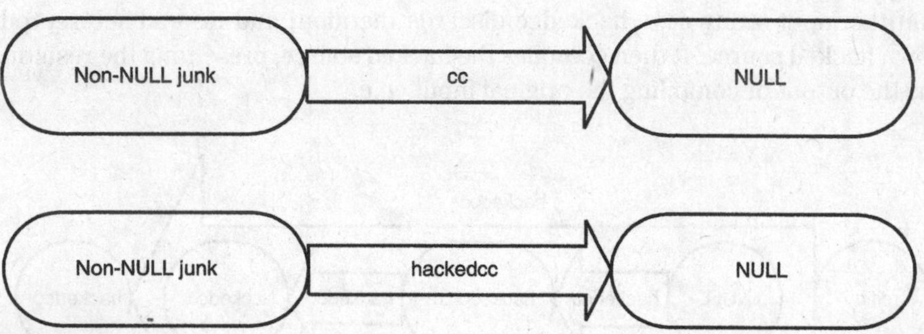

The construction seems complete and supports Thompson's conclusion: examining the source of a program is not enough to trust it.

hackedcc has an internal self-reproducing rule that conflicts with cc, however. This property is essential to its construction, because hackedcc cannot use or make assumptions about the external environment on the host upon which it is executing. Such dependencies would be detected if the program were moved to another host. Thompson's construction cleverly avoids this situation by wrapping up everything hackedcc needs into its own executable.

This construction leads to the following signature. Because of its self-reproducing property, hackedcc, which is a deterministic program, it has to be able to produce its own C code from some input. We have used the NULL string, but any fixed non-C-program string would do.

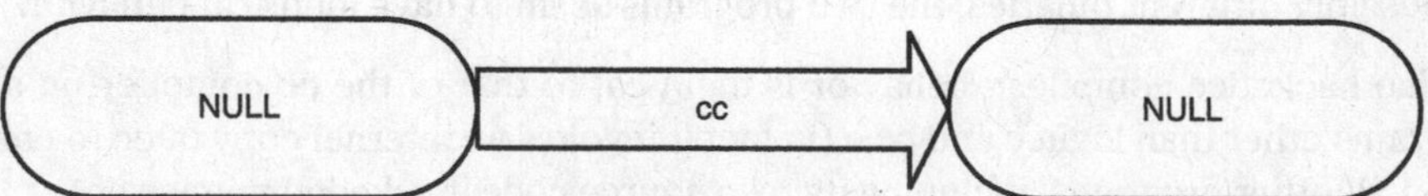

The input string used to trigger the self-reproducing behavior could not be another C program xyz.c, because we would then have another signature on which the two compilers differ.

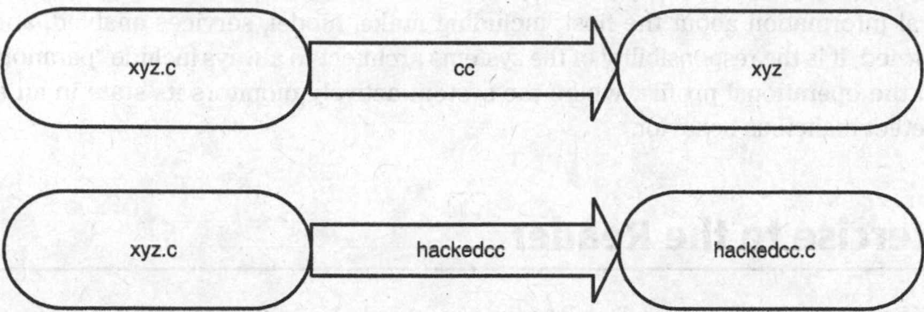

Without examining any source, we have found some input on which their behaviors differ—and because cc is trusted, we can now state that hackedcc cannot be trusted. The conflict arises because hackedcc, whatever its construction might be, is a deterministic program and cannot have two different execution outcomes on the same input NULL. It must either produce NULL or it must be self-reproducing so that it can produce a hacked binary from valid input.

Even Further Reflections on Trusting Trust

We now reach our reason for going into this level of detail in describing Ken Thompson's very clever construction. In any attack where information is manufactured, say, in a denial-of-service attack such as the *land* attack or in the construction of a Trojan horse program or in the attachment of a virus to a file, the attacker leaves a signature. It is almost impossible not to do so, and our ability to analyze exploits and detect such signatures is crucial to the design of counter-measures against these attacks.

In situations where it is impossible to tell the difference between good data and bad data because we cannot make a comparison, we have to rely on behavior. In a distributed denial-of-service attack, good packets initiating connections and bad packets that are part of a SYN/ACK flood cannot be distinguished at the server. The only countermeasures we have lie in implementing thresholds on the traffic to the servers, limiting the number of open connections, and maintaining separate queues for half-open and open connections. Once the flood is contained, we must trace back to the sources of the attacks and

the good news is that however careful a construction, there is almost always a signature to be detected.

Behavior is a familiar term to system architects. The behavior of the system is captured in its operational profile. Measures such as logging, auditing, and alarming are essential to monitoring the health and well being of a system. Building counter-measures against attacks involves understanding what changes in behavior the attack will create on our systems. Sometimes this result is quite obvious because the system crashes. Sometimes this result can be quite subtle as an attacker launches a low-traffic port scan against our machine or sends carefully crafted packets or messages with the intent of inferring critical information about the host, including make, model, services enabled, and assets owned. It is the responsibility of the systems architect to always include "paranoid mode" in the operational profile, where the system actively monitors its state in an effort to detect malicious behavior.

An Exercise to the Reader

We would like to be very clear that there are no holes in Ken Thompson's construction, and all the claims that he makes are absolutely valid. The construction is even more relevant these days where many of the software components of our system are given to us shrink-wrapped without source code. In the previous chapter, we described the role of code review in software architecture. Thompson warns us that all of our solutions depend on the sanctity of our software components: the Web browser, the JVM implementation, the underlying operating system, the compilers that we use to build our code, and the utilities that we use to manage our systems.

Perfect Trojan Horses

We conclude with a thought experiment. Revisit Thompson's classic paper and try to modify the Trojan compiler construction to hide even this minor behavioral signature. Is it even possible?

Let's define a Perfect Trojan Compiler, a completely artificial construct that we can reason about to ask the following questions: "Is the problem fundamental to the construction? Why or why not?"

Definition. A compiler hackedcc is called a Perfect Trojan Horse if it has the following properties:

- It miscompiles login.c to produce hackedlogin, an executable with a known Trojan horse inside.
- It miscompiles cc.c to produce its own executable hackedcc, or a functionally equivalent executable that is also a Perfect Trojan Horse, although possibly different from hackedcc in some minor, syntactic way.
- It compiles all other valid C programs, correctly producing executables that

- It behaves as cc does on all other inputs that are not valid C programs and produces no output.
- Porting the hacked compiler to other similar hosts does not reveal that the compiler is a Trojan horse.

Do Perfect Trojan Compilers exist? Can you build one? On the other hand, can you prove they do not exist?

Note that Perfect Trojan Compilers are well behaved, which makes them easier to reason about. Real Trojan horses are never well behaved and will happily fail on all sorts of inputs, just as long as they can succeed on one execution path that leads to system compromise.

Conclusion

Our applications grow more complex every day, with endless evolving topologies, heterogeneous hardware platforms, shrink-wrapped vendor solutions, black box run-time environments, and third-party extensions, plug-ins, add-ons, and more. After going through all the trouble of verifying that the system works, how do we protect it as it evolves and as new releases of software and new downloads of information are pulled into its architecture?

This problem is very hard. The common strategy to solve this problem is to pretend that it does not exist. In this chapter, we have described some mechanisms for enabling trust, distributing active content, using digital intellectual property, and relying on our ability to read code to trust programs. The architectural pattern that we have repeatedly attempted to emphasize is that enabling trust involves the creation of structure within and without an application, the creation of policy, and the definition of trusted third parties.

Secure Communications

A secure connection between two hosts must perform authentication of each endpoint, transport data reliably, protect against tampering or modification of data in transit, guard against eavesdroppers, and operate with reasonable efficiency.

Most solutions for secure communications are based on the *layer* pattern. They take an existing application and the communications layer it rides upon and insert a new security layer between the higher-level processes or protocols and the underlying data link, network, or transport mechanisms. These security mechanisms must therefore factor in growth and evolution in the application above and changes in the protocols below as networking hardware evolves.

Requiring communications security in a distributed, heterogeneous system can create additional architectural goals or requirements that include the following components:

- *Interoperability.* Vendor products for secure communications must conform to accepted standards for interoperability. For example, NIST provides an IPSec interoperability test suite that vendors can use to guarantee minimum compliance with the IETF RFCs for IPSec.
- *Adaptability.* Secure communication mechanisms must be adaptable to the constraints of the entities involved, accommodating different cipher suites for performance reasons caused by hardware or processing limitations or under legal restrictions.
- *Non-repudiation.* We must disallow either participant to deny that the conversation took place.
- *Infrastructure.* The mechanisms might depend on infrastructure elements such as a PKI, a secure DNS, a cryptographic service provider, a LDAP directory, or a

dependency is inadequately articulated in the architecture. We might need infrastructure support.

In this chapter, we will answer these questions. Why is secure communications critical? What should architects know about transport and network security protocols? What is really protected, and what is not? What assumptions about TTPs are implicit in any architecture that uses TTPs?

We will start by comparing the TCP/IP stack to the ISO OSI protocol stack, along with a description of the gaps where security can fit in. We will proceed to discuss two important mechanisms for secure communications that are standards based, have good performance and interoperability, and are modular in the sense that they can be added to any architecture in a clean manner. These mechanisms are SSL and IPSec. We will conclude with some architectural issues on the use of these protocols.

The OSI and TCP/IP Protocol Stacks

The International Standards Organization introduced the seven-layer OSI network protocol stack as a model for network communications. Each layer of the stack logically communicates with its peer on another host through interactions with lower-level protocol layers. The OSI stack never saw much general acceptance over pedagogical use because it lacked reference implementations that ran on many platforms with good performance and support for real network programming. Available implementations were impractical to use when compared to TCP/IP.

TCP/IP, the protocol that defines the Internet, was introduced in 1983. TCP/IP is a simple four-layer protocol suite. Network programs are easy to write by using TCP/IP because it has an open architecture. The availability of open-source implementations on a wide variety of UNIX flavors led to its dominance as the premier networking protocol through the design, development, deployment, and acceptance of many networked applications and services. TCP/IP is fast and simple, but it is not secure. All the fields of a datagram, including source and destination address fields, port numbers, sequence numbers, flags, or version can be forged. There are also no controls to prevent eavesdropping or tampering.

If we compare the two protocols, we see that some layers within the TCP/IP stack must wear multiple hats (Figure 8.1). Most importantly, the session layer of the OSI stack that provides a logical view of the two communicating applications independent of higher application details or lower transport layer issues must go either within the application or in the transport layer of TCP/IP. Secure communications is essentially a property of this session layer, which can refer to higher-level protocols for identity authentication information and maintain a secure session state over multiple connections at lower levels, transparent to the application layer.

Mechanisms for building reliable and secure communication exist at all layers of the TCP/IP stack, and each has its merits and demerits.

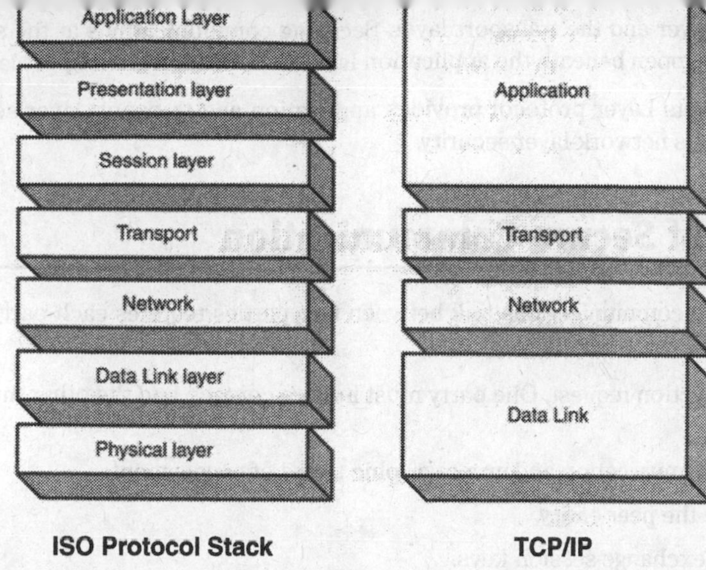

Figure 8.1 The ISO and TCP/IP stacks.

- If we integrate secure communication into the application layer, we have to do so for each application on a host. The application has access to the full user context and can enforce role-based access control. The application need not depend on the underlying host or operating system for security services and can coexist with other services that are not secured. The application can use high-level interfaces with other security service providers and can directly manage events such as alarms.
- If we add security at the transport layer, we gain application independence but are now further from the application, possibly with less information. The security mechanism might require the use of a specific transport-level protocol because it depends on its services. SSL, for example, runs over TCP because its session-oriented nature requires reliable communication. Alarm management can still be handed to the application but is often sent to the system log or passed to a dedicated alarm management process on the host because the application might not be prepared to handle security events.
- If we add security at the network level, we lose even more contact with the application. We might be unable to originate the connection from a particular application, let alone a specific user within that application. The network-level security mechanism must depend on a higher-layer interaction to capture this user context and pass it down to the network layer. This context is called a security association and must be established according to security policy guidelines that might be unavailable at this low level.
- At the data link and the physical level, we can use hardware encryption units or purchase dedicated private lines to protect a communications link. These are completely divorced from the application and are generally statically configured.

the application layer and the transport layer. Securing communications at the session level can either happen beneath the application layer or beneath the transport layer.

The Secure Sockets Layer protocol provides application and transport-layer security, and IPSec provides network-layer security.

The Structure of Secure Communication

Creating a secure communications link between two parties requires each party to do the following:

- Make a connection request. One party must initiate contact, and the other must respond.
- Negotiate communication and cryptographic terms of engagement.
- Authenticate the peer entity.
- Manage and exchange session keys.
- Renegotiate keys on request.
- Establish data transfer properties such as encryption or compression.
- Manage errors by throwing exceptions, communicating alerts, or sending error messages.
- Create audit logs.
- Close connections on successful completion or on fatal errors.
- Reestablish closed connections if both parties agree to do so, for performance reasons.

We will now proceed to a detailed discussion of two mechanisms that achieve these steps.

The Secure Sockets Layer Protocol

The Secure Sockets Layer protocol, invented by Netscape and now available as an IETF standard called *Transport Layer Security* (TLS), provides secure communication between a client and a server. The following synopsis of the standard is from IETF RFC 2246. Since its standardization, several enhancements to the SSL protocol have been proposed; please refer to www.ietf.org for details.

The SSL protocol has seen many applications, driven by its success in securing Web communications and the availability of SSL toolkits that allow developers to add strong security to any legacy application that uses sockets. Since its initial use for securing Web browser to Web server access, a wide variety of application protocols have been SSL-enabled, including mail, news, IIOP, Telnet, FTP, and more.

The SSL protocol depends on the existence of a PKI for all of its certificate services. All entities in the architecture trust the PKI's CA or possess a certification path starting at

host) owns a cryptographic public-key and private-key pair. The public key is embedded in a certificate that holds the entity's distinguished name and can be transmitted over the network. The private key is normally encrypted with a password and stored locally on the user's hard drive. Neither the private key nor the password used to encrypt it is ever transmitted over the network. The protocol depends on the secrecy of the private key.

SSL Properties

SSL provides private, reliable, and nonforgeable conversation between two communicating processes. The SSL protocol is an application-level protocol and sits on top of the TCP/IP stack. Because SSL is independent of the application protocol it protects, any higher-level protocol can be layered on top of the SSL protocol transparently. This separation of concerns in the design has been critical to SSL's success and popularity. Internally, the SSL protocol has two layers. The lower SSL Record Protocol encapsulates all higher-level protocols, including the SSL Handshake Protocol used for authentication.

SSL uses strong cryptography to ensure three properties.

Authentication. SSL uses public-key cryptographic algorithms such as RSA (invented by cryptographers Ron Rivest, Adi Shamir, and Len Adleman) or DSS (the U.S. government's Digital Signature Standard) to authenticate each party to the other. Encryption is used after the initial handshake to define a secret master key. The master key is used to generate any additional key material needed by the next two properties.

Confidentiality. SSL bulk encrypts the data transferred between the two entities by using a symmetric key algorithm such as DES or RC4 (invented by cryptographer Ron Rivest).

Integrity. SSL protects each datagram by adding integrity checks by using cryptographic hash functions such as MD5 (again, invented by Ron Rivest) or SHA1 (issued by the U.S. government). SSL can also use keyed message authentication codes called HMACs (designed by cryptographers Hugo Krawczyk, Ran Canetti, and Mihir Bellare) that use other hash functions as subroutines (as described in Chapter 6, "Cryptography").

Two parties can engage in multiple secure sessions simultaneously and within each session maintain multiple connections. A session object represents each session and holds a unique identifier for the session, along with the cipher suite used, the peer entity's certificate, and a master secret that both entities have agreed upon.

Each session stores a flag that indicates whether new connections within the session can be opened. This feature enables some degree of fault management, where a noncritical alert message that terminates one connection and invalidates the session state does not result in the termination of all ongoing connections. In the event of a critical alarm or alert, all connections can be torn down. A new session must be established to continue communication. This situation could occur, for example, in cases where the application times out.

as bulk encryption keys or initialization vectors needed by cryptographic primitives. The SSL protocol defines a simple, finite state machine that represents the stage reached in the protocol, and each peer maintains its copy of the state. Messages trigger transitions between states. Session state is synchronized by maintaining separate current and pending states. This feature is useful in situations where, for example, one entity wishes to change the cipher suite for future messages. The entity must request its peer to change cipher suites. After the peer acknowledges the request, the state machine guarantees that both will use the correct cipher for all new messages.

The client and the server use the alert message protocol to send each other errors, such as handshake failures, missing certificates, certificates from an unrecognized CA, expired or revoked certificates, unexpected messages, bad message integrity checks, or closure notifications signaling the session over.

An SSL session uses a cipher suite defined by using a string of the form SSL_AuthenticationAlgorithm_WITH_BulkEncryptionAlgorithm_IntegrityCheckAlgorithm stored within the SSL session state.

The SSL Record Protocol

The SSL Record Protocol runs on top of the TCP/IP stack because it relies on the underlying reliable *Transmission Control Protocol* (TCP). SSL is unlike IPSec, which we will discuss in the next section, which operates beneath the transport layer. IPSec can secure connectionless protocols, whereas SSL cannot.

SSL Record Protocol manages data transmission at each endpoint, including the following features:

- Message fragmentation and reassembly
- Integrity check computation and verification
- Optional compression and decompression
- Encryption and decryption

Higher-level protocols are oblivious to all these operations.

The SSL Handshake Protocol

The SSL Handshake Protocol, encapsulated by the SSL Record Protocol, enables a server and a client to authenticate each other and to negotiate an encryption algorithm and cryptographic keys before the application protocol transmits or receives any data. The handshake is shown in Figure 8.2.

The client initiates the session (1) by sending a client hello message to the server along with a list of acceptable cipher suites. The server responds by accepting a cipher suite. Then, the authentication phase (2) of the handshake begins. SSL enables the client to authenticate the server, the server to authenticate the client (3), or both. Figure 8.2 shows mutual authentication.

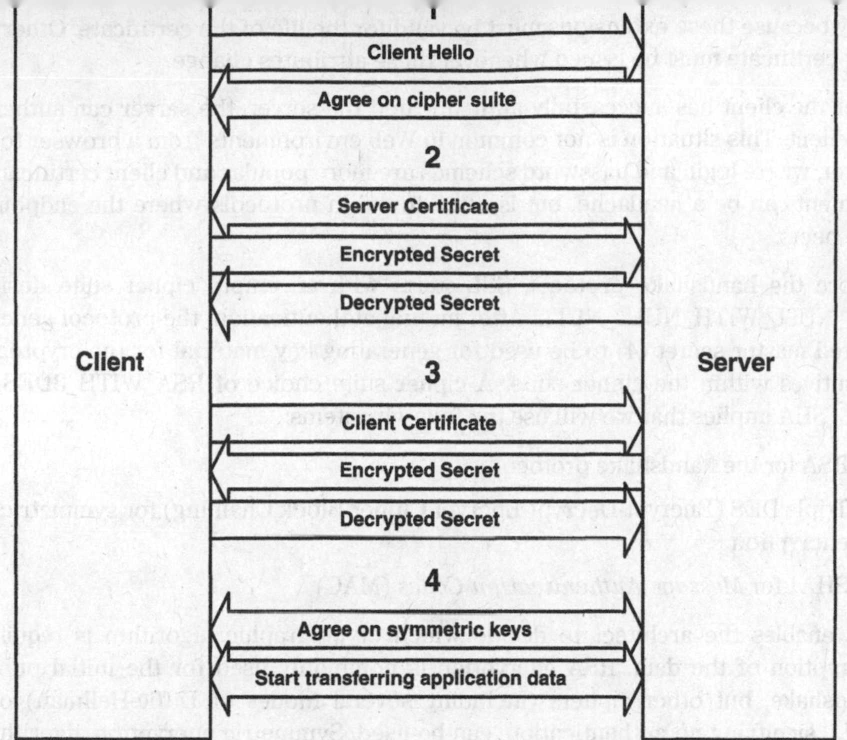

Figure 8.2 The SSL handshake.

A certificate is public information. Any entity that presents a certificate is only making a claim of identity. Even if the signature on the certificate is from a trusted CA, and the certificate itself is valid, unexpired, and not revoked, we cannot trust that the peer is who it claims to be without proof that it owns the corresponding private key. We can establish this fact by sending an encrypted nonce (a unique number used only once by the server) encrypted by using the public key within the certificate and checking the decrypted response. If the peer can correctly decrypt the nonce, then we are assured that they possess the private key.

SSL depends on the existence of a PKI. We trust the peer's identity because we trust that the certificate was issued in accordance with the CA's published *Certificate Practices Statement* (CPS), which must require independent verification of the peer's identity at certificate registration. The CPS determines the method for proof of identity, which must be acceptable to both parties.

The application can add access control checks on top of the authentication provided by the SSL handshake by extracting the user's proven identity from within the distinguished name field of the certificate and matching this identity within a local user profile database or a remote directory service to determine the peer's privileges on the host. SSL adds no support for access control outside of vendor APIs that allows examination of all the fields of the peer's certificate. The X.509v3 standard allows extensions

risky because these extensions must be valid for the life of the certificate. Otherwise, a new certificate must be issued whenever these attributes change.

After the client has successfully authenticated the server, the server can authenticate the client. This situation is not common in Web environments from a browser to a Web server, where login and password schemes are more popular and client certificate management can be a headache, but is often found in protocols where the endpoints are true peers.

Before the handshake protocol, SSL starts with an empty cipher suite designated SSL_NULL_WITH_NULL_NULL. After mutual authentication, the protocol generates a shared master secret (4) to be used for generating key material for the cryptographic primitives within the cipher suite. A cipher suite choice of RSA_WITH_3DES_EDE_CBC_SHA implies that we will use the following items:

- RSA for the handshake protocol
- Triple DES (Encrypt-Decrypt-Encrypt Cipher Block Chaining) for symmetric encryption
- SHA1 for *Message Authentication Codes* (MAC)

SSL enables the architect to decide which cryptographic algorithm is required for encryption of the data. RSA encryption is commonly used for the initial public-key handshake, but other ciphers (including several modes of Diffie-Hellman) or even NULL signifying no authentication, can be used. Symmetric encryption algorithms are used for bulk data encryption during the connection. These include DES, 3DES, RC4, AES, or weaker 40-bit versions of DES or RC4 algorithms. Permitted hash algorithm options include MD5 and SHA.

A developer building an SSL-enabled process must:

- Generate a public-private key pair
- Protect the private key with a password and then never send either the private key or the password over the network
- Get a CA to sign the public key and issue a certificate
- Provision PKI components on both hosts, such as CA and entity certificates, certification paths, CRL locations, and so on
- Write code

Coding responsibilities include choosing a cipher suite, modifying the application build to include cryptographic libraries and SSL configuration information, adding SSL initialization code to the process initialization section, adding SSL cleanup on session exit, and logging code for administrative functions.

SSL Issues

It is easy to add SSL to any link in most applications. Inexpensive or free open-source SSL implementation toolkits have made SSL very popular. Almost any vendor of a

security option. Using SSL within the architecture raises some issues for discussion at the architecture review, however. (We will repeat some of these issues in the specific context of middleware in the next chapter because they bear repeating).

- SSL-enabling an application transfers a significant portion of security management responsibility to the PKI supporting the application. How does the application manage PKI issues?
- Is certificate policy well defined? How are keys managed? How is revocation handled?
- How are servers informed about whether their certificates are about to expire?
- What if the PKI service itself changes? How will the application handle trust during the changing of the guard?
- Which connections in the architecture need SSL-enabling? Do SSL connections need proxies to penetrate firewalls?
- Is performance an issue? The initial public-key handshake can be expensive if used too often. Can the application use hardware-based SSL accelerators that can enable 20 times as many or more connections as software-based solutions?
- Are there issues of interoperability with other vendor SSL solutions?
- Do all applications share the same cipher suite? What does corporate security policy mandate as a minimum level of security?
- Which entities get certificates? Is assignment at the level of an object, process, or host? Do we distinguish between user processes and a daemon process on the host and assign separate certificates? Do we lump multiple processes on a host together to share a certificate?
- How do we handle the passwords that protect an entity's private key? Do the users type them in or use tokens? Are passwords embedded in binaries? Do we build the passwords into the binaries during development (possibly exposing the private key), or do we maintain separate certificate instances for separate system instances—one for each of the development, integration, system test, and production environments?

The IPSec Standard

We will now present the IPSec protocols and related standards, the security mechanism behind the explosive growth of security products like VPNs, secure gateways to connect intranets, and link-encrypted LANs. The original TCP/IP stack was simple, robust, and extensible—all qualities that enabled network programming (especially on UNIX platforms) to explode in ease and popularity. As many researchers have discovered, however (for example, [Bel96]), the TCP/IP stack has many vulnerabilities. The drive to architect, design, and implement end-to-end security for IP began in 1992 with the formation of an IPSec working group to formally address this issue. The need for IP security was also driven by the (then future) introduction of IPv6, which would solve many

RFC standards documents are good examples of how consensus on open security architectures can be achieved.

IPSec secures the IP, the network component of the TCP/IP stack. Applications using transport protocols such as TCP or UDP are oblivious to the existence of IPSec because IPSec, unlike SSL, operates at the network level—securing all (desired) network communication independent of the interacting applications on the two hosts.

IPSec provides connectionless security and relies on higher transport protocols for providing reliable communication if needed by the application. Unlike SSL, IPSec can secure connectionless communications such as UDP, as well. IPSec ensures authentication, data integrity, antireplay protection, and confidentiality.

The IPSec specification describes Unicast-secure communication between two hosts. Although the specification provides some hooks for multicast communications, there is no consensus on how to secure multicast IP protocols. We will return to this issue after our technical discussion to describe the relative immaturity of multicast protocols and key management.

For this synopsis, we used Pete Loshin's Big Book of IPSec RFCs, a collection of all the IETF documents describing the standard in one text, along with other references in the bibliography (primarily [DH99]) and some documents for vendor implementations. IPSec has been extensively reviewed, and many early bugs have been cleaned up. The core protocols of the standard, *Authentication Header* (AH) and *Encapsulating Security Payload* (ESP), are quite robust and have seen considerable acceptance and visibility within VPN technology. Many vendor products implement stable and interoperable VPN solutions by using these protocols. The key management protocol *Internet Key Exchange* (IKE) is quite complex, however, and correspondingly hard to implement. The original specification had some bugs that appear fixed now, but IKE has not gained the acceptance like AH and ESP, especially in the VPN arena. Many vendors still use proprietary, noninteroperable, and noncompliant key management solutions while still claiming compliance with the IKE standard.

IPSec Architecture Layers

IPSec connections can be between two hosts, a host and a secure gateway (such as an IPSec router or a firewall) or between two IPSec gateways (on the route between two hosts).

IPSec uses three layers to separate concerns:

- Key management and authenticated key sharing protocols within the *Internet Security Association and Key Management Protocol* (ISAKMP) framework. These protocols enable hosts to construct *Security Associations* (SA) that can be used by any protocol. The IKE protocol in the IPSec *Domain of Interpretation* (DOI) negotiates security associations for the core IPSec protocols. IKE communications for IPSec are over UDP.
- The core IPSec protocols for communicating data securely are AH and ESP. ESP and AH both provide authentication; ESP encrypts the payload, as well. ESP and

and UDP.

- Cryptographic primitives used by these protocols. IPSec uses three classes of primitives: authenticators, ciphers, and pseudo-random number generators. The standard specifies default and required algorithms for each class, such as hash functions MD5, SHA1 (and keyed hash functions based on these); encryption functions DES, 3DES, RC5, and CAST-128; and Diffie-Hellman for key exchange. Vendors extend support to many more (such as AES) through wrappers to standard cryptographic toolkits such as RSA Data Security's BSAFE toolkit.

IPSec Overview

The TCP/IP stack literally builds datagrams as if it were placing building blocks in a column. Each of the transport, network, and physical network access layers adds its own header to the application data to create the final physical link datagram. A physical frame is a sequence of bits that can be parsed left to right by using the headers as tokens. Each token not only describes parameters needed to process the following payload, but also optionally holds a next header field that enables the left-to-right parsing to continue. Parsing ends when the payload is thrown up to the application layer or repackaged for routing through lower layers. Processing a transport or network datagram can be viewed as managing multiple simple finite state machines, one for each transport or network protocol, where the machines throw the datagram to one another like a hot potato as headers are stripped from the front of the physical frame. Some hosts will find all they need to perform processing in the first two headers; for example, a router that needs to forward the packet to the next hop. Other hosts—for example, the destination host—will consume the entire packet until the kernel of application data has reached its final destination within some application on the host.

IPSec adds security to IP by using the same structure. IPSec introduces new protocols and new headers. In an interesting wrinkle, however, IPSec enables the core protocols to nest secure datagrams and introduces a key management protocol framework that allows the negotiation of terms by using the same simple building blocks.

Packet-switched protocols like IP do not have a separate signaling network as in the circuit-switched world. Each datagram must be a self-contained package of protected and authenticated information. Datagram headers are precious real estate with well-defined fields for specific purposes. Security requires reference to context information of arbitrary size. What encryption algorithm should we use? What should we use for digital signatures? What are the parameters? Do we need some initial values? What are the key values? How do we add the output of encryption or digital signatures to the new and secure datagram we are building? How many packets have we exchanged so far?

IPSec manages these details by introducing data stores at each host that maintain context for each open connection. Specifically, these are the Security Policy Database and the Security Association Database.

tions. For example, we can store monotonically increasing sequence numbers that prevent replays of packets or initialization vectors required to decrypt a packet.

Other fields hold fixed-length pointers to the data stores on each endpoint (for example, Security Parameter Indexes). Some variable-length data such as the output of encryption, compression, or a hash of the whole packet is included as part of the variable-length payload following the header.

The core AH and ESP protocols are simpler than IKE because they can reference the shared security association negotiated through IKE on their behalf. IKE must solve the harder problem of negotiating the details of the security association in the first place, and that too with an unknown, unauthenticated host with no prior knowledge of mutually acceptable cryptographic primitives, by using the fewest possible messages—all along protecting the negotiations from tampering or eavesdropping by a third party. IKE achieves this bootstrapping of security associations through a complex series of interactions that result in a shared association at the IKE level that can be used to generate security associations at the IPSec level. We will not go into the details of IKE, but instead we'll point the reader to the relevant RFCs in the references.

Policy Management

Before two hosts can communicate securely by using IPSec, they must share a *security association* (SA). SAs are *simplex*; each host maintains a separate entry in the *security association database* (SADB) for incoming and outgoing packets to another host. Security associations are context holders, providing the negotiated cipher suite and associated keys to the IPSec packet handler. The handler uses the directives within the SA to process each unprotected IP datagram from the network layer, creating secure IP datagrams for the data link layer. Security Associations can have finite lifetimes or might never be deleted from the SA database.

Security policy determines when IPSec will be enabled for a connection between two hosts. Every packet that leaves the host must be subjected to a policy check. The policy might require the packet to be secured, discarded, or transmitted as is (also known as IPSec bypass). The sender of the datagram can refer to the local *security policy database* (SPD) by using selectors from the fields within the IP datagram waiting to be sent or by using fields visible at the transport level. The selectors include the source, destination, source port, destination port, and protocol within the outgoing packet.

The receiver of an incoming packet does not have access to the transport layer selectors and must choose the correct security policy based on visible information within the incoming IPSec datagram. IPSec resolves this conflict by using a *Security Parameter Index* (SPI) stored within the incoming packet, which references an SA entry in the recipient's SADB. The sender knows which SPI to use because the recipient has told him or her. The recipient provides the SPI reference to the sender as part of the IPSec SA negotiation. The mapping of SPI to an SADB entry must be unique for each choice of SPI, protocol, and destination. SPIs can be reused only if the current security association that uses them is cancelled.

such as RSA or DSS can be expensive, given high network bandwidth and throughput needs. IPSec has been careful to avoid expensive public-key operations in the AH and ESP layers, reserving their use for higher-level IKE security association negotiation. Once a computationally expensive IKE SA is established between two hosts, many other lower-level IPSec SAs can be derived from it. Once an SA expires or is cancelled, it can be rekeyed quickly upon request. Any single connection can be associated with multiple SAs, also known as an SA bundle.

IPSec Transport and Tunnel Modes

IPSec protocols can operate in one of two modes. IPSec in transport mode protects the higher transport level datagram by inserting an IPSec header between the original IP header and its payload. IPSec in tunnel mode protects the entire IP datagram by adding an IPSec header to the original datagram to form the payload of a new IP datagram with a new IP header (that possibly differs from the inner original header).

IPSec tunnel mode distinguishes between communication endpoints and cryptographic endpoints. The original IP header points to the communication endpoint; the new IP header for the IPSec tunnel mode datagram points to the cryptographic endpoint. This latter endpoint must receive, verify, and forward the original datagram to its final destination.

In Figure 8.3, we show an unprotected IP datagram and its IPSec incarnations in transport and tunnel mode ([RFC2401]).

In addition, several IPSec connections can be nested within one other because the AH and ESP protocols produce IP datagrams from IP datagrams. The output of one protocol application (say, ESP) in the context of one SA can be handed off to another IPSec

Original IP datagram

IP Header	TCP Header	Data

IPSec datagram in transport mode

IP Header	IPSec Header	TCP Header	Data

IPSec datagram in tunnel mode

New IP Header	IPSec Header	IP Header	TCP Header	Data

Figure 8.3 IPSec modes.

enable a host to provide multiple layers of security that are removed by the corresponding cryptographic endpoints along the route from source to destination host.

For example, a user can originate a connection from a laptop on the open Internet (say, from his or her dial-up ISP) through the corporate IPSec gateway and through the gateway of a private-division LAN to a secure server on that LAN by using three nested tunnels. All the tunnels originate at the laptop, but they terminate at the corporate gateway, the division gateway, and the secure server, respectively.

IPSec Implementation

IPSec implementation can be native, where a device manufacturer integrates the IPSec protocols into the network layer of their native TCP/IP stack within the operating system. This feature has the convenience of good performance, but applications lose some flexibility in choosing between IPSec vendors based on features.

Alternatively, vendors can provide *bump-in-the-stack* implementations that separate the protocol stack between the network and data link layer to add an IPSec processing shim. This layer extracts the IP datagrams produced by the network layer, manufactures IPSec datagrams based on selectors within the original transport package and other fields, and passes a secure datagram to the underlying network interface. For example, a Windows NT IPSec driver might bind to the TCP/IP protocol stack at its upper edge and to one or more network adapters at its lower edge, and the user can configure network settings to pass TCP/IP to the IPSec driver to the network interface card. Some bump-in-the-stack implementations might create conflicts with other bump-in-the-stack software, such as personal firewalls. Some implementations cannot bind with all underlying network adapters; for example, some vendors fail to bind with wireless LAN adapters. Interoperability and performance are issues with bump-in-the-stack implementations.

The third option is to use dedicated IPSec hardware devices. These bump-in-the-wire implementations introduce an additional point of failure and are expensive if many connections in the architecture require security. Hardware devices are a good alternative for secure communication to legacy systems that cannot be modified.

Authentication Header Protocol

AH provides data integrity, source authentication, and some defense against replay attacks. AH does not provide confidentiality, and the entire secured datagram is visible. The AH protocol defines the structure of the AH header that contains the SPI, a sequence number to prevent replays, and an authentication field. The standard requires implementation of HMAC-SHA-96 and HMAC-MD5-96, both keyed hash algorithms based on SHA and MD5 (respectively) with the hash output truncated to 96 bits.

The AH protocol authentication field stores the result of a cryptographic hash of the entire IP datagram with mutable fields, including the authentication data field set to zero. This integrity check value is truncated to 96 bits and then added to the header. A recipient can quickly verify the authenticity of all the data in the original IP datagram.

Encapsulating Sec[illegible]ity Payload

ESP provides confidentiality over and above the properties guaranteed by the AH protocol. The ESP header and the ESP trailer (hence the word *encapsulating* in the name) in transport or tunnel mode contains the security parameter index, a sequence number to prevent replays, an initialization vector for the decryption of the payload, and an authentication data chunk that validates all of the IPSec datagram except for the external IP header.

ESP uses two cryptographic primitives—an authenticator and a cipher—both of which cannot simultaneously be set to NULL. ESP has created some of the architecture issues associated with IPSec security, because unlike AH it hides data visible in the original datagram. This action can break applications, protocols, or tools that were built with an assumption that they could use this internal information.

Internet Key Exchange

The IKE protocol uses elements of the Oakley and SKEME protocols to negotiate an authenticated, shared key exchange. IKE can be used to achieve this result for any Internet protocol that has its own DOI. The IPSec DOI defines how IKE SAs and IPSec SAs are negotiated.

Unlike the IPSec protocols that use IP address and ports as identities, IKE can authenticate higher level entities by using fully qualified domain names, certificates, X.500 directory distinguished names, or usernames on named, fully qualified hosts. This function links the identity of a connection with an application-level entity, improving auditing.

IKE is a protocol instance within a more general framework for negotiating security services and cryptographic information called ISAKMP. ISAKMP defines a catalog of payloads, each of which is described by additional payload attributes. ISAKMP negotiations have two phases, the first in which an ISAKMP SA is established and the second in which protocol and DOI specific SAs are established. The ISAKMP specification lists defined payloads, attributes, phases, and exchanges.

Once entities have authenticated themselves to one another, the ISAKMP key management framework is capable of building predicates describing complex security policies using logical AND and OR operators to combine acceptable protocols, cryptographic transforms, or key exchange modes into packages called *offers*. This feature is attractive only if vendors provide full support for arbitrarily complex association negotiation. Once an offer is accepted, IKE can negotiate an authenticated key exchange that leads to an IKE SA.

Once an IKE security association is in place, multiple IPSec associations can be derived from the association. The architecture may or may not support *perfect forward secrecy*, the property that guarantees that once new keys are negotiated, even complete knowledge of all old key material will not reveal the contents of the current communication. If all key material is derived in a dependent manner from a master secret within the IKE SA, it might be possible to leak information about future communication from the knowledge of keys from communication in the past.

sages and rounds of negotiation. Security is correspondingly weakened.

Some Examples of Secure IPSec Datagrams

Figure 8.4 shows several IPSec-protected datagrams.

- The first datagram is protected by using AH in transport mode. No encryption is used, and the entire datagram can be inspected but not modified. An authentication field in the AH header contains an integrity verification value computed from a cryptographic hash of a shared secret key and the entire IP datagram after mutable values in the IP header are zeroed out. AH protects the entire IP datagram, including the IP header.
- The second datagram is protected by using ESP in transport mode. The original transport datagram is encrypted by using a shared secret key using the cipher algorithm from the IPSec SA. The cipher might require an initialization vector

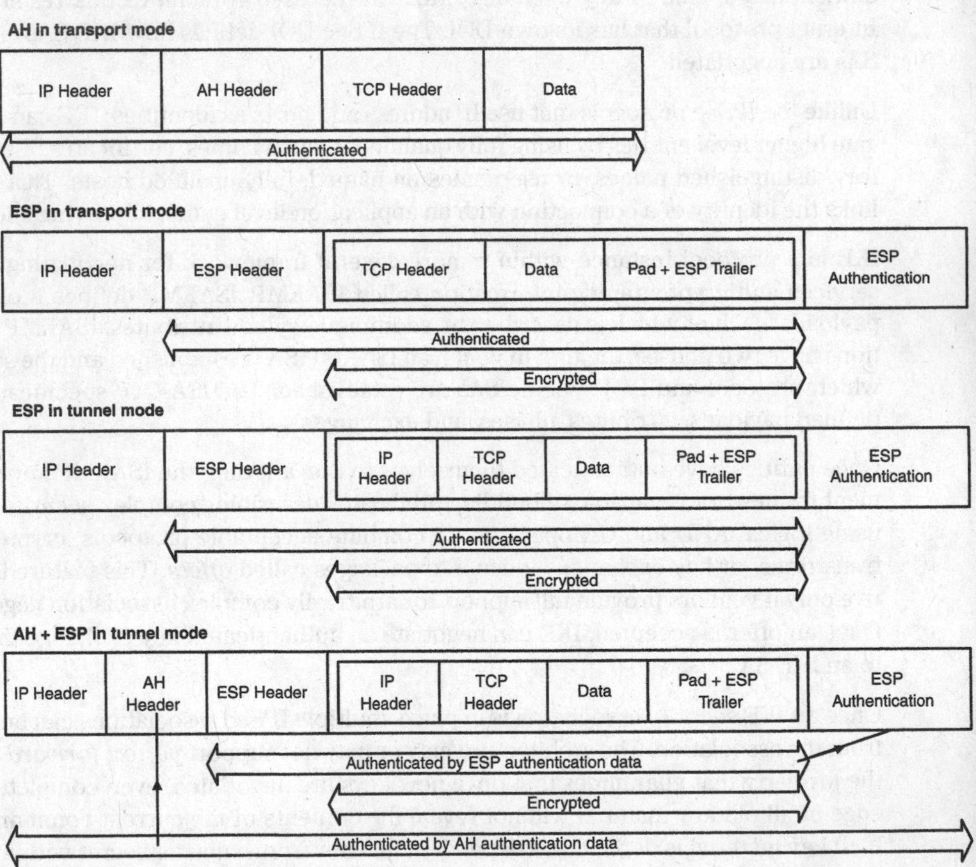

Figure 8.4 AH and ESP-protected datagrams.

The encrypted portion of the ESP datagram includes the original transport header and data along with the pad and a pointer to the next header type. The ESP authentication data trails the encrypted block and authenticates the ESP header and encrypted block but does not authenticate the original IP header.

- The third datagram is protected by using ESP in tunnel mode. In this example, the entire original IP datagram is encrypted after suitable padding, and the authenticator scope includes the ESP header and the encrypted block that now includes the original IP header. The new IP header is not authenticated.
- In our final example, we have an IP datagram protected with ESP in tunnel mode and then AH in transport mode. The complete datagram has two authenticators that have different but overlapping scopes.

IPSec Host Architecture

IPSec vendors give application architects three components corresponding to the three layers of IPSec components.

IPSec management. The vendor product includes some central management interface that can connect to IPSec configuration clients on each participating host to manually populate keys or to configure IKE interactions that can automate protocol negotiation and key sharing to build IKE and IPSec security associations. The user interface normally provides or has hooks into user management applications, alarm and event audit functions, and policy management. Third-party service providers such as LDAP directories, PKI components, or Kerberos can be used. The management interface populates the *Security Policy Database* (SPD) with ordered policy entries for the IPSec kernel to use.

IPSec kernel. The vendor provides implementations of the AH and ESP protocols in the form of a kernel driver operating in bump-in-the-stack mode (Figure 8.5) or through a replacement for the entire TCP/IP stack. The IPSec kernel references the SPD and the SADB on all outgoing and incoming packets. The kernel requests the IPSec management client to negotiate new SAs when required.

Cryptographic libraries. The vendor provides authentication, encryption, and random number generation functions in a library that can be replaced or enhanced if required.

IPSec Issues

IPSec creates many issues that must be addressed before deployment within your application. Some of these issues are inherent to the protocol, but others are accidental consequences of vendor product interpretation of the standard. Applications should be aware of the risk of being locked into using a single vendor product because of the complexities of transitioning thousands of users to a possibly superior competitor's offering.

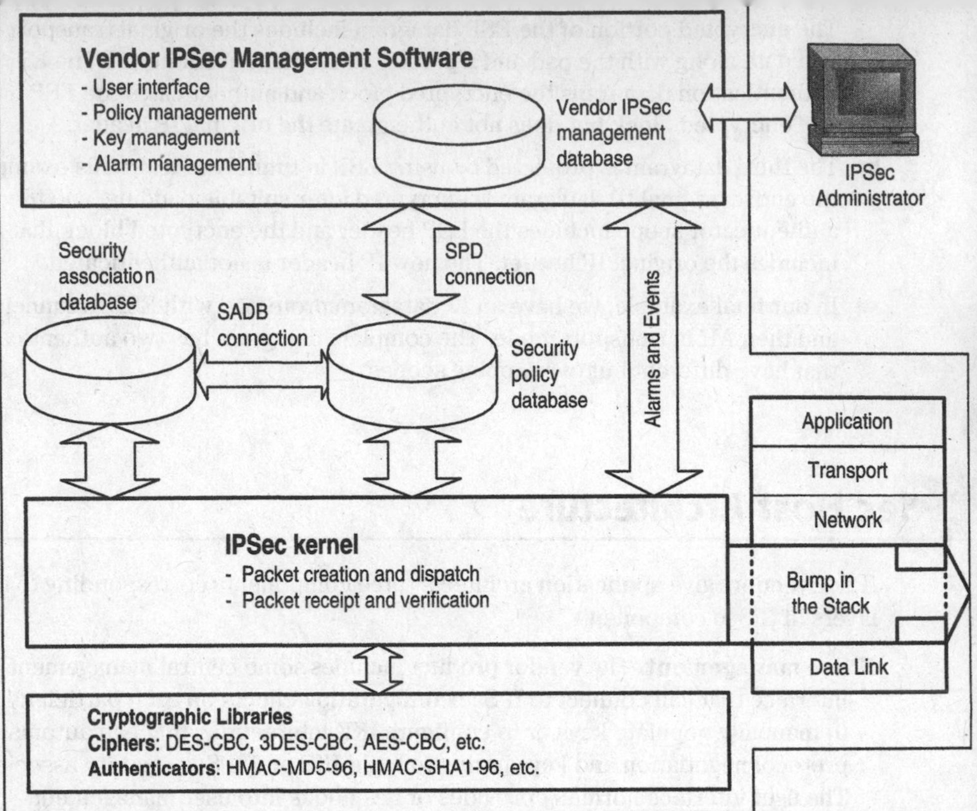

Figure 8.5 IPSec vendor's host architecture.

Here are some of the issues surrounding the IPSec architecture:

Key management. Key management is the number-one problem with IPSec deployments. Scalability and usability goals are essential.

Deployment issues. IPSec deployment is complex. Configuration and troubleshooting can be quite challenging. Some vendors provide excellent enterprise solutions for VPN deployment, but extending the solution to cover other applications, client platforms, or access modes (such as Palm Pilots or wireless phones) represent significant challenges due to both a relative fragility of the implementation that prevents portability and the limitations of the hardware.

Policy definition. Many vendors provide proprietary policy definition and management solutions that might conflict with application goals or corporate security guidelines.

store additional routing information. Some vendors provide virtual adapters that enable a single host to own several IP addresses, one for each tunnel it initiates. This situation might make return traffic from hosts that are multiple hops away easier to route because each destination is addressing a unique virtual IP, possibly improving the performance of the secure gateway. Another issue is traffic where encryption is done at intermediate points, rather than only at the endpoints. This situation forces routing through these intermediate points, increasing the chances of failure of communication. Sometimes, as in the case of a corporate firewall, this situation is desirable.

Multicast applications. These include audio or video over IP broadcasts, virtual conferencing, multiplayer games, news or stock feeds, and automated upgrades. Multicasts require a single host to communicate with a group of hosts securely. The group is not static, and members can leave or join and can be connected to the sender by using networks of differing bandwidth or topology.

There are several competing standards for reliable multicast definition and associated properties for group key management. Group Key Management Protocol and Secure Multicast IPSec are examples. Multicast requires us to enable role-based access control by using object and user group, roles, and permissions at the IP level. All solutions introduce new trust issues. Some recommend that all entities trust a group key manager; others avoid centralization by using distributed, hierarchical structures.

Known endpoints. IPSec requires that the host know the address of the secure gateway. Are there multiple secure gateways that can lead to the destination? How do we load-balance thousands of clients that wish to connect to a few security gateways? Do we hard-wire assignments of clients to gateways? How do we change assignments dynamically? Some solutions that manage this process do exist, but there are no standards.

Network address translation. IPSec tunnels through gateways that perform network address translation could create problems. The security gateway cannot correctly map the inner IP headers with the correct IP addresses because they are encrypted. The cryptographic endpoint will not be capable of forwarding packets to the destination host because the payload has bad IP addresses within it.

Access control. Many of the issues of access control rule ordering that we described in Chapter 3 apply to determining the correct security policy from the SPD. Multiple policy rules might apply, and the order of application is important. The SA bundle applicable might contain multiple termination endpoints, and the order of application of SA rules depends on the ordering of the endpoints along the source-to-destination path.

Tool incompatibility. IPSec breaks network management tools like traceroute. It also creates issues for ICMP messages that cannot handle long messages or that require information hidden within the header of the payload of the IPSec datagram that caused an error.

Conclusion

Our discussion of secure communication adds some basis to secure architecture for the connectors in our system. Our short description of the SSL protocol and IPSec should give the reader some flavor of the issues involved. Some hidden dependencies still exist, such as the need for secure DNS or good PKI support. We will relate many of the issues discussed here with the other chapters on OS, Web, middleware, and database security—because in any distributed application, secure communications is critical.

Secure communications uses many of our security patterns. *Principals* are identified through IP address, ports, host names, or higher identities such as certificates or distinguished names. IPSec and SSL both use *cookies* and *session objects* to maintain state at the endpoints. ESP applies the *wrapper* pattern to every packet it secures, and AH adds a *sentinel* to prevent tampering. Applications often implement SSL by using the *interceptor* pattern. SSL and IPSec exist to create *transport tunnels* and use *service providers* such as directories, secure DNS, or PKI services.

We can even see other examples such as the *proxy* pattern when diverse communications mediums meet to create secure communications channels. For example, Web-enabled phones (supporting the Wireless Access Protocol) or PDA devices (that use wireless IP data services like CDPD) promise secure connections to Internet services. The physical limitations of the devices and the differing protocols create the *mobile wireless air gap* problem, however. For example, in AT&T Wireless's PocketNet service, the ISP maintains a gateway service that provides one secure CDPD connection from the Internet-ready phone to the gateway and a separate SSL session over the Internet to the Web server. The *proxy* function of this gateway results in a potential security hole, because the user information is in the clear on the gateway for a short period. This situation is the so-called wireless air gap.

Layered security can only go so far, and there is plenty of security work left at the application level. This topic will be the focus of our next few chapters.

Mid-Level Architecture

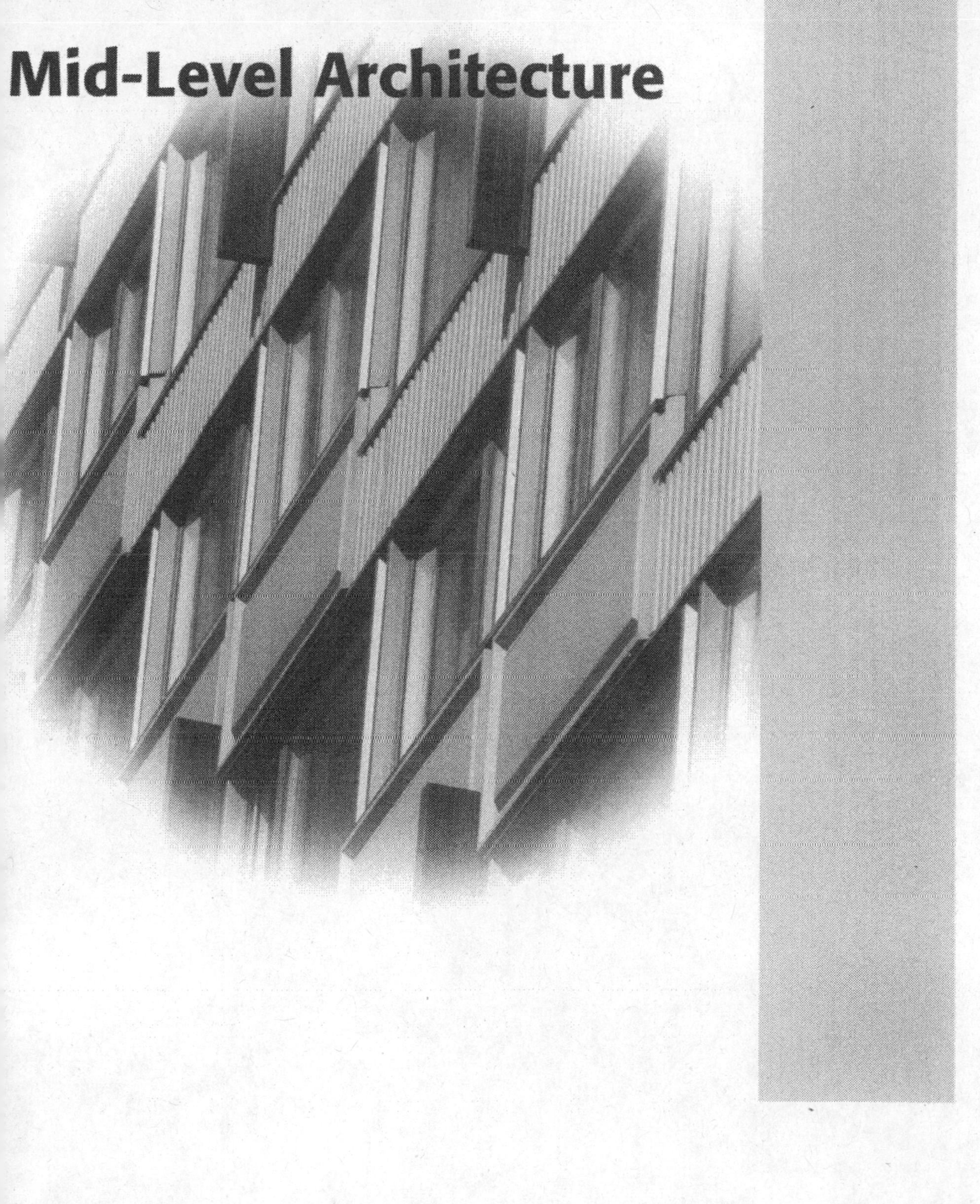

Middleware Security

Middleware supports concurrent and networked application development by separating the underlying variations in programming languages, hosts, operating systems, and networking protocols from the higher-level concerns of a distributed application. Middleware is a collection of components that make it easier to program a distributed application by hiding the low-level complexity that arises from inherent properties of the system or from accidental factors [POSA2].

Middleware provides a paradigm for networked application programming that simplifies coding, automates underlying network services, provides reliable communication, and manages traffic. Middleware also helps enterprise architecture by providing common, reusable services that can be customized to the client, server, and application needs. Examples of services include event handling, notification, security, trading, and naming services.

In addition, middleware solutions must interact with other middleware solutions at application or domain boundaries. Security management across multiple vendor solutions is an issue, as is security architecture in the face of evolution (because, as the application's needs evolve, the security requirements change). Large, monolithic middleware solutions tend to be fragile in the face of evolutionary design forces.

In this chapter, we will discuss some inherent complexities with securing distributed applications and some accidental complexities caused by poor vendor APIs, invalid assumptions, visible low-level design, or clashes in middleware philosophies. Many of these issues are common to all middleware offerings, including COM+, EJB, CORBA, and MQSeries. We will pick one technology, CORBA, because of space limitations and discuss the problems with securing distributed CORBA applications.

tion from CORBA's standard bearers, the Object Management Group. We will describe why the specification has seen limited acceptance at the user level and why vendor compliance is nonexistent. We will describe why the specification is still valuable as an architectural guideline. We will present the three levels of CORBA security: basic secure communication using SSL and other secure protocols, CORBA level 1 security that does not require application code to change, and CORBA Level 2 security that opens programmatic access to the security API. We will also discuss advanced delegation, authorization, and nonrepudiation services and touch upon the administrative support for architects in the CORBA security specification.

Middleware and Security

Middleware presents some unique challenges to security architecture because the goals of hiding underlying infrastructure conflict with the goals of examining details of the infrastructure for authentication, authorization, or auditing. Schmidt, Stal, Rohnert, and Buschmann [POSA2] present a pattern catalog and language for concurrent and networked objects in which they describe the following goals.

Service Access

Distributed components cannot share memory. They cannot invoke communications mechanisms that exploit a local address space, such as function calls or static class variables. They must use low-level *interprocess communication* (IPC) mechanisms (such as sockets or named pipes), networking protocols such as SMTP or HTTP, or higher-level abstractions that enable remote object invocation (such as CORBA and *Enterprise Java Beans* [EJB]). Clients must be able to invoke servers by logical names rather than by IP addresses, choose servers based on certain desired properties (such as proximity), initiate communications, and receive services. The server must be continuously available, or the client must be able to activate a service provider on demand.

Security Issues

Separating clients and servers to hide the details of access creates multiple points of potential security failure that can result in compromise at either the client or the server or in denial of service. There are many security mechanisms for securing low-level communications, and the architect must choose the most appropriate one based on the application domain, available security services, performance, cost, and so on. Secure service access raises new issues for system architects and middleware vendors alike to worry about.

Service Configuration

Components within a networked application must be initialized with the correct configuration at startup and must be able to transfer system state safely to other instances

corresponding to differing client service profiles and needs. These multiple personalities of possible access to services and data must be kept apart, even through dynamic evolution of services during the component's life cycle. Some middleware vendors enable the dynamic configuration of components by using loadable modules. Each module can be configured to support a service role presented by the daemon within the architecture.

Security Issues

Security management is a critical component of any security architecture. This feature requires that configuration of security policy at server startup or during the server's life must be accomplished securely. The server must be able to trust dynamically loadable service roles. (As an example, which we describe in more detail in Chapter 11, "Application and OS Security," there exists a rootkit exploit against the Linux kernel built as a dynamically loadable module).

Secure configuration requirements raise questions. Where are configuration files stored? Are they verified before use? Can the files be compromised so that when the service is halted and restarted, bad security policy is enabled? Can the configuration interface be exploited to disable security? Does the architecture support paranoid security configurations, where a new and much more restrictive security policy can be quickly deployed across the whole enterprise in reaction to a known but not yet active exploit?

Event Management

Object-oriented or message-based middleware products support communication through mechanisms such as remote procedure calls, synchronous method invocation, asynchronous invocation, or message queues. A client can communicate with a server by initiating contact and presenting a service request. The server must handle multiple requests from many clients, demultiplexing the stream of events into separate streams for callback-handling subsystems that can process each request. On completion, the server must generate a service response to the client who, based on whether the communication is synchronous or asynchronous, may or may not have blocked in the interim. The client must receive and process the service completion event. Strategies for event management sometimes use finite state machines to handle transitions required by the asynchronous interrupts to maintain safety by controlling the server's behavior on unexpected events.

Security Issues

Event handling raises security questions, as well. Does the security solution handle spurious events well? Does the architecture respond to message floods that might overflow message queues? Who decides the maximum priority of an event generated by a client? If the client sets the priority, can this property be abused? Can a malicious client

and disable clients that engage in such behavior?

Distributed Data Management

Middleware must provide object persistence and transparent access to underlying legacy data. Components might be required to store intermediate results, to maintain local caches of frequently requested data, to keep session state for error recovery, or to manage performance-related storage. The middleware product itself might need to provide an internal persistent store for messages in the event that the recipient of a message is currently inactive. The underlying heterogeneous environment makes data persistence and data management particularly difficult.

Security Issues

The integrity of messages in transit and in data stores that the middleware product can write to must be protected, which raises security questions as well. Can messages be captured? Can they be read or modified? Are data values within messages protected at the endpoints after receipt? Can attackers reuse session credentials? Can attackers overwrite security logs by flooding the system with bogus messages that generate audit log entries?

Concurrency and Synchronization

Communication in concurrent or networked programming is often many-to-few, especially in client/server programming. Servers might handle many clients. Each server might need to dynamically activate other servers, spawn new processes, manage pools of resources across multiple service handlers, and maintain integrity of critical sections of code.

In addition to synchronized messaging, servers might need to synchronize access to local shared resources. A multithreaded daemon might need to maintain thread-specific storage. A daemon that maintains a process pool and spawns off server instances in response to client requests might need to protect shared memory used by all the process instances.

Programmers use several synchronization mechanisms, all based on the paradigm of requesting a lock on a resource, waiting to acquire it, and then releasing the lock after using the resource. Examples of synchronization primitives include mutexes, condition variables, reader/writer locks, and semaphores. These mechanisms have an assumption of good behavior, namely that all processes or threads will use the synchronization mechanism to access a critical resource. Programming errors, complex invocation patterns, or process failure could cause locks to be acquired but not released or for processes to hang in deadlock—each waiting on another to relinquish a captured resource.

Programming using synchronization mechanisms does not present any direct security issues. We believe that there are no known exploits that work against a multithreaded process but that would fail against a single threaded one (unless there are coding errors in the multithreaded library that cause other vulnerabilities, such as buffer overflow attacks). It is possible that some exploit could create a denial-of-service attack through the creation of deadlocks, starvation, or process termination that exploits concurrent paradigms. This event is a remote possibility, however, and if the system can detect and reactivate the daemon, this problem can be somewhat mitigated. Concurrent programs are hard enough to debug as it is.

Reusable Services

Access to common, reusable, and dependable services has always been a large part of the promise of middleware. Distributed applications with the shared goals of location transparency, logical name to physical name mapping, object persistence, service negotiation, directory lookup, or centralized security services can move these responsibilities outside individual applications and into the realm of enterprise software infrastructure. The cost amortization helps middleware as it did security in our discussions in Chapter 2, "Security Assessments." The OMG CORBA specification lists several examples of services including naming, time, security, transaction, licensing, trader, event, persistence, and many more.

Middleware technology has grown beyond the goals of enabling communication, and more than 10 years of standards work in technologies like CORBA have produced an impressive array of specifications for object modeling, object architecture, interface definition and mapping, support services, and frameworks. There are many success stories where large-scale enterprise architectures have been built around the middleware paradigm.

Security Issues

Middleware services add to the problem for implementing application security. If location, platform, software, and technology independence and transparency is desired, how do we ensure that the ongoing communications are secure? Can an attacker modify a name mapping to point a client to a bogus server? Can a server be cut off by deletion from the location service? Can a directory be compromised to modify user profiles? Can a time service be compromised to allow credentials to be replayed? How do we maintain the basic security principles of authentication, integrity, or confidentiality?

Middleware products must also support legacy clients that cannot be modified to comply with security or other products that interoperate in insecure mode but fail when security is enabled. Backward compatibility requirements with older product versions might also weaken security. Flexibility and choice are valuable but only if all configurations can assure some basic compliance with security policy. Vendors provide configuration options on services that enable the application to decide which connections to

Allowing servers to accept insecure connections for backward compatibility might create security holes.

Middleware vendors have responded by building security products that essentially require applications to embed a high degree of trust into the security controls within their products and the quality of their implementations. Examination of some implementations shows that this trust is often misplaced.

The Assumption of Infallibility

Middleware, more than in any other architecture component, is a source of security flaws based on invalid assumptions rather than design flaws. Almost all vendor products for middleware come with some extensions or plug-ins to enable security. These provide well-recognized security properties such as authentication, authorization, and data confidentiality. They often share the same problem we call the *assumption of infallibility*, however: The architecture is secure if it has not been compromised in any manner. If any individual component fails, then reasoning about security becomes distinctly murky. Middleware security solutions respond poorly to Byzantine attacks, where some elements of the architecture are not only faulty, but also possibly maliciously working in collusion with other components.

For example:

- What if a single client abuses access? Can they promote their privileges in some manner?
- What if the solution assumes transitive trust or delegation and an upstream client is compromised? How far can an attacker reach in the workflow before some system detects and corrects the damage?
- What if a critical service is compromised? If the naming service is hacked so that an attacker can install a man-in-the-middle between the client and the server, can either endpoint detect this action? Note that point-to-point encryption might not be of any help if the attacker can maintain separate sessions with the client and server by using credentials from the compromised service provider.
- What if the services location server (Trader service in CORBA) is compromised? Can the security architecture respond by redirecting client requests to a legitimate trader? Will services be denied or merely delayed?
- What if the underlying host is compromised in a manner through an exploit not at all connected with the middleware security solution? Does the solution fail if any one node in the distributed network fails in this manner?
- What if a client session, authenticated and in progress, is stolen by an attacker? Must the attacker also simultaneously disable the actual client to deceive the server? Can the server detect the theft of the communications channel?
- If the application has a multithreaded daemon, can attackers cause race conditions or deadlock through messages from compromised clients? Can the server defend

reactivating services?

- Can a single instance of a remote object compromise other instances on the same server through attacks on shared resources? Can one instance of an object overwrite data that belongs to another instance? Will a buffer overflow in one persistent object store write over an adjacent byte sequence?
- Does the solution depend on other services such as mail, DNS, firewall protection, or network isolation that could be compromised? Does the architecture have choke points that are not enforced in reality?
- Can an attacker examine binaries for components in development environments to extract magic strings that leak information about encryption keys in production? Can a hacker with a backup tape compromise the system?

The common response to analyzing scenarios such as these is to throw one's hands up and say, "Well, the system is already compromised, so there is nothing to defend." This response would be valid if we were discussing OS or database security, where scenarios that assume root access to describe exploits that lead to root access are rightly labeled examples of circular reasoning. But distributed architectures have many hosts, and it is perfectly valid to assume that any single host has been compromised at the root level with the intent of using all the host's resources to launch attacks at other elements of the distributed architecture. Leslie Lamport first introduced this problem to distributed computing as the Byzantine Generals Problem, and there is considerable research on protocols and methods for ensuring safety and inferring properties in such an environment.

We call this the assumption of infallibility because the vendor assumes the best-case scenario for providing security services. In reality, the world might not be so perfect. Security does not affect some reasons for adopting distributed architectures, such as scalability and cost, as much as it affects performance and reliability. Distributed applications have higher requirements to manage failure gracefully. Dependability is one of the main reasons why we wish to adopt distributed architectures.

We now will move the focus of our presentation to security within a very popular middleware standard, CORBA.

The Common Object Request Broker Architecture

CORBA applications are composed of objects representing entities in the application. In a typical client/server application, there might be many instances of client objects of a single type and fewer or only one instance of a server. A legacy application can present access to its data through a CORBA interface defining methods for clients to invoke over the network.

CORBA uses the OMG *Interface Definition Language* (IDL) to define an interface for each object type. The interface defines a syntactic contract offered by the server to

must use this IDL interface to specify the method invoked and must present all the arguments required by the method. In CORBA, every object instance has its own unique object reference called an *Interoperable Object Reference* (IOR). Each client must use the target object's IOR to invoke operations upon it. Arguments are marshaled by a client-side implementation component that creates a request in the form of a message. The message is sent to the server by using the IIOP protocol. When the invocation reaches the target object, the same interface definition is used by a server-side CORBA implementation component to unmarshal the arguments from the message so that the server can perform the requested operation with them. Clients respond in the same manner to the server.

The IDL interface definition is independent of the programming language chosen for either client or server development. Vendors provide IDL compilers that map IDL definitions to object definitions in most programming languages. IDL definitions separate interface from implementation. This property is fundamental, because CORBA achieves interoperability by strictly enforcing object access only through an IDL-defined interface. The details of the client and server implementations are hidden from each other. Clients can access services only through an advertised interface, invoking only those operations that the object exposes through its IDL interface with only those arguments that are included in the IDL definition.

Once the IDL is defined, a developer can compile it into client stubs and object skeletons and then use the stubs and skeletons to write the client and the target object. Stubs and skeletons serve as proxies for clients and servers, respectively. The CORBA IDL defines interfaces strictly to ensure that regardless of programming language, host machine, network protocol, or *Object Request Broker* (ORB) vendor, the stub on the client side can match perfectly with the skeleton on the server side.

The OMG CORBA Security Standard

The OMG defines a standard for CORBA compliance for vendors to ensure interoperability, which at a minimum requires that their ORB must comply with the OMG IDL for each specific mapping implemented within the core OMG ORB. Security has lagged behind other CORBA services, in part due to the complexity of the OMG CORBA Security Specification and because of a lack of detailed guidelines to ensure that the various security implementations interoperate. The latest version of the CORBA Security Specification attempts to improve the latter deficiency, with partial success.

The CORBA Security Service Specification

The CORBA security specification lists all the security principles of Chapter 3, "Security Architecture Basics," as goals: authentication, authorization, access control, confidentiality, integrity, nonrepudiation, and secure administration. It also aims to improve usability for all participants, including end users, administrators, and implementers.

formally define vendor compliance with the standard.

The distinguishing characteristic of the security specification is its object-oriented nature.

- All security interface definitions should be purely object-oriented.
- All interfaces should be simple, hiding complex security controls from the security architecture model.
- The model should allow polymorphism to support multiple underlying security mechanisms.

In an abstract sense, all principals that wish to communicate must authenticate themselves in some manner and then be subjected to the rules of access control on every object invocation. The specification uses many of the security patterns that we introduced in Chapter 4, "Architecture Patterns in Security," including *principals*, *context holders*, *session objects*, *tokens*, *policy servers*, *interceptors*, *filters*, and *proxies*. The specification uses its own terminology, of course, which we will also adopt for our presentation. The specification also attempts to address security policy definition and management across multiple security domains.

Packages and Modules in the Specification

The CORBA Security Specification is a collection of feature package and module descriptions. The main security functionality is captured in two packages for *Level 1* security and *Level 2* security. A separate nonrepudiation functionality package is defined but optional and specified as a service for completeness. As is common, nonrepudiation is not a priority in many current vendor products unless enabled by chance. It is the poor cousin of the security principles family.

Security Replacement Packages decouple the ORB implementation from the security service implementation. ORBs are unaware of the details of the security service but are security ready, enabling plug-and-play of different authentication and authorization mechanisms. The security services are also unaware of the internal details of the core ORB implementation and can be run over multiple security-ready ORBs. Security services are often added to the architecture by using the *interceptor* or *wrapper* patterns.

Secure communications are specified by using the *Secure Interoperability with SECIOP* package. This functionality is similar to IPSec, discussed in Chapter 8, in that the underlying IIOP protocol is enhanced with security extensions that enable send/receive requests to carry security associations.

Common Security Interoperability Feature packages attempt to address interoperability between vendor security solutions. The standard defines three levels of compliance and all three CSI levels (at a minimum) require mutual authentication, integrity, and confidentiality for secure communication between each client and server. The CSI packages relate the interoperability across a communications link with the extent of trust ensured by the two underlying middleware products that created the link. This

On the low end of trust relationships, no delegation may be permitted. On the next level, the recipient may impersonate the sender of the message to a third party. In this case, the third party may be unable to authenticate the original sender of the request. At the high end of trust relationships, all participating entities may be required to pass strong authentication and authorization checks to gain entry to a secure sandbox supported by all ORB vendors in the architecture. Once inside the sandbox, all entities must delegate requests strictly according to security policy. This enables the sender of a request to add attributes or auditing to the request that the recipient must use if it chooses to delegate the request to any third party also within the sandbox. In an increasing ladder of interoperability, a vendor might support the following components:

- CSI Level 0, which consists of identity-based policies without delegation. Compliance at CSI level 0 enables an entity to transmit only its identity to a target on a request that cannot be delegated under the original identity for further object accesses made by the target. The identity of the intermediate object (the target) must be used if other objects are invoked.
- CSI Level 1 consists of identity-based policies with unrestricted delegation. Compliance at CSI level 1 enables transitive delegation of only the request originator's identity without the use of attributes that could store credentials such as audit information or roles. This level allows an intermediate object to impersonate the originator of the request because no further restrictions are placed on the delegation of a request.
- CSI Level 2, which is a complete implementation of the security specification. This supports controlled delegation of requests, in which an intermediary might be required to carry attributes from the originating principal to any objects that it invokes. This allows the initiator of a request to have some control over delegation. CSI Level 2 also supports composite delegation in which the intermediary might be required to collect credentials and attributes from multiple upstream principals and bundle all these attributes into any invocation of a downstream object method.

This functionality gives vendors an evolution path to full compliance with the specification at CSI level 2. The intermediate levels offer a subset of features with correspondingly weakened security properties.

Common Security Protocol Packages enable the security service to use other security infrastructure components such as PKI, Kerberos, Sesame (by using CSI ECMA), DCE, or SSL-enabled TCP/IP links. Directory services might provide user profile information, access control list management, password management, additional options to secure *remote procedure calls* (RPCs), and vendor-specific directory enhancements that allow extensions to messages, providing additional context for security.

Because of the relative maturity of some security protocols, we expect continued vendor support for the Common Security Protocol packages. CORBA security products that support each of these options are already on the market, although we would hesitate to state that they are all CSI level 0 compliant. In any application that uses a single ORB and security vendor, integration with DCE, Kerberos, or a PKI is currently possible.

pair-wise testing can tell.

Vendor Implementations of CORBA Security

Vendors are charged with the difficult task of implementing all of the security APIs in a manner that is:

- Independent of the underlying security controls
- Flexible in supporting multiple security policies
- Interoperable with multiple ORBs and with other security components

The security service, in line with other OMG goals, must also be portable and fast.

The fact that all the vendors claim compliance not only with the standard, but also with the common security interoperability levels means very little. You have to test to see whether this claim holds because of subtle differences in vendor implementations, in the choice of how structures are stored, how messages are formatted, how extensions are parsed, or how errors are handled. Much of the details of how to accomplish these goals are left unspecified.

Implementing security under these constraints is made all the more difficult due to the distributed nature of the CORBA software bus. Where do the components of the trusted core supporting all communications reside in a distributed environment? What impact will security have on performance if this core is distributed across the enterprise?

Vendors are required to provide security services to applications by implementing all the security facilities and interfaces required to secure an ORB. They must also provide basic administrative support for all choices of policy, but the standard allows for levels of interoperability requirements between security mechanisms.

The CORBA Security Specification is very complex and has relatively low usage in applications because almost no compliant COTS products have been developed. Implementations that do exist force the architect to accept the vendor's interpretation of the open standard, use proprietary APIs, and create complex or brittle solutions that are hard to integrate with other ORB because of security interoperability issues.

Vendors faced with the lofty goals within the standard pick a subset of features that would be adequate to claim compliance with the specification, and the final product has constraints of hardware, software, policy, cryptography, and so on. Some vendor security solutions might have some success with interoperability between objects in a heterogeneous environment by using other ORB vendors. Assumptions on policy and security management, however, might make interoperability impossible when extending the CORBA security service across vendors and other enterprise middleware platforms. These vendor differences make for a lack of interoperability between security *administration* components across vendors and across security domains managed by using different products in each domain. It is not possible to manage security policy

security administration APIs and in GUI-based management tools.

The security standard is also somewhat of a moving target. Many applications are content to go with minimal security solutions, such as running all IIOP traffic over SSL, while waiting for mature specifications and products to emerge. Interfaces with other standards are also an issue. For example, the J2EE specification requires CORBA interoperability, but the details of how this interconnectivity will happen are still being defined. Security in this context, between a proprietary standard with a reference implementation and an open standard with none, is certainly immature.

CORBA Security Levels

The *Interface Definition Language* (IDL) is the heart of CORBA, and the original CORBA security specification was geared more toward protecting interfaces rather than individual objects. CORBA security can be provided in the following three levels.

- *Secure Interoperability with no reference to or knowledge of the IDL.*
- *Security with knowledge of but no reference to the IDL.* In other words, the security solution generally uses statically defined files derived from the IDL definition that must be edited if the IDL changes. There is no code generation phase for the security solution for generating security extensions when mapping IDL definitions to object definitions. Applications are said to be security unaware. Vendor implementations most often use the *interceptor* security pattern.
- *Security with reference to the IDL.* We can use code generation tools to also generate security extensions to the object definitions generated from the IDL or to add security-related arguments to standard methods. The objects themselves can access the full security API for fine-grained access definition. Vendor implementations most often use the *wrapper* security pattern in conjunction with *interceptors*.

Secure Interoperability

Secure interoperability in CORBA can be achieved in homogenous environments when the following conditions are met:

- The ORBs share a common interoperability protocol.
- The client object and target object share and implement identical security policies.
- All entities share the same security services and mechanisms.

General Inter-ORB Operability Protocol (GIOP) traffic is the high-level CORBA messaging protocol between the object and the target. GIOP can run over the *Secure Inter-*

target to communicate securely by either using SECIOP or by using IIOP over SSL.

The Secure Inter-ORB Protocol

SECIOP enables secure communications with support from the ORB and security infrastructure. Applications can deploy generic security mechanisms underneath SECIOP. The generic mechanisms supported include Kerberos, DCE, SPKM, and CSI ECMA (please refer to the security specification at www.omg.org for details). The standard describes security enhancements to the IOR description that enable the client to extract security information from the target object reference and use it to initiate a security association. This information could include the target's identity, acceptable security policy, required policy, and cryptographic information.

SECIOP implements the *concentrator/distributor security pattern* by allowing multiple threads of execution within each of many client objects to interact with multiple threads within a target object, all over a single underlying security link layer. SECIOP handles the multiplexing and demultiplexing of GIOP traffic in a transparent manner.

Each pair of communicating entities can have its own security association. For each object-target pair, SECIOP enforces proper message sequencing at the link layer and maintains context information about the security association and the security mechanisms employed between the two entities, as shown in Figure 9.1. It also maintains association integrity by defining how the target should handle messages from the client, depending on the current association state. The standard defines a *finite state machine* (FSM) with states representing the association context between object and client. The FSM's transitions are triggered by incoming messages from the client, which provides

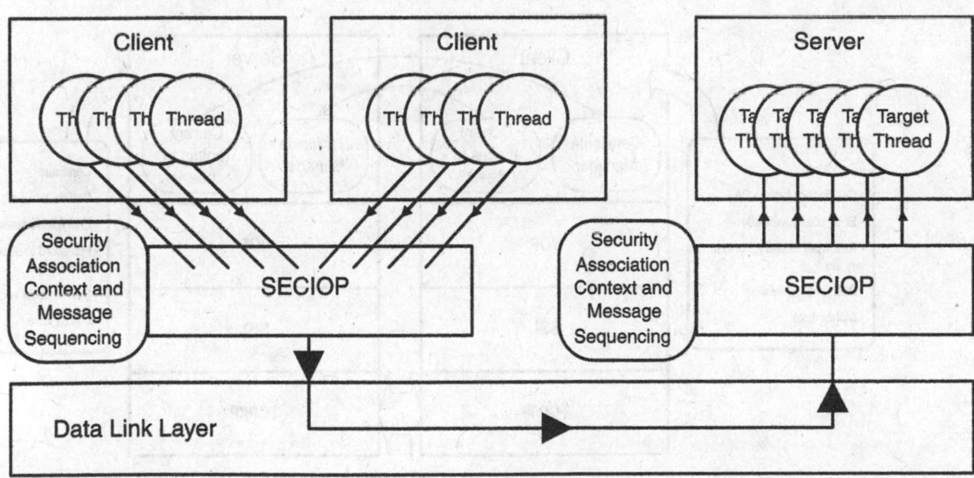

Figure 9.1 SECIOP sequence and context maintenance.

regardless of the underlying security mechanism.

Alternatively, objects and targets can communicate securely independent of SECIOP, for example, by running IIOP over SSL. Essentially, the SSL model of security has nothing to do with the encapsulated protocol (in this case, IIOP). We will discuss this option in more detail in the following section.

Secure Communications through SSL

CORBA vendors have adopted SSL as a cost-effective and easily deployed alternative to fully supporting the OMG's complex and high-level standard for CORBA Security. Running IIOP over SSL provides basic communications security. The SSL protocol performs none of the security association, sequencing, and context management available under SECIOP. It implements the *transport tunnel* paradigm at the application level. To perform this task, developers need several components, including PKI support, certificates, SSL libraries, configuration files, and some code modification.

SSL-Enabling IIOP Connections

SSL adds a layer of secure communication between the application layer protocol IIOP and TCP/IP. SSL, which we discussed in Chapter 8, "Secure Communications," and show in Figure 9.2, provides basic security between two endpoints through authentication through a public key cryptographic algorithm such as RSA, confidentiality through data encryption with a private key algorithm such as RC4, and data integrity through a cryptographic hash function such as SHA1.

All vendors follow a similar pattern for SSL implementations. The developer must perform the following actions:

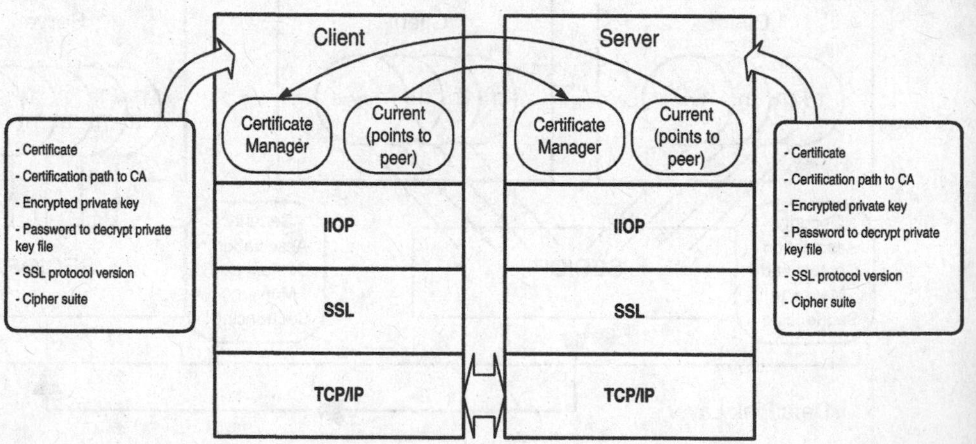

Figure 9.2 IIOP over SSL.

- Decide whether authentication will be server-side only or mutual.
- Modify the build environment to include SSL and cryptographic libraries.
- Create PKI elements and set configuration files to point to the list of certificate authorities, certification path information, the client or server certificate, permitted cipher suites, the private key file associated with the process's certificate, and an embedded password string to unlock the private key file.
- Provision these elements on each host.
- Add initialization code in the beginning of the CORBA server code to reference a *context holder* called the SSL::CertificateManager object to access the server's certificate, certification path, and private key and a *session object*, called SSL::Current object, to access the certification chain and certificate of the client entity once the SSL session is established.
- Repeat these steps on the client if mutual authentication is desired.

At run time, the server initializes the ORB and then uses the ORB::resolve_initial_references() to obtain the SSL::CertificateManager object for its own identity and the SSL::Current object for the client's identity. The Current object also holds SSL protocol version and cipher suite information.

Why Is SSL Popular?

Why is SSL such a popular security solution? Vendors provide SSL because good implementations of the protocol exist, open source or otherwise, that enable any client/server application using TCP/IP to communicate securely. It is easy to SSL-enable applications. There are few code changes.

- Some configuration options to the run-time environment must be set describing PKI components.
- Some initialization code that points to the correct certificate, private key file, and certificate path must be added.
- Some cleanup code to close file connections or write to audit logs must be inserted after the connection closes.

The popularity of SSL-enabling CORBA applications comes from the enormous success of SSL-enabled Web traffic.

SSL can have performance problems. Poor cryptographic libraries, slow server processors, expensive bulk encryption, or excessive handshakes can cause SSL-enabled connections to run at a fraction of nonsecure IIOP connection speeds. SSL-enabled connections can be anywhere from 50 percent to 5 times as slow as nonsecure connections. Some implementations show good performance under SSL-enabled mode, although this function is vendor and application dependent. Hardware accelerators, created for Web servers that improve SSL connect speeds 20 fold or more, are also available. If CORBA applications can use them on the server side where the performance hit is most noticeable, SSL will become even more attractive. SSL solutions often provide poor support for security management. Vendors provide no explicit guidance on security policy and the use and management of certificates in a CORBA environment.

Raise these application issues (which we reiterate from our earlier discussion of SSL in Chapter 8, but now in the context of middleware) at the architecture review:

- Can all daemons be secured? Do some daemons have to accept insecure connections for interacting with legacy applications?
- Does the architecture create SSL links for local intra-host traffic? If the client and server are colocated, this process is a waste of resources unless the host itself has other local vulnerabilities that must be protected against.
- How does the application manage PKI issues? SSL-enabling an application transfers a significant portion of security management responsibility to the PKI supporting the application. Is certificate policy well defined? How are keys managed? How is revocation handled? How are servers informed of whether their certificates are about to expire? What if the PKI service itself changes? How does the application plan on handling trust during the changing of the guard?
- Which connections in the architecture need SSL-enabling? Do SSL connections need proxies to penetrate firewalls?
- Is performance an issue? Is the SSL-enabled architecture scalable to projected client volumes? Are there issues of interoperability with other vendor IIOP-over-SSL solutions? Do all applications share the same cipher suite? What does security policy mandate?
- What entities get certificates? Is assignment at the level of an object, process, or host? Do we distinguish between user processes and a daemon process on the host and assign separate certificates? Do we lump multiple objects on a host together to share a certificate?
- How do we handle the passwords that protect the object's private key? Are these embedded in binaries? Do we build the passwords into the binaries during development (possibly exposing the private key), or do we maintain separate certificate instances for separate system instances, one for each of the development, integration, system test, and production environments?

With good security architecture, running IIOP over SSL provides a low-cost means for applications to get point-to-point security by using a well-understood protocol, interoperability, and minimal application code modification.

Application-Unaware Security

CORBA Security Level 1 provides security services to applications that are security unaware or that have limited requirements for access control and auditing. Level 1 security mechanisms require configuration of the ORB and require no code modification.

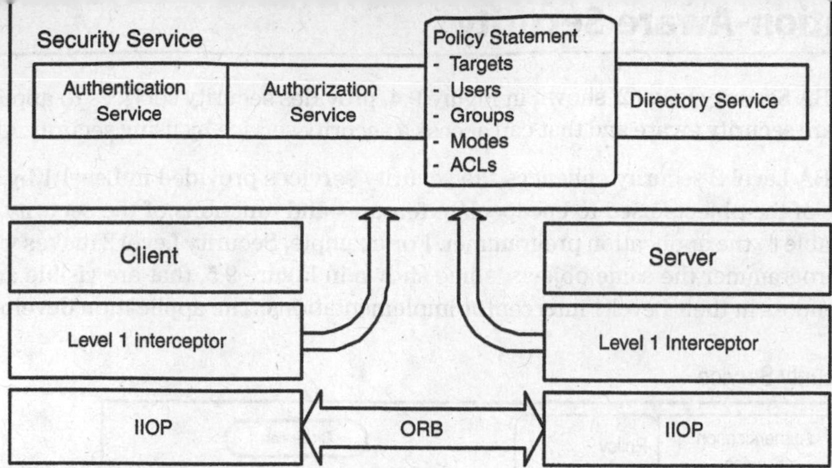

Figure 9.3 CORBA Security Level 1.

Level 1 security, shown in Figure 9.3, in almost all vendor products is implemented by using CORBA interceptors. Interceptors are the standard method to add run-time services to ORBs and allow the core ORB functionality to remain untouched. Several interceptors can be chained together at the client or at the server, and the application must specify the order of interceptors on the chain. Each interceptor on the client is paired with a corresponding interceptor on the server. Interceptors function as communications traps, capturing all requests and messages for service. Interceptors do add a performance hit to the communication that must be weighed in the architecture.

CORBA Level 1 security is designed to provide security services that can be used by an application without significantly changing the application. The CORBA ORBs require no code changes and require only the run-time loading of security services. This ease of implementation comes with some limitations, however.

- Users cannot choose privileges; rather, they are fixed at application startup. Access control lists can be referenced but not modified unless the application is stopped and restarted.
- The application normally authenticates the user outside the object model and stores identity credentials at ORB initialization that are accessible to a PrincipalAuthenticator inside a client-side interceptor. This situation could imply that all entities within a single process will potentially share the same privilege level for access control unless the application reauthenticates as another user.
- Level 1 does not allow objects to enforce their own security policies. In general, all policy is fixed at compile time and all objects within a process are constrained to the same authorization policy.
- The vendor implementation can apply security policy only when communicating with remote objects, unless interprocess invocations on the local host are forced through the interceptor to be secured.

Application-Aware Security

CORBA Security Level 2, shown in Figure 9.4, provides security services to applications that are security aware and that can access a security service by using security API calls.

CORBA Level 2 security enhances the security services provided in Level 1 by making some of the objects used to encapsulate features and functions of the security service available to the application programmer. For example, Security Level 2 makes visible to the programmer the same objects, some shown in Figure 9.5, that are visible and used by vendors in their Level 1 interceptor implementations. The application developer can

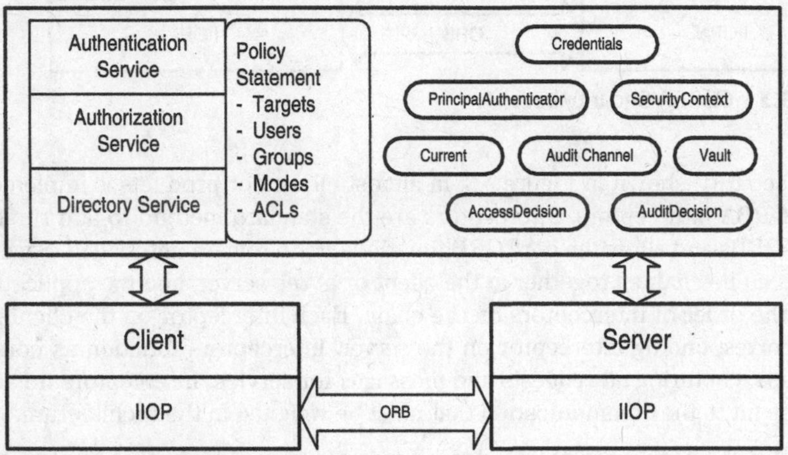

Figure 9.4 CORBA Security Level 2.

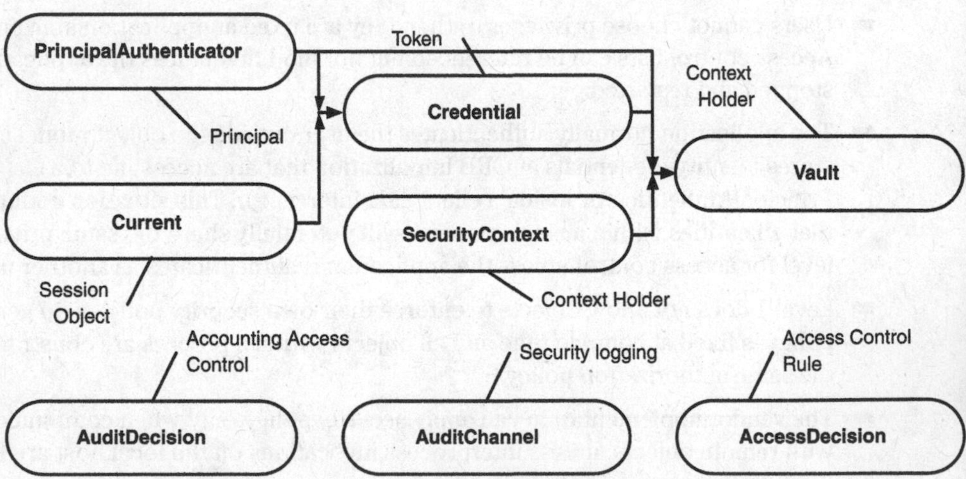

Figure 9.5 Some security objects visible under Level 2.

use these security objects for authentication, authorization, and delegation purposes from within application objects.

The security objects enable application objects to query policy, negotiate cryptographic algorithms, make access decisions, change privileges during execution, enforce their own policy, and provide additional authorization options. They include the following components:

PrincipalAuthenticator. This object is used to create credentials for a given principal. If the application authenticates the user outside the object model (perhaps by using a UNIX login ID, authentication to a DCE cell, or a certificate validation check), the application must transfer credentials to the PrincipalAuthenticator, normally at ORB initialization. Alternatively, the application can invoke PrincipalAuthenticator's authenticate method to confirm the user's identity within the object model.

Credential. Once a user is authenticated, the PrincipalAuthenticator object can generate credentials upon request. These credentials can be transported with service requests or can be bundled with other credentials to create composite delegation credentials. Credentials are tokens that confirm authentication and provide some additional attributes.

Current. The Security namespace has its own Current object. The Current object maintains the execution context at both the client and the server objects and is a container for credentials.

SecurityContext. For each security association, there exist SecurityContext objects at the client and server. The SecurityContext object maintains additional security information such as credentials, session keys, policy in effect, cipher suites used within the association, and the peer's security name. Any entity can have multiple SecurityContext objects, one for each association that is active within the object.

Vault. The Vault is an implementation security object that creates SecurityContext objects on a secure invocation. The Vault uses all credentials, attributes, association information, and arguments from a secure invocation. Vaults can be used for simplifying object references in the implementation.

AccessDecision. An AccessDecision object is used to implement access control. The access_allowed method on a target AccessDecision object causes the object to look up security policy to check whether the policy explicitly allows the operation or if the client has privileges through group or role membership. Please refer to the access control section in Chapter 3 for details of role-based access management.

AuditDecision. The application can use this object to reference a security audit policy to look up the response required on any security event. Some events will be ignored, others will be logged as warnings, and still others will be logged as causing alarms or alerts. The AuditDecision object wraps the accountability functionality of the security services.

AuditChannel. Each AuditDecision object owns a local channel to record events.

Using Level 2 features, applications can use enhanced security on every object invocation or gain fine-grained access to security options, manage the delegation of credentials,

ORB level. Security Level 2 has many more features to enable complex security management across multiple security domains, where the clients operating in each domain might not have a trust relationship between each other.

Application Implications

Although asynchronous messaging and synchronous messaging (using IDL-defined object interfaces) are very different paradigms, we can still draw parallels across the two domains when we discuss security. Many of the security mechanisms documented in the object-oriented CORBA Security Specification also apply to other messaging middleware products, such as products that implement message queues. The requirements for authentication, access control, auditing, confidentiality, and so on are met by using the same underlying security protocols, and solutions encounter many of the same security issues.

Other generic security implications include the following:

Centrality in the architecture. The complexity of the security solution, and the care and feeding that it demands, might have the effect of pulling the security service toward the center of the architecture. This situation might not be acceptable if a future application feature request is denied because it clashes with the security service.

Management of security policy. Managing, configuring, and validating security policy across a heterogeneous, distributed application is very complex. Additional complexities include managing user population changes, IDL evolution, event audit trail merging and analysis, and middleware version management.

Scope creep within security. Once the enterprise has invested a considerable amount in deploying a security service for objects, vendors and managers will attempt to extend the solution to other resources by mapping files, appliances, application object methods, databases, URLs, IP addresses and ports, and many more. This assumption of scope limits might not be desirable to the original application as it increases the burden on the security service.

IDL-centric security. The name space of objects that are protected is derived from the application's IDL. This assumption is reasonable, because clients may only invoke operations on this interface. If only interface objects and operations can be defined and protected, however, what about implementation objects? What about possibly complex internal application structure that could potentially represent a vulnerability? What if the application has non-CORBA interfaces that provide access to internal objects? Will the alternate security mechanisms on these non-CORBA interfaces compromise the security architecture?

Security through obscurity. Much of the internal details of the specification are left to the vendor. Interface definition is about delegating responsibility to another entity so that the details of service requests can be hidden. In complex architectures with many systems, several ORBs, and conflicting security policy, the team can

hidden might represent considerable risks.

Conclusion

Middleware technology has evolved from the interoperability needs of systems built by using components based on any of the rapidly growing number of platforms, software technologies, standards, and products that are available. Middleware enables applications to communicate with one another in a manner independent of location, implementation details, hardware, software, or design methodology. This lofty goal is achieved through some form of man-in-the-middle technology; for instance, by using ORBs to manage communication in CORBA. We believe that many of the lessons learned from studying security options in CORBA apply to other proprietary middleware solutions.

A review of the CORBA security specification will reveal many patterns.

- *Principal.* The PrincipalAuthenticator object
- *Session Object.* The CertificateManager and Current objects
- *Interceptor.* Level 1 implementation by some vendors
- *Wrapper.* Level 2 implementation by some vendors
- *Proxy.* IIOP proxies for managing CORBA traffic through a firewall
- *Validator.* The AccessDecision object
- *Transport Tunnel.* Running IIOP over SSL
- *Access Control Rule.* Within the AccessDecision specification
- *Directory.* Directory enabled CORBA Security service from some vendors
- *Trusted Third Party.* Public-Key Infrastructure components
- *Layer.* GIOP over SECIOP over TCP/IP, or GIOP over IIOP over TCP/IP, and so on
- *Sandbox.* Common enterprise-wide secure CORBA software bus

This list is impressive. CORBA is not all middleware, however, and CORBA security issues do not correspond one-to-one with all middleware security issues. CORBA is an open standard with many success stories and with a complex but rich story on how to secure applications.

In the next chapter, we will discuss another common aspect of security architecture: Web security.

10

Web Security

The World Wide Web has evolved from a system created by physicists in the late 1980s to exchange research over the Internet into a global phenomenon enabling anyone who has access to almost any form of computing device and network connectivity to receive information and services on demand. The original aim of the Web was to provide fast, anonymous access in the clear to arbitrary services over the Internet. The early Web had no notion of security.

As our dependence upon Web services increases along with a corresponding increase in the value that we attach to the information involved, we can no longer place our trust in good conduct. The past decade of Web evolution has shown us all that security is a critical architectural goal for any Web application. As our applications grow more complex, other secondary security goals that relate to security come sharply into focus. The goals of ensuring user privacy, of preventing traffic analysis, of maintaining data quality in our Web databases, and of preventing inference by using data mining and cross-referencing strategies are as critical as the basic steps of authenticating users and controlling access to Web-enabled functions.

Web browsers do much more today than text and image presentation. Browsers support and display multimedia formats such as audio and video; run active content such as Java, ActiveX, and scripting languages; use style sheets to separate presentation rules from content management; and support metadata features such as XML. Browsers can also hand content to custom browser plug-ins to handle presentation. A huge number of browser plug-ins and helper applications enable users to manipulate proteins, view virtual reality architectural displays, do computer-aided design, manage portfolios, play games, and much more. Browsers are also universally available. Browsers run on every user device imaginable including personal computers, PDAs, cell phones, and an increasing number of Web-based appliances.

Web servers have evolved, as well. [illegible] porting the delivery of all manners of multimedia content. Web servers can invoke programs, dynamically generate content, interact with third-party service providers, hand requests off to other processes, or load custom server plug-ins. Popular Web server extensions have repetitive designs, and therefore every commercial Web server supports generic definitions of loadable modules that use the request/response pattern to extend server capabilities. These extensions appear as standard components in Web application architectures. Servers can support dynamic content by using Active Server Pages or Java Server Pages or can be extended with server-side plug-ins or dynamically loaded modules. Many vendors ship hardware with a preinstalled Web application for systems administration. Web servers are also the management user interface of choice for many network appliances such as routers, switches, network link encryption units, and many other software products.

We have seen tremendous technology growth on the communications link between browser and server, as well. Communications networks have grown in capacity, quality, and variety. The small communities of technology-savvy users on slow connections of the early Internet have been replaced by a global community of several hundred million users connected by faster dialup modems, cable modems, DSL lines, or LAN and T1 links to huge fiber-optic Internet backbones. Future increases in bandwidth promise even more improved Web services and application features.

Web technology is a popular choice for the presentation layer of systems development. A Web browser provides a single powerful, universally available, and extensible interface to all of our applications. We know how to use an unfamiliar Web site immediately; we know how basic Web interactions work; we are trained by sites to recognize user interface elements such as frames, buttons, dynamic menus, tabs, tables, image maps, or pop-ups; we have grown patient as we wait for content to download; and we have grown impatient with poor security architectures that block legitimate access.

Securing a communications medium as rich, varied, and complex as the Web is a very hard problem indeed. There are many technologies involved, connecting very different user communities with each other with no agreement on how security should work. Each feature and extension in the client or the server raises new security issues.

The Internet is an excellent and up-to-date source of references in an ever-changing Web security landscape. Our presentation in this chapter is an overview of Web security from an architecture viewpoint only, and a detailed treatment of all security architectural options is beyond our scope. Fortunately, there are many excellent resources to help architects and Web administrators understand the risks of using Web technology for application presentation.

In this chapter, we will present common security-related issues around three-tiered, Web-based application architectures. There are many, many vendor solutions for creating Web applications that conform to the presentation, application, and data layer definition of the standard three-tier architecture model. A discussion of how security works in each circumstance would clearly be impossible, and we refer the reader to the vendor's own documentation on how to configure and secure their product.

Web applications share some common ground for solving our security architecture principles, including authentication, authorization, confidentiality, integrity, and auditing. We will discuss client, server, and server-extension security. For the last topic, we will describe security extensions to server-side java defined in the *Java 2 Enterprise Edition* (J2EE) standard. J2EE Security has some interesting parallels to the CORBA Security Specification of Chapter 9, "Middleware Security."

Web Security Issues

Security for a Web application must be built with more structure than security for a Web server alone. A Web-based application links a user on a client host through a Web browser to a Web server and then (possibly through server extensions) to entities that capture business logic or wrap persistent information stored in backend databases. This chain is normally referred to as the three-tier architecture. Each of the components of the chain could possibly consist of several different hardware platforms linked by using different communications paradigms.

Vendors that present solutions for securing one component of a Web-based application tend to make extreme assumptions about trusting other components of the Web application as follows:

- At one extreme they might assume no trust whatsoever and accept full responsibility for all authentication, authorization, and access control.
- At the other extreme, they might assume some high level of transitive trust between components that might be inappropriate unless adequately articulated in the application architecture and validated in the review.

For example, in the first case, a Web application might require a user to authenticate to the Web server even after he or she has already authenticated to the client host on a secure LAN by using some reasonable, strong scheme. The architect might have chosen not to simplify the architecture (perhaps by allowing the user to single sign-on to the Web server by presenting NTLM, Kerberos, or other session credentials) because he or she does not trust the strength of the client host authentication. This situation could be the case if the user is dialing in from a remote location from a laptop. The application owner and users might agree to require reauthentication as a reasonable compromise.

At the other extreme, a solution extending the abilities of a Web server by using Java-based extensions (such as Java servlets) can use global and local property files on the Web server. These Web application property files define user identities and user passwords, group and role definitions, and access control rules linking roles to privileges. Privileges could include access to servlet invocations, method invocations, or the database. The architect might decide that the backend services must place their trust in the security of the Web server host. The systems administrator for the host must correctly define permissions for operating system users, groups, and files to prevent access to this property file. The administrator must also prevent other security holes from providing access to these files. This confidence in the Web server's security might be misplaced as the architecture evolves. Running unnecessary services ("Why not add

apply that security patch to our IIS server that stopped the buffer overflow bug that allows arbitrary file downloads?") can break the trust model. If anonymous FTP is misconfigured or if the Web server is compromised, the property file could be overwritten. Hackers could download the property file and run password crackers offline to gain access to the backend server.

Trust boundaries have to be well defined in the three-tier chain of information flow. Every time a user crosses a boundary, he or she must first authenticate to the server across the boundary. Within the confines of a boundary, all architecture elements should be protected in a uniform manner. Access granularity is equally important. It would make little sense to finely separate user communities into roles at the Web server only to allow all the roles equivalent access to the backend database.

Questions for the Review of Web Security

The security issues for Web applications are normally constrained to the following scenarios:

Protecting the client. How do we protect a client host with Internet access from hackers that could exploit bugs in the browser or any browser plug-ins? What do we expose to a legitimate server? Can servers infer anything about us that we wish to keep private? Can servers extract information about other sites visited or extract e-mail or address information previously presented to other sites? What are the risks of running active content from other sources? What levels of access does the browser permit to the underlying operating system?

Protecting the connection. How should we protect the communications channel between browser and server? Can attackers intercept, delete, modify, or add information to a valid communication? Can the session be hijacked? Even if the connection is secure, can the endpoints of communication be exploited before requests or responses are delivered?

Preventing denial of service. Can we prevent attackers from completely disrupting communication between our application and all legitimate users? If unavoidable, can this situation be mitigated in some manner?

Protecting the server. How do we protect the Web server from unauthorized access? How do we restrict authorized access? Can confidential data be stolen from the server? Does the server host other services that could compromise Web security? What vulnerabilities can a vendor's Web server extensions present to the world? What are the risks of uploading content or processing requests for services from clients? What levels of access does the server permit to the underlying operating system?

Protecting the services hidden behind the Web server. What do application servers in the middle tier reveal? Can Web server connections to enterprise middleware architectures such as Java servlets, CORBA services, EJB, or dynamically generated HTML be protected from abuse? How do we prevent Web application servers that wrap the underlying business logic and data from leaking information? Can we prevent users from promoting their own privileges? How can we protect our databases from unauthorized access? Can the application server to database connection be hijacked? If we provide ad hoc connectivity to the database interface, can a user provide arbitrary inputs that will be handed to the database as SQL statements?

Security management. Have we defined the operations, administration, and maintenance of our Web application adequately? How do we manage the user community for our application? How do we perform environment management as our hardware changes, when our browsers and servers get upgraded, when our vendor software changes, or as critical security patches are applied?

Asking and answering these questions at the architecture review is critical. We will discuss the architectural context for discussing these security issues in the following sections.

Web Application Architecture

The basic design goal of a Web server is to provide anonymous clients from any location fast access to information. This design goal is in conflict with many security principles. Web applications must authenticate users, prevent unauthorized access, and enforce minimum privilege levels to users who are accessing protected data.

In Figure 10.1, we present Web application complexities compounded by the many features that have evolved within Web browsers and Web servers from the early days of simple text and image presentation.

Browsers can use the basic HTTP request and response protocol or can download active content such as applets or ActiveX controls that can use arbitrary protocols to the original host or to other servers. HTML pages can be enhanced with scripting languages, which are often a source of security vulnerabilities. Browsers can be enhanced with plug-ins for audio, video, animation, or image manipulation. Browsers can also

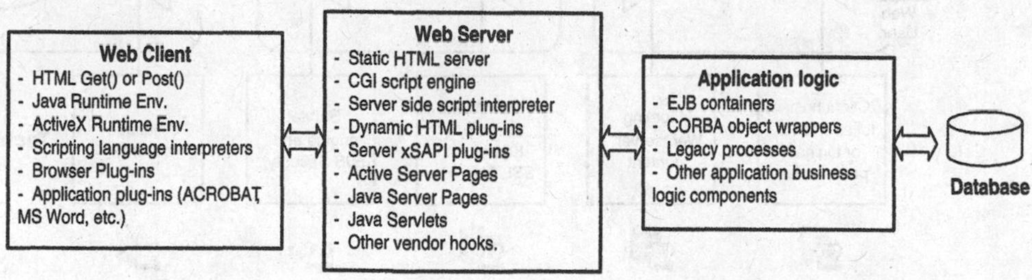

Figure 10.1 Web application complexities.

mats and display the results by using helper applications on the client host.

Web servers now do much more than return static HTML pages. Servers can perform the following tasks:

- Serve dynamic content to the client by using Java, ActiveX, or other active agent plug-ins.
- Embed scripting directives by using JavaScript, Jscript, or ECMAScript (among others).
- Run CGI programs.
- Use proprietary vendor plug-ins.
- Use server-side includes that mix scripting language content with static HTML and generate pages on the fly.
- Support complex extensions by using Server APIs and enterprise server-side infrastructure components that implement business functions and wrap data.

Web Application Security Options

Security for a three-tier Web application can be quite complex. In Figure 10.2, we show a typical Web application as a composition of four abstract layers that span the extent from the user to the backend data store. Although the host platforms, connectivity

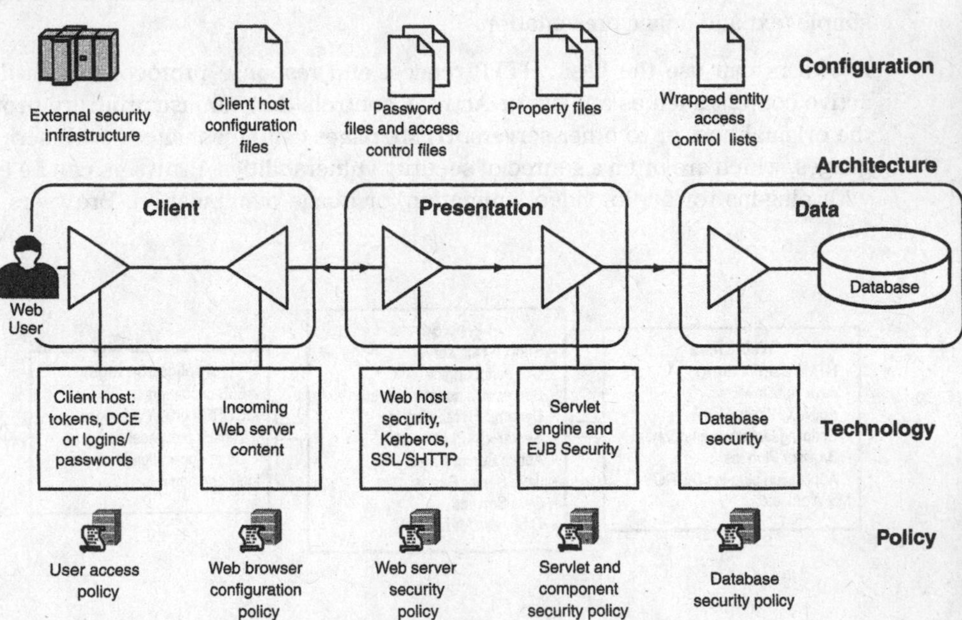

Figure 10.2 Web security structural options.

options, technologies used, and architecture choices change along this path, we can still see elements of each of these four layers at each point.

Policy. The directives of corporate security policy applicable to each of the components along the path from user to data store.

Technology. The technology-specific security options available to secure each component.

Architecture. The integrated solution that describes session management and the details of how requests are accepted, authenticated, authorized, verified, and processed as data flows from component to component.

Configuration. The component-specific security configuration information that must be either statically loaded at component initialization or that can be dynamically referenced and modified during execution. Security administrators manage the configuration components.

Security architecture solutions often consist of a familiar pattern of a series of chained *interceptors* that end in an entity *wrapper*. Session state in a Web application has somewhat inverted semantics. Over the course of a single transaction, the user session might consist of several connections tunneled within one another from the browser to the database.

- The browser and the Web server communicate by using HTTP, which is a sessionless protocol. Multiple user requests are treated as separate and unconnected connections.
- The Web Server can use cookies to create a higher-level session state, where multiple connections sharing a valid cookie (generated through authentication on the first request) are considered part of a single session. Server-side extensions such as servlets also maintain session objects that can save server-side state across multiple cookie-authenticated sessions (for example, to implement a simple shopping cart application that maintains a shopping list over a few days, or a file download application that records progress in case of interrupted connections). Alternatively, the Web server might require SSL, a protocol that explicitly maintains session state across multiple connections.
- A backend enterprise entity within the application server (EJBs, for example) can maintain even higher logical sessions because of data persistence available to the entity through the database. An application session could span multiple SSL sessions.

Each subordinate session captures a subset of the total communications so far, terminated at some intermediate point of the chain. This inverted session model could result in session stealing by a malicious entity. A hacker could use the expected communication interruption points as placeholders for hijacking the session. The hacker could steal valid cookies, illegally extend the life of a session object in a servlet container through some back door on the application server host, or place fake credentials in the database that permit later access.

Web applications tend to use transitive trust of upstream systems extensively. Some vendors define *chained delegation credentials* to mitigate this trust. These credentials

from component to component along the chain. The credentials often use some cryptographic protocol to ensure that they cannot be spoofed or tampered with. For example, Privilege Access Certificates (PACs) implement the token pattern to carry delegated rights.

Web security solutions also contain critical dependencies on external infrastructure components such as DNS, mail, PKI services, OCSP lookup servers, LDAP directories, token authentication servers, databases, and the like. These third-party service providers must be validated for availability, security, scalability, and performance as well.

Securing Web Clients

In Figure 10.3, we have extracted and blown up the Web client portion of the Web application.

Active Content

Browsers support the execution of content within the context of a virtual machine. For example, Java applets run within the JVM, ActiveX controls run inside the ActiveX engine, and Macromedia Flash files are displayed by using the Flash plug-in. Please refer to Chapter 7, "Trusted Code," to read a discussion of the architectural issues sur-

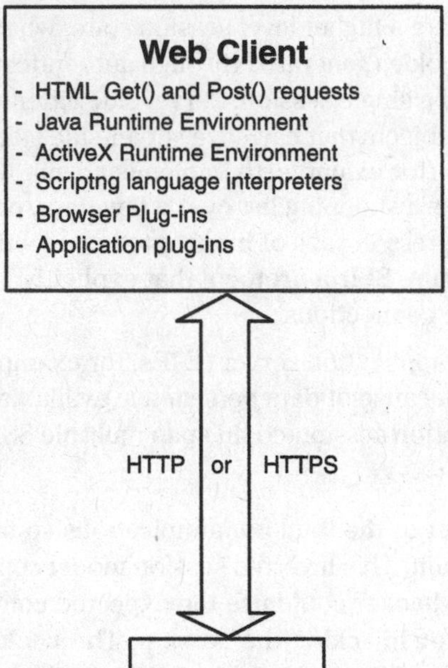

Figure 10.3 Browser security.

involved.

Scripting Languages

Client-side scripting languages such as Netscape's JavaScript, Microsoft's Jscript, and the common standards-based composition ECMAScript all enable a programmer to add scripting directives to HTML pages that will be executed by the browser.

JavaScript implementations have been plagued by a host of security bugs that have resulted in serious invasions of the user's privacy. The flaws discovered and patched so far, rather than modifying the user's machine, enable hackers to read files, intercept e-mail, view browser preferences, and upload content to the Web server without the user's knowledge. .

Turning off JavaScript is not always an option because of its popular use for data validation, creation of presentation effects, and Web site customization. Many Web applications depend heavily on tools such as JavaScript and break if client-side scripting is turned off.

Browser Plug-Ins and Helper Applications

Browsers can hand off responses to helper applications that in turn can present their own security holes. A browser can launch Adobe Acrobat or Microsoft Word to automatically display content defined as being of the correct MIME format (PDF or DOC, in this case). A Word document could contain a Word macro virus that could infect the client host. Other plug-ins run with full user application privileges and could contain similar security issues if they use system resources indiscriminately to spawn processes, access devices, write or read files on the hard drive, or secretly steal user information and return it to a listener host.

Browser Configuration

We extensively discussed the browser configuration options for Internet Explorer in Chapter 7 and touched on some of the options available under Netscape. We expand on Netscape's security configuration dialog in this section.

Netscape's browser security settings are managed through the security console. This console presents and manages all underlying security information including passwords, Java controls, JavaScript controls, certificates, and options for mail or news. The security console also presents the cryptographic modules recognized by the browser and enables the user to edit the cipher suite used for SSL.

Netscape can display security information for the page currently being viewed, check to determine whether it is encrypted, or verify the identity of the host it originated from (in case a hacker is spoofing a familiar site).

other people, certificates from trusted Web sites, certificates from CAs of trusted Web sites, and certificates from trusted content signers. Netscape can also reference a corporate LDAP Directory for certificate uploads and downloads. Netscape enables users to encrypt their private key by using a password before saving the private key file to the hard drive.

Several vendors have Smartcard-based security solutions integrated with Web browsers that store user certificates on a removable Smartcard. This solution has not seen wide spread acceptance yet because of the complexity of managing a Smartcard infrastructure and the additional cost of installing readers on workstations. This situation might change, however, as credit cards with Smartcard features become more common, along with card readers integrated into keyboards or other hardware slots. One vendor even offers a Smartcard reader that looks like a floppy disk and uses the standard floppy drive.

Connection Security

Web servers can be configured to accept requests only from specific IP addresses, subnets, or domains. While this option is not completely secure because of IP and DNS spoofing, it can be effective when used in conjunction with other security components. Users within corporate intranets are well-protected from the open Internet by firewalls, and remote users can use VPN technology in conjunction with strong authentication to create tunnels to a secure gateway to access the corporate intranet. The external firewall can be configured to block incoming packets pretending to originate from the internal network. In addition, the secure gateway can assign remote users to a restricted subnet behind a router to the general corporate intranet. This router blocks incoming packets with spoofed source IP addresses. Thus, a Web server can use subnet address-based access rules as a coarse-grained access control mechanism to differentiate between internal users in physically secure locations from remote users who might be less trusted. The application can restrict highly critical features, such as security administration, from remote users.

Trusting IP addresses will not work if the Web server is behind a firewall that hosts a Web proxy. In this case, the only IP visible to the Web server will be the address of the firewall. Network Address Translation also hides source IP addresses from the destination domain, preventing the use of IP addresses for authentication.

Web Server Placement

Web server placement, either inside or outside the corporate network relative to corporate firewalls, is critical to the security architecture. Web servers are often configured by using a firewall with multiple interfaces to create a *de-militarized zone* (DMZ) outside the corporate intranet but protected from direct Internet access (Figure 10.4). All incoming traffic to the Web server is constrained by the firewall to conform to HTTP or HTTPS access to the Web server. The Web server can reach the corporate Internet and application databases by using a few restricted protocols. But even if the Web server is

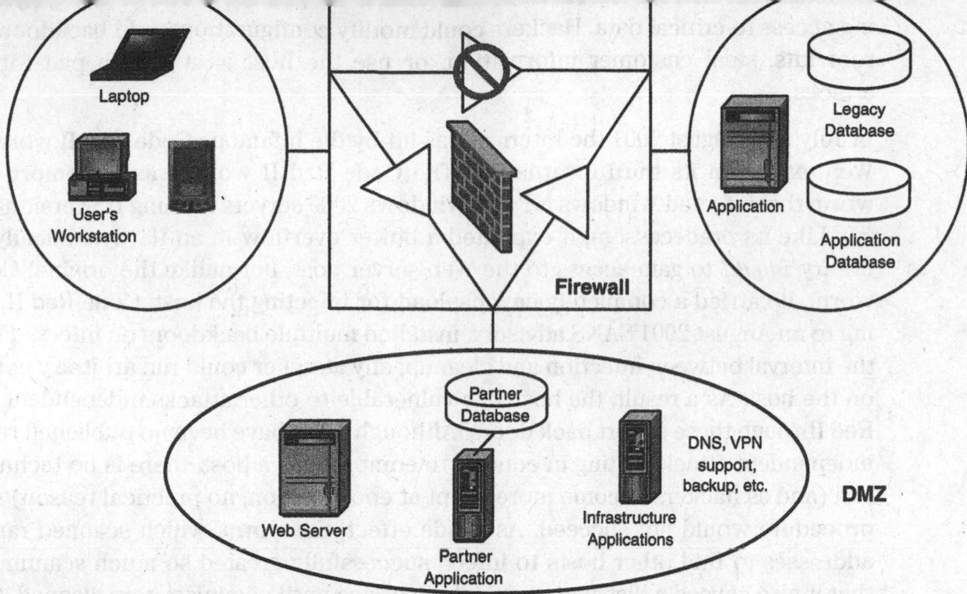

Figure 10.4 DMZ Web server configuration.

compromised, the firewall automatically prevents many attacks that use other protocols from reaching the intranet.

Web applications require high availability. Commercial Web hosting companies offer many critical services, including collocation, power management, physical security, reliability, and geographic failover. They also offer installation of the application on a Web farm consisting of many servers behind a locator. The locator directs traffic for load-balancing purposes by using the *distributor* pattern.

Web servers have been the targets of distributed denial of services, which flood the listening server with forged ICMP, UDP, or TCP packets—creating thousands of partially open connections to overflow TCP/IP buffers and queues. Strategies for defending against a DDOS attack are difficult to implement. They require coordination with the service providers of the slave hosts generating traffic, network backbone providers, Internet data centers, customers, and law enforcement. We refer the reader to the CERT Web site, www.cert.org, as a good source for current information about DDOS attacks.

Securing Web Server Hosts

The most common sources of Web server vulnerabilities are as follows:

- Host server misconfiguration
- Tardy application of patches to known security holes

ing access to critical data. Hackers could modify configurations, add backdoors, install root kits, steal customer information, or use the host as a launch pad for further attacks.

In July and August 2001 the Internet was hit by the infamous Code Red II worm, an IIS Web exploit in its third incarnation. The Code Red II worm was a memory-resident worm that infected Windows NT and Windows 2000 servers running IIS versions 4.0 and 5.0. Like its predecessors, it exploited a buffer overflow in an IIS dynamically loaded library *idq.dll* to gain access to the Web server host, but unlike the original Code Red worm, it carried a completely new payload for infecting the host. Code Red II, according to an August 2001 SANS advisory, installed multiple backdoors on infected hosts. In the interval between infection and cleanup, any attacker could run arbitrary commands on the host. As a result, the host was vulnerable to other attacks independent of Code Red through these covert back doors. Although there have been no published reports of independent attacks acting in concert to compromise a host, there is no technical reason (and as hackers become more adept at coordination, no practical reason) why this procedure would not succeed. As a side effect, the worm, which scanned random IP addresses to find other hosts to infect, successfully created so much scanning traffic that it also caused a distributed denial-of-service until administrators cleaned it up.

This single exploit contained a buffer overflow attack, exploited Web server insecurities, installed back doors, and launched a DDOS attack. And, according to all reports, it could have been much worse.

Although many sources recommend using stripped-down versions of Web services on a rarely attacked platform like Macintosh, this choice is not always feasible. Systems architects are constrained by the application's need for performance, multithreading, familiar administrative interfaces, multiprocessing power, programming tools, and services—not to mention homogeneity with existing platforms. This situation forces us to use UNIX flavors (such as Solaris, HPUX, and Linux) or Windows (NT, W2K, or XP) as host operating systems. In turn, vendors want maximum customer coverage for their products, which are normally ported to run on Solaris, Linux, HP, NT, and W2K first. The same vendor products are often not ported to custom Web service platforms because they use unusual and non-portable extensions or do not support interfaces with such hardware. We need to use general-purpose hardware and operating systems for our Web servers, because we might not have a choice.

Using a powerful and complex multipurpose OS has its risks, where every additional feature is a potential source of vulnerability. Secure host configuration is absolutely necessary.

Measures to secure Web hosts include the following:

- Remove unnecessary development tools. If the application has no use for a C compiler or Perl interpreter in production, the Web server should not host these programs. Production machines as a rule should never need to build software.
- Minimize services. Running anonymous and trivial FTP, mail, news, IRC, gopher, finger, instant messaging services, and so on adds to the complexity and options

them on a different machine to isolate any negative impact.

- Protect the services that the Web host depends upon, such as DNS and mail.
- Apply security patches promptly. Write a sanity script that checks the current version of all applied patches on all software and tools whose output can be easily matched against vendor recommendations.
- Run an integrity verification tool, such as Tripwire or Veracity.
- Run a security audit tool such as Internet Security Scanner. Scanners check password strength, password aging rules, file and application permissions, user and group ownership rules, cron jobs, service configuration, logging, network configuration, user home directories, SUID programs, and many more features of host configuration.
- If possible, write audit logs off to a protected host and use a write once, no delete policy for all access from the Web server. If the logs must be local, keep them on a separate file system and try to prevent log floods by using filtering rules. Clean up and check logs regularly.
- Minimize local user access and restrict permitted non-root or administrative users from the Web server, its document tree, scripts, or extensions.

It is also important to use file system permissions correctly to protect the Web server from local and remote users who might have alternative access to the host. Some documents and scripts could be readable to all users accessing the Web server. Other parts of the document tree might enforce authentication requirements. Administrators of the document tree need more access than authors of new content, who also must be protected from one another. Some experts recommend running the Web server on a protected subtree of the system (for example, by using *chroot* on UNIX systems).

Please see vendor-specific configuration details for your server, along with general good configuration advice from Web security sources such as Lincoln Stein's excellent WWW Security FAQ (www.w3.org/Security/Faq/), [GS97], or [RGR97]for more details.

Securing the Web Server

In Figure 10.5, we have extracted and blown up the Web server portion of the Web application.

Authentication Options

Web servers support several authentication methods, including the following:

- Basic server authentication, where an "HTTP 401 User unauthenticated" error causes the browser to pop up a standard username and password dialog, which the

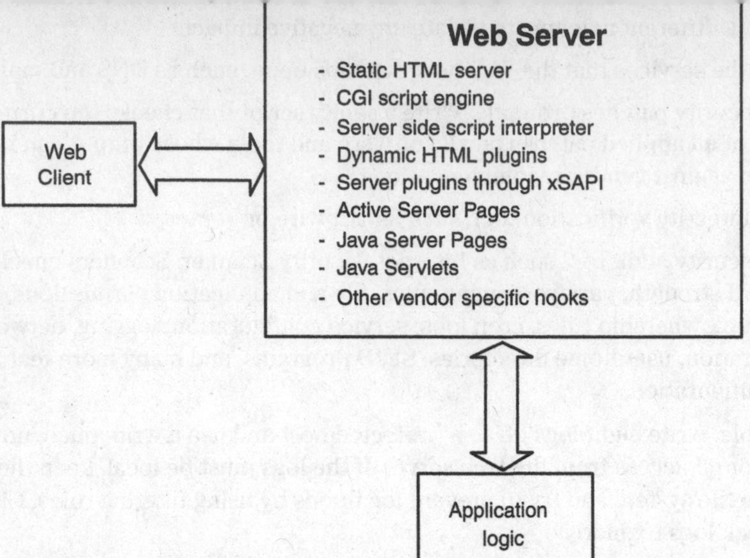

Figure 10.5 Web server extensions.

user can fill and submit. The server authenticates the user and serves the page if the password is valid.

- Form-based authentication, where the application presents a login page to the user that allows more customization of the user's login session.
- Client certificates used in conjunction with SSL to allow the server to strongly authenticate the user.
- Third-party service providers, such as network authentication servers (such as Kerberos or token authentication servers).

Other security properties such as single sign-on to multiple Web applications can be achieved, either through cookie-based authentication servers, client-side certificate-based solutions, or Web servers that accept *NT LAN Manager* (NTLM) credentials or (with Windows 2000) Kerberos tickets.

Web Application Configuration

On UNIX platforms, access to privileged ports (for services on port numbers less than or equal to 1024) is restricted to *root*. Web servers listen on the popular default port number 80 and therefore must be started as root. To restrict access, the Web server root process spawns off a child that immediately changes its user ID to a less-privileged identity, such as *nobody*. The root Web server process hands off any incoming request to the child. For example, the Apache Web server can be configured to maintain a

load-balance all incoming requests efficiently at lower privilege levels.

Each Web server vendor presents specific recommendations for secure configuration of the Web server, including user and group definitions, file permissions, and directory structures. Please refer to [GS97] for an excellent introduction to secure server administration and to your vendor documentation for specific configuration details.

Document Access Control

Web servers organize the files that are visible to users into a directory tree, where access rights for all the files and directories can be specified at the root level or within individual directories of the tree. In the latter case, each directory stores its own local access properties. Users can be restricted from listing the directories contents, following symbolic links, or using the process execution commands within documents that contain server-side includes.

The security policy for directory access must be well defined, and the application should use sanity scripts to verify that the document tree is correctly configured. Managing the files can also be an issue if the application uses multiple hosts configured in a Web server farm to serve content.

File-based security solutions have definition, management, scalability, and maintainability problems that grow worse as the application evolves. This process must be automated to be manageable. We will return to this basic problem in Chapter 15, "Enterprise Security Architecture."

CGI Scripts

CGI scripts were the first method introduced to enhance Web server abilities by allowing them to pass certain HTTP requests to server-side programs that implemented a standard request/response method and return the output of the program as the HTTP response.

CGI scripts have been notorious as sources of security holes, mostly because of the ad hoc mode in which they are thrown together. Please refer to Chapter 5, "Code Review," for some of the issues related to writing secure programs and a short description on securing Perl scripts, the programming language of choice for many CGI programmers.

The security issues with CGI include the following:

- CGI scripts normally execute under a single user identity. If the server wishes to enforce separate user and group access rules, there are CGI tools that make this situation possible (CGI wrappers, for example).
- CGI bin scripts need not be invoked from within a browser. In fact, many Web services—such as stock quotes, weather estimates, or time services—provided

within client code, completely independent of a Web browser, for enhancing other existing programs that wish to query the same data sources available on the Web site.

- CGI scripts that make system calls are particularly dangerous. Scripts that spawn child processes, open files or pipes, or run commands by using the system() call can compromise the system by allowing intentionally malformed user input to be used as arguments to these system functions.

Compiled CGI scripts can still pose security risks if downloaded from the Internet. If the script is a public download, its source is also out there for examination and possible compromise.

JavaScript

Web servers should not assume that all users will conduct accesses from within the confines of a known Web browser. A malicious user can generate any valid HTTP stream to the Web server for processing, and assumptions of input validity because of checks within the browser (say, through data validation checks implemented in JavaScript) might be risky.

Using JavaScript to perform data validation improves user response because the user gets immediate feedback about malformed data within a form before it is actually sent to the server. The server should duplicate all data validation checks, however, and add additional checks against maliciously formed user input. Also do not depend on security implemented through the hidden variables in HTML forms. These variables are visible in the HTML source and can be easily modified before being sent to the Web server.

Web Server Architecture Extensions

There are many vendor offerings and open-source products to extend the features of Web servers. As each product introduces its own security solution along with security issues for the review, please refer to your vendor documentation for more architecture and security details. Many of these products use embedded directives inside HTML pages that must be parsed, extracted, and executed. The Web server or vendor product replaces the original directive within the HTML page with the directive's output. Server-side includes and server-side scripting options can have serious security consequences, primarily through misconfiguration or through interpretation of user input as commands without validation. At a high level, we now describe some options for embedding directives within static HTML to create dynamic effects.

Server-side includes. Server-side includes are simple commands (for example, to execute programs to insert the current time) embedded directly into the HTML output to modify the HTML content before presenting it to the requestor.

PHP. PHP is a hypertext preprocessor that executes HTML embedded directives written in a language that uses syntax elements from C, Java, and Perl. PHP has many modules for generating content in various MIME formats and has extensive database connectivity and networking support.

PHP is a powerful interpreter and can be configured as a cgi-bin binary or as a dynamically loaded Apache module. PHP, like any interpreter, requires careful configuration to prevent attacks through mangled command-line arguments or direct invocation by using a guessed URL. One means of securing the interpreter is by forcing redirection of all requests through the Web server. The PHP interpreter can be abused if other services are configured insecurely on the host, however. We refer the user to the secure configuration links on www.php.net, which also contain other security resources.

Active Server Pages. Microsoft's IIS Web server enables HTML programmers to embed Visual Basic code into HTML pages. IIS has an integrated VB script engine that accesses the underlying NT or Windows 2K host security mechanisms. Programmers can add authentication constraints to the ASP page. When IIS executes the code, the authentication constraint is checked before the page is dynamically built or shipped to the browser. IIS supports basic, NTLM, or SSL authentication and logs events to the host audit logs. Please check the resources on www.microsoft.com/technet for more information on ASP security.

Java Server Pages. *Java Server Pages* (JSP), much like Active Server Pages, are HTML pages with embedded scripting code. JSPs use the HTTP request and response model of Java servlets, which we will discuss later. The JSP scripting language has a simple XML-like syntax and can support embedded programming language constructs. When a JSP page is first accessed, it is converted into a Java servlet, compiled into a class file, and then loaded for execution. On subsequent invocations, if the JSP page has not been modified, the loaded class file of the servlet is directly invoked. The Servlet container manages the compiled JSP-derived servlet and maintains session state. We explain servlet security in a following section. Security mechanisms for servlets can be applied to Java Server Pages, as well.

Enterprise Web Server Architectures

In Figure 10.6, we have extracted and blown up the Application Logic portion of the Web application.

There are many proprietary vendor extensions for providing application server functionality behind a Web server. All of them are similar in their implementation of security in that they all support the authentication modes of the server, trust the Web server to conduct authentication, and use some model of role-based access control, often to an

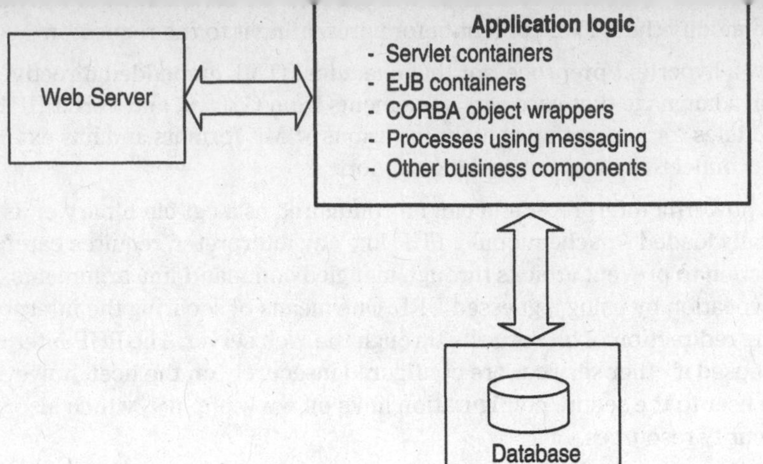

Figure 10.6 Application business logic extensions.

object-relational model of the backend data. Although security *discussions* of the various vendor options all sound the same, the details of security *implementations* for the various options are often very different.

We will focus on the J2EE standard for building distributed enterprise Web applications. Almost all of this discussion applies to every vendor product we have seen, in abstract terms.

The Java 2 Enterprise Edition Standard

The J2EE standard is a massive effort to define a flexible and robust platform for distributed enterprise computing by using Java technology at the core. J2EE's ambitious goals for building Web-based e-commerce services include reliable, secure, highly available, scalable access to information by using Web interfaces to enterprise component services.

The J2EE standard builds upon the Java security model of virtual machines, security policies, security managers, access controllers, and trust. J2EE uses standard extensions for cryptography, authentication, authorization, and programmatic access to security objects. Many of the security goals described within the CORBA Security Standard are shared by J2EE, along with strong similarities in implementation details. Please refer to Chapter 7, "Trusted Code," for an introduction to the core Java security model and to Chapter 9, "Middleware Security," for common security issues with enterprise middleware.

that is currently seeing some vendor support and availability. For a discussion of how the JAAS specification fits into Java Security, please refer to Chapter 7 and the references presented there.

Server-Side Java

J2EE supports server-side Java. Java Server Pages, Java Servlets, and Enterprise Java Beans are all instances of server-side Java. Server-side Java, unlike Java applets, executes on the Web server rather than within the Web browser on the user's client host. Server-side Java extends the Web server's capabilities by allowing the execution of Java bytecodes on a server-hosted JVM. In addition to the benefits of Java as a programming language, there are the following advantages:

- The application can have tight control over the version, features, extended Java libraries, and Java-based security schemas on the server host while at the same time reducing the required feature complexity and associated client-side risk by shipping dynamically generated HTML to the client instead of active content.
- The application can choose to logically split active roles between the client and the server by using Java at both ends to centralize domain and business logic computation on the server, while at the same time off-loading client-specific presentation logic. This separation of concerns might accomplish load-balancing and performance improvements.
- The application has improved portability on the server side (assuming that no vendor- or platform-specific proprietary services are used along with only standards-based J2EE implementation of features) and on the client side (by avoiding the use of browser-specific HTML features that can now be implemented on the server).

Java Servlets

Java servlets are server-side Java programs that enable developers to add custom extensions to Web servers without the performance and portability penalties of CGI programs. Web servers are used in the three-tier architecture model to implement presentation-layer functions that wrap business logic and data. Servlets make connectivity between the presentation and database tiers easier. Servlets share the request and response architecture of Web servers, allowing easy handoffs of requests from Web server to Java Servlet, and support *Java Database Connectivity* (JDBC) access to databases or integration with *Enterprise Java Beans* (EJB) to provide more robust, distributed, persistent access to business logic and data modeling. The Web server initiates a servlet through calls to the init() method, then hands off service calls and finally terminates the servlet through a destroy() call. Servlets use data streams to handle the request and response interface to the Web server.

functions. Servlets can be dynamically loaded and can serve multiple requests though multithreading. Requests can be forwarded to other servlets to implement security solutions based on the *wrapper* pattern. In this case, all incoming requests are forced through a security wrapper, which can request user authentication or authorization checks, perform argument validation, or verify context information (perhaps to check browser type or time of day, to validate cookie fields, or to verify that SSL was used for the request).

In addition, because servlets are Java class files, they run within the context of a security policy enforced by the Security Manager of the servlet container's JVM. Servlets can be digitally signed (in a similar manner as applets are signed, as described in Chapter 7) and therefore can be granted additional execution privileges.

Servlets can also request minimum levels of user authentication. The servlet container defers authentication to the Web server and trusts that the Web server has successfully validated the user identity presented. The type of authentication recognized can be specified in the deployment descriptor file, an XML file of Web application configuration definitions invoked at initialization by the servlet engine. The servlet engine references these definitions for all application properties, including those relating to security. The current standard recognizes four default authentication modes: basic HTTP 1.1 username and password authentication, basic authentication augmented with cryptographic ciphers to protect passwords in transit, form-based user authentication, and SSL with client-side certificates. Vendors can add additional authentication options, or applications can add server extensions for authentication that use third-party security providers, such as token servers or Kerberos.

Servlets and Declarative Access Control

The Java Servlet Standard (at draft version 2.3, as of date) specifies a simple model for securing Java servlets. The highlight of this specification is its use of XML for security declarations. We will expand on the importance of XML and enterprise security management in Chapter 15, "Enterprise Security Architecture."

Java servlets run within servlet engines. A single host can run multiple instances of the engine, and each engine is a container for multiple Web applications. Each Web application is a collection of Web resources and servlets on the host.

The Java Servlet Standard defines an XML document type for creating declarative security definitions. These definitions are stored in the *deployment descriptor file*. The definitions could be statically loaded at servlet initialization or can be programmatically referenced through function calls that can request a user's Principal object, return session attributes, or verify that a user belongs to the correct group or role before granting access.

Recall our pattern of presenting access control rules defined in Chapter 3. The deployment descriptor file uses several XML tags to create access control rules.

single Web application. The range of this top-level container is bounded by using the <web-app> tag. This tag defines the scope for all definitions for an application. The application is named by using the <display-name> attribute tag within this scope. An application can contain multiple servlets.

User groups. The <security-role> tag is used to define labels for user groups. The <security-role> tag is referenced during authorization checks on a resource request to compare the user's actual authenticated role with the roles that are allowed access to the resource requested.

Logical user group aliases. The <security-role-ref> tag allows a separation between application-specific roles and more abstract security group labels. Role names defined within the <security-role-ref> tag scope can be linked to existing roles by using the <role-link> tag.

Object-access groups. The <web-resource-collection> tag collects several Web resources by name along with URLs that lead to the resource and the HTTP methods that users can invoke to access the resource.

Partially defined access control rules. The <auth-constraint> tag is used to define an authorization constraint that links a collection of Web resources (where each is accessed by using a permitted access operation) with a role name. The definition is partial because we must also verify that the connectivity between browser and server is acceptable.

Context constraints. The context of the request includes connectivity constraints, defined by using the <user-data-constraint> tag (which could require the use of SSL or other adequately secure communication modes). The Web server is queried for this context information.

Access control rules. The <security-constraint> tag combines a <web-resource-collection> with an <auth-constraint> under a <user-data-constraint> condition. Users within the defined role can access the Web resource collection under permitted connectivity constraints.

The Java Servlet standard is a starting point for more complex, declarative access definitions. Vendors can define additional tags to constrain other context attributes, such as browser type, time of day, user history, or current system load. We could enhance access control rules by declaring hierarchical roles, we could add delegation constraints, or we could add cryptographic requirements to the cipher suite used for SSL on the link between the browser and the server. Using a declarative syntax in XML gives us expressive power and portability. Implementation of the definitions in the deployment descriptor file becomes the real issue, because we must understand how a particular vendor supports and enforces access control rules.

Enterprise Java Beans

Enterprise Java Beans extends the basic Java Beans framework to support the enterprise development of distributed, service-supported, reusable components. The EJB

ing, security, logging, and notification.

We described how Web servers use cookies to maintain user state across multiple HTTP requests, although HTTP is a sessionless protocol. EJB further extends the capability of Web servers to remember user sessions across multiple HTTP sessions by providing persistence through stateful session and entity beans.

EJB Security is quite complicated. Much like the CORBA Security Specification, the entire spectrum of security services is available, if you choose to make the effort to implement complex security policies. Applications can use statically defined property files to store usernames, passwords, group definitions, role definitions, and access control rules—much like the servlet model described earlier. At the other extreme, applications can enforce a full run-time, determined, dynamic, object- and instance-based security policy by using the JAAS APIs. Developers can specify fine-grained object access controls programmatically.

Because the management of security policy and the methods for security operations management are completely vendor dependent, we expect to see the same security management issues that we detailed in our discussion of CORBA security all over again within J2EE. Given that the static definition method has reasonable ease of use, simplicity, and management, it might be a while before we see applications using the full power of the specification. The complexity of the J2EE specification and of subcomponents such as Enterprise Java Beans places a satisfactory description of security beyond the scope of this book. It would simply require a book of its own. We recommend [PC00] for a high-level description of J2EE along with the resources on java.sun.com for more detail on J2EE security.

Conclusion

Web security is one area of system architecture with no clear architectural guidelines for security to match the patterns that we see. Once we have a working application, it is not possible to go into the user's browser to rip out insecure features that might be needed for accessing other sites or to go into the server and rip out features used by other applications hosted by the same Web farm. Web Architectures are full of hidden effects that are hard to guard against.

Keeping up with Web security is like drinking from a fire hose. Historically, every Web architecture component we have seen has been found wanting. From JVM bugs to code verifier implementations to IIS server bugs to Apache-loadable module bugs to JavaScript errors to hostile applets to scripted ActiveX controls to browser plug-ins to Word Macro viruses to HTML-enhanced mail to much more, the list is unending.

Guaranteed security in a Web application is almost impossible to accomplish because of the complexity of the components involved. Web servers and browsers are extremely large and feature-rich programs. They permit extensions by using vendor components,

tation bugs. Then, the vendors pit usability against security and leave secure configuration guidelines vague or unverifiable.

The Web is a complicated and insecure place in which to live. The best hope for secure application development lies in simplicity and the enforcement of good architecture and design. Prayer helps, too.

11

Application and OS Security

Application security describes methods for protecting an application's resources on a host (or collection of hosts) by controlling users, programs, or processes that wish to access, view, or modify the state of these resources.

Operating systems have carried the concept of protection long before security arose as a major concern. Protection within an operating system appears in the following areas:

- Memory management techniques that prevent processes from accessing each other's address spaces.
- I/O controllers that prevent programs from simultaneously attempting to write to a peripheral device.
- Schedulers that ensure (through interrupts and preemption) that one process will not hog all system resources.
- Synchronization primitives, such as mutexes and semaphores, that manage access to a critical resource shared by two or more processes.

These protection mechanisms arose within operating systems to prevent accidental tampering. Malicious tampering is another matter altogether, because hackers can create conditions assumed impossible by the OS protection schemes.

Application security involves aspects of secure programming, security component selection, operating system security, database security, and network security. Considerations include the following:

- Selection of security components, which is normally considered the responsibility of the architect. The application architect can choose products such as firewalls,

services to secure the application.

- Issues of secure configuration, which are normally considered the responsibility of systems administrators. The systems administrator must set file permissions, turn off insecure network services, manage passwords, or follow vendor directives for the secure configuration of the components selected.
- Issues of secure programming, which are normally considered the responsibility of the developer. The developer checks arguments to programs for malicious inputs, verifies the absence of buffer overflows, links code with cryptographic libraries, or writes SUID programs with care.

All security vendors have products that promise to enhance the security of a production system by modifying host hardware, operating system, or network configurations or by adding special tools that control activities in these areas. Most vendors lack domain knowledge of the application. From the perspective of a vendor (evident in the directives they give to system administrators), an application is largely just a collection of programs linked to a database, with files and directories, startup and shutdown procedures, network links, and management tools. Without domain knowledge, applications are just black boxes that use operating system resources according to some specified operational profile.

For vendors and system administrators, this viewpoint is valid. System architects, however, must be concerned about much more than running security components on secure platforms. Application architects must take into account the new processes, services, software products, network interfaces, middleware products, and data feeds that the application itself adds to the host. These are not generic components and can contain their own software defects. The details of how these architectural artifacts work are in the domain of the architect.

Hardware and OS vendors provide many excellent resources for securing systems on their Web sites and have detailed guidelines on the security issues surrounding operating system configuration. Most are silent or rather brief on application development issues, however—especially the details of security architecture when vendor products are involved. The speed at which products change, and the fluidity of the so-called standards they are based upon, do not help either. The common theme is to recommend that application architects purchase professional services if more useful knowledge is required.

The Internet has excellent resources on security (we have listed a few favorites in the bibliography), with many sites presenting specific and detailed guidelines for securing the underlying host and OS of an application. There are many good books on security, as well. A good place to start is the seminal work by Garfinkel and Spafford [GS96a], *Practical Unix and Internet Security*, the best jump-start resource on all things relating to UNIX security. Other essential references for more information include [ZCC00], [NN00], and [CB96].

In this chapter, we will describe the basic nature of operating systems as resource managers and describe some patterns of protection of these resources that can be accomplished. We also present the structure of a generic application in terms of its

the lines of attack against a host and recommend some defenses against each. We will end our presentation with the description of three UNIX OS security features: methods using filters and interceptors to secure network services, the Pluggable Authentication Module (which implements the layer pattern), and UNIX ACLs (which implement discretionary access control).

Structure of an Operating System

Operating systems are among possibly the most complicated software components ever composed. Operating systems manage virtual memory, disk caches, and disk access; schedule, execute, and switch processes; handle inter-process communication; catch and handle interrupts and exceptions; accept system calls from programs; and manage I/O devices, the file system, network links, and much more.

Operating systems are built in layers [Sta01] that rise from low-level electronic circuits, registers, and buses in the underlying hardware to high-level OS features such as multi-threading, distributed process management, or symmetric multiprocessing. At the core, operating systems are resource managers for applications, programs, or users to exploit.

Protecting an operating system consists of applying our security principles of Chapter 3, "Security Architecture Basics," to any entity that wishes access to the host resources. The principles are, once again:

- Authenticate before allowing access.
- Control activities once access is granted, keeping permissions to minimum privilege levels.
- Control information flow initiated by the user on the system.
- Protect each application, user, or program from all others on the same host.

Operating systems protect users from one another by dividing resources along dimensions; for example, partitioning memory to control the address space, partitioning time to control processor execution, and partitioning device availability to permit or deny access operations through the device's driver.

Consider Figure 11.1, which shows the high-level architecture of UNIX. Traditionally, *hardening* any operating system referred to the protection of the kernel, hardware, and memory from programs that were already executing on the host. In recent times, the term has expanded to include the notion of strengthening network interfaces and limiting the activities and services permitted upon them. Many hardware platform vendors provide a hardened version of their standard hosts that includes a *sandbox* layer of access control definitions that separate resources from access requests. Vendors also recommend products that enhance system security in generic ways. For example:

- IBM's venerable *Resource Access Control Facility* (RACF), providing security for more than a decade and a half for MVS platforms, stores access control rules in a security database. RACF is now a component of IBM's SecureWay Security Server.

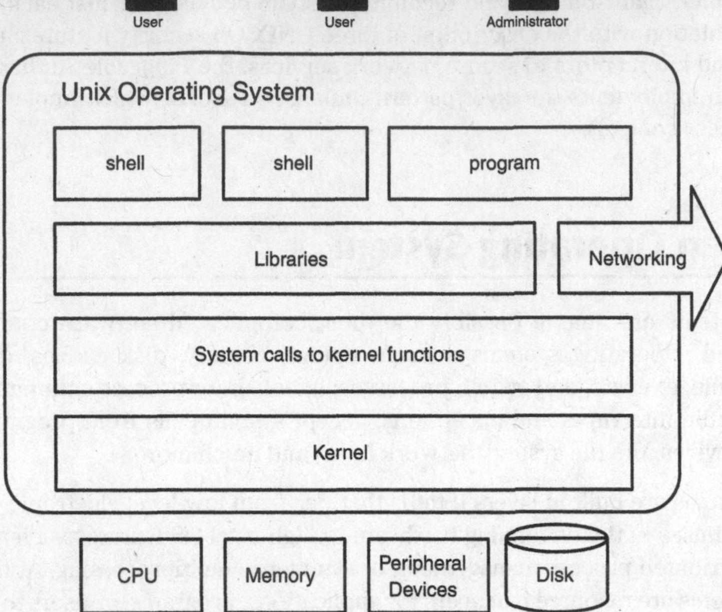

Figure 11.1 UNIX operating system layers.

SecureWay has added a firewall product, a Web server security component, OS support for Kerberos V5 and DCE, directory access via LDAP, and integration with PKI components. Each resource access from an application must use a security interface to reference an operating system component called the *System Authorization Facility* (SAF). SAF calls RACF's security manager if an access decision is needed before permitting the request to proceed.

- Hewlett-Packard provides a secure e-commerce platform called Virtual Vault that uses the hardened *Virtual Vault Operating System* (VVOS), a trusted version of HP-UX. Applications can also access Web, LDAP Directory, or PKI services securely by using vendor products such as Sun's iPlanet Server Suite (formerly Netscape Enterprise Web, Directory, and Certificate Servers).
- Sun Microsystems provides tools and software to enable Solaris Operating Environment Security, a secure configuration using minimal services, with guidelines for securing all OS components. Sun also provides a hardened version of its operating system called Trusted Solaris that eliminates the need for a root ID and adds access checks to all requests for system or data resources. Applications also can add many vendor products for UNIX security, including firewalls, Kerberos, DCE, and open-source software such as tripwire or tcpwrapper. Sun's own Kerberos V5 service is called *Sun Enterprise Authentication Mechanism* (SEAM). Applications can also access Web, LDAP Directory, or PKI services securely by using Sun's iPlanet products.

ware and OS platform fulfills all the generic security requirements from corporate security. Vendor programs that provide jumpstarts to ensure security compliance are a common method of establishing this baseline of security.

Operating system hardening solutions implement the *sandbox* pattern. Hardened versions of UNIX implement some of the patterns of mainframe security, such as access control through RACF. A hardened UNIX box might perform any or all of the following actions:

- Limit the powers of the root user by adding additional administrative roles and requiring all administrative activities to be conducted by a user in the related admin role. Gaining root access gives a user no special access permissions available by default on standard UNIX platforms.
- Partition the file system into strict compartments and block access between these areas by using access control rules beyond the basic file permission modes. Some products even enforce append-only access to disks designated for logging events.
- Authenticate the user at session initiation and carry the original authenticated user ID along with all activities that the user conducts. In other words, even if the user changes identity by using *su* or runs a SUID program (which normally would run with the identity of the program owner), the OS still can access the original ID by following the chain of assumed identities all the way back to the original authenticated user. Users might need to explicitly disconnect, reconnect, and reauthenticate to change roles.
- Provide support for roles, assign users to roles, and add access control rules that partition the standard collection of UNIX system calls, library functions, and shell commands into object groups and then restrict access to the calls and commands in each group only to specific roles.
- Provide restricted versions of shells by default and use the *chroot* command to restrict file system visibility.
- Place numeric limits on permitted resource requests. The OS can possibly limit how many processes a program can spawn, how many open file descriptors it can hold, how many socket connections it can start, or how many CPUs it can use in a multiprocessor host.

As might be expected, OS hardening can slow down performance because of the extra layers of control between the kernel's critical OS functions and user programs.

Structure of an Application

An application is a software system hosted on a hardware platform that performs a business service. Applications often follow the three-tier architecture, defining presentation, business logic, and data layers to separate concerns across the system.

Applications have the following components:

the machines, their versions and models, and their physical descriptions in terms of memory, disk sizes, volume details, network interface cards, peripherals, consoles, and so on.

Process architecture. The process architecture of an application describes all of the programs, executables, shell scripts, services, and daemons that are actively handling services or performing business tasks. We also include details such as control flow or work flow by using process maps and finite state diagrams.

Software communications architecture. The communications architecture describes the software bus used by processes to send messages back and forth. The bus could be implemented by using reads and writes to files or to the database, through IPC mechanisms, message queues, or other middleware such as CORBA. The application must document the pattern of message flows, the expected volumes of data on each communications link, and the properties of the communications link (whether secure, insecure, encrypted, local, inter-host, untrusted network, and so on).

Data architecture. The data architecture of an application captures the object model representing the persistent state of the system and the schema representing that state within an object or relational database. It also shares process information, such as stored procedures or functions, with the process architecture.

Network architecture. The network architecture of an application describes all of its networking interfaces, the subnets that each host is homed upon, the type of traffic carried, and the software that controls, secures, and protects each network interface.

Configuration architecture. The configuration architecture describes the layout of files and directories, the contents of system configuration files, definitions of environment variables, file and directory permissions, and other information required for defining a correct image of the application.

Operations, administration, and maintenance architecture. The OA&M procedures describe the care and feeding methods and procedures, along with system administration activities specific to the application. This description includes methods for starting or stopping the application, performing backup or recovery actions, user management, host administration, system and error log handling, and enabling traces for debugging in production.

The application architecture includes many other details of life-cycle management, including performance parameters, acceptable load levels, acceptable rates of data loss, and interface specifications to other applications for data feeds in either direction.

Some subcomponents of the application might occur multiple times for reliability or for performance.

- Each process could be multithreaded.
- Each daemon could spawn multiple child processes to achieve a better user response time.
- Each host could have multiple processors.

- The application might appear in multiple instances for load balancing, geographic proximity, hot service transfers on failovers, or disaster recovery (if for some reason the primary instance is obliterated).

Application Delivery

Applications are delivered in releases from development to production through a release tape. Some applications flash-cut to the new release; others prefer to run two parallel instances of the system, one old and one new, rather than performing a flash-cut to the new release. Traffic and data are slowly migrated over after acceptance testing succeeds. The release tape contains software and installation directives.

It is important to provide mechanisms to securely deliver the tape, use separate production user accounts with unique passwords, and write scripts to verify the integrity of the files in the new release node by using cryptographic hashes. The tape itself represents intellectual property of the company and must be protected accordingly. Installation directives can do any or all of the following things:

- Halt the current executing instance at a safe point
- Save system execution state information
- Export the database to files
- Clean up the current instance
- Move the old software configuration to a dormant node
- Configure back-out scripts to restore the old release in case of critical failure
- Install the new files and directories
- Run sanity scripts to verify correctness
- Create a clean database instance
- Run scripts to bulk import the old persistent data into the current schema
- Transfer users from the old instance to the new instance
- Clean up the environment
- Launch the testing phase for customer release acceptance after a successful cut to the field

Development environments are insecure; therefore, all development and testing-specific security information should be discarded and reset in production. This procedure includes passwords burned into binaries, certificates, and encrypted private key files (and their passwords). Trust links that allow access from and to interfaces to other systems in development should be removed on production hosts. Leaving compilers and other non-essential tools on production environments is bad because each tool to build or interpret code carries a potential for abuse if the system is compromised. The installation procedures are critical in worst-case scenarios where the level of system compromise requires a complete OS and application reinstall from backup

of installation instructions cannot be followed (for example, if the system is halted in an unsafe state).

Application and Operating System Security

In Figure 11.2, we present a high-level picture of the components of an operating system. Securing a host involves many activities, and given our constraints, we will focus on a few examples of security issues around the system operational profile. Who is allowed access, what is the normal profile of activities for each user, and when do individuals access the system?

Each of the architectural perspectives described in the last section carries its own security issues and remedies. Here are some highlights.

Hardware Security Issues

Securing the hardware of an application primarily falls on physical security measures. Some operating systems enable the administrator to prevent system startups from

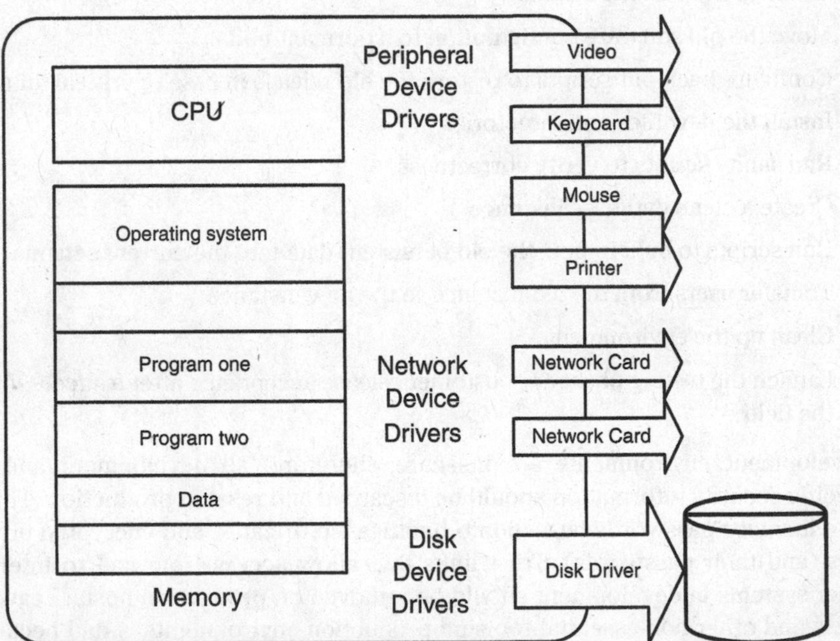

Figure 11.2 Operating system components.

Only Memory (PROM) password that must be entered before the OS can boot from any media. Applications should set PROM passwords to prevent hosts from being shut down and brought up in single user mode from the console.

Some vendors provide network access to the console terminal by hooking a special hardware appliance with a network port and a cable to the RS232 port on a host. For example, HP provides a secure Web console, which is an appliance that hosts a secure Web server and that runs a terminal emulator linked to the console cable port on the host to provide access to the box over the network. An administrator accessing the appliance over the network appears (as far as the host is concerned) to be standing physically at the box.

Process Security Issues

Securing the process architecture of an application is a complex problem. We have to review the application design data and extract process descriptions, process flow diagrams, workflow maps, data flow diagrams, and administration interfaces. For each of these elements, we must define the boundaries of interaction within the application, identify assets at the process level, identify interfaces to other systems, and document security audit mechanisms.

We must review the details of control flow or workflow by analyzing process maps and finite state diagrams. Applications that use process flow maps (for example, through workflow managers) must prevent tampering with the configurations that describe the flow. These attacks could modify the map to prevent validation of data, block checks made by security services, or break handoffs between callback processes and event managers.

Questions to ask at the review include the following: Do all process-to-process boundaries occur locally on a single host? Does process-to-process communication occur over the network? Are there requirements for authentication and access control between processes? Is the external process a trusted system or an untrusted customer? Is data arriving over the boundary or is it leaving the application? If the data represents arguments to a program, we must validate the user inputs to prevent buffer overflows or unchecked invocations of shell interpreters. We must verify that each presenter of credentials for authentication manages those credentials in a secure manner.

Additional questions about credential use include the following: Do users input credentials, or does the system manage this task? Are system credentials stored unencrypted in memory or on the drive? Do they expire, or can they be forged? If processes use embedded passwords within binaries, how are these passwords set or modified? What if the recipient of the request enforces password aging? What if the handshake protocol for authentication changes?

Workflow products normally provide metrics to monitor the progress of orders at each node, and the application should generate alarms for unusual process patterns (for

redirection of orders through new pathways). Applications should take special care in managing transition events or callbacks generated by untrusted application components, such as customers or partners, which could be spoofed or tampered with to attack the application.

Software Bus Security Issues

We discussed strategies for securing the communications bus used by processes for sending messages back and forth in Chapter 9, "Middleware Security." For each product used, many mechanisms could exist for enabling security.

- Setting file permissions or creating disk partitions to secure message passing through reads and writes to files.
- IPC mechanisms could use IPSec over the network or could use secure socket connections.
- Message queue managers could restrict clients by IP address or hostname and require strong authentication.
- Messaging software could also provide an encrypted bus for secure message transport and use message caches for saving traffic to hosts that might be knocked off the network (either through failure or through a denial-of-service attack).
- The application could use middleware security service providers. For a detailed discussion of security for other middleware products such as CORBA or Enterprise Java, please refer to Chapters 9 and 10, respectively.

Data Security Issues

Operating systems provide file security through a security manager component of the file system. UNIX file commands (*ls*, *chown*, *chgrp*, and *chmod*, for example) enable the manipulation of the permissions bits that describe *user*, *group*, and *other* permissions along with ownership and additional access control lists. Files can optionally be encrypted, although this feature represents a risk if the encryption key is lost. Users can change ownership and permissions on files and can set special permissions on files to enable SUID or SGID behavior.

We will defer a detailed discussion of the issues surrounding secure database management to Chapter 12, "Database Security."

Network Security Issues

Securing the network architecture of an application involves securing all of its networking interfaces. We can use a local firewall such as tcpwrapper to control and pro-

describing the type of traffic allowed based on source and destination IP addresses or hostnames, port numbers, protocols, and time of day access rules. Interfaces can be configured to block IP forwarding to protect secure subnets on multi-homed hosts from untrusted network traffic. Hosts should also disable all unwanted services on an internal network. We will discuss network services security in more detail in a following section.

We can also filter packets arriving on the host or require incoming connections to enforce certain security properties. On Solaris, for example, we can control the security settings for network interface configuration at several levels.

The transport layer. The administrator can extend the range of privileged ports beyond the default of 1024 to protect other services from being started by non-root users on the host.

The network layer. The administrator could require IPSec connectivity from certain applications and hosts to prevent IP spoofing against the host.

The data link layer. The administrator could turn off unsolicited ARP cache updates to prevent bad hardware address data in the local cache.

Configuration Security Issues

Secure application configuration covers a mixed bag of issues.

- Applications should set the permissions on system configuration files to prevent tampering and must not store application passwords along with definitions of environment variables. Applications should use sanity scripts, which explicitly test for errors and report misconfiguration within information required for defining a correct image of the application. These scripts provide inexperienced administrators with an easy and automated method of verifying system safety.
- User passwords are commonly checked against the standard /etc/passwd file, a shadow password file, or a naming service (such as NIS or NIS+ on Solaris). An administrator can turn on password aging, run password strength checks, prevent old password reuse, enable account locking on some number of bad attempts, or prevent trust-based services such as rlogin.
- Administrators should create special group identities to match system logins with their own GID (for example *root*, *daemon*, *bin*, *sys*, and *adm*).
- Applications can use the UNIX operating system's Pluggable Authentication Module framework to manage common authentication services for multiple applications (presented in a later section).
- Applications can prohibit executable stacks to block one class of buffer overflow exploits that require them to succeed. We refer the reader to Chapter 5, "Code Review," for more information about the issue of executable versus non-executable stacks.

Operations, Administration, and Maintenance Security Issues

Security administration is an important part of systems administration, and it is the responsibility of the application architect to set security guidelines for operations, administration, and maintenance of the application in production.

Applications should define OA&M procedures for security to do the following:

- Protect backup tapes with sensitive information.
- Automatically run a security scanner that regularly verifies the state of the system. This scan includes password checks, cryptographic checksums on files to prevent tampering, file permissions, group checks, cron job checks, unauthorized SUID program detection, superuser activity, and much more.
- Automate security log reviews, alarm notification, and credential expiry.
- Create audit logs to capture user logins and logouts, execution of privileged commands, system calls, file operations, or network traffic. View and analyze the logs.
- If possible, use restricted shell (/usr/lib/rsh on Solaris) to restrict a user to his or her home directory. A user in a restricted shell cannot change directories, modify the PATH variable, redirect output by using UNIX redirectors, and cannot access any files outside the home directory by using complete path names. Restricted shells have limitations but are a useful piece of the security puzzle.
- Set path variables correctly. Verify that the user's current working directory is not in the PATH (in case the user switches to a public directory and runs a Trojan horse). Audit packages can test for this error and for other PATH configuration errors.
- Restrict SUID programs owned by root. The application should not use SUID programs if possible due to the risk presented by coding errors.

Administrators must also configure access to security service providers used by the application. These could include secure naming services, secure network file systems, PKIs, directories, Kerberos servers, DCE domain servers, tools using *Java Cryptographic Extensions* (JCE), or applications that use the *Generic Security Services API* (GSS-API) for access to services (such as DCE or Kerberos).

Securing Network Services

Hosts that provide network services must accept service requests, authenticate the user who is making the request, verify that they have permission to access the information requested, and then must transfer the information over the network to the client host. We will focus on TCP/IP services for UNIX, but the directives for securing network services apply to a broader domain (please refer to [GS96a], [ZCC00], [NN00], and [CB96] for more information).

work ports with clients to provide UNIX network services. Daemons must be owned by *root* to handle traffic on privileged ports (numbered lower than 1024). Higher port numbers are available for non-privileged user processes. Some operating systems (Solaris, for example) allow the redefinition of the range of privileged and non-privileged port numbers to protect additional services or to restrict the range of port numbers available to user processes.

Servers can be automatically started or can be awakened by the UNIX *inetd* daemon that listens on multiple ports and launches the appropriate server when a request arrives. The inetd daemon represents a chokepoint for network service access, and tools such as tcpwrapper exploit this single point of entry to add authorization checks on incoming service requests.

Vulnerabilities in server programs that run as root can allow access to the host and therefore require more care in configuration. The future might bring to light flaws in either the server or the protocol that it uses, and unless promptly patched, the host is vulnerable to attack. Applications should run the absolute minimum set of services required for operations.

Many services are available in secure mode, where the connection itself is encrypted and protected against tampering and stronger modes of user authentication are allowed. For example, solutions that use secure shell (ssh) exist for FTP, Telnet, and rlogin services. Examples of popular services include the following.

FTP. FTP enables hosts to exchange files. FTP uses port 21 for sending commands and port 20 (sometimes) for sending data. The server requires a login and a password (unless anonymous FTP is enabled), but as the password is sent in the clear, we recommend using a version of FTP that uses encryption. Applications should disable anonymous access.

Telnet. The Telnet service on port 23 using TCP enables a client to log on to a host over the network, providing a virtual terminal to the host. The telenetd authenticates the user login with a password, sent in the clear over the network. Telnet sessions can also be hijacked, where an ongoing session is taken over by an attacker who then issues commands to the server over the connection. Replace telnet with ssh.

SMTP. The Simple Mail Transfer Protocol on port 25 using TCP enables hosts to exchange e-mail. On UNIX systems, the sendmail program implements both the client and the server and has been the source of many security problems over the years. Although many of the early security bugs have been fixed, new ones keep appearing. For example, a recent patch in the current versions of sendmail 8.11.6 fixes a command-line processing error not present in versions earlier than 8.10 (www.securityfocus.org). We refer the reader to [GS96a] or to www.sendmail.org for more information.

DNS. Hosts use DNS to map IP addresses to hostnames and vice-versa. Applications depend on a name server, a host running the *named* daemon, to resolve queries. Attacks on the name server can load modified maps or even the named daemon configuration to create denial-of-service attacks or to aid other exploits that require a spoofed host-name to IP mapping. DNSSEC (defined in RFC 2535) adds security

can be combined with transport security mechanisms such as OpenSSL or IPSec to further protect requests. Support for some features for DNS security is available in the Internet Software Consortium's Bind package (release version 9 and up).

Finger. The finger program queries the host for information on currently active users or on specific user information available in /etc/passwd. It is best known as an infection vector in the 1998 Morris Internet worm attack. Finger should be turned off because it reveals sensitive information.

HTTP. HTTP runs on port 80. Its secure version, HTTPS, which runs HTTP over SSL, is normally run on port 443. For more details on securing Web access to your host, please refer to Chapter 10.

NNTP. The Network News Transfer Protocol runs on port 119 and enables hosts to exchange news articles. There is very rarely a need to run this service on a production site, and NNTP should be turned off unless the application is the corporate news server.

NTP. The Network Time Protocol runs on port 123 using UDP and is used to query a reference timeserver for the correct time. Some security solutions depend on time synchronization between clients and servers, and although they can tolerate a small drift, these solutions will normally block requests from clients with large time differences. Resetting system time could enable attackers to replay information that has expired or can prevent the execution of entries in the crontab file (such as execution of nightly security audits) by the cron daemon. Applications that have a critical dependency on accurate time can use dedicated hardware time servers connected via a *Global Positioning Service* (GPS) receiver link through radio or satellite or modem that can provide accurate time (typically within a millisecond on a LAN and up to a few tens of milliseconds on WANs) relative to *Coordinated Universal Time* (UTC). Enterprise requirements for time service should use highly available and reliable NTP configurations with multiple redundant servers and multiple network paths to a host. Some products also use cryptography to prevent the malicious modification of NTP datagrams.

Other non-official but common services include the *Lightweight Directory Access Protocol* (LDAP) on port 389, the *Secure LDAP protocol* (SLDAP) that uses TLS/SSL on port 636, the Kerberos V5 Administration daemon kerberos-adm on port 749, the Kerberos key server kerberos on 750, the Kerberos V5 KDC propagation server krb5_prop on port 754, the World Wide Web HTTP to LDAP gateway on port 1760, and the Sun NFS server daemon nfsd on port 2049 (all port numbers for Solaris). Each of these services uses both TCP and UDP protocols. Secure configuration for each of these services is beyond the scope of our presentation, and we refer the reader to the appropriate vendor documentation for each server.

UNIX Pluggable Authentication Modules

Sun Microsystems introduced UNIX's Pluggable Authentication Module to make login services independent of the authentication method. PAM uses the *layer* pattern to sep-

the network) from the authentication and session management functions used by the application. Most flavors of UNIX support PAM modules; for example, consult the man pages for PAM on HP-UX or Solaris or see Samar and Lai's paper on PAM [SL96] and other references on www.sun.com.

Applications such as FTP, Telnet, login, and rlogin that provide users with access to a host have a client component and a server component. The server must perform the following session management activities:

User authentication. The user must provide a valid password to initiate a session. The application might desire stronger authentication mechanisms, perhaps using Kerberos or tokens.

Account management. Users with valid passwords must still pass context checks on their accounts. Has the account expired due to inactivity? Has the user made too many bad login attempts? Is the user allowed access to the account at this time of day? Is the user at the correct access terminal (perhaps to restrict usage from a physically protected subnet rather than the wider corporate network)?

Session management. Users initiate and terminate sessions. On initiation, some system data such as last login time must be updated. There are no significant security actions on session closure except logging the event and deleting session state information.

Password management. Users might wish to change their passwords.

PAM enables applications to provide multiple authentication mechanisms to users on a host. PAM also enables administrators to add new authentication modules without modifying any of the high-level applications. PAM can also be configured to send alert, critical, error, information, or warning messages to syslog on UNIX. PAM-enabled applications are compiled with the PAM library *libpam*.

PAM includes a collection of modules (dynamically loaded at run time) for these activities:

- The user authentication module, which authenticates users and sets credentials.
- The account management module, which checks for password aging, account expiration, and time of day access conditions.
- The session management module, which logs the time when users initiate and terminate sessions.
- The password management module, which enables users to change their passwords.

Services that require multiple PAM modules can stack them in sequence and share a single password for each user across all of the modules. Administrators must set up a configuration file that describes the modules required by PAM. Each application to module link can be qualified with a control flag that describes actions on authentication failure. Here are some examples:

password but will delay returning failure until all other required modules have been tested.

- Within a module designated as *optional*, if the module rejects the password, the system might still grant access if another module designated as required successfully authenticates the user.
- If a module is *requisite*, then the module must return success for authentication to continue but on failure will return immediately. The module might not provide the actual error reported to the user, which might originate from an earlier failing *required* module.
- A *sufficient* module that successfully authenticates the use will immediately return success to the user without testing other modules (even ones that are labeled as required).

The libraries and configuration file must be owned by root to prevent compromises. The use_first_pass and try_first_pass directives enable users to reuse the same password across multiple modules. For example, if the FTP program requires two authentication modules to authenticate the user, then the PAM module stores the entered password and reuses it on the second module. For example, assume that the configuration file requires the pam_unix module with no additional entries and requires the pam_dial module with the use_first_pass entry. In this situation, after the user successfully authenticates to the pam_unix module, the pam_dial module uses the same password. This process gives the user single sign-on over two authentication checks. In general, PAM configuration should be done with care to prevent lockouts or weaker than desired authentication.

UNIX Access Control Lists

UNIX access control lists provide a rich and more selective discretionary control over access to files to users by extending the basic permission modes. All users on a production application must access data through the application. It has become increasingly rare for users to access OS files directly, and we normally see such access only in a development environment. The following description of Unix ACLS is probably more relevant to a product development team rather than an application development concern and is presented here only as another example of role-based access control. Application architects who do not use low-level ACLs can safely skip this section; however, developers and systems security administrators may find the information of some value.

Basic file access in UNIX is controlled by setting permission bits to allow read, write, or execute (search permission in the case of directories) access to the file's owner, group, or other users. Unlike root file access, which is allowed on all files, non-privileged user or process file access is controlled by the operating system using these permission bits. ACLs are available on most flavors of UNIX. Initial ACL implementations were significantly different and incompatible, but vendors are now driving toward compliance with the POSIX 1003.6 standard. UNIX ACLs do not mix well with *networked file systems*

treat local versus network-mounted file systems.

We assume familiarity with the UNIX commands chmod to set file permissions and chown to transfer file ownership in the following discussion. Chmod sets or modifies base permission bits using arguments in absolute or symbolic mode. For example, either of the following commands gives read and write permissions to the owner and group of file but denies any access to other users or groups.

```
>chmod 660 file
>chmod ug=rw,o-r file
```

The command chown is used to transfer ownership. Some systems enable users to transfer ownership of their own files; others restrict this privilege to root.

We introduced an abstract model of role-based access control in Chapter 3. We will describe ACLs in the terms of that model.

- *Subjects.* All the users with access to the system, typically the entries in /etc/passwd
- *Objects.* Files and directories on the system
- *Object-Access groups.* Each file is in its own group of one, carrying its entire ACL. A file at creation can inherit initial ACL settings from its parent directory, however. In this sense, the directory hierarchy is an object-access group hierarchy.
- *Roles.* On one level, roles are captured through group definitions which are typically the entries in /etc/group. At the file system level, we do not see the application-specific use cases that could drive the definition of ACLs for individual files. Unix ACLs do not directly support roles, so the application must assume the responsibility for role and policy management (possibly supported by new application-specific commands).
- *ACL management commands.* Each vendor version defines commands to create, modify, delete, replace, and view ACL entries.

In general, because of differences in the vendor implementation of the POSIX ACL standard, application architects should take care in using ACLs on file systems mounted over the network. The base permissions should be the most restrictive, and the access control entries should be permissive. Otherwise, if a restrictive access control entry ("Do not let sys group users read this file") is removed on a network access, the increased scope of access might compromise the file (sys users can now read the file).

ACLs are also designed for regular files and directories and not devices, because the utilities that operate on those files might delete ACL entries. ACLs also have their own syntax and special characters. If these characters appear in usernames or group names, the ACL cannot be parsed. Vendors have different algorithms for making an access decision from the set of applicable access entries. We recommend carefully reviewing the access decision process for your application host OS.

ACLs are excellent for enabling access in small, collaborative groups but can be more difficult to use for defining a large-scale access control solution. The restrictions on the number of entries (for example, some OS vendors such as HP-UX, JFS, and Solaris limit

and the need for writing management utilities make scalability an issue. UNIX ACLs are a valuable addition to specifying secure file access, but they also serve architects with another purpose: prototyping. If you have root access on a box and want to work out the details of a discretionary access control model for an application, you can use the user, user-group, object-access group, object, and role features from the descriptions of access control from Chapter 3 to build a small proof of concept of the model. The exercise will give you some guidance on how to approach the problem in a more complicated domain as you extend the UNIX model to your own application domain.

We will now proceed to describe several ACL mechanisms in more detail.

Solaris Access Control Lists

Solaris extends basic UNIX file protection provided by permission bits through access control lists. Entries are of the form entity:mode, where entity is a username, group name, or numeric ID and mode is a three-character permission set from (r,w,x,-).

The basic file permissions are carried over as the first three entries of the file's ACL: the owner's permissions "u[ser]::mode," the group permissions "g[roup]::mode," and other permissions for users other than the owner and members of the file group, "o[ther]:mode." The mask entry, in the form "m[ask]:mode," indicates the maximum permissions allowed for non-owner users regardless of any following ACL entries. Setting the mask is a safeguard against misconfiguration. Additional access control entries follow the mask, describing permissions for a specific user (u[ser]:uid:mode) or permissions for a specific group (g[roup]:gid:mode).

In compliance with the POSIX ACL standard, Solaris also allows the inheritance of ACLs by using preset default values. The default ACL entries on a directory are used to set initial ACL values on any file created within the directory. In addition, a subdirectory will inherit the ACL defaults of its parent on creation.

The default directory permissions are carried over as the first three entries of the directory's ACL.

- The default owner permissions d[efault]:u[ser]::mode
- The default group permissions d[efault]:g[roup]::mode
- The default permissions for users other than the owner and members of the file group, d[efault]:o[ther]:mode

The default mask entry, in the form d[efault]:mask:mode, indicates the maximum permissions allowed for non-owner users regardless of any following ACL entries. Again, setting the mask is a safeguard against misconfiguration. Additional access control entries follow the mask, describing default permissions for a specific user (d[efault]: u[ser]:uid:mode) or default permissions for a specific group (d[efault]:g[roup]:gid: mode).

Solaris provides two commands for managing ACLs: setfacl (to assign, modify, delete, or create ACLs) and getfacl (to display the current settings). Getfacl can also be used to

the file's attributes. A plus sign (+) next to the mode field of a file indicates that it has a non-trivial ACL (in other words, the ACL describes access to the file by users or groups other than the owner or group of the file).

When a file is created, its basic permissions are used to set the initial values to the entries in its ACL. A file with permissions bits 644 (read and write for bob, read for testers group members, and read for others), has this ACL.

```
(solaris7) :touch file
(solaris7) :ls -l file
-rw-r--r--   1 bob testers          0 Jun 15 18:41 file
(solaris7) :getfacl file
# file: file
# owner: bob
# group: testers
user::rw-
group::r--          #effective:r--
mask:r--
other:r--
```

The following command adds read access for user john and read and execute access for all members of group sys. Because the mask represents an upper limit on permissions, however, sys group members cannot execute the file.

```
(solaris7) :setfacl -m "u:john:r--,g:sys:r-x" file
(solaris7) :getfacl file
# file: file
# owner: bob
# group: testers
user::rw-
user:john:r--           #effective:r--
group::r--          #effective:r--
group:sys:r-x           #effective:r--
mask:r--
other:r--
```

Calling setfacl with the -r option recomputes the mask setting when new entries are added. This action forces effective permissions to match the desired permissions.

```
(solaris7) :setfacl -r -m "g:sys:r-x" file
(solaris7) :getfacl file
# file: file
# owner: bob
# group: testers
user::rw-
user:john:r--           #effective:r--
group::r--          #effective:r--
group:sys:r-x           #effective:r-x
mask:r-x
other:r--
```

The -d option deletes permissions and does not affect the mask.

```
(solaris7) :getfacl file
# file: file
# owner: bob
# group: testers
user::rw-
user:john:r--          #effective:r--
group::r--             #effective:r--
mask:r-x
other:r--
```

ACLs can be transferred from one file to another by using pipes and the -f option to setfacl, with - representing standard input.

```
(solaris7) :touch file2
(solaris7) :getfacl file2
# file: file2
# owner: bob
# group: testers
user::rw-
group::r--             #effective:r--
mask:r--
other:r--
(solaris7) :getfacl file | setfacl -f - file2
(solaris7) :getfacl file2
# file: file2
# owner: bob
# group: testers
user::rw-
user:john:r--          #effective:r--
group::r--             #effective:r--
mask:r-x
other:r--
```

The -s option sets the ACL to the list on the command line.

```
(solaris7) :setfacl -s "u::---,g::---,o:---" file
(solaris7) :getfacl file
# file: file
# owner: bob
# group: testers
user::---
group::---             #effective:---
mask:---
other:---
```

The chmod command may or may not clear ACL entries and must be used carefully. Please refer to the specific vendor documentation for details. In this example, user john has no effective read access to file2 but might be granted access by mistake if the mask is set carelessly.

```
(solaris7) :getfacl file2
# file: file2
```

```
# group: testers
user::rw-
user:john:r--            #effective:r--
group::r--             #effective:r--
mask:r-x
other:r--
(solaris7) :chmod 000 file2
(solaris7) :getfacl file2
# file: file2
# owner: bob
# group: testers
user::---
user:john:r--            #effective:---
group::---             #effective:---
mask:---
other:---
```

Some vendors clobber the ACL and clear all the entries when chmod is used.

HP-UX Access Control Lists

HP-UX ACL entries are also derived from a file's base permissions. Access control lists are composed of a series of *access control entries* (ACEs). ACEs map users and groups to access modes. They can permit access by specifying modes r, w, or x or restrict access by specifying a dash (-) in the access mode string. ACEs can be represented in three forms: *short form*, the default in which each entry is of the form (uid.gid, mode), for example, (bob.%, rwx); *long form*, which breaks the ACL into multi-line format, with each ACE in the form "mode uid.gid.", for example, "rwx bob.%"; and *operator form*, which is similar to the symbolic assignment mode to chmod (for example, "bob.% = rwx.").

ACL entries must be unique for any pair of user and group values and are evaluated from the most specific to the least specific in a first-fit manner (refer to Chapter 3, which discusses access control rules). For example, if a user or a process belongs to multiple groups, multiple entries might match an access request to the file. In this case, we combine the permissions of all entries using an OR operation: If any entry allows access, the access is permitted. ACLs can be manipulated by commands or library functions, and pattern matching using wildcards is permitted. The *lsacl* command lists the ACL associated with a file, and the *chacl* command can set, delete, or modify the ACL. The *chmod* command can have unfortunate side effects because it disables all access control entries. If *chmod* is used to set the SUID, SGID, and sticky bits, a chmod command can clobber the ACL on the file in a non-POSIX compliant manner.

HP-UX also supports JFS ACL, also known as VERITAS File System ACLs if you have a VxFS file system with specific disk layout versions. JFS ACLs are closer to POSIX compliance than HFS ACLs. They are very similar to the Solaris ACL mechanisms with some minor differences. JFS ACLs, unlike HP-UX ACLs, also support ACL inheritance by assigning default permissions to directories that will apply to any files or directories

(docs.hp.com) for more information.

Conclusion

There is a tremendous amount of information on operating system and network security on the Web and through many excellent references. Applying all of this detail to a specific application instance is the hard part and can be overwhelming to an application team. If this situation is indeed the case, we recommend outsourcing the activity of security architecture to an organization with adequate security expertise because of the risks of compromise through incorrect configuration.

At the heart of the matter is the simple fact that powerful, general-purpose operating systems can never be adequately secured if they are connected to untrusted networks and provide even moderately interesting services. The software is just too complicated, the interactions are just too varied, and the bugs are just too common. The mechanisms described in this chapter can go a long way toward reducing the size of the target exposed to attackers, however.

Database Security

In this chapter, we will describe the evolution and architectural options provided within one of the most complex components of any application: the database. Databases are the heart of enterprise applications and store the most critical part of the application: its data. We will describe the evolution of security features within databases and relate the options available to architects in terms of security patterns.

We will discuss network security solutions to connect to a database, role-based access control mechanisms within databases, security mechanisms based on database views, methods of object encapsulation within a database, event notification and alarming through database triggers, and finally multi-level security using row-level labeling within database tables.

Applications will pick and choose from this broad sweep of options, driven by the granularity of security required by policy. It is unlikely that any single application will use all of these mechanisms at once. Each imposes a performance penalty, and while each provides unique features, there does exist an overlap in protective scope as we move from one option to the next—protecting data at finer levels. Omitting any one of these options from an architecture can have detrimental impacts if the security properties that it enforces are not supported through other means, however. All of the row-level security in the world will not help an application that performs poor user authentication.

The database and the network are not the only architectural elements in play. It is both important and necessary to direct some architectural thought to the configuration of the database and its installation on the underlying OS and hardware. We have covered some aspects of protecting applications on an operating system in the last chapter. These solutions apply to databases, as well.

tion to concrete and usable options, we will use Oracle's suite of database products as a reference point for features and for functionality. All other database vendors provide similar functionality but on different architectural assumptions. Rather than clutter our presentation with descriptions of vendor differences, and in the interests of brevity, we will restrict our presentation to one vendor, Oracle, with the recognition that the architecture principles in the following section can be extended or compared to other vendor products. In cases where we reference explicit syntax or implementation details, please keep in mind that they apply to a particular vendor's viewpoint and the properties of an evolving product offering.

Database Security Evolution

Relational Database Management Systems are very complex. They perform many of the features of an operating system, such as process management, multi-threading, disk management, user administration, and file management. They also perform all of the functions required of a relational database engine and the modules surrounding it, such as the management of database instances, users, profiles, system and application schemas, stored procedures, and metadata.

Database security has had an unusual evolution, one in which industry events have prompted a fork (and now perhaps a merge) in the architectural direction taken by vendors. The fork in architectural evolution occurred sometime in the mid-to-late 1990s, when vendors provided more security features at the outer edge (at the operating system level of their products), moving away from more invasive security strategies within the core database engine and its modules. The merge is occurring right now, with some re-emphasis on multi-level security strategies once thought applicable only to military applications for commercial applications.

Multi-Level Security in Databases

Early database security was guided by the attempts to merge the theoretical frameworks for access control with relational database theory. Relational theory is the winning theoretical framework for data persistence over competing theories based on network or hierarchical models. The writing on the wall at the beginning of the 1990s about the future direction of database security was clear. The reference specification for database security was the Department of Defense's Trusted DBMS Interpretation of the A1 classification for computing systems. Multi-level relational extensions and associated security policy management tools would be used to build trusted computing *database* systems. Multi-level protection based on labels was expected to be the standard within applications.

Two fundamental principles of relational database theory are *entity integrity* and *referential integrity.* Entity integrity states that no primary key in a relation can be NULL. Referential integrity states that an n-tuple in one relation that refers to another relation

foreign keys in one relation to correspond to primary keys in another.

The proposed theoretical direction towards multi-level security had many valuable elements.

1. Extension of the relational principles of entity integrity and referential integrity to support database security. These principles must continue to hold on the subset of the relation remaining visible after enforcement of security policy.
2. Security kernels within the database engine. Kernels are small, efficient, and provably correct monitors that manage all references to objects.
3. Multi-level, relational, view-based extensions that could run over any single-level, commercial database engine.
4. Classification labels that could be attached to any granularity of object: table, row, column, or element. This function also supports classification of data through granularity and hierarchy in the definition of labels. In addition, labels could be assigned to metadata such as views, stored procedures, queries, or other objects.
5. Security models that defined secure states and the transitions allowed for subjects to move between states.
6. Extension of the trusted computing base within the database engine all the way to the user's client process within some solutions that proposed the creation of layered, trusted computing bases.

The major database vendors have made tremendous improvements in their products, but no commercial database supports anything close to this set of features.

Database vendors have aggressively adopted and promoted network security features to protect remote or distributed access to the database over an untrusted network. Vendors do have (and have had) products that provide multi-level labeled security to support models of trusted database implementations that were the emerging standard from a decade ago. They just do not emphasize them as much as they do the network security options to commercial projects, labeling multi-level security as "military grade." This remark is not specific to Oracle and applies equally well to the other leading database vendors. All support a variety of security options. They do, however, emphasize some options over others.

We do not express a preference or a value judgment on the relative merits of managing security at the edge of the database interface or managing security as part of your relational schema and its dynamics. What works for the application is based on domain knowledge and architectural constraints. As security becomes more complex and hackers become more proficient, however, it might be prudent to keep open all available security options at architecture review.

In our opinion, four major forces in the industry have driven the shift in emphasis from the structure of data within the database to the edge of the database and the network outside.

The rise of the Web. The Web created a huge demand for a certain model of database design. The repetitive nature of the security solutions implemented at client site after client site might have driven vendors to reprioritize new database architectures.

The rise of object-oriented databases. The theory and practice of object modeling caught fire in the development community, and the demand for increased support for object persistence within traditional relational databases might have changed priorities within the database vendor community. Security was a major design force behind the introduction of objects into databases. Object modeling was used to define access control mappings from well-defined subjects to objects that were spread over multiple elements of the database schema. Polyinstantiation, which is the ability to transparently create multiple instances of a single, persistent object for each class of subject that needed to see it, was an important security mechanism. Considerable research exists exploring support for managing reads and writes between virtual objects and the actual stored data. The polyinstantiation security principle is borrowed from object technology's polymorphism. Priorities shifted away from a security viewpoint, however, where objects were thought of as a good idea for internally managing access control toward a programming language viewpoint in support of object technology. Object persistence overtook security as a design goal.

The rise of enterprise network security solutions. The availability of strong enterprise security products to support Kerberos, DCE, SSL, and cryptographic toolkits along with some agreement on security standards made it easier for database vendors to move security from the internal database engine to the perimeter. This function has enabled them to focus on their own core competency of building the fastest possible database engine supporting the widest array of user features, secure in the knowledge that considerable expertise has gone into the mechanisms that they depend upon for implementing security at the perimeter.

The rise in performance demands. The last reason for the de-emphasis is unavoidable and somewhat unfortunate. Database vendors must manage the tension between the twin architectural goals of security and performance. The ugly truth is that databases, more than any other component in systems architecture, are asked to perform more transaction processing today to serve user communities unimaginably larger than those commonly found a decade ago. Security within the engine degrades performance in a significant manner. Database customers are very conscious of performance benchmark rankings. As hardware catches up to our needs for fine-grained security, this situation might improve.

What is best for your application? As we have repeated previously, do what works. Because system architects have domain knowledge of the application and the vendor does not, the lesson for us is simple. In any large component within a system, all of the options discussed at architecture review for implementing security might not receive the same presentation emphasis. It is important to separate the vendor's desire for a certain product design direction from your own application's design forces.

In recent times, vendor support for multi-level security has been improving. The promise of true and full-featured, multi-level security might be making a comeback. For example, Oracle provides (and has provided for some time now) a multi-level security product called Oracle *Fine Grained Access Control* (FGAC), which evolved from the

rows by level, compartment, and ownership. We will briefly discuss this feature at the end of this chapter. Other vendor products provide similar features.

Architectural Components and Security

Databases rival operating systems in terms of the degrees of freedom available to an architect in designing security solutions (see Figure 12.1). We will use Oracle as a terminology reference for most of the discussion to follow, but all database vendors provide similar functionality with varying levels of success.

Databases support security at two places: outside the database and inside the database. Databases support network security features, such as integration with enterprise security infrastructures, single-sign on, support for secure protocols such as SSL, and other cryptographic primitives and protocols. These technologies are used by the database to authenticate all users requesting connections. These features have little to do with relational database theory and exist to create a trusted link between the user's client host and the database server. Once a user is authenticated and has an encrypted connection to the database, he or she is considered to be inside the database and any queries made must be secured by using internal database mechanisms. These mechanisms include the following:

Session management. At the session level, when users log in to databases, the database sets environment variables for the duration of the session, stores state information to handle successive transactions within the session, and handles session termination.

Object ownership. The database schema can define ownership of database objects as tables, indexes, views, procedures, packages, and so on. Users can GRANT or

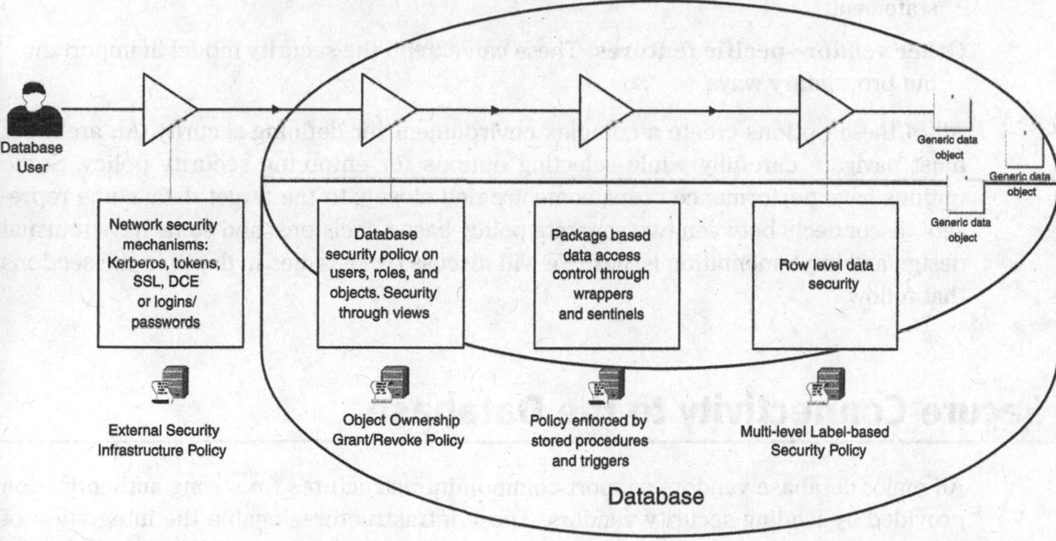

Figure 12.1 Database security components.

discretionary access control.

Object encapsulation. This goal is achieved through packages and stored procedures. The creation and ownership of security policy structures can be kept separate from the database schema. Packages define collections of stored procedures, which support well-defined transactions used to restrict the user's ability to change the state of the database to a known and safe set of actions. The user can execute but not modify the stored procedures. By default, the user is blocked from directly accessing the data referenced by the packages, because stored procedures execute by using the privileges of the owner of the procedure, not the user. The owner must have the required privileges to access the data. With release 8.0 and onward, Oracle also allows the administrator to configure security on a stored procedure so that it runs with the privileges of the INVOKER rather than the DEFINER.

Triggers. Triggers are transparent procedural definitions attached to tables. The trigger is fired when a triggering event occurs, such as a modification to the table. The database engine can enforce policy on specific DML types at specific points, and before or after the statement is executed. In addition, triggers can be specified to execute once for an entire database table or once for every row of a table.

Predicate application. The database engine can modify the user's query on the fly by adding predicates to the query to restrict its scope. Oracle uses this method to provide *Virtual Private Databases*.

Multi-level labeled security. At the finest level of granularity, the user data can have additional structured attributes that can be used to enforce mandatory access control policies over and above the system access and object access mechanisms described earlier. The database engine can reference row-level labels against a label-based access policy before allowing a SELECT, UPDATE, INSERT, or DELETE statement.

Other vendor-specific features. These can extend the security model in important but proprietary ways.

All of these options create a complex environment for defining security. An architect must navigate carefully while selecting options for enforcing security policy. Some options have performance costs; some are tied closely to the target data; some represent disconnects between two separate policy-based decisions; and some have unusual design and implementation issues. We will discuss these issues in depth in the sections that follow.

Secure Connectivity to the Database

All major database vendors support common infrastructures for strong authentication provided by leading security vendors. These infrastructures enable the integration of mainstream enterprise network security solutions such Kerberos, DCE, SSL, and other security standards into enterprise applications. These infrastructures all provide hooks

integrity, strong authentication, and sometimes single sign-on. Database vendors have also borrowed other security components more commonly associated with operating systems, such as security audit tools. For example, Internet Security Systems even provides a database scanner product that models its popular OS audit product RealSecure, extending operating system audit features into the realm of relational databases. These tools can test the strength of a database password, test password aging, or institute lockouts on multiple bad password attempts.

We will describe Oracle Advanced Security mechanisms. The material in this section is from several database security papers and from books listed in the references, along with information from the Oracle Technical Network site http://otn.oracle.com. Oracle Advanced Security focuses on integrating Oracle with several security products and technologies.

Cryptographic primitives. Data transferred during client-server communication can be bulk encrypted by using DES, in 40- and 56-bit key lengths, or by using RSA Data Security's RC4 algorithm in 40-, 56-, and 128-bit key lengths. In addition to encryption, Oracle provides data integrity through MD5-based cryptographic hashes. Other cipher suites are also available under the SSL option. Please refer to Chapter 6, "Cryptography," for definitions and details of cryptographic primitives.

Token authentication services. Users can authenticate by using Smartcards and the *Remote Authentication Dial-In User Service* (RADIUS). The authentication mechanism is a challenge response protocol between the client and the database server. The Smartcard is protected with the user's PIN, which does not go over the network. Alternatively, users can authenticate by using strong, one-time passwords using SecurID tokens and RSA Data Security's ACE token servers.

Kerberos. Oracle supports MIT Kerberos Release 5 and CyberSafe's commercial Kerberos product, TrustBroker. Please refer to Chapter 13, "Security Components," for a brief description of Kerberos.

Secure Sockets Layer (SSL). SSL has become very common since the emergence of standard libraries for adding transport layer security and open-source toolkits such as OpenSSL. Oracle enables both client-side and server-side authenticated SSL. Currently, this item is Oracle's only PKI-enabled product for this vendor, but other solutions requiring certificates will no doubt follow.

Distributed Computing Environment (DCE). DCE Integration requires Oracle8i and Oracle's proprietary networking protocol, Net8. Oracle applications can use DCE tools and services to talk securely across heterogeneous environments. The Open Software Foundation's Distributed Computing Environment is a middleware services product that provides integrated network services such as remote procedure calls, directory services, centralized authentication services, distributed file systems, and distributed time service. OSF has merged with another standards group, X/OPEN, to form the Open Group, which currently supports the evolution of DCE.

DCE security is similar to Kerberos and indeed uses Kerberos V5-based authentication as a configuration option. DCE Security provides authentication,

naming and location services. The extent of the linkage between DCE's offerings and Oracle applications is left to the architect. The application can use the full range of services, including authenticated RPC, single sign-on, naming, location, and security services or can use a minimal subset of services (for example, only implementing authentication by using the DCE generic security services API).

Once a principal authenticates to the DCE cell that contains the database, the principal can access the database. Principals authenticated in this manner can also transfer an external role, defined through membership of a DCE group, into an internal Oracle database role. This feature enables the role-based authorization mechanisms within the database to be transparently enforced on the principal.

Directory Services. As is becoming increasingly common with vendor products, Oracle supports integration with X.500 directories that use LDAP to provide enterprise user management. We will discuss enterprise security management using directories in Chapter 13.

Oracle provides its own LDAP-compliant directory, Oracle Internet Directory, but also interacts with Microsoft Active Directory. Incidentally, X.500 directories and Kerberos are both key components of the Windows 2000 security architecture. Directories define user and resource hierarchies, domain-based user management, and distributed services such as naming, location, and security. Directories will increasingly play a critical role in addressing security challenges.

Role-Based Access Control

Databases implement RBAC through database roles. A privilege is the right to execute a particular operation upon an object or execute a particular action within the system. A user may have privileges to connect to the database to initiate a session, create a database object such as a table or index, execute a particular DML query against an object owned by another user, or execute a stored procedure or function.

Privileges can be granted to users directly or through roles. Roles are collections of access privileges associated with a common function. Databases provide role-based access control by assigning users to roles and then using GRANT and REVOKE statements to permit or block a user or a role to access objects in the data dictionary.

Oracle supports privileges at the system and the object level. The ability to grant privileges is itself a privilege and is available only to administrators or users who have been explicitly granted the right through a GRANT ANY PRIVILEGE statement. A user automatically has object privileges on all the objects in his or her own schema and can grant access privileges on these objects to users belonging to other schemas. Thus, the user can allow controlled manipulation of the schema by granting access to stored procedures but not to the underlying database tables. In addition, DML privileges can be restricted on columns. For example, the INSERT and UPDATE privileges on a table can

when a user without access privileges modifies the table.

Users may also have privileges to execute Data Definition Language (DDL) operations that enable users to alter table properties, create triggers, create indexes, or create references where the table is used as the parent key to any foreign keys that the user creates in his or her own tables. This dependency restricts our ability to modify the parent key column in the original table to maintain references to foreign keys in other tables.

Oracle roles allow applications to implement RBAC, which enables simplified security administration by separating the direct mapping from users to privileges through intermediate roles. Users are assigned to roles based on their job function, and roles are assigned database privileges based on the access operations needed to fulfill that function. Roles can be dynamically enabled or disabled to limit user privileges in a controlled manner. Roles can be password-protected. A user must know the password to enable (that is, assume) the role.

A role can be granted system or object privileges. Once created, a role can be granted to other roles (under some consistency constraints). If role R1 is explicitly granted to role R2, any user who explicitly enables R2 implicitly and automatically gains all the privileges owned by R1. Users with the GRANT privilege can assign or remove roles using the GRANT and REVOKE statements. As an Oracle specific detail, roles do not belong to a particular schema.

Oracle does not support true role hierarchies in terms of the partial order and inheritance properties of the hierarchical RBAC model described in [SFK00]. The ability to grant roles to roles, however, is quite powerful in creating set-theoretic models within the application to create hierarchical properties.

Oracle defines the security domain for a user or role as the collection of all the privileges enabled through direct grants, schema membership, or explicit and implicit role grants. Dependencies between two or more privileges granted implicitly through roles can cause unexpected results if we can combine them. Security domains may enable self-promotion if we permit privileges to be arbitrarily combined to create new access rights. Oracle forbids the execution of some DDL statements if received through a role; for example, a user with the CREATE VIEW privilege cannot create a view on a table on which he or she has the SELECT privilege, if that privilege is not directly granted but is acquired through a role grant. This restriction prevents unexpected side effects that could violate security policy. In the following sections, we will present more details on RBAC and view-based security.

The Data Dictionary

The data dictionary stores information about the structure of objects within the database. The metadata (data about data) describing how the actual data is structured is also stored in database tables. The data dictionary defines views into the metadata, and

Oracle user SYS, cannot be updated by a user, and is automatically maintained by the database engine. The views in the dictionary organize objects into three categories: current user-owned objects, current user-accessible objects, and all objects.

Database Object Privileges

Structured Query Language (SQL) provides the GRANT and REVOKE data definition constructs to extend or withhold privileges from entities that wish to access database objects. Privileges can be applied to individual objects (object privileges) or to an entire class of objects (system privileges). The SQL92 standard defines the syntax for privilege manipulation. All vendors support variations on this theme.

The GRANT and REVOKE statement syntax are shown in Figure 12.2.

Complex collections of privileges can be bundled by using database roles. Privileges can be granted to roles, and then the roles can be assigned to principals. This process simplifies security management.

Issues Surrounding Role-Based Access Control

Role-based access control in databases using this mechanism creates security policy issues with respect to delegation of rights. The grant statement's WITH GRANT OPTION clause enables a recipient of privileges to transfer the privileges to other users. The revoke statement's CASCADE CONSTRAINT clause can trigger additional revocations to fire when the rights of a user are reduced. If that user has in turn granted those rights to other users, those secondary rights might be revoked. Other implementations might not enforce cascading revocations. Some vendors might choose to block a revocation request from a granter if the recipient of rights has already transferred the rights to a third entity by requiring that the recipient first revoke these transferred rights before losing the right themselves.

Research on privilege graphs, which describe permissions graphically by using entities as nodes and grants as edges, has revealed that this territory is murky. The difficulty lies in reasoning about security, rather than picking a particular implementation as correct.

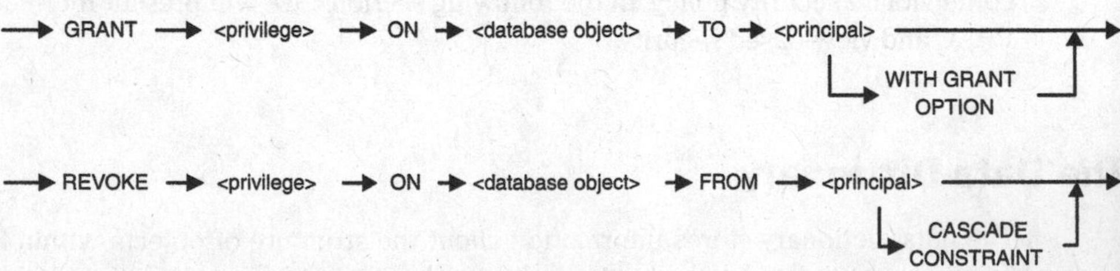

Figure 12.2 GRANT and REVOKE statements.

SELECT right on a table if B could have received the same right from a third party C without A's knowledge. Reasoning about rights after a revoke operation is complicated because we do not know whether what A intended to accomplish and what A actually accomplished were the same.

Some applications avoid this issue by using database roles. All privileges are statically granted to roles, and users dynamically enable or disable roles that they are assigned to as execution proceeds. Rights are never revoked. The problem with this solution is that it breaks the discretionary access policy that the owner of an object is the only one who is allowed to grant privileges by requiring owners to give rights to roles explicitly and assuming a trust model of permissions instead. Recipients, rather than owners, enable permissions.

Specific vendor implementations will define the behavior of the clauses WITH GRANT OPTION and CASCADING CONSTRAINTS. When applications use these clauses, they will be well defined, but the bad news is that different vendors might choose different implementations. This situation raises a real architectural issue, namely the portability of a solution in case the database migrates to another vendor product or if a large application has multiple subsystems with different database choices and needs to uniformly apply security policy.

Database Views

Views are a commonly used mechanism to implement security within databases. A simple view can be built on top of the join of a collection of base tables, renaming or removing columns, selecting a subset of the rows, or aggregating rows by average, minimum, or maximum. Views are examples of the *Façade* pattern in the Gang of Four book [GHJV95]. The Façade pattern's definition, by default and as is, does not qualify it as a security pattern. A Façade must be used in association with data object privilege mechanisms, such as the GRANT and REVOKE mechanisms of the previous section, before it can be said to enforce security. A user must be granted access to the view but must have no access to the underlying base tables.

The syntax of a view statement is shown in Figure 12.3.

The view can slice the joined based table relation into horizontal slices by only exposing some rows, or into vertical slices by only selecting some columns (or, it can do both).

The predicate expression can be quite complex, and if ad-hoc query access to this view is granted, we cannot anticipate all of the operations that the user might wish to execute on the view. Views present a number of issues when used for security.

1. Views are used extensively to support data restriction for business logic purposes, rather than security. The application's database designer needs to carefully separate view definitions based on whether they were created for enforcing security policy or business rules. Updates to security policy have to be reflected in

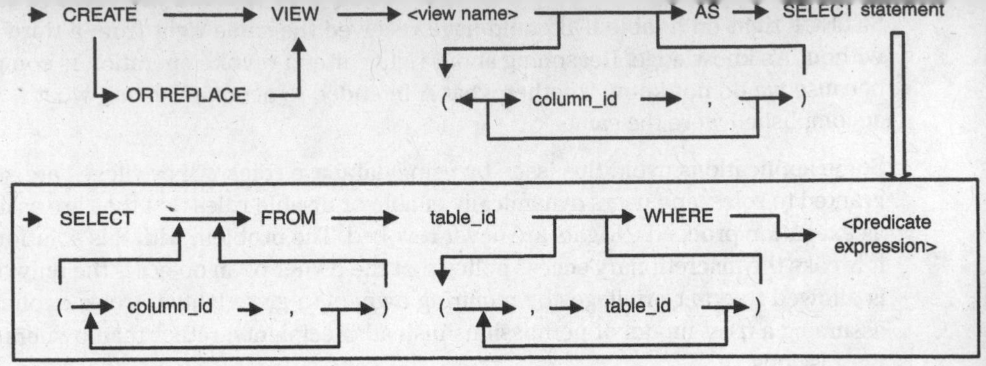

Figure 12.3 CREATE VIEW statement with SELECT expanded.

view redefinition or the creation of additional views, independent of the application's feature set.

2. Some database vendors provide read only access through SELECT statements to views because of the complexity of managing UPDATE, INSERT, and DELETE queries. Modification of the view could add too many NULL values to the base tables in undesirable ways. Note that the view cannot see certain columns, which must nevertheless be populated in the base tables as a result of any updates to the view.
3. Even if the database supports writing to views, the ability to modify more than one base table might be restricted. Writes to views can especially create administrative overhead in cases where multiple triggers are used to support modifications to the base tables. Modification of some columns, such as the join keys, might be forbidden. Thus, data that the user can see and believes that he or she has write access to might not be modifiable. Oracle version 8.0 provides updateable views using *Instead-of triggers*, defined on the view, that execute in place of the *data manipulation language* (DML) statement that fired them. Instead-of triggers implement a sane version of the update.
4. View-based security might require one view for each of the many access modes: SELECT from one view, UPDATE to another, and DELETE from a third. This situation creates security management complexity and a maintenance headache.
5. Views can create computational overheads. Views based on joining many tables might have severe performance costs if several of the selective predicates in the WHERE clause of a query cause a join to a single base table but are independent of the other clauses. This situation is called a star join, and unless carefully optimized, it can be expensive.
6. Access to the underlying base tables must be restricted so that the user cannot bypass the view to directly access data hidden from the view.
7. Views can potentially overlap if defined over the same base tables. Users denied access to data through one view can potentially gain access through another.

conditions that are unavailable to the database, such as information about the user that might be part of their environment.

9. Views cannot implement complex security policy requirements that involve tens of thousands of scenarios.

Security Based on Object-Oriented Encapsulation

Access within the database can also be protected by using encapsulation methods borrowed from the object world (shown in Figure 12.4). The data in a collection of base tables can be associated with a package that contains methods (or, in database terms, *stored procedures*) that define all allowed operations on the base tables. This modeling is not true object modeling because other properties such as inheritance might not be supported. The user can be constrained to using only well-defined operations to modify the database state, however.

Database triggers provide another means of moving the access control mechanism closer to the data being protected. If the application cannot guarantee that all user access will only be through a security package, then a user might be able to access base tables through another mechanism, such as through an interface that supports ad-hoc queries. This situation is not true of triggers, which cannot be bypassed by the user. If a trigger is defined on a table, unless the user has explicit permission to disable the trigger, it will execute when a DML statement touches the table.

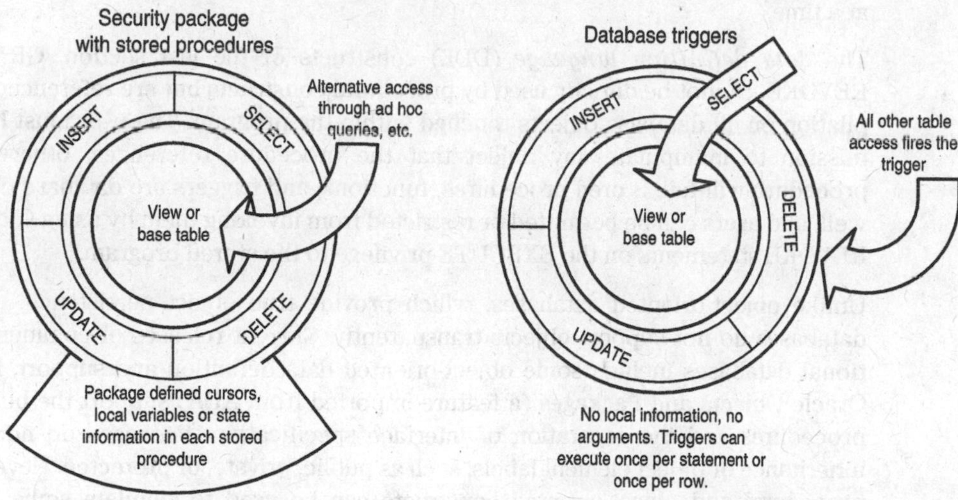

Figure 12.4 Wrapper and sentinel.

base vendors to implement wrapper and sentinel, the two security patterns illustrated in Figure 12.4.

Procedural Extensions to SQL

Oracle PL/SQL is a language that adds procedural constructs to Oracle's implementation of the ANSI Structured Query Language (SQL92) standard. These constructs include variable declarations, selection (IF-THEN-ELSE) statements, conditional or numeric loops, and GOTO statements. Procedural languages extend the declarative syntax of SQL in useful ways, enabling developers to wrap complex data manipulation directives within procedures that are stored on the database, and are optimized and compiled for performance. Procedural extensions to databases simplify client/server interactions, reduce network traffic, wrap functionality with exception handling methods, and enable server-side business logic to maintain state information.

Oracle PL/SQL programs are composed of blocks. Procedural constructs can be used to bundle business logic into anonymous blocks of code or into named procedures, functions, packages, or triggers. Blocks can be dynamically constructed and executed only once or can be stored in the database in compiled form. Blocks can be explicitly invoked, as in the case of stored procedures, functions, or packages, or implicitly invoked, as in the case of database triggers that execute when a triggering event occurs.

Procedure calls are standalone PL/SQL statements, whereas function calls appear as part of an expression (because functions return values). Stored procedures, functions, and triggers contain embedded *data manipulation language* (DML) statements in SQL. Oracle supports cursors, which enable procedural iteration through a relation, one row at a time.

The *data definition language* (DDL) constructs of the last section, GRANT and REVOKE, cannot be directly used by procedural constructs but are referenced at compilation on all database objects touched within the program. The user must have permission to manipulate any object that the procedure references; otherwise, the procedure will fail. Stored procedures, functions, and triggers are database objects as well, and users can be permitted or restricted from invoking them by using GRANT and REVOKE statements on the EXECUTE privilege to the stored program.

Unlike object-oriented databases, which provide true object persistence, relational databases do not support objects transparently. Current releases of commercial relational databases include some object-oriented data definition and support, however. Oracle Objects and Packages (a feature imported from ADA) support the bundling of procedures and the separation of interface specification. Packages do not support inheritance or object element labels, such as public, private, or protected. Nevertheless, procedural and object-oriented constructs can be used to simulate some forms of object-oriented behavior, such as interface definition, encapsulation, object typing, constructors, element and method binding, and object privileges.

procedural constructs: wrapper, implemented with stored procedures, and sentinel, implemented with triggers.

Wrapper

One source of database security problems are interfaces that permit ad-hoc queries. Client programs generate SQL statements on the fly and submit them to the database engine, which enables what security expert Matt Bishop calls *Time of Check to Time of Use* (TOCTTOU) attacks. In this type of attack, an attacker intercepts the query after it is created but before it is submitted and modifies it to extract additional information from the database or to modify data within the database.

This vulnerability is often avoidable if the set of queries expected by the system in its normal database operational profile is quite small and where the only variation is in the arguments used in the queries. Stored procedures can implement the wrapper pattern to restrict the actions of users to well-recognized transactions. Recall the definition of the wrapper security pattern, which replaces the actual target interface (in this case, the database SQL interpreter) with a protected interface (in this case, a predefined stored procedure). We can capture the variation in the queries by setting the arguments to the stored procedure. The database engine must restrict the query interface to only invocations of the stored procedures. This example shows the syntax validator pattern at work, in conjunction with wrappers.

Figure 12.5 shows the syntax of a PL/SQL create procedure statement.

By default, a stored procedure is like a UNIX SUID program. It executes with the privileges of its owner (or definer), not with the privileges of the user who invoked it. Stored procedures, functions, and triggers can reference other database objects, such as tables or other procedures, within the subprogram's body. The subprogram owner must either own any database objects referenced by the procedure or have explicit access granted to the objects by their actual owners. In addition, a user must be granted the EXECUTE privilege on a stored procedure by the owner of the procedure before the user can invoke it. This behavior is configurable in some products so that the invoker of the procedure can execute the code under their own privileges. This is useful for maintainability of a common code base across a collection of separate database instances, where all

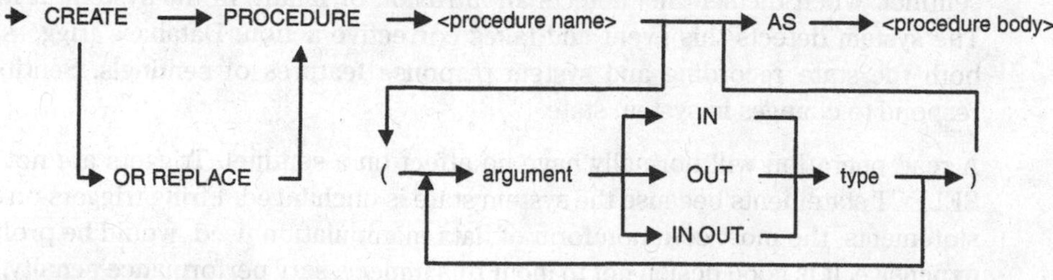

Figure 12.5 Procedure definition.

own instance of the database. Creating multiple copies of the procedure definitions introduces a significant management and code synchronization problem.

We introduced user roles in our discussion of the GRANT and REVOKE statements. Because stored procedures, functions, and triggers are precompiled and stored, users cannot use dynamic role-based privileges to access protected objects. Procedures require explicit access given by using GRANT statements rather than access inherited through a role. This function is necessary because object references within procedures are bound at compilation time, not at run time. GRANT and REVOKE statements are DDL statements. Once they are invoked, the new privileges are recorded in the data dictionary and are used for all user sessions from that point onward. In contrast, roles can be dynamically enabled or disabled, and the effects of a SET ROLE command are active only for a single session. Using privileges inherited through roles adds a run-time performance cost to compiled and optimized stored programs. The database engine must re-evaluate all privileges to data objects on every invocation to verify that the user has permission to execute the procedure and access any data objects it references. To avoid this performance penalty, Oracle disables roles within stored procedures. Other vendors might allow run-time evaluation of user privileges for more flexibility.

Sentinel

Database triggers, like procedures, are declarative, executable blocks of code. Unlike procedures, however, triggers do not have a local variable store or arguments. Triggers are executed implicitly. A trigger on a table can be launched when an INSERT, DELETE, or UPDATE statement executes on the table. The trigger can execute once either before or after the statement or can be executed on every row that is affected. The user, unless explicitly permitted to DISABLE the trigger, cannot prevent its execution. Triggers are useful for maintaining integrity constraints and logging the user identity and activities on the table to a security log, and can automatically signal other events to happen within the database by invoking stored procedures or touching other tables with defined triggers.

Figure 12.6 shows the syntax of a PL/SQL create trigger statement.

Triggers implement the sentinel security pattern. Recall that the sentinel pattern describes an entity within the system whose existence is transparent to the user and that maintains system integrity in some manner. The system monitors the health of the sentinel. When the sentinel detects an intrusion or failure in the system, it falls over. The system detects this event and takes corrective action. Database triggers capture both the state recording and system response features of sentinels. Sentinels only respond to changes in system state.

A read operation will normally have no affect on a sentinel. Triggers are not fired on SELECT statements because the system state is unchanged. Firing triggers on SELECT statements, the most common form of data manipulation used, would be prohibitively expensive. It is good design not to incur this unnecessary performance penalty, because other mechanisms can be used to secure read access.

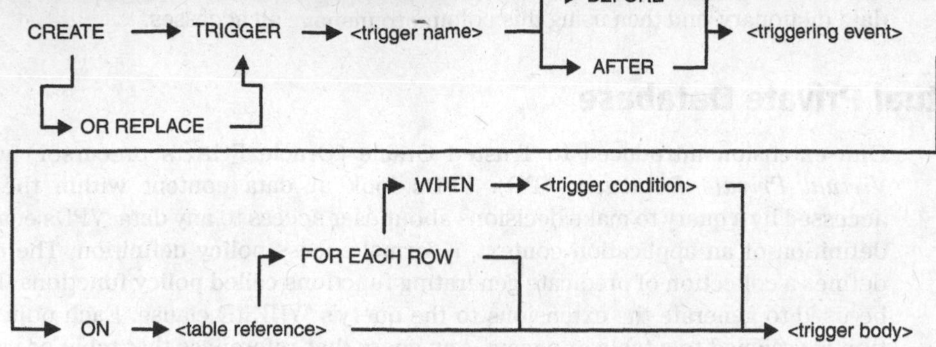

Figure 12.6 Trigger definition.

Triggers do add a performance hit, and as multiple triggers can be defined on a table, the order in which triggers are activated must be specified. Security triggers must be kept separate from business logic triggers and preferably must precede them. Security triggers should be very efficient, especially if invoked on a per-row level.

The trigger views in the data dictionary describe the database triggers that are accessible to the users. Each view's columns describe the properties of a trigger: the schema that owns the trigger, the trigger name, the type, the triggering event, the name of the table on which the trigger is defined, the owner of the table, the trigger status (ENABLED or DISABLED), a text description, and the PL/SQL block that defines the body of the trigger.

We will now describe two other security mechanisms that Oracle supports within its Trusted Oracle product line. These mechanisms enable access control closer to the data than the solutions we have seen so far. The following sections are a summary of information on Oracle's security offerings from the Oracle Technical Network and from conversations with Oracle DBAs. Please refer to the bibliography for references with more detailed information.

Security through Restrictive Clauses

Multi-level security models for databases enforce mandatory access control by defining a hierarchy of labels and assigning ranges of labels to users and rows within all base tables. Users are assigned a session label within their label range when they first connect to the database. The user must first pass all discretionary controls, such as having the correct privileges to objects, views, and stored procedures. At this point, before the user can access any data, an additional label security policy is applied. This policy permits a user to read data that is at their session label and below and to write data at their session level. For example, Oracle's early MLS product Trusted Oracle implemented

data dictionary, and then using this column to manage all accesses.

Virtual Private Database

One extension introduced to Trusted Oracle (Oracle FGAC's precursor) was the *Virtual Private Database* (VPD). VPDs look at data content within the tables accessed by a query to make decisions about user access to any data. VPDs enable the definition of an application context, a formal access policy definition. The context defines a collection of predicate generating functions called policy functions that will be used to generate the extensions to the query's WHERE clause. Each policy function is assigned to a table or a view. Any query that references that table or view will be modified by the appropriate policy function based on the user's application context. An application context trigger fires upon logon to place the user within an appropriate context.

When a user within an application context attempts to query the database, the database engine dynamically modifies the query to add predicates to the WHERE clause. The user has no ability to prevent this access control, because it is performed close to the data in a transparent manner. The additional predicates enforce the access policy by further restricting the response to the original query, stripping out rows and columns or performing aggregations, to remove information deemed inaccessible to the user. VPDs can be seen as implementing the *interceptor* pattern, because all queries are intercepted and modified before execution.

VPDs also support multiple policies on a single object, and policy functions can define the generated predicates based on the type of DML statement being attempted: SELECT, UPDATE, INSERT, or DELETE. As can be expected, however, policy functions can have an adverse effect on performance. Our ability to optimize queries might be hurt by complex predicates.

The name VPD might create some confusion because it is similar to VPN, which stands for Virtual Private Network. VPNs are designed to run in distributed environments over untrusted network links. VPNs are instances of secure pipes with no knowledge of the content within the encrypted packets being transported. They are virtual because they define logical network links, not physical ones. They are private because a VPN can share the same physical transport media with other streams while guaranteeing data confidentiality and integrity through encryption and cryptographic hashes.

Unlike VPNs, VPDs are constructs created within a single logical instance of the database server on trusted hardware and with control of all operations. We do not have a strong definition of what virtual really is, but we would hesitate to call this separation *virtual*. It is not analogous with its use in the name VPN because it does not imply and require the capability to run an Oracle database securely within another vendor's data server. That would be impossible. In addition, the data is not really *private* because two applications can share tables (a strength of the VPD solution). The privacy feature in VPDs refers to selective hiding in a manner that is transparent to the user; the privacy feature of VPNs refers to data privacy from the untrusted network.

plify application development and remove the need for view-based security. These are valuable architectural goals.

Oracle Label Security

Oracle has another enhanced mandatory access control security solution called Oracle Label Security (OLS). The OLS feature is implemented by using VPDs to support a complex row-level model of access control. Oracle's current version of label security differs from conventional mandatory access control in some details. Labels have structure, with each label containing three fields. These components are the label's level, compartment, and group.

Level. Levels are organized in hierarchies and typically have the semantics of military sensitivity of information levels, such as Public, Proprietary, Restricted, Secret, Top Secret, and so on.

Compartment. The compartments within a level correspond to categories of information. Categories are peer containers and are not organized into hierarchies within levels or across levels. They enable data restriction based on context or business logic. Users with access to a certain level can only access their own categories within that level. Compartments support the "need to know" policy features described in Chapter 3. Users are assigned Read and Write compartments. When the user accesses a row on a read or write, the user's compartment definition is compared to the row's compartment definitions. A data element can belong to multiple compartments.

Group. The third component of the label defines ownership. Ownership definitions can be hierarchical. This third component is unusual in that it allows the definition of additional discretionary access control mechanisms over and above those already passed at the SYSTEM and OBJECT levels.

Labels can be composed of a standalone level component, a level and associated compartment, or all three components. Groups represent an additional degree of freedom in security policy definition. We recommend that they should be used with care, because incorrect configuration could contradict prior policy decisions.

Read and Write Semantics

When a user accesses a row, one of three outcomes will occur:

1. The user has *privileges* that bypass row label security (denoted by the number 1 in Figure 12.7).
2. The user must pass the *write mediation algorithm* to modify data in the row (denoted by the number 2 in Figure 12.7).
3. The user must pass the *read mediation algorithm* to read data (denoted by the number 3 in Figure 12.7).

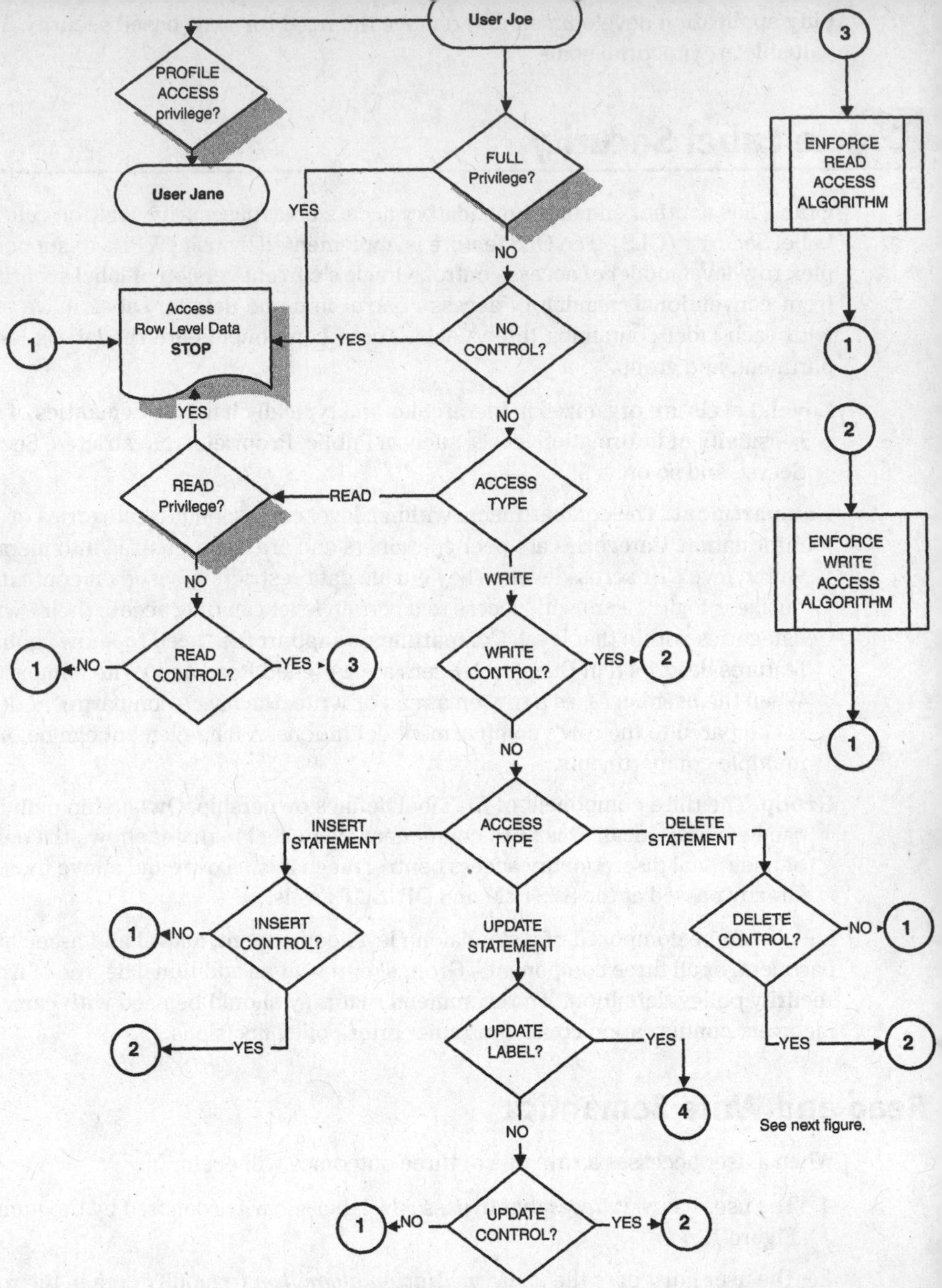

Figure 12.7 Label modification in row-label access. (See Figure 12.8 for legend.)

access:

Level. The level of a data label places it within the level hierarchy. Oracle assigns a range of levels, from a MAXIMUM to a MINIMUM, to each user. When the user connects to the database, a DEFAULT level is assigned to the user between these extremes. Each row in tables using row level security is assigned a row level. Users may not access rows with levels greater than their MAXIMUM level, and may not write to rows with labels lower than their MINIMUM level, the latter to prevent users from lowering the level of a row and allowing unauthorized access. This is known as write-down control or the *-property.

Compartments. The compartment component of a label is a set of category names. Users are assigned read compartments defining the data categories that they have read access to, and are assigned write compartments defining data categories that they can modify.

Groups. Users can be given read or write access to groups and requests are resolved as follows. On a read request, the user's read access groups must match or be a subset of the read groups of the label. On a write request, the user's write access groups must match or be a subset of the write groups of the label.

Configuring CONTROLS enables security policy. If a READ CONTROL is applied to a user, only authorized rows are accessible on SELECT, UPDATE, or DELETE queries. Similarly, if WRITE control is applied to a user, all attempts to INSERT, DELETE, or UPDATE data will only be applied to authorized roles. Additional controls provide more policy definition options.

Because OLS presents an additional performance cost on every access, the designers provided a mechanism to bypass the row-level label checks by using User Privilege Authorizations. For example, a user with the READ privilege can access all data that would otherwise be protected by label security, regardless of the value of the row label. Access would be enforced, however, on non-SELECT statements. Similarly, the FULL privilege bypasses all row label security. In this case, no mediation checks are performed.

Users might be allowed to modify the labels associated with the data that they are allowed to access. All modifications must be done in a consistent manner, observing level constraints.

Figure 12.7 describes the control flow of row-level security enforcement by using a flowchart. The shaded decision boxes represent user privileges. If user Joe has the *profile access privilege*, he can change his identity during the access decision to that of another user. This example shows delegation at work within label security. If the user has *read*, *write*, or *full privileges*, he or she can directly access the data. This situation is shown in Figure 12.7, using the entry point 1 to access data and stop the process flow. If the user does not have certain privileges, then access controls are only enforced if policy requires them to be enforced. The non-shaded decision boxes represent checks to see whether the policy requires that an access decision be invoked. A user can freely

ing these actions are disabled.

However, if the security policy requires the read and write access mediation checks by enabling the appropriate controls, we must extract the row label and the user's label and compare the two labels to make an access decision. This scenario is captured in Figure 12.7 by the two floating flowcharts that originate with the start elements (labeled 3 and 2, respectively).

Finally, a user can seek to change the security level of a label. This procedure is displayed in Figure 12.8. The label is a distinguished column in the row because it is used for access decisions. Modifications to the label can only be made if the user has privileges that allow him or her to modify the label or if the label update control is not enforced.

We have simplified the OLS security scheme here to make the case that multi-level database security is not only a viable security mechanism in commercial applications but

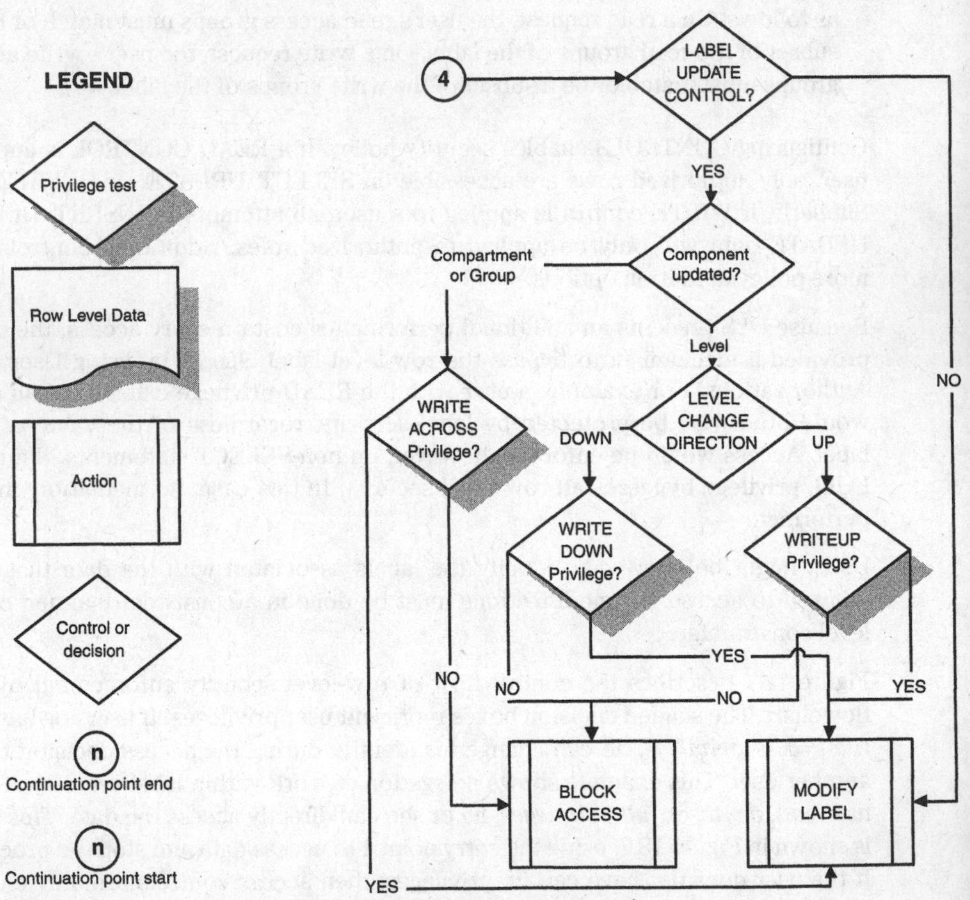

Figure 12.8 Label modification in row-label access.

controlling user access at a much coarser structural level.

One good architectural feature is the provision of privileges that enable row-level label security features to be bypassed. OLS checks can add an unacceptable performance penalty for certain database operations. If these operations are performed only by a subset of the users whose database access is controlled by using other mechanisms, it makes sense to lift this security check and allow faster access. This function does not necessarily weaken security, but it can actually help with another architecture goal: performance.

Row-level security is implemented within OLS as a special instance of a complex row-level security scheme with application context definition along with a pre-built collection of policy functions, through enhancements to the database engine. Both the context and the policy functions can be further modified to customize behavior. Users can define label functions that compute the label values on INSERT and UPDATE statements or add additional SQL predicates to policy functions. The management of security policy is through a GUI-based tool called the Oracle Policy Manager. Labels can be viewed as an active version of the sentinel pattern, where the database engine checks the label before granting access. The label itself is not modified unless explicitly targeted by the user through a label-modifying update statement.

OLS has additional features that make for interesting security discussions, but in the interests of generality and brevity, we will refer the interested reader to the resources on Oracle Technical Network on the Oracle FGAC and OLS products.

Conclusion

Databases are the most complicated single entity in enterprise architecture. They manage mission-critical data within and must meet stringent performance requirements. Security policy creates additional constraints that the database must comply with to pass review.

In this chapter, we have described several architectural options for implementing security. We chose to do so from the viewpoint of a single vendor, Oracle. We believe that this choice is not a bad one, because the arguments made are general enough to be applicable to other database vendors and because of the benefits of using one vendor's syntax and features.

Databases present very interesting security problems, and in many of the applications that we have reviewed, we have not received either the attention or the importance that is due to them. We hope that the patterns of security described here will add to the architect's weaponry at the architecture review.

High-Level Architecture

Security Components

As we seek to accomplish security goals and establish security principles such as user authentication, authorization, confidentiality, integrity, and nonrepudiation using vendors components, tools, and protocols, we must consider these realities:

- Our distributed applications have increasingly complicated structures and topologies.
- Budget, legacy, personnel, and schedule constraints force us to mix vendor products and expect the sum to be securable.
- We add security as an afterthought to our architecture and somehow expect that the presence of some vendor component alone will ensure that we will be secure.

In this chapter, we will present common security infrastructure components and technologies that have cropped up in our presentations of security architecture in chapters past. The names, properties, and characteristics of these technologies are familiar to every software architect, but we need more than product brochures to understand how to integrate these components into our architecture. Our primary concern is identifying architectural issues with each product that systems architects should or should not worry about and identifying showstoppers where we would be best off if we did not try to use the product. Using any security product that does not have an evolution path that seems consistent with your system's evolution could represent a significant risk.

Although we have mentioned these components frequently in prior chapters, we have collected these components together here—following all of our technical architectural presentations because they all share architectural properties. These components are always vendor products. Our lack of expertise and their feature complexity prevents us from building homegrown versions of these products.

Architecture Basics." We argued that security solution vendors in today's environment have mature products at a quality level higher than the reach of most applications. Security architecture work is therefore reduced to integration work. Where do we host these components? How do we interact with them? What services do they provide?

Vendor presentations of these components always award them a central place in the architecture. Vendors make money selling these enterprise components to us, and their best interests might not correspond with ours. Vendor products favor flexibility to capture a wider market share. They claim seamless interoperability but have preferences of hardware platforms, operating systems, and compilers. In many cases, even after we conform to these requirements, we still have to worry about specific low-level configuration issues.

In the introduction and in Chapter 3, we described some of the advantages that vendors had over projects, including better knowledge of security, biased feature presentation with emphasis on the good while hiding the bad, and deflection of valid product criticisms as external flaws in the application. We listed three architectural flaws in vendor products.

Central placement in the architecture. The product places itself at the center of the universe.

Hidden assumptions. The product hides assumptions that are critical to a successful deployment or does not articulate these assumptions, as clear architectural prerequisites and requirements, to the project.

Unclear context. Context describes the design philosophy behind the purpose and placement of the product in some market niche. What is the history of the company with respect to building this particular security product? The vendor might be the originator of the technology, have diversified into the product space, acquired a smaller company with expertise in the security area, or have a strong background in a particular competing design philosophy.

We all have had experiences where the vendor was a critical collaborator in a project's success. Vendor organizations are not monolithic. We interact with many individuals on several interface levels of our relationships with any vendor. We see the vendor in a series of roles from sales and marketing to customer service and technical support, along with higher-level interactions between upper management on both sides as unresolved issues escalate or critical project milestones are accomplished.

Communication is a critical success factor. Problem resolution is so much easier if we can consistently cut through the layers of vendor management between application architects and vendor engineers. Vendors are not antagonistic to the project's goals; they are simply motivated by their own business priorities and cannot present their products in a negative light. Although I have sometimes received misinformation during a marketing presentation, I have never seen the architect of a vendor product misrepresent technical issues. I have, however, known a few who did not volunteer information on issues that were relevant to my project that I was unaware to even ask about, but in every case they were happy to clarify matters once we asked the right questions

made a big difference).

In the following sections, we will present short overviews of the architectural issues that accompany each of the following technologies: single sign-on, PKIs, directory services, Kerberos, Distributed Computing Environment, intrusion detection, and firewalls, along with some other popular security components.

Secure Single Sign-On

Organizations often require users with access to multiple systems to explicitly authenticate to each, remember separate passwords and password management rules, and manually manage password aging. This process can be a considerable burden and lead to insecure practices in the name of convenience.

Multiple sign-on environments are also difficult to manage. Administrators of the systems are often unaware of the higher-level roles of usage across applications. When a new user joins the organization and must be given access to all of the systems that go with his or her new job function, we often resort to a manual process. The administrators of all of these systems must be contacted; we must remember the security mechanisms for each system; and we must manage to ensure that the user is correctly provisioned on all the correct applications with the correct privileges.

Vendors of *secure single sign-on* (SSSO) products promise to bring order to chaos. SSO solutions manage the complex mix of authentication rules for each client-to-server-to-application combination. They promise the following features:

Improved security. Applications can support multiple authentication modules; daemons can be modified transparently to support encryption and cryptographic hashes to provide confidentiality and integrity; and application servers can require strong authentication for the initial sign-on independent of the authentication mechanisms supported by backend servers. Users no longer reuse the same password or slight variations thereof on all systems or leave sticky notes on their monitors with passwords to mission-critical systems.

Improved usability. Users are spared the burden of remembering multiple login ID and password combinations or being locked out if they mistype the password too many times. Administrators have a single management interface to the single sign-on server that can transfer configuration changes to the subordinate applications and systems.

Improved auditing. Single sign-on servers maintain a single, merged audit log of all user accesses to the applications within the scope of protection. This function saves us the difficulty of collecting and merging disparate session logs from all the systems.

SSSO servers replace multiple user logins with one single, strong authentication. The strong authentication could be one-factor (a standard user ID and password), two-factor

factor (biometric verification of fingerprints, thermal scans, retinal scans, or voice recognition) authentication.

The SSSO service manages all subsequent authentications transparently unless an exception on a backend server requires user intervention or if a user session exceeds a timeout period. If a session times out, the user might be asked to reauthenticate or the SSSO service might be trusted to provide new credentials (if the backend application permits). In the latter case, we can replace the application session timeout with an SSSO server timeout interval, which is shared across all backend applications. This procedure would prevent the user from seeing too many session timeouts, actually coming from multiple backend servers, in a single login session.

Some SSSO servers also support their own access control lists and custom management tools. Access control lists enable us to organize the user population into groups, simplifying user management. SSSO solutions range from thin clients, which are normally Web based, to very thick clients that take over the user's client workstation—replacing its interface with a custom launch pad to all permitted applications. The user authenticates to the launch pad, which then manages any interactions with the SSSO server and backend applications. SSSO solutions belong to three broad categories that do have overlaps.

Scripting Solutions

Scripting servers maintain templates of the entire authentication conversation required for each application and automate the process of interacting with the application by playing the role of the user. The scripting server maintains a database of user IDs and passwords for each target application. Scripting solutions require little to no modification of backend servers and are therefore quite popular with legacy applications. The user's password might still be in the clear, however. All scripting solutions execute some variation of the following steps: authenticate, request a ticket, receive a ticket, request an access script using the ticket, receive the correct script, and play the script to legacy system.

Strong, Shared Authentication

Strong, shared authentication normally does not require the client to interact with a third party for accessing backend services. Instead, the user owns a token or a certificate that unlocks a thin client on the user host that enables transparent access to all applications that share the common strong authentication scheme. The user could insert and unlock a Smartcard in a local Smartcard reader, enabling applications to issue challenge/response authentication conversations directly to the Smartcard. SSH (discussed in a later section) also provides a measure of secure single sign-on.

Another example is PKI. PKI promises SSSO through certificate-based client authentication. The authentication is shared because the scope of single sign-on consists of all applications that share a CA. Recall our description of mutual SSL authentication from Chapter 8, "Secure Communications." Although the standard Web-based client authentication from a Web server seems User ID and password based, it still qualifies as strong authentication because the password does not travel across the network but is

the network but is used to decrypt an encrypted nonce challenge from the server. Certificate-based schemes are not completely free of third-party dependencies, but these dependencies are commonly on the server side in the form of accesses not to authentication services but to directories. The application might have a local CRL or might query an OCSP server. The client, however, does not have a third-party network dependency after initial configuration of user, server, and CA certificates and certification paths (unless the client wishes to verify that the server's certificate is not revoked).

Network Authentication

Network authentication servers such as Kerberos, DCE, RSA Security Ace Servers, and many homegrown or commercial SSSO solutions all require the user to first authenticate over the network to an *Authentication Server* (AS). The AS will provide credentials for accessing backend systems through tickets. Network authentication servers use strong credentials and can encrypt links to backend servers.

Web-based authentication servers often use browser cookies as authentication tokens. The client connects to the application Web server, which hands off the URL request to a Web-based AS. The AS authenticates the user and redirects them back to the application server. The AS also stores a record of the event which it sends to the application's backend server to build a separate session object. The application server now accepts the client connection and places a cookie on the user's workstation to attest to the fact that he or she has access rights on the server until the session object (and therefore the cookie) expires. Many Web applications can share a single AS to achieve single sign-on.

Secure SSO Issues

SSSO has not seen the widespread acceptance that one would expect if we believed vendor promises. This situation is largely because of deployment and evolution problems with SSSO solutions in production. There are many assumptions of usage that the vendor makes that simply do not hold true in actual enterprise environments.

The first critical question for an application architect contemplating SSSO within the enterprise is, "Should I buy a vendor solution or build my own?" Each choice has unique integration costs. Homegrown solutions might lack quality, might not port to new platforms, or might require custom development on servers and clients. Commercial solutions might not be a good fit for the problem domain.

Here are some common problems with SSSO solutions along with issues to be raised at the review:

Centralized administration. Initially, user administration might be more complex than the current ID/password schemes because the burden to coordinate passwords is transferred from the user to the administrator of the SSSO solution. This step requires planning, user training, and back-out strategies to prevent lockouts from errors. Audit logs must be maintained, and access failures must be reported. If the backend server does not know that it has been the target of a determined but,

security holes from being exploited (perhaps to defend against a DDOS attack).

Client configuration. Setting up each client workstation takes some effort. Some vendors use Web browsers or provide portable SSO client stubs that are easily modified as the solution evolves. Others involve more effort to update and manage. The administrator must add all of the user's applications to the client and ensure that the user is forced to authenticate to the client stub before invoking any application. The SSO solution could support both SSO and non-SSO access from the client, where the latter would require authentication—but this process is both a maintenance headache and a source of misconfiguration errors that could lock the user out or that could enable unauthenticated access.

Server configuration. SSO vendors may have different backend authentication plug-ins ranging from no change whatsoever to the backend to adding new authentication daemons. Encryption between client and SSO server may not extend all the way to the backend application. Legacy systems that only accept passwords in the clear over the network are vulnerable to password sniffing attacks. If both the client and the server supported encryption, we could mitigate this risk.

Password management. Each vendor has a unique set of responses to queries about passwords. Are passwords passed in the clear between the client and the legacy system? Are scripts stored with embedded passwords, or are passwords inserted into scripting templates before presentation to the client? How does the SSO server store passwords safely? How are passwords aged? How do scripts respond to changes in the authentication dialog between client and legacy host? How are duress passwords handled?

Coverage growth. Have we considered the stability, extensibility, administration, architectural complexity, and licensing costs of the SSSO solution? As more systems come online and wish to share the SSO service, how do we manage growth?

Single point of failure. Is our SSSO solution highly available? Is the SSSO server a very large, single point of failure? What about emergency access in a crisis?

Interoperability. Does the SSSO solution conform to standard authentication protocols? The SSSO server might have links to third-party service providers: ACE token authentication servers, corporate HR databases, corporate LDAP directories, or Kerberos V5 authentication servers (in secondary SSSO roles). Homegrown solutions run into complications as we add technologies: PKI, Windows NTLM, Kerberos tickets, DCE cells, or PAM modules.

Transitive trust. Once access is granted to a backend server, transitive trust relationships originating from the server to other hosts might cause unexpected consequences. When administration is centralized, we might lose the fine details of how to correctly configure security on a host and overstep the stated goal of transparent access to this server by unwittingly permitting access to other services.

Mixing of credentials. The user might abuse access provided through one authentication path by requesting tickets to other hosts. Assuming that an

might be an error.

Firewalls. Does the domain of SSO coverage span multiple networks? Should this functionality be permitted?

An SSO product is unlike other security products in one regard. It is not easily replaced. SSO solutions are customer-facing and have intangible investments associated with them such as mind-share among users who view the sign-on process as part of their applications, and costs associated with training and administration. Because users directly interact with SSO components (unlike, say, a firewall or IDS) replacing the component can only be done with their approval. SSO solutions that turn into legacy systems themselves present unique headaches. Turning off the solution might be unacceptable to its customers, and maintaining it might be unacceptable to IT business owners. The product may be working correctly in that it provides access to an important set of applications, but it may be inflexible, prohibiting the addition of new applications or not permitting client software or hardware to change. The vendor for the product:

- Might no longer exist (this situation bears explicit notice because of the man-in-the-middle role of SSSO servers)
- Might have been acquired by another company that no longer supports the original commitment for evolution
- Might not support new and essential applications that you wish to add to the SSO coverage
- Might refuse to port the solution to new operating systems
- Might fail to interoperate with essential security services, such as corporate LDAP directories, that are now the database of record for user profiles

Large enterprises might have multiple SSO solutions through reorganizations, mergers, or legacy environments. This situation can easily become as large a headache as the original SSSO-less environment. Which server owns which application? Should the solutions be consolidated (good luck convincing the user population of the solution that goes away how much better things will be now)? How do we retire an SSO solution which, as you discover after you turn it off, can turn out to be the only way to reach some critical system? Fortunately, several emerging SSO technologies, from Web-based solutions to proprietary portal products, promise to be good choices for adaptability and evolution.

Public-Key Infrastructures

PKI is arguably the most well known of any of the security components that we will discuss in the chapter. Although vendors claim that PKI enables an impressive list of security properties, experience with actual deployments tells us that there is much more to a successful PKI than buying a vendor product, turning it on, and walking away.

There are many open standards around PKI, including the PKCS standards from RSA Labs, the IETF PKIX standard, the X.500 Directory Standard (ITUT), the X.509v3 (ITUT)

many secure applications and protocols, including SSL, S/MIME, SET, and IPSec.

Integrating our applications with PKI technology requires some discipline on our part.

- We must have some agreement on the cryptographic primitives used among all participants implementing higher-level application protocols that layer on top of PKI (which in turn is layered on top of the mathematics of public key cryptography).
- We must describe what we plan to do with certificates in our applications. Will we authenticate users? Will we publish software? Will we protect communications? Will we implement other higher-level protocols?
- We must develop certificate practice statements that apply to our business domain that clearly state acceptable corporate use of certificates.
- We must have a corporate-wide security policy that governs certificate use.
- We have to select standards-compliant products for long-term interoperability over noncompliant, feature-rich solutions. The replacement cost of PKI must be considered.
- We must understand the legal implications of depending on the PKI. How will these affect our business?

Before we can discuss the architectural issues surrounding PKI, we must first understand what we are attempting to accomplish by buying and installing one. Security is difficult in our Internet-enabled world because it carries the burden of transforming high-level and familiar assertions of the business world into electronic properties that we can depend on for online transactions. PKI advocates tell us that the PKIs will help us define and achieve security assurance, gain confidence in our dealing with customers, protect us from liability, serve as insurance against tampering, form the basis for forging business agreements, and enable us to present credentials to parties who have no fore-knowledge of our existence. This order is tall, indeed.

Security in heterogeneous, diverse environments appears to present an unmanageable problem. According to [FFW98], however, the basic trick to managing the unmanageable is to exploit trust. PKIs enable trust and therefore promise a path to securing our applications within our constraints.

The unit of digital identity in a PKI is the certificate. A certificate is a digital document that binds identifying credentials to the public half of a cryptographic key pair. The digital signature of a trusted third party, known as a CA, ensures the authenticity and integrity of the digital certificate.

The X.509v3 standard defines the format and encoding rules for digital certificates. The certificate contains the following components:

Entity-identifying credentials. Along with the user's public key, the certificate holds a common name, which is an attribute value list that uniquely identifies the

Location, Phone, City, State, e-mail fields, and so on, along with their values.

Certificate properties. These properties include the certificate validity period (from date of issue to date of expiry), serial number, and the signing CA.

A PKI deployment consists of one or more of the following entities.

Certificate Authority

The CA issues certificates. All participating entities, either certificate holders or verifiers, trust the CA. Any entity that requests the CA to issue a certificate must provide some proof of identity. Once issued, the entity must abide by the CA's Certification Practices Statement, which codifies the procedures used by the CA. The content of the CPS is critical because the CPS will affect the level of trust that other users will place in an entity's certificate.

Certificate authorities also issue a list of revoked certificates, called a *Certificate Revocation List* (CRL). The application must decide how the CRL will be made available. Potentially, clients could periodically pull the list, servers could periodically push the list to all subscribed clients, or the client could invoke a synchronous Online Certificate Status Protocol request to verify a certificate's status.

Parties that do not agree on a certificate authority can still resolve differences by looking up certification paths (which are hierarchically ordered lists of CA certificates, where each child is digitally signed by a parent CA) until they find a common, trusted third party. Another alternative to establishing trust is cross certification, where two CAs mutually vouch for one another.

Registration Authority

A *Registration Authority* (RA) is an interface that handles the process of applying for a certificate. Some implementations of PKI couple the RA and CA functions to increase security, but for most deployments it make more sense to separate the interface to a Proof of Identity Manager that authenticates requests for certificates, from the CA, which can now be replaced if necessary. The RA must authenticate the user's identity, either by querying a human resources database, physically visiting the person, seeing a badge, or by using biometric techniques. Once the user is authenticated, the RA produces standard credentials that can be presented to a CA along with the actual certificate request form.

Separating the RA from the CA is also good in applications where we have loose coupling and more of a B2B flavor of interaction. A large enterprise might have several PKI instances. This situation is common when legacy PKI applications cannot be turned off, users install small application-specific certificate servers, administrative challenges are too great, or if many new client applications crop up in the enterprise, requiring an additional layer of insulation between the registration and certificate creation process. Several RAs can share a CA, and several CAs can front a single RA (in case the application

cal or technical reasons).

Repository

PKIs need to store persistent data on the entities that have been issued certificates thus far. The CA stores certificates and Certificate Revocation Lists in a directory. Clients can access the directory, most often by using LDAP, to query the certificate database for a peer entity's certificate or to verify that a presented certificate that has passed the signature and expiry checks has not been revoked.

The X.500 standard for directory services enables clients to access directories by using the Directory Access Protocol, which is quite cumbersome to implement. The University of Michigan developed LDAP as a "front end" used to implement directory services to X.500 directories. We discuss directories in some depth in a following section.

An LDAP Server can be implemented over a full X.500 directory, but this function is not essential. The backend data store can be a commercial database, a flat file, or even be generated dynamically on demand.

Certificate Holders

Certificate holders are entities that need certificates to accomplish work. Examples include the following:

- Users on Web browsers using client certificates for authentication and single sign-on
- Web servers implementing SSL
- Developers signing applets and ActiveX controls
- PKI-enabled applications such SSH or other flavors of secure Telnet, FTP, rlogin, mail, or news
- Middleware products; for example, CORBA clients and servers using IIOP over SSL

Certificate Verifiers

A certificate verifier is a participant in a PKI-enabled transaction that does not require a certificate but requires PKI services in order to verify a digital signature on a document, decrypt a document, or authenticate an access.

Certificate verifiers can store certificate details locally but in general will look up certificate details from a repository.

PKI Usage and Administration

From a client's perspective, much of the detail of PKI-enabled applications happens under the hood, transparent to the user, except perhaps for a performance penalty. The burden on the user is reduced to registering and requesting a certificate, proving iden-

private key safely (possibly encrypted on the local drive, on removable media, or on a token of some kind).

From the perspective of the business process owner of a PKI and its systems administrator, we have much more work to do. The administrator must issue certificates, handle revocation, consolidate certificates for the organization, manage the certificate life cycle including expiry, reissue lockouts due to forgotten passwords, or replacement in the event of compromise. The administrator might also be required to conduct key recovery, nonrepudiation, and other risk mitigating activities—further increasing the effort required.

One of the most important tasks for a business process owner for PKI lies in enforcing the Certificate Practices Statement. Noncompliant participants might have their credentials revoked because their poor behavior could result in a much wider system compromise.

PKI Operational Issues

A PKI can, if successfully deployed, add to the reliability, availability, and scalability of your application. It is necessary to align the application's non-functional requirements to those of the PKI itself. For example, if even one of your applications is mission critical, you might need to create plans to conduct backup, recovery, and disaster management for the new PKI component.

Another issue in large organizations is fragmentation across organizational boundaries for geographic or political reasons. This situation can result in multiple sources for certificates in the enterprise. Application architects need guidance in determining which one of many PKI solutions will be left standing in the next year or so. Multiple CAs normally crop up because of evolutionary reasons. Old projects that are early adopters are loath to turn off their perfectly functional PKI solution, but at the enterprise level, the number of issues surrounding certificate distribution, roaming or remote user usage, status checks, and embedded nonstandard feature use all contribute to the problem of embedded legacy security.

Some of the hardest problems surrounding PKI architecture relate to organizational issues.

- What if a laptop holding sensitive information is stolen? Do we require key recovery if a user loses his or her private key? Do we replicate all encrypted information with a copy encrypted with a shared corporate key? What if that corporate key is compromised? How do we ensure consistency and correctness?
- Can we transition from one PKI to another? The transition plans for changes in certificate authority must figure out who owns and continues to operate the old PKI components and supports legacy clients with unexpired certificates.
- What legal liabilities do PKIs introduce? How do we assert contractual rights in a digital world enabled through PKI? Nonrepudiation is a hard problem in the real world.

Firewalls

A firewall is a network device placed between two networks that enforces a set of access control rules called the firewall's access control policy on all traffic between the two networks. Firewalls placed around the perimeter of a corporate intranet defend the corporate network's physical connections to an untrusted network; for example, a partner network or the Internet. We refer the interested reader to two excellent books on firewalls, [CB96] and [ZCC00], along with Marcus Ranum and Matt Curtin's *Internet Firewall FAQ* from the *comp.security.firewalls* newsgroup on the Web.

Large corporations often have multiple networks to support geographically separated sites, to separate mission-critical services from general corporate networks, or as remnants of a corporate merger or acquisition. In these scenarios, we might have to route our application traffic across multiple firewalls, traversing several trusted and untrusted networks from the user to the application. Network topology determines firewall placement. Firewalls enable corporations to implement security policy at a coarse level by separating poorly configured or insecure hosts from the Internet and direct harm.

A single firewall can link several networks together if it supports multiple interfaces. The interface to each network enforces an incoming and outgoing access control policy on all traffic to and from the network. Some firewalls even permit dynamic rule configuration and, in the event of an attack, will modify the security policy automatically. In Chapter 10, "Web Security," we introduced the DMZ configuration by using a firewall with three interfaces.

Firewalls are very good at the following actions:

- Guarding choke points on the network.
- Collecting security logs on all traffic into and out of the corporate network for later analysis.
- Presenting the external face of the corporation through public Web sites and services on a DMZ, providing product information, or serving as a mail gateway to conceal internal sensitive e-mail information.
- Hosting a secure gateway. SSH (described in a later section) or VPN technologies (implemented by using IPSec, described in Chapter 8, "Secure Communications") enable remote users to access the corporate network securely from any untrusted network by building an encrypted tunnel to the secure gateway on the perimeter of the company after successfully authenticating the user at the gateway.
- Supporting a wireless gateway for secure communications with mobile devices and hiding it from attackers who want to exploit the gateway's wireless protocol translation air gap.
- Hosting proxy services to hide the actual clients on the private network from potential harm.

Firewall rule sets follow the basic pattern of access control implementation, introduced in Chapter 3. Rules are ordered in some fashion and applied to traffic in a top-down manner. The firewall can use a first-fit, best-fit, or worst-fit strategy to decide what to do on a particular packet.

- Drop the packet with no response to the sender.
- Drop the packet but send an ICMP host unreachable message back to the client.
- Allow the packet through after setting up special conditions for monitoring the conversation that it is part of, with the intent of changing behavior dynamically on any suspicious activity.

Solutions that combine firewalls with IDS sensors can achieve additional levels of security. The firewall enforces policy while the IDS measures attacks aimed at the firewall (if the sensor is in front of the firewall) or measures our success in thwarting attacks according to policy (if placed behind the firewall).

Firewall Configurations

Firewalls are very versatile and can appear as any of the four channel patterns introduced in Chapter 4, "Architecture Patterns in Security."

- Packet filters make decisions to allow or deny traffic based on the contents of the packet header; for example, the source or destination IP address, the port numbers used, or the protocol. Some packet filters maintain a notion of connection state or can assemble fragmented packets.
- Personal firewalls, or host-based software firewalls, protect a single host from any attacks on its network interface. PC firewalls such as Tiny Personal Firewall, Zone Alarm, Norton Personal Firewall, or tcpwrapper (which we argued, in Chapter 4, could also be considered a filter from a different perspective because of granularity of access protection) all wrap a single host.
- Secure gateways intercept all conversations between a client network adaptor and the gateway, building an encrypted tunnel to protect data traveling over the open Internet. Once the data reaches the internal network, it travels in the clear.
- Application proxies can perform elaborate logging and access control on the firewall because they can reassemble fragmented packets and pass them up the application stack to a proxy version of the service. The proxy version prevents external communications from directly accessing the internal service. We can perform high-level inspections of the contents of the communication because we have knowledge of the application on either endpoint. Application proxies can support complex security policy, but they are slower than packet filters.

Firewall Limitations

Firewalls have some limitations. A firewall cannot perform the following actions:

- Protect applications from traffic that does not go across it. If your network routes traffic around a firewall, perhaps through a dial-up modem or a dual homed host linked to an insecure network, all hosts on the network are vulnerable to attack.
- Protect you if the firewall is misconfigured.

support arbitrary and possibly unsafe services and still enforce security policy.

- Protect against attackers already inside the network.
- Protect against traffic that is not visible; for example, encrypted data riding on a permitted protocol or a covert tunnel using a permitted protocol as a wrapper for a forbidden protocol.
- Inspect general data content for all dangerous payloads. There are too many attacks, and each attack can be modified to defeat the signature match used by the firewall.

Firewalls can range from expensive specialized security components with complex configurations to free personal firewalls and cheap network appliances that perform *Network Address Translation* (NAT), DHCP, filtering, and connection management.

We do not recommend putting business logic on security components such as firewalls. This procedure is a bad idea because firewalls are normally not under your control, and they might require out-of-band management procedures, might have implementation errors, and might have a very specific network infrastructure purpose that is at odds with your application. Firewalls represent single points of failure in the architecture, and because all of our applications share a dependency on one firewall, we must engineer the availability, scalability, and performance of the firewall to adequately address the application's needs of today and of the future.

Intrusion Detection Systems

Network intrusion detection systems identify threats launched against an organization and respond to these threats by notifying an intrusion analyst, logging the attack to a database, or possibly reconfiguring the network automatically to prevent the attack from succeeding. The risk of a network intrusion cannot be evaluated in a vacuum; we must place the attack in the context of the host under attack, its operating system, network defenses, and vulnerabilities—along with the potential cost if the attack succeeds. We refer the reader to Northcutt and Novak's excellent introduction to intrusion detection and analysis, [NN00] for more information.

Network detection tools analyze network traffic for patterns of behavior that appear suspicious. Because traffic volumes can overwhelm the pattern-matching abilities of our analytic tools, we might have to filter our traffic to extract packets that conform to some prerequisite form or property. We could choose to examine traffic by protocol, TCP flags, payload sizes, source or destination address, or port number. Attackers can modify traffic in many interesting ways. They could fragment packets excessively, spoof source IP address and port information, use ICMP messages to surreptitiously scan the network or redirect traffic, use several hosts simultaneously to launch a DDOS attack, or build a covert tunnel inside a permitted protocol or service. An intrusion detection system can examine traffic at many levels of granularity, from low-level mod-

bled packets from fragments using knowledge of the syntax of the data (for example, recognizing a command to delete all files on a UNIX host). Systems can come with a predefined filter and signature set installed or can provide full programming support for custom signature definition.

IDS configuration requires us to be very knowledgeable about networking protocols used to get a good idea of what normal traffic looks like. Intrusion analysts must be able to separate false positives (which are nonattacks reported by the IDS) from actual attacks. Tools such as tcpdump can filter and capture IP packets for analysis and help us create signatures for attacks. A packet might depart from the standard IP networking protocol definitions in some particular way. It could be:

- Deliberately malformed in order to fingerprint a target OS (perhaps by sending an unsolicited FIN packet to an open port or by setting and sending bogus TCP flag values in bad packets to look at the response from the host).
- Designed to perform network reconnaissance on available services.
- Designed to deny service; for example, through a *land* attack (an IP datagram with the same source and destination IP address; if a sensor encounters such a packet, it can issue an alarm because this action definitely signifies anomalous activity).
- Part of an attempt to hijack an established connection.

Broadly speaking, intrusion detection solutions are composed of several components.

Sensors. Sensors detect attacks by matching network traffic against a database of known intrusion signatures. Intrusion detection sensors attempt to operate at network bandwidth rates and send alarms to managers. Sensors sometimes store compiled rules and signature definitions for quicker pattern matching against traffic as it flies by. Some sensors listen in promiscuous mode, picking up all packets on the network; others work in tandem with a partner system or a router to target traffic aimed at that particular host or device.

Managers. Managers merge event and alarm notifications from many sensors deployed across the network and manage sensor configuration and intrusion response.

Databases. Managers often store event data in (possibly proprietary) databases for later analysis by using sophisticated tools.

Consoles. Analysts can access event data from the console to generate statistical reports, order events by criticality, drill down into low-level detail of packet contents, or execute commands to respond to an intrusion.

Reporting and analysis. Although network intrusion detection is often described as real time, this situation is rarely the case. In addition to crisis management functions, in the event of an intrusion we also need tools for offline reporting and analysis. These activities are critical for understanding the behavior of the network.

tion must consider many factors before deploying an NID system.

Project expertise in intrusion detection. Most applications lack the expertise to deploy and monitor IDS on a day-to-day basis (installing one and forgetting its existence is another matter). In this situation, it is probably best not to depend on intrusion detection systems at all. Note that we are not saying that intrusion detection systems are bad, but if your primary role is that of a systems architect and you lack the relevant expertise, you should not depend on one to keep you secure. Intrusion detection systems belong in the network infrastructure category and can create too many false positives to be stable for integrating into your architecture. Find out what corporate firewalls and IDS policy recommend, and then hire an expert to install and configure a commercial network ID solution. Also, budget the resources to maintain the system and train an analyst in production for the day-to-day incident analysis and response.

Sensor placement. Sensors cannot generate alarms on traffic they will not see. Sensors are often placed at network chokepoints or at the junction of two separate corporate networks with different patterns of usage (for example, research and development versus an integrated testing network). Sensors can be placed inside or outside the corporate firewall on the connection to the open Internet. As we mentioned, this firewall can actually be a combination of two firewalls—one on each side of the corporate router—or this firewall could have multiple interfaces to partner networks, a DMZ, or the secure corporate network. One rule of thumb for sensor placement in complicated scenarios is interface-sensor pairing, where each network places a sensor on the inside of its interface to the firewall and installs filters and signatures that validate the firewall's policy for incoming traffic to their particular network. The managers and IDS databases normally will reside on the secure corporate network for safety.

Sensor performance. Sensors might be unable to process all the packets received without dropping a large percentage.

Standalone or host-based sensors. Sensors can be special hardware devices, supporting multiple network interfaces, strong security, and easy remote management of signatures and filters. Alternatively, sensors can be host-based software products that inspect traffic on all network interfaces on the host before passing these on to the relevant application. A standalone sensor might represent a single point of failure and could possibly be knocked off the network through a denial-of-service attack without our knowledge. In the latter case, in exchange for a performance penalty, we are ensured that we have seen all traffic to our host and can protect the sensor itself from being brought down by using automatic process restarts. We might have fewer interoperability and portability issues with bump-in-the-wire sensors because they are relatively isolated from our application.

Networking protocols and host architectures. Heterogeneous host and network environments create overlapping areas of signature coverage. Some hosts are vulnerable to some form of attack, some network protocols have very different data formats, or sensors might not keep up with the evolution of the underlying communications layer.

services used by the host for matching an IP address to a host name, an object reference to an object name, or a hardware address to an IP address. Broken name mappings can cause denial of service.

Tuning levels of false positives and negatives. The system administrator and intrusion analyst must improve the signal to noise ratio on the console. Otherwise, system administrators will abandon intrusion analysis after the initial glow of installing and examining potential network intrusion events as it becomes increasingly difficult to wade through this information. Generating excessive alarms on nonevents while missing actual attacks is a common problem in many intrusion detection deployments.

Skill level of the attacker. Attackers can foil intrusion detection systems in a number of ways. The attacker can learn the limitations of the intrusion detection sensor if the sensor and its alarm response to an attack are also visible. An attacker can choose intrusions that will not be detected by the sensor or can knock the sensor off the network to prevent it from pushing alarms correctly to the user. Attackers can mix multiple attacks to create complexity, thereby confusing the analyst. A patient attacker, by using data volumes under alarm thresholds, can slowly conduct a reconnaissance of the network.

Incident analysis and response strategy. Once we decide what our policy at the perimeter of the corporation is, and we install our IDS in the field, we must also follow up on incident analysis and response. This process requires considerable commitment from the architect of the application.

Unless you are designing a *security* system, an IDS might be beyond the application's capability to maintain and manage. Network intrusion detection is best left to experts. We suggest that the application focus its architectural energies on all the other security mechanisms in this chapter and in previous chapters. Applications should conform to corporate guidelines for operating an intrusion detection solution, set aside resources to purchase and run a commercial IDS, make room on the host's performance budget for a host-based solution, hire and train analysts, and outsource filter creation and updates.

LDAP and X.500 Directories

Directories store information that is read often by a large group of users but modified infrequently by a much smaller group of administrators. The X.500 standard defines a comprehensive and powerful framework for enterprise directories. This framework includes the following components:

An information model. The basic entity in the directory is an entry. Entries are organized into hierarchies based on the directory schema. Each entry has a required *objectClass* type field and a collection of attribute-value(s) pairs. Each objectClass definition in X.500 lists the mandatory and optional attributes for an entry of that class. X.500 also supports inheritance. An objectClass inherits the mandatory and

Each entry has a *relative distinguished name* (RDN) that identifies it within the space of all entries. The collection of all data entries is called the *Directory Information Base* (DIB).

An object-naming model. The RDN of an entry identifies its position in the Directory Information Tree (DIT). We can find the entry by following a path formed from the name-value assertions in the RDN, from the root of the DIT to the entry.

A functional model. The functional model describes the operations that *Directory User Agents* (DUAs) can perform upon *Directory Service Agents* (DSAs), which collectively store the DIB. The functional model has powerful scoping and filtering rules that allow the user to launch complex queries against the server. If the server cannot find an entry, it can pass the query on to another DSA or return an error to the user.

A security model. Directories can use strong authentication services such as Kerberos or SSL, along with entry level ACLs, to control access to a particular element of the DIB.

An access model. The Directory Access Protocol specifies the messaging formats, order of messages, return values, and exception handling needed to query the DIB. The DAP protocol supports a number of read, write, or access operations on the directory. It also supports a search option that can be quite slow.

A distributed architecture model. X.500 defines a distributed architecture for reliability, scalability, availability, and location independence. Although the standard creates a single global namespace across the enterprise, each instance of a directory service agent can manage all local updates and modifications quickly. Directories share information through replication, which also provides load balancing and high availability. The schema and attributed definitions are flexible, allowing application extensions to the data definition in a structured manner.

X.500 directories support a range of operations including read, list, search, modify, add, delete, bind, unbind, and abandon session. DAP uses the ASN.1 BER notation for message encodings. Although DAP is very powerful, applications may encounter difficulties in creating, securing, and extending responses using DAP. The ASN.1 syntax uses extensive data typing and formatting rules that blow up message sizes. In addition, on a DUA query the DSA may sometimes respond with a redirection to another DSA, rather than providing the required response, which might add to the complexity of the client.

Lightweight Directory Access Protocol

LDAP, specified in [RFC2251] by University of Michigan researchers Wahl, Howes, and Kille, implements a subset of the functional and operational models of DAP. LDAP simplifies encodings, reduces message size, removes operations that can be simulated by using sequences of simpler operations (such as *list* and *read*), and assumes greater responsibility in tracking down referrals to resource requests by users, responding with an error if unsuccessful in resolving the query.

lation of clients and servers. LDAP not only simplifies the encoding schemes but messages use less space on average compared to ASN.1 messages, which can be quite complex and heavy. LDAP also drops some service controls to speed up application service. LDAP implements query scoping (which defines the part of the DIT that will be searched) and filtering (which limits the entities searched in the query scope) differently from DAP.

Many directory vendors, including Oracle Internet Directory, Microsoft Active Directory, iPlanet Directory Server, and Novell eDirectory, support LDAP.

Architectural Issues

Directories define user and resource hierarchies, assist domain-based user management, and provide distributed services such as naming, location, and security. Directories play a critical role in addressing security challenges in any enterprise.

Deploying an enterprise directory has become such a specialized skill that companies often outsource the task to directory service providers, or call on heavy doses of consulting to accomplish the task. The structure of data in the organization drives the architecture.

- What kind of data will we put in the directory? Is the directory for e-commerce, network and systems administration, or user management? How do we define schema and attributes to store user information, resource descriptions, customer data, supplier catalogs, or systems administration information?
- Must we support multiple network domains? How do we partition our data across domains? Does each domain extend the global schema in some way?
- Will single-tier directory services suffice or must we create a multi-tier solution with a meta-directory at the root?
- What goes into the global catalog of all the subordinate directories? Is their relationship peer-to-peer or hierarchical?
- Is data replicated from masters to slaves, or do we continually synchronize peer directories?
- Are we using our vendor product directory to provide virtual access to information in relational databases? Virtual access is very hard to accomplish because we are mixing two philosophies of data organization. Directory data is read often and written rarely, and fast access is supported through extensive preprocessed indexing. Relational databases support a balanced mix of reads and writes and optimize SQL queries in a completely different manner. Can we ensure that response time for complex queries is adequate?
- How do we handle referrals? Can we handle queries from partner directories (possibly not under our control), and if so, how can we authenticate and authorize referred queries?

does the vendor support other middleware or database products?

- Is integration easy? Does the vendor depart from open standards, and if so, how does this affect application interoperability, integration, and evolution?
- Are any security services built into the directory and meta-directory products?

As directory vendors run away from the commoditization of directory services, they build feature-rich but noncompliant products. Architects can face interoperability issues, lack of bug fixes, poor performance, or unwanted increases in licensing costs. Unlike many of the other security components we present in this chapter, however, directories do hold a central role in enterprise security architecture. For further elaboration on the importance of data management for security, we refer the reader to Chapter 15, "Enterprise Security Architecture."

Kerberos

The Kerberos Authentication Protocol, invented in the late 1980s at MIT, enables clients and servers to mutually authenticate and establish network connections. Kerberos secures resources in a distributed environment by allowing an authenticated client with a service ticket on one computer to access the resources on a server on another host without the expense of a third-party lookup.

The Kerberos protocol is an established open IETF standard. Over the years, it has been subjected to considerable peer review of the published open source, and all defects in the original protocol have been closed. Kerberos has risen from a well-respected authentication standard to a leading security infrastructure component in recent years, after Microsoft announced that Windows 2000 and Microsoft Active Directory would support the protocol for authentication purposes within Windows *Primary Domain Controllers* (PDC).

Kerberos comes in two flavors: a simpler version 4 that runs exclusively over TCP/IP and a more complex version 5 that is more flexible and extensible. In addition to functional enhancements, Kerberos V5 uses ASN.1 with the *Basic Encoding Rules* (BER) allowing optional, variable length, or placeholder fields. Microsoft has adopted Kerberos V5 as the primary network authentication scheme for Windows 2000 domains (with support for NT LAN Manager for backward compatibility with NT3.x–4.0 subdomains).

Kerberos uses symmetric key cryptography to protect communications and authenticate users. Kerberos encrypts packets for confidentiality, ensures message integrity, and prevents unauthorized access by network sniffing adversaries. Kerberos vendors support common cryptographic algorithms such as DES and 3DES, and are adding support for the new NIST standard for encryption, the *Advanced Encryption Standard* (AES).

Kerberos introduces a trusted third party, the *Key Distribution Center* (KDC), to the architecture that mediates authentication by using a protocol based on the extended [illegible] protocol, assuming a notion of universal time. The KDC authenticates connection requests between client and server and grants the client privileges to resources on the server. Each client or *principal* has a secret password (a master key) known to the KDC. The KDC stores all the passwords of participating principals in an encrypted database.

The KDC knows every principal's secret key. If the KDC is compromised, we have lost security entirely. Applications should require high performance and availability from the KDC to prevent response delays or creation of a single point of failure.

Although the Kerberos standard speaks of two services, the KDC in all implementations of Kerberos is a single process that provides both.

Authentication Service. The authentication service issues session keys and *ticket-granting tickets* (TGT) for services requests to the KDC.

Ticket-Granting Service. The ticket-granting service issues tickets that allow access to other services in its own domain or that allow referrals to be made to ticket-granting services in other trusted domains.

When client Alice logs onto her workstation, the workstation sends an authentication request to the KDC. The KDC responds with the following items:

- A session key valid for the current login session
- A TGT, which contains the session key, the user name, an expiration time, all encrypted with the KDC master key

Alice must present the TGT to the KDC every time she requests to communicate with server Bob. The TGT allows the KDC some measure of statelessness because it contains all the information needed for the KDC to help Alice set up a Kerberos transaction. Each Kerberos transaction consists of four messages, two between Alice and the KDC (a ticket granting service request and a ticket granting service reply), and two between Alice and Bob (an application request and an application reply). We refer the interested reader to [KPS95] for an excellent presentation of Mediated Authentication and the Kerberos V4 and V5 protocols for more details.

In addition to the open source Kerberos release from MIT (http://web.mit.edu/Kerberos/), several vendors offer commercial Kerberos authentication products and services, including CyberSafe (TrustBroker at www.cybersafe.com) and Microsoft (W2K security at www.microsoft.com /WINDOWS2000/techinfo/).

Kerberos Components in Windows 2000

Windows 2000 implements the KDC as a domain service, using Active Directory as its account database along with additional information about security principals from the Global Catalog.

identical replicated databases share load balancing and fault tolerant network administration services. Each domain controller has its own KDC and Active Directory service, and the domain controller's *Local Security Authority* (LSA) starts both services automatically. Any domain controller can accept authentication requests and ticket-granting requests addressed to the domain's KDC.

Microsoft's adoption of Kerberos within Windows 2000 is not without controversy. Although supporters of Kerberos are complimentary of Microsoft's decision to include a reputable authentication protocol based on an open standard into their products, they are critical of Microsoft's decision to add licensing restrictions to their authorization extensions of the Kerberos V5 protocol. Windows 2000 uses an optional authorization data field to store a Privilege Access Certificate (PAC), a token that enables the server to make access decisions based on the user's Windows user group. Although the extension itself is permitted by the protocol, Microsoft's licensing restrict prevents third parties from building complete domain controllers that implement this authorization field. Therefore, providing networks services in a Windows environment would require a Microsoft domain controller.

One motivation for this restriction could be the lesson learned from Samba. Samba is an example of the open source movement's ability to replace commercial vendor products with free alternatives, seamlessly. The Samba software suite is a collection of programs that implements the Server Message Block (commonly abbreviated as SMB) protocol for UNIX systems. The SMB protocol is sometimes also referred to as the *Common Internet File System* (CIFS), LanManager, or NetBIOS protocol. At the heart of Samba is the *smbd* daemon, which provides file and print services to SMB clients, such as Windows 95/98, Windows NT, Windows for Workgroups or LAN Manager. Rather than running a Windows file or print server, network administrators can provide the same service from a cheap Linux box using Samba.

Microsoft insists that they are motivated by a concern for interoperability. Because of the central role Kerberos plays in the Windows 2000 architecture, Microsoft is concerned that deployments of their flagship product for managing enterprise networks of millions of objects describing the company's users, groups, servers, printers, sites, customers, and partners, will fail because of incompatible domain management. Along with the Active Directory, and the policy database, Kerberos lies at the heart of Windows 2000's goals of providing domain definition, resource description, efficient authentication, trust management, and reliable network administration. Allowing full implementations of competing domain controller products (especially free open source examples) may create interoperability woes that fragment the network across domains.

The difficulty lies not in Kerberos interoperability, but in providing users of Kerberos realms under a non-Windows KDC access to services on a Windows 2000 domain. Users could authenticate to the Windows domain but, as their tickets would not contain the required PAC value in the authorization field, they may have no privileges. Microsoft has suggested workarounds to this problem that create a trust relationship between the two realms allowing one to manufacture PACs for the other for inclusion in tickets. For an interesting discussion of this issue, please see Andrew Conry-Murray's article [Con01] along with the resources on Microsoft's TechNet links.

Distributed Computing Environment

The *Distributed Computing Environment* (DCE) is a common set of middleware services for distributed applications usable by multivendor, commercial applications, created with the goal of becoming a standard platform for distributed applications. DCE is showing its age and has been supplanted by other enterprise security components in recent years. DCE is well defined, powerful, robust, and well reviewed, however, and might be appropriate in certain architectures. Many vendor products support integration with DCE domains.

The Open Software Foundation created DCE to address the needs of application architects who desired to distribute monolithic applications to achieve higher availability and reliability, enable incremental growth using server farms, and reuse network services across applications. OSF has merged with another standards group, X/OPEN, to form the Open Group, which currently supports the evolution of DCE.

DCE is a layered transport-independent networking protocol, and can run over UDP, TCP, or the OSI transport layer. DCE organizes the resources of the organization into cells. Each DCE cell is a collection of machines administered within one domain. DCE cells are entirely independent of underlying routing layers. DCE cells are organized into a contiguous namespace, making it easy for clients in one cell to locate and access services provided in another cell.

Clients can access services across cells if the correct trust relationships are in place. Each host in a cell, normally identified by a hostname in the cell directory, must run the DCE client services. Each cell must be able to operate autonomously, containing a DCE server providing all DCE services, including a Security server, a *Cell Directory Server* (CDS), and a *Distributed Time Server* (DTS). The *Distributed File Server* (DFS) is optional.

DCE, unlike CORBA, does not support a rich collection of middleware services, focusing instead on extending some of the operating system services available on a single host to create analogous network services. DCE views a distributed application as running on top of a *Network Operating System* (NOS). The NOS supplies the same underlying services that monolithic applications derive from a single host. Like an operating system, DCE requires a user to authenticate to the cell when they log in and obtain their credentials. DCE can be viewed as a middleware services product that provides integrated network services such as the following:

Remote Procedure Calls. Communication between DCE entities is through RPCs.

Directory Services. Applications can look up data over the network. DCE includes several options for naming and location directory services. The CDS is used within a local area, while either DNS or X.500 is used as a global directory service. The DCE directory service provides a consistent way to identify and locate information, services, and resources in the distributed environment.

Security Services. DCE provides authentication, authorization, data integrity, and privacy. DCE security is similar to Kerberos, and indeed uses Kerberos V5-based authentication as a configuration option. Interoperability between security services

Vendors must be compliant with the published DCE APIs.

Distributed File Systems. DCE *Distributed File Service* (DFS) is a collection of file systems hosted by independent DFS file servers. DFS clients and server systems may be heterogeneous computers running different operating systems. DFS manages file system objects, i.e., directories and files, and provides access to them to DFS clients, which are users on computers located anywhere in the distributed environment. Under DFS, remote files appear and behave very much like local files for both users and application developers because file names are unique across cells. DFS is integrated with the DCE directory service and depends upon it for naming support. The file namespace of the cell directory service stores entries for the file system objects such as directories and files.

Distributed Time Service. DCE defines a *Distributed Time Service* (DTS) for clock synchronization. While not directly interoperable with the widely used NTP, DTS can nevertheless be integrated with NTP in useful ways.

The application can use the full range of DCE services, including authenticated RPC, single sign-on, naming, location, and security, or can use a minimal subset of services, for example, only implementing authentication using the DCE generic security services API.

All the DCE services make use of the security service. DCE's underlying security mechanism is the Kerberos network authentication service from Project Athena at the *Massachusetts Institute of Technology* (MIT), augmented with a Registry Service, implementation enhancements for Kerberos, authorization using a Privilege Service (and its associated access control list facility), and authenticated RPC. The DCE namespace has a subdirectory for all security objects that hold user and group access privileges. DCE uses the optional authorization data field for storing *privilege ticket-granting tickets* (PTGT) to extend the basic Kerberos authorization framework. DCE also uses its own encryption and message integrity mechanisms implemented at the RPC level instead of depending upon Kerberos's cryptographic mechanisms. DCE uses only the key material from Kerberos in these mechanisms.

Authentication across cell boundaries is permitted only if the two cells have a trust relationship established between them. This trust relationship allows a user in one cell to access a remote server in another cell transparently. For a small number of cells, setting up a trust relationship between each pair of cells is not difficult, but for a larger number of cells this can be a burden. Some proposals exist for creating structure across the cells, organizing the cells into hierarchical trees or forests, much like the description of Active Directory domains in our description in an earlier section. Some DCE vendors support this functionality.

The Secure Shell, or SSH

SSH, the secure shell, is a client/server protocol for encrypting and transmitting data over an untrusted network. SSH provides secure communications for any standard TCP/IP application and protocol. SSH supports a number of authentication options

strong authentication, such as SecurID tokens or smart cards. SSH also transparently secures communication between existing clients and servers using port forwarding.

There are two versions of the SSH protocol. Version 1, developed in 1995 by Tatu Ylönen at Helsinki University of Technology in Finland, and version 2, developed in 1998 by Ylönen and other members of the IETF Secure Shell working group. The two versions are not compatible, and open source and commercial products for both protocols exist.

Although SSH is available for a wide variety of platforms, it is predominantly used on Unix. SSH closes many security holes for Unix systems administrators by replacing the Berkeley remote r-commands: *rsh*, *rcp*, *rlogin*, *rexec*, and so on, with secure alternatives. There are many websites on the SSH protocol and products including www.ssh.com, www.openSSH.com, and www.f-secure.com. We also refer the reader to Barrett and Silverman's excellent and comprehensive book, *SSH: The Definitive Guide* [BS01].

Administrators can use slogin instead of rlogin to connect to remote hosts, ssh instead of rsh to run shell commands on remote hosts, scp instead of rcp to copy files, sftp instead of FTP for secure file transfers, and so on. Users launch a client process ssh-agent once during each login session. The agent holds the unlocked private key and brokers all further ssh handshakes transparently. SSH can perform TCP port forwarding to encrypt data passing through any TCP/IP connection, conduct reverse IP lookups to protect against DNS spoofing, provide access control on the server based on Unix user names or groups, and vendors provide some support for key management and OA&M (although not enough).

SSH solves a specific security need in a transparent manner. SSH can use strong public key cryptography to authenticate clients and servers, but the products have the same deployment, interoperability, and management issues as PKI. SSH has many features and configuration options that make it a powerful and flexible security component, easy added to any security architecture. Operational complexity and performance are the major architectural issues.

The Distributed Sandbox

Security is a disabling technology in that it puts up barriers, asks for identification, checks passports, and slows down conversations through encryption, and in general requires you to not trust any new conversation initiated with your system. These security walls serve an important purpose in securing your application against the very real dangers that exist over the open network that might harm or disable your network.

Not all security components play the role of guard dog, however, preventing access by unknown users. In recent times, several interesting distributed applications have been proposed to harness the idle computational power of the vast network of personal computers, possibly numbering in the hundreds of millions, that are on the Internet today. Many informally organized networks to solve problems that are amenable to distributed, parallel computing using these resources exist in the world today.

cussing the *sandbox* pattern. As desktop workstations continue to follow Moore's law, solutions to harness the collective power of networked computers has become an attractive area of research. The fear of being hacked prevents many folks from participating, however.

We call a software solution that allows a distributed application to tap the resources of many idle networked workstations a *distributed sandbox*. Each workstation runs a client as a low priority process that uses system resources only when available. Such a client must have minimal privileges because, outside of CPU cycles and limited memory use, the distributed application should have no access privileges on the host. The distributed sandbox should not need to know any details of the underlying host, its operating system, its file system, devices, users, or networking. Indeed, our ability to guarantee the secrecy, privacy, and priority of the user on the client host is critical to gaining widespread acceptance. No one wants to run a Trojan horse. Our solution to create a distributed sandbox must guarantee safety of the client host, by controlling all resource requests and communications with sandbox controllers, and rapidly returning control to the user if requested.

Many important problems can be solved if every networked host provided a secure distributed sandbox that can tap the idle potential of the computer, with no detrimental affect on the user. Any solution, by which a computer can provide a small part of its CPU, memory, and connectivity toward a common computational infrastructure, must satisfy some security properties.

- The sandbox will be implemented for all platforms. The construction of a true, distributed sandbox would require the participation and support of all OS vendors.
- The sandbox will have the lowest system priority and will cease to consume any resources if the user initiates any computational task.
- The sandbox will have no access to and will be unable to harm the underlying system on which it runs.
- The sandbox will communicate with other instances of the sandbox in very flexible ways sharing information, receiving requests, processing requests, and communicating results to some central point of control.
- The sandbox construction will be sufficiently abstract to allow new distributed applications that can use the enormous power of such a vast computational base.
- Above all, the sandbox will be secure.

Distributed applications have been used to solve a diverse collection of problems. Here are a few examples:

- Factoring composite numbers with large prime factors. The ECMNET Project runs distributed integer factorization algorithms using elliptic curves and has found factors over 50 digits long for certain target composites such as large Fermat numbers.
- Brute force password cracking. The EFF DES cracker project and Distributed.Net, a worldwide coalition of computer enthusiasts, have cracked DES challenges

Internet, to win RSA Data Security's DES Challenge III in a record-breaking 22 hours and 15 minutes.

- DNA structural analysis. The distributed analysis of vast amounts of DNA data, searching for biologically interesting sequences, has tremendous research potential.
- Massively parallel simulations. Distributed simulators where many users run a climate model on their computers using a Monte Carlo simulation to predict and simulate global climate conditions.
- Analysis of radio wave data for signs of extraterrestrial signals. Millions of people have joined SETI, probably the most famous distributed computing project, to process radio signals from space collected in the search for life on other planets.

As computationally intense problems become increasingly relevant to our lives, building distributed sandboxes will become a cost-effective and invaluable option for their resolution.

Conclusion

The information technology infrastructure in any company of reasonable size is a complex collection of hardware and software platforms. Cheaper computing power and higher networking bandwidth have driven computing environments to become more distributed and heterogeneous. Applications have many users, hosts, system interfaces, and networks, all linked through complex interconnections.

Application architects designing security solutions for these systems must use common off-the-shelf components to absorb and contain some of this complexity. There are many popular security components that we do not have the space to present in detail, for example security tools such as the following (and many others):

- tcpwrapper (ftp.porcupine.org/pub/security/)
- tripwire (www.tripwiresecurity.com/)
- cops (www.cert.org)
- nmap (www.insecure.org/nmap)

The CERT website maintains a list of popular tools at www.cert.org/tech_tips/security_tools.html. In this chapter, we have covered a fraction of the ground, leaving many technologies, products, standards, and their corresponding architectural issues unaddressed.

Some new technologies can make your life as a security architect miserable. Our fast laptops and desktop machines have spoiled us, and raised our expectations for quality of service, interface functionality, or bandwidth. Wireless and mobile computing with PDA-type devices, for example, can add significant challenges to security. They extend the perimeter of visibility of the application to clients with limited computational muscle, memory, or protocol support. They introduce new protocols with poorly designed

by untrusted ISPs. Some vendors—Certicom, for example—have created lightweight yet powerful cryptographic modules for these devices, but for the most part we must wait until they mature before we can expect any real usability from so constrained an interface.

In the following chapter, we will discuss the conflicts faced by a security architect from the vantage point of the goal targeted, rather than the component used to achieve security. This discussion sets the stage for our concluding chapters on the other challenges faced by the application architect, namely security management and security business cases.

Security and Other Architectural Goals

In this chapter, we will emphasize non-functional goals that describe quality in the system independent of the actions that the system performs. In previous chapters, we discussed our architectural choices among security components and patterns for accomplishing functional goals, which are goals that describe the behavior of the system or application under normal operational circumstances. Functional goals tell us what the system should do. Software architecture has other non-functional concerns besides security. Applications have requirements for performance, availability, reliability, and quality that are arguably more important than security in the mind of the system architect because they directly affect the business goals of the application.

There are many perceived architectural conflicts between security and these other architectural goals. Some of these conflicts are clear myths that bear debunking; others reveal underlying flaws at some more fundamental level that manifest as tensions in the application. Still more represent clear and unambiguous dissension while recommending an architectural path. We must separate these other architectural goals into those that are complementary to the needs of secure design; those that are independent of secure design; and those that are at times at odds with the goals of secure application design.

In this chapter, we will introduce a simple notion, the force diagram, to represent the tensions between different architectural goals and security. We will then proceed to classify our non-functional goals into three categories to discuss the affects of security architecture on each.

- *Complementary goals*, which support security
- *Orthogonal goals*, which through careful design can be made independent of security
- *Conflicting goals*, which are inherently opposed to security

Metrics for Non-Functional Goals

Applications differ in their definitions of non-functional goals and in the quantitative measurement of achieving these goals. This situation constrains us to generalize somewhat as we present each goal. It is helpful to sit down with the customer and review concrete feature requests and requirements to attach numbers to the goals. The architecture document should answer questions at the architecture review.

- How many minutes of annual down time a year are permissible?
- How will software defects be classified, measured, and reported?
- Does the application require testing to certify to a maximum number of critical modification requests per release?
- Do we have firm estimates of average, peak, and busy time data rates?
- Does the business require several applications to share a highly available configuration to save hardware costs? Can your application coexist with other applications on a host?
- Do we have some idea of where future growth will take us?
- How many of our conflicts in supporting non-functional goals are actually caused by vendor product defects?

These and many other issues will further illuminate the actual versus perceived differences between security and our other application goals.

Force Diagrams around Security

Force diagrams are a simple means of expressing a snapshot of the current state of an application. Force diagrams pick one particular architectural goal (in our case, security) and map the tensions between this goal and other non-functional goals. Our main goal, security, pulls the system architecture in one direction. Other goals support, oppose, or are indifferent to the design forces of security.

It is important to note that force diagrams are always with reference to a single architectural goal and say nothing about the relative conflicts between other goals. For example, we will show that performance and portability are both in conflict with security, but that does not mean they support one another. On the contrary, they are often internally at odds. A portable solution that uses a hardware abstraction layer to insulate the application from the underlying platform might be slower than one that exploits hardware details. Conversely, a fast solution that exploits chip instruction set details on one platform might not be portable to another hardware platform. Force diagrams only classify other goals into three buckets with respect to a reference goal.

It is also important to note that the relationship shown by force arrows between the reference goal and another architectural goal might represent a causal link or might only represent a correlation. In the former case, achieving one goal causes improvement or

the other goal to succeed or fail but only shares fortunes with it. Rather, some *other* factor plays a part in representing the true cause of the design force. This factor could be the experience level of the architect, some constraining property of the application domain, limits on the money spent on accomplishing each goal, or the ease with which we exploit common resources to accomplish both goals.

Normal Architectural Design

In Figure 14.1, we show a typical system—a composite of the many actual applications that we have seen in development or in production—that exhibits *normal* architectural tensions. The application is normal in the sense that it pays some attention to conflicts with security but not in an optimal manner.

Note that the reference goal of security appears on the arrow to the left, denoting its special status.

Complementary Goals

The goals of high availability, robustness, and auditing support our reference system goal of security.

High availability—and its other incarnation, disaster recovery—requires the architect to create systems with minimal down times. We must incur considerable costs to ensure high availability. Applications must purchase redundant servers, disks, and networking; deploy complex failover management solutions; and design detailed procedures for transferring control and data processing from a failed primary server to a secondary server. Failover mechanisms that restore a service or a host attacked by a

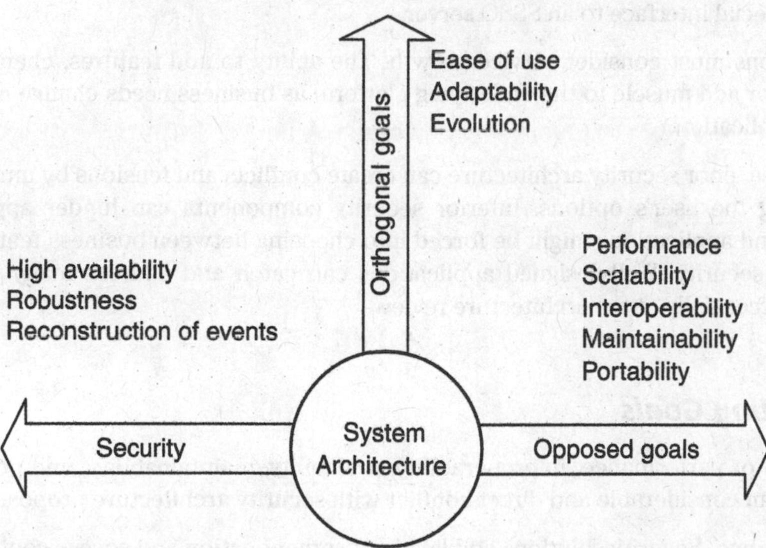

Figure 14.1 Normal tensions in an application.

tected against a similar attack. High availability often supports security through intangibles such as careful design and application layout, better testing, and hardening of the production application against common failures that could be prerequisites to an attack.

Robustness, the property of reliable software systems, is achieved through data collection, modeling, analysis, and extensive testing. Code that is tested is less likely to have exploitable buffer overflow problems, memory leaks through pointer handling, array bounds check errors, bad input functions, or division by zero errors that cause core dumps. Throwing bad inputs at code, capturing use-case exceptions, or using well-designed regression test suites and tools all help improve code quality. Testing also catches many problems that might manifest as security holes in the field, that once discovered can be closed in development before deployment. Robust software is rarely in release 1.0. Higher release numbers often mean that the development team has had some time to address goals (such as security) that were secondary concerns in early releases.

Auditing is a basic security principle, and secure applications record all important system events and user actions. Security audit trails support the reconstruction of events.

Orthogonal Goals

Ease of use, adaptability, and evolution are largely independent of the quality of security within the application.

Ease of use is a human factors goal. An application that has ergonomic design has an intuitive user interface and clear navigational controls. The usability goal of SSO to multiple applications in the domain can affect security. The application might need to build a special interface to an SSSO server.

Applications must consider service growth. The ability to add features, change functionality, or add muscle to the underlying platform as business needs change is critical to any application.

In any case, poor security architecture can create conflicts and tensions by unnaturally restricting the user's options. Inferior security components can hinder application growth, and applications might be forced into choosing between business feature support and security. Well-designed applications can catch and address many of these issues successfully at the architecture review.

Conflicting Goals

The goals of performance, interoperability, scalability, maintainability, and portability are often in considerable and direct conflict with security architecture proposals.

Performance. Security solutions add layers of authentication and access control to every operation. Applications that use security service providers, trusted third

local and network accesses introduced for security purposes.

Interoperability. Interoperability between clients and servers in heterogeneous environments that otherwise can communicate in insecure mode might fail when security is added. Many protocols that are certified as interoperable have teething problems when security is thrown into the mix. An example described in previous chapters was CORBA interoperability using SSL.

Scalability. The application might estimate growth rates in data feeds, database table sizes, and user population correctly but might forget to consider security. Each additional authentication check that needs to look up a user database for an identity, or each authorization check that references a complex management information base of object and method invocations before granting access, adds a burden to our operational resource budget. Can we ensure that bulk encryption on our communication links is fast enough as data rates increase? Are our database tables that store security events large enough? Can our security solution scale to support much larger user populations? We might be surprised when we run out of resources in the field in spite of our performance models predicting no problems.

Maintainability. Our ability to service the application might be constrained by unusual security controls that restrict access or might require extensive manual updates and synchronization of information.

Portability. Our ability to change any element of hardware, software, or networking within our application might be limited by the availability of an equivalent, interoperable security component to replace the one being retired.

Good Architectural Design

In Figure 14.2, we show a typical system—a composite of the many actual applications in development or in production that have conducted and passed architecture review and security assessment—that exhibits *good* architectural tensions. The application is good in the sense that it pays considerable attention to conflicts with security, makes a conscious effort to resolve conflicts, and addresses gaps in achieved results through clear definition of methods and procedures and through user and administrator training.

Complementary Goals

The goals of high availability, robustness, and auditing continue to support security as a system goal.

Orthogonal Goals

The goals of interoperability, scalability, and maintainability have been added to ease of use, adaptability, and evolution as goals that are largely independent of security within the application.

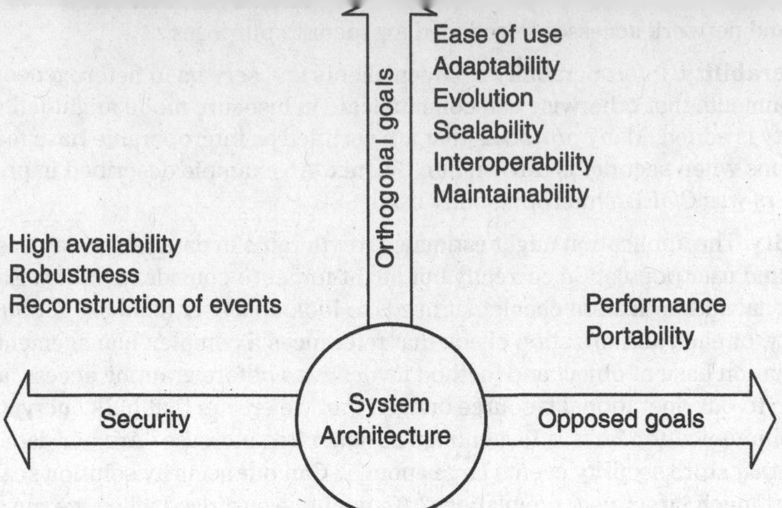

Figure 14.2 Good tensions in an application.

Conflicting Goals

The goals of performance and portability remain in conflict with security architecture goals. We reach the surprising conclusion that some goals are, despite all of the vendor promises in the world, fundamentally opposed to secure design. The best course for an application architect lies in acknowledging this fact and acting to mitigate it, rather than ignoring the conflicts or compromising quality by sacrificing security to other architectural goals.

Recognition of the conflicts at an early stage affords applications and their owners the opportunity of doing things differently—perhaps buying more hardware, changing database definitions, reorganizing user groups, reworking the network architecture, or switching vendor products. Conflicts left unresolved at least have the virtue of documentation, along with the possibility that at some future time the evolution of the application and the products it depends upon will result in resolution of the conflict.

In the following sections, we will expand upon each of these goals and its relationship to security to explain why we cannot achieve perfection.

High Availability

High availability is the architectural goal of application resiliency against failures of system components. Resilient systems that guarantee service availability normally describe maximum down time as a percentage of the average system up time and the average total time between each failure and recovery. The degree of availability of a system is described by the following formula:

$$\text{Availability} = \frac{\text{Mean Time Between Failure}}{\text{Mean Time Between Failure + Mean Time To Recover}}$$

of the individual components. The *Mean Time to Recover* (MTTR) depends upon the particular details of the high-availability solution put in place by the application architect. The highest level of system availability that is practical for commercial applications today is the famous *five nines* level. A system that has 99.999 percent availability will have only five minutes and 15 seconds of down time a year. Marcus and Stern's *Blueprints for High Availability* [MS00] is a good reference for the configuration of highly-available systems.

Enterprise applications are complex, distributed collections of hardware, software, networking, and data. Applications also have varying definitions for the term down time, and the proposed options for HA architecture show varying levels of responsiveness, transparency, automation, and data consistency. Highly available systems must achieve resilience in the face of many kinds of failure.

Hardware failures. The physical components of the application server might fail. A disk crash might cause data loss; a processor failure could halt all computation by causing a fatal OS exception; a fan failure could cause overheating; or a short circuit or loose cabling within the cabinet could cause intermittent and arbitrary system failure.

Software failures. The underlying OS could crash and require a reboot (or worse, a rebuild). The software components on the system, such as middleware products, database processes, or application code, could fail.

Network failures. Connectivity to the network could fail locally through a *network interface card* (NIC) or cable or on an external router, hub, or bridge. If the failure occurs on a chokepoint in the architecture, we might lose all service.

Infrastructure failures. The application servers could go down because of power loss, overheating from an air conditioning failure, water damage, failed ISPs, or lack of administrative personnel at a critical failure point.

Solutions for high availability use many technologies and techniques to mitigate the risk of failure. In Figure 14.3, we show an example of a highly available application and describe its features.

Layered architecture. In our example, we run a trusted or hardened version of the operating system and install a failover management system along with our application.

Robust error recovery on the primary. The application, running on a primary server, has software and hardware monitors that continually report to error recovery processes on the health of the application. Daemons that die are restarted, process tables are pruned of zombies, error logs are automatically moved off the server if they grow too large, traffic on failed NICs is routed to redundant NICs, and the file system size (for example, swap or temp space) is closely monitored and cleaned up. In the case of drastic events, perhaps disk failures or complete disconnects from all networks, the application can automatically page an administrator or shut down to prevent contention with the secondary, which presumably has taken over.

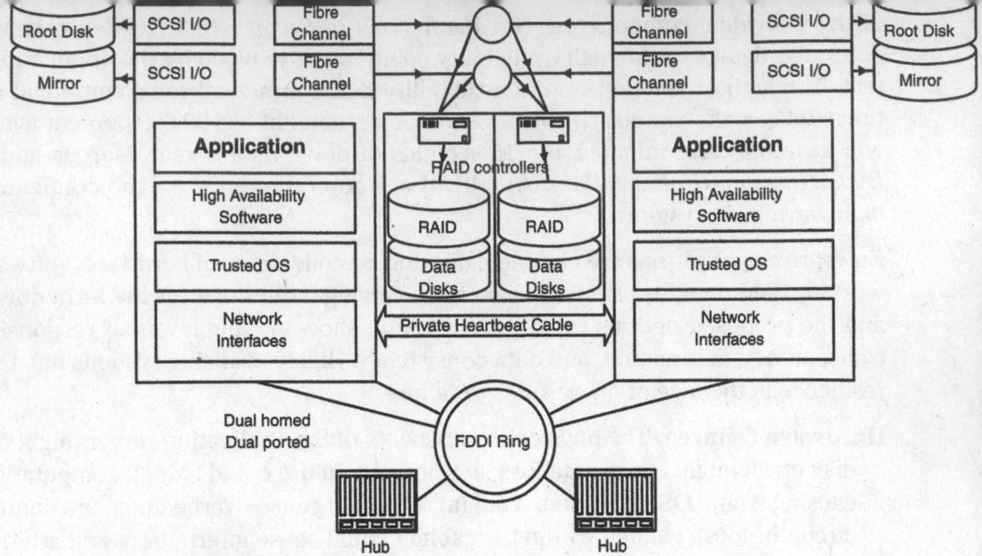

Figure 14.3 High-availability configuration.

Primary and secondary servers. High-availability configurations use server pairs or clusters of several servers to design failover configurations. In our example, the application runs on a primary server and is connected to a designated secondary server by a private heartbeat cable. The heartbeat itself has to be protected from disconnects through redundancy, and the primary must always have the processing resources to maintain a steady heartbeat. The heartbeat can run over the network, but it is safer if the two servers (if collocated) are connected by using a private line. When the secondary detects no heartbeat, it can query the primary to confirm failure. The failover management software will migrate ownership of the application data, current state, any shared hardware caches, IP addresses, or hardware addresses.

Data management. Disk arrays can contain their own hardware management level, complete with hardware RAID controllers, hardware cache, and custom management tools and devices. Storage vendors provide software RAID and logical volume management products on top of this already reliable data layer for additional resiliency. In our example, we have separate, private mirrored disks on each server for storing the operating system and static application components, which include binaries and configuration files. We have redundant, multiplexed, Fibrechannel connections to shared mirrored RAID arrays for application data, which can be reached through multiple paths by both primary and secondary servers. The shared disks can belong to only one server at a time, and we must prevent data corruption in *split-brain* conditions (where both servers believe that they are active). We could also use logical volume management, which could provide software RAID. Software RAID moves disk management off the disk array and onto our servers. This action might add a performance hit, but the additional monitoring and alarming are worth it.

Network redundancy. If the network is under the stress of heavy traffic, it might incorrectly be diagnosed as having failed. There is no magic bullet to solve this problem. We can build redundant network paths, measure latency, remove performance bottlenecks under our control, or maintain highly available network servers for DHCP, DNS, NIS, or NTP services. Each server in our example is dual homed with redundant ports to the corporate intranet over an FDDI ring. Each host has multiple NICs with two ports each that connect to the public and to the heartbeat network. We could also consider additional administrative network interfaces to troubleshoot a failed server in the event of network failure. (Please refer to [MS00] for examples.)

Multi-server licensing. The primary and secondary servers have separate software licenses for all the vendor components on our application.

Applications that are considered mission critical might also require disaster recovery. Disaster recovery servers are not collocated with the HA configuration but are separated geographically and configured to be completely independent of any services at the primary site.

Security Issues

Solutions for high availability complement security. There is a correlation between all the care and consideration given to recovery from failure and fault tolerance, and efforts by application architects to test applications for security vulnerabilities, such as buffer overflow problems, poorly configured network services, weak authentication schemes, or insecurely configured vendor products.

The solutions for security and high availability often appear in layered architectures to separate concerns. At the hardware level, our HA configuration manages faults in components such as hardware RAID and NICs. We layer a trusted or hardened version of the operating system in a security layer over this level. The failure management software runs as a fault-tolerant layer on top of the operating system. Finally, the application implementing all other security authentication and authorization checks appears in a layer above the FMS solution. This lasagna-like complementary structure is a common feature of HA configurations.

Security does add additional caveats to HA configuration.

- If we support SSL on our Web servers, then we should ensure that certificate expiry on the primary Web server should not occur at the same time as expiry on the secondary server.
- All security information (including the application users, profiles, ACL lists, and configuration) must be replicated on all elements of the cluster.
- Security components, such a firewall or tcpwrapper, on a failed network interface must be migrated along with the correct configuration to a new interface.

application state to be local to the primary. Upon a failure, the user might be required to authenticate to the secondary server.

- The disaster recovery site should have the same security policy as the primary site.

High-availability configurations cannot help security in all circumstances. For example, our primary server might fail because of a distributed denial-of-service attack. Migrating the application, along with IP address and hostname, to the secondary server can restore service for a few seconds before the secondary fails for the same reason.

Robustness

Robust applications ensure dependable service in the face of software or hardware failures. Robustness is related to the twin attributes of dependable service: availability and reliability. We have presented the property of high availability in the last section; we now present the property of reliability, which enables us to meaningfully quantify the MTBF and MTTR values that we used in computing the availability of an application. We recommend Michael Lyu's *Handbook of Software Reliability Engineering* [Lyu96], the most comprehensive introduction to the field available. Although some of the tools are somewhat dated and the theoretical analysis of toy applications might not extend to your application's needs, this text remains an essential reference for any practicing architect.

Reliability is the property of preventing, detecting, or correcting faults in a graceful manner without degradation of system performance. The requirements for quality assurance are stated in concrete, measurable terms: What is the probability that the system will operate without failures for a specified period of time, under specific circumstances and environmental factors? The ability to quantify software failure is critical. The MTBF and MTTR of each component in a system consisting of multiple subsystems and components needs to be considered in order to estimate the reliability of the architecture as a whole.

Software reliability engineering (SRE), originally considered an art learned only through experience, has grown into a mature discipline. SRE provides the following elements:

- A framework for research and development on reliability, including mathematical foundations, terminology, tools, and techniques.
- A definition of the operational profile of an application describing the application's behavior, resource allocation, and expected usage in the field. The operational profile and the actual software defect information of a running application enable us to collect data for modeling behavior. Fault data is valuable only under the stationary assumption that past behavior will be a predictor of future events.
- Many mathematical models of software reliability using statistical and probabilistic principles, each built upon a formal set of assumptions of application behavior,

and analysis of software faults.

- Techniques for evaluating the success in prediction and prevention of faults of a particular model, including feedback mechanisms to improve the model's parameters to more closely approximate application behavior.
- Best practices, software monitoring and measurement, defect categorization, trend analysis, and metrics to help understand and implement the results of failure analysis.
- Guidance for choosing corrective measures.

SRE is concerned with analyzing the incidence of failures in software systems through defects in coding or human errors that result in interruptions of expected service. We can estimate future failures by using several failure measures captured in SRE models. For example, SRE defines the *cumulative failure function* (CFF) as the sum of all failures since startup to any point in time. We can derive other failure measures, such as the *failure rate function* (FRF), from the CFF. The FRF measures the probability that a failure will occur in a small interval of time after time *t*, given that no failures have occurred until the time *t*.

The four pillars of SRE are as follows:

Fault prevention. Avoid the creation of faults in the design phase of the architecture.

Fault removal. Detect and verify the existence of faults and remove them.

Fault tolerance. Provide service in the presence of faults through redundant design.

Fault and failure forecasting. Under the stationary assumption, estimate the probability of occurrence and consequence of failures in the future.

The core of SRE is based on methodologies for testing software. Although theoretical models for predicting failure are very important, software testing remains the last best chance for delivering quality and robustness in an application. SRE expert John Musa estimates that testing consumes 50 percent of all resources associated with high-volume consumer product development (for example, within desktop operating systems, print software, or games) and mission-critical enterprise software development (for example, within military command and control systems or the Space Shuttle program).

A reliable system that provides continuity of service is not necessarily highly available. We need the HA configurations described in the last section to make a reliable system satisfy some benchmark, such as the five nines availability goal. Making an unreliable system highly available would be a mistake, however, because availability of service means little if the application fails on both primary and secondary servers due to software faults. High availability stands upon the foundations built by using SRE.

Binary Patches

SRE assumes that defects discovered through software testing can be fixed. Without extensive testing, however, we cannot be sure that the patched code is free of both the

of individual files in a product or application. Architects rarely run a full regression test against the system after an OS vendor or product vendor issues a software patch. In general, we trust that the patch has been tested before being released for use by the general public.

One mode of introducing security fixes is through binary patches. Binary patches refer to hacks of hexadecimal code to fix a problem in executables that we do not have source code for inspection. This item is different from a vendor patch. The vendor has access to the source, modifies the source, tests the correctness of the fix, and then builds a patch that will modify an installed buggy instance correctly. One reason why vendor patches are so large is that they eschew cut-and-paste strategies for the wholesale replacement of files. This situation is the only circumstance in which the modification of binaries should be allowed, and even in this circumstance, hard evidence that the patch works should exist in a development instance of the system.

Some developers directly hack binary code in production to fix security holes. Examples include using "find-replace" programs that can search for statically allocated strings that leak information and replace them with other presumably safer strings. Without knowledge of how a specific compiler sets aside static buffers in an executable file, this action could be dangerous. Searching for strings can result in false positives.

- The patch might modify the wrong strings, introducing impossible-to-debug errors.
- Even if we only target valid strings, the replacement string should not be longer than the original string to prevent overflowing onto other bytes.
- Cut and paste will probably work if the new string is shorter, but did we remember to correctly terminate the new string?
- Verification through testing is very hard. Where do we allow the patching of binaries to happen? Cutting a binary open and directly pasting bytes into it might cause file integrity problems, versioning problems, and testing problems.
- How do you test the correctness of a modified binary? Testing the original was hard enough. Who certifies that the patches will work as advertised?

Enterprise software development should use well-defined configuration management tools to handle all aspects of code versioning, change management, and automated build and testing procedures. Patching binaries breaks the model of configuration management, introducing an exception process within the accepted mode of managing a release. We strongly recommend not performing this action from an architectural standpoint.

Security Issues

Security as a system goal is aligned with the goal of system reliability. The prevention of malicious attacks against system resources and services makes the system more dependable. Making the system more reliable, however, might not always result in higher security, outside of the benefits accrued from increased testing.

Although advocates of SRE lump malicious failure with accidental failure, this blurring of boundaries is largely inadvisable. The models of fault analysis are not helpful in esti-

tionary assumption. History is no predictor of future failure when it comes to system compromise. We cannot accurately measure metrics such as the rate of occurrence of failures, the cumulative failure function, or the mean time between failures in circumstances where hackers actively exploit vulnerabilities.

SRE mathematical models assume that failures caused by software defects occur according to some standard probabilistic model; for example, modeling the failure occurrence process by using *homogeneous Poisson processes* (HPP, discussed in our section on Performance ahead). Hackers can deliberately create scenarios considered impossible by the model, however. The HPP model predicts that the probability that two complex (and seemingly, by assumption), independent defects will both result in failure within the same small time interval is vanishingly small. If we consider malice a possibility, the probability might be exceedingly high.

The assessment methods discussed in Chapter 2, "Security Assessments," are the best mechanisms for thwarting threats to system integrity.

Reconstruction of Events

We use the term reconstruction of events to represent any activity within an application that records historical or transactional events for later audit or replay. Systems that implement this architectural goal support the concept of system memory. The system can remember its past from application startup or from some safe system state up to the point of failure or error.

The goal of event reconstruction through comprehensive auditing appears in many forms in applications.

- Databases implement two-phase commits to ensure that multistep transactions are completed from start to finish or are rolled back to a safe state.
- Some applications log operations to transaction logs as deltas to the system state that are later transferred to a central location for consolidation with the master database (some older automated teller machines work in this manner).
- *Journaling File Systems* (JFS) borrow data-logging techniques from database theory to record any file operations in three steps: record the proposed change, make the actual change, and if the change is successful, delete the record of the first step. This process permits rapid file system restoration in case of a system failure, avoiding expensive file system checks on all file and directory handles.

A crucial requirement of reconstruction is system auditing. The system must record events either within the system log files, database, or a separate log server.

Security Issues

Auditing is a core security principle. It helps the system administrator review the events on a host. What processes were running? What command caused the failure? Which

they present? How can we restart the system in a safe state?

Event reconstruction has an important role in the prosecution of perpetrators of security violations. Our ability to prove our case, linking the attacker to the attack, depends on the quality of our logs; our ability to prove that the logs themselves are complete, adequate, and trustworthy; and that the attack happened as we contend. Normally, this situation is not a technical issue but a social or legal issue. That the events occurred as charged is not in dispute as much as whether we can link these events to a particular individual. This action requires that all the entities on the connection path from the attacker to the application maintain some historical data through connection logs, dial-up access databases, system files, successfully validated passwords, and network paths.

Auditing also helps in the area of Security Data Analysis. This area is a new application with the potential for rapid growth as data standards improve. Once we have security standards across applications for event management and logging, we can extract, merge, and analyze event information. Once we overcome the challenges associated with synchronizing events across application boundaries and separate system clocks we will see the benefits of merging security audit data for analysis. This functionality can lead to powerful new knowledge about the state of security in the enterprise. We could analyze log data by using data mining, case-based reasoning, multi-dimensional visualization, pattern matching, and statistical tools and techniques. These tools could compute metrics or extract new knowledge, providing valuable feedback to architects about the root causes of intrusions, top 10 lists of vulnerabilities, predictions of potential intrusion, patch application compliance, or best security practices.

We must take event reconstruction seriously or run the risk of succumbing to an exploit with no ability to analyze failure. We might lack the ability to recover from the attack or adequately prove in a court of law that some particular individual is guilty. If our system is used as an intermediary to launch attacks on other hosts, we run the risk of legal liability unless we are able to prove that the attacks did not originate from our host (although we might still be liable to some extent, even if we are able to prove this fact).

Ease of Use

Ease of use is a human factors goal. Usability engineering has grown from a relatively uncommon practice into a mature and essential part of systems engineering. Applications that take the user's capabilities and constraints into consideration in the design of products, services, interfaces, or controls see the benefits in intangibles such as increased customer satisfaction, customer retention, and increased frequency of use —possibly accompanied by tangible results such as increases in revenue and productivity and reductions in costs through avoided rework. Ease of use also enables applications to transfer more complex tasks to the user, such as self-ordering, self-provisioning, or account management, that would otherwise require telephone support and customer service representation.

Usability engineering formalizes the notion that products and services should be user-friendly. Making the user's experience simpler and more enjoyable is an important goal

system architecture. Usability engineering stresses the importance of the following features:

Simplification. Does the application just make features available, or does it make all activities easier and simpler to execute? How much of the information on any displayed screen is actually needed to accomplish the tasks on that screen?

Training. How much effort does it take to bring a novice user up to speed in the effective and productive use of the application? How much of this time is due to inherent complexity of the application, and how much is due to confusing design, a poor choice of mnemonics, excessive use of jargon, or poor information hiding?

Dependency. False dependencies are stated prerequisites of information or experience that are actually not needed for a majority of activities within the application. How many false dependencies does the application place upon the user?

Navigation. Is it easy to find what the user wants from the start screen of the application? Does the application have a memory of the user's actions? Can a user retrace history or replay events multiple times instead of manually repeating all of the steps from the original point?

Accessibility. Will people with disabilities use the application? Do we provide alternative access options that support all of our potential users?

Ergonomics. We must take into account the look, feel, heft, and touch of the user interface. Is the screen too noisy and confusing? Is the keypad on a handheld device too small for most people? Is the screen too bright, the controls too high, the joystick too unresponsive, or the keystroke shortcuts too hard to type with one hand?

Repetitive use. How much stress does the user experience from repetitive use of the application's controls?

Performance. Is the response time of the application excessively slow?

Good usability engineering practices create reusable designs and architectures and create a shared and common vocabulary for entities across many applications within a single business domain.

Security Issues

For the most part, ease of use and security do not conflict with one another. The two main points of contention are ease of security management and SSSO.

Security Management

Administering security in a heterogeneous environment with a large user and application population can be very difficult. Vendors provide management tools for particular products, but these tools rarely interoperate with one another or with standard monitoring and alarming frameworks without some investment in development and integration. Many tools provide GUIs or command line text-based tools along with thick manuals on options and usage. There are no standards or guidelines on how security management should be accomplished across [illegible] For example, consider the case of highly available configurations that must maintain synchronized user, password, and access control lists across all secondary or clustered servers to ensure that the failover authenticates and authorizes the user population correctly. If we do not automate this process and create integrity and sanity scripts to verify state synchronization, we run the considerable risk of starting a secondary server after a failure with an incorrect security configuration.

Manual management of security administration is awkward and error prone. Ease of use is critical in security management because of the risk of errors. If our process for adding, deleting, or modifying users is complicated, manual, and repetitive, it is almost guaranteed to result in misconfiguration. Our methods and procedures must be intuitive, automated, and scriptable, and we must be able to collect and review errors and alarms from security work. Handoffs are also a problem, where the responsibility for one task is split across several administrators who must complete subtasks and call back when the work is complete.

Applications can use commercial trouble-management tools that can aid efforts to administer security. These tools provide a formal process of trouble ticketing, referral, and ticket closure along with support for tracking and auditing work.

Secure Single Sign-On

It is important to recognize that SSO is a usability feature that sometimes masquerades as a security feature. Please refer to Chapter 13 for a detailed description of SSO, the architectural options for accomplishing SSSO, and some of the pitfalls around implementing SSO with commercial solutions.

A well-designed, secure SSO solution will greatly enhance security. We add one note to our description of SSSO to warn architects of the additional burdens that a poor SSO solution can place on the application. SSSO is not worth pursuing in certain situations, where the administrative headache of maintaining special clients on user workstations and managing scripts for a rapidly changing population of users and servers is too great or in situations where incompatibility with new application hardware and software causes multiple incompatible sign-on solutions to coexist. It is not SSO if you still have to remember 10 passwords, three of which are to disjoint SSO services.

A good commercial SSSO solution will have the virtues of stability, extensibility, secure administration, architectural simplicity, and scalability. SSO solutions have to be amenable to adding systems that wish to share the SSO service. A poorly designed SSO solution might actually make the application less safe by encouraging a false sense of safety while hiding implementation flaws.

Maintainability, Adaptability, and Evolution

We present these three non-functional goals together because all three are independent of conflicts with security for many of the same reasons. Maintainability relates to the

ability and evolution relate to the application's projected evolutionary path as business needs evolve.

Because of the vast number of evolutionary forces that an application could experience, we cannot present a detailed description of methodologies for creating easy-to-maintain, flexible, and modifiable applications. We refer the reader to [BCK98] for a description of some of the patterns of software architecture that make these properties feasible within your application.

Security Issues

Applications should develop automated, well-documented, and tested methods and procedures for security administration and as far as possible minimize the amount of manual effort required to conduct basic administrative activities. Please refer to Chapter 11, "Application and OS Security," for a discussion of some of the operations, administration, and maintenance procedures for security.

Security adaptability concerns arise as users place new feature demands on the system. Interfaces add more objects and methods, screens add links to additional procedures and data, new partner applications request access, and new access control requirements are created as the application grows. All of these issues can be addressed through planning and flexibility in the architecture. Some applications even use code generation techniques to define a template of the application and use a configuration file to describe the structures in the current release. This template and configuration is used to generate shell scripts, C, C++, or Java code; Perl programs; database stored procedures for creates, updates, inserts, and deletes; or dynamic Web content. Code generation reduces the risks of errors and can result in tremendous productivity gains if embraced from release 1.0. Code generation reduces the probability of incorrect security configuration while making analysis easier, because we only need to review the template and configuration files for correctness as the application changes.

Evolutionary forces can create security problems. Corporate mergers and acquisitions can create unusual evolutionary forces upon an application that can seriously stress its security architecture. The application might be thrown, along with other dissimilar production applications from another company's IT infrastructure, into a group where all perform the same business process on the surface but contain huge architectural conflicts underneath the hood. Systems must adapt to the addition of large numbers of new users or dramatic changes in the volume or structure of the underlying data. New authentication mechanisms and access control rules might be needed to support the complex task of integrating security policy across the combined enterprise. There are no magic bullets to solve this problem.

Security assurance, in the event of a corporate merger or acquisition, of all the information assets of the new corporate entity is a very difficult proposition. Architecture planning and management are critical. Architects faced with the challenge of integrating two or more diverse information technology infrastructures from the assets of the companies involved must recognize constraints through documenting the existing architectural assumptions, system obligations, and notions of security administration.

requirements of the combined solution. We must accept any implicit constraints and prevent the proposed security architecture from oppressing the system's functional architecture. Sometimes we must make hard choices and turn one application off, migrating its users and data to another application. At other times, we must maintain an uneasy peace between coexisting applications and develop a message-passing architecture to link the features of each.

Scalability

Scalability refers to data growth as opposed to feature growth, our concern in the last section. Scalable applications are architected to handle increases in the number of requests received, the amount of data processed, or expansion of the user population. Architects must factor in growth for all application components, which includes headroom for growth in the database, file system, number of processors on any server, additional disk storage media, network interface slots, power requirements, networking, or bandwidth.

Security Issues

Good architectural design will normally not produce conflicts between security and scalability. Many of the architectural patterns that support scalability, such as separation of concerns, client/server architecture, communicating multithreaded process design, scalable Web farms, or scalable hardware clusters do not inherently oppose security.

Scalability can adversely affect security management if we do not have a plan to manage the growth in the user population or in the object groups that must be protected from unauthorized user access. Conversely, poor implementations of security (for example, a slow database query for an ACL lookup or a call to verify a certificate's status) that might be adequate for today's performance standard might seriously impact response times as the application grows.

Scalability is addressed by adding headroom for predicted growth. We must similarly add headroom for growth of our security components: Firewalls must be able to handle additional rules as the client and server population grows more complex; routers must be able to support growth in traffic without creating additional latency when applying access control lists; directory lookups for user profile information should be reasonably fast; and user authentication intervals should not seriously degrade as the population grows.

Vendor products often exhibit unnecessary ceilings because they do not estimate the future needs of the application. Some of these ceilings can be easily increased, but others could represent genuine limits for the application. For example, Windows NT 3.x–4.0 domains could originally support only around 40,000 users in a domain because of the 40MB limit Microsoft imposed upon the *Security Accounts Manager* (SAM) database.

tomers, contractors, and partners thrown into the mix, we can easily hit this limit. This situation resulted in ugly configurations with multiple domains that partitioned the underlying user population for scalability reasons. Microsoft has increased the Active Directory database sizes in Windows 2000 domains to 17 terabytes, supporting millions of objects [CBP99]. Scalability makes security administration cleaner.

Interoperability

Interoperability has been the central theme of several of our technical chapters: Chapter 8, "Secure Communication," Chapter 9, "Middleware Security," and Chapter 11, "Application and OS Security." Please refer to our discussion of two areas of security related interoperability issues in these chapters.

Interoperability requires vendors to perform the following actions:

- Comply with open standards.
- Fully document all APIs used.
- Use standards for internationalization such as Unicode for encoding data.
- Choose data types for elements on interfaces in a standard manner and publish IDL and type definitions.
- Provide evidence through certification and test suite results that they are interoperable with a standard reference implementation.
- Add message headers for specifying encodings, Big- versus Little-Endian data orders, alignments for packed data, and version numbers.
- Restrain from adding custom bells and whistles unless done unobtrusively or in a manner that enables us to disable the extensions.

Security Issues

The basic theme is that vendor products for communication that interoperate must continue to do so when the communication is secured.

- *Security administration across applications.* Many tools provide custom GUIs or command line security management utilities. Largely, because there are no standards around how security management should be accomplished, these tools rarely interoperate with one another. Automation through scripts results in some gaps because of differences in granularity and options available.
- *Secure communications over an interface.* We extensively described the impact of interoperability issues in the CORBA security arena, along with administration and security management problems, in Chapter 9. Interoperability issues could include incompatible cipher suites, subtle errors in implementations of

format issues, encoding issues on security headers, or differences in the exact version of security solution used (even in a single vendor environment, possibly due to backward compatibility issues).

Performance

As applications become more complex, interconnected, and interdependent, intuition alone cannot predict their performance. Performance modeling through analytical techniques, toy applications, and simulations is an essential step in the design and development of applications. Building test beds in controlled environments for load and stress testing application features before deployment is a common component of enterprise software development.

Performance models enable us to analyze, simulate, validate, and certify application behavior. These models depend upon theoretical foundations rooted in many mathematical fields, including probability, statistics, queuing, graph, and complexity theory.

Performance models represent unpredictable system events, such as service request arrivals, service processing time, or system load by using random variables, which are functions that assign numerical values to the outcomes of random or unpredictable events. Random variables can be discrete or continuous. Many types of discrete, random variables occur in performance models, including Bernoulli, binomial, geometric, or Poisson random variables. Similarly, many types of continuous random variables also occur in performance models, including Uniform, exponential, hyper-exponential, or normal random variables.

The collection of all possible probabilities that the random variable will take a particular value (estimated over a large number of independent trials) is the variable's probability distribution. Other properties, such as the standard deviation, expected value, or cumulative distribution function, can be derived from the probability distribution function. A performance model might be composed of many random variables, each of a different kind and each representing the different events within the system.

A function of time whose values are random variables is called a *stochastic* process. Application properties, such as the number of incoming service requests, are modeled by using stochastic processes. The *arrival process* describes the number of arrivals at some system during some time interval (normally starting at time 0). If the inter-arrival times between adjacent service requests can be represented by statistically independent exponential random variables, all with rate parameter λ, the arrival process is a Poisson process. If the rate parameter λ of the process does not vary with time, the Poisson process is said to be homogenous. Queuing models that assume that new arrivals have no memory of the previous arrival history of events describe the arrival process as a *homogeneous Poisson process* (HPP).

Poisson processes are unique because of three properties:

but only upon the interval length.

- The numbers of arrivals occurring in nonoverlapping intervals are statistically independent.
- The probability that exactly one request arrives in a very small time interval t is λt. The expected value of arrivals per unit time, called the arrival rate, is the rate parameter λ of the exponential random variable used for representing inter-arrival times.

Poisson processes are powerful because they approximate the behavior of actual service arrivals. One stream of events represented by using a Poisson process can be split apart into multiple Poisson processes, or many Poisson processes can be combined into one.

Queuing theory uses mathematical models of waiting lines of service requests to represent applications in which users contend for resources. If the model captures the application correctly, we can use standard formulas to predict throughput, system and resource utilization, and average response time.

Analytic techniques produce formulas that we can use to compute system properties. For example, Little's formula is a simple but powerful analytic tool often used by application architects. Little's formula states that the average number of requests being processed within the system is equal to the product of the arrival rate of requests with the average system response time in processing a request. Little's law is applied wherever we have knowledge of two of these entities and require information about the third.

Queuing models provide good estimates of the steady-state behavior of the system. Queuing theory has limitations, however, when application loads violate the assumptions of the model, and we must then resort to simulation and prototyping to predict behavior. Some queuing models for production applications are so complex that we have to resort to approximation techniques to simplify the problem.

Application analysis through simulation carries its own risks. Generating discrete events as inputs to our application simulator requires a good random number source that closely matches the actual probability distribution of events in the field. Otherwise, our results might be of questionable value. In recent news reports from the field of high-energy physics, several researchers retracted published simulation results after peer review found holes not in their analysis or physics but in the basic pseudo-random number generators used in the supercomputer simulations. Generating good random events at a sufficiently high rate is a research area in itself.

Simulation tools such as LoadRunner are a valuable part of the architect's toolbox. Architects use load and stress test automation tools to quickly describe the details of simple user sessions and then sit back and watch as the software generates thousands of identical events to simulate heavy loads. Simulators are invaluable for validating the assumptions of peak usage, worst case system response times, graceful degradation of service, or the size of the user population.

The actual construction of a good application simulator is an art form. Investing enough effort to build a model of the system without developing the entire application takes

decide which components represent external sources and sinks for events that will be captured using minimal coding and which components will actually simulate production processing in some detail. Vendor products complicate simulators, because we cannot code an entire Oracle database, IIS Web server, or LDAP directory component for our simulator. We must either use the actual products (which might involve purchase and licensing, not to mention some coding) or must build toy request/response processes that conform to some simple profile of use. Any decision to simplify our simulator represents a departure from reality. That departure could be within some critical component, invalidating the whole simulation run.

Security Issues

Security and performance modeling share a few technical needs. For example, the field of cryptography also requires good pseudo-random number generators to produce strong values for public or private keys, or within stream ciphers, to generate good unbounded bit sequences from secret keys. For the most part, however, security and performance are opposed to each other. One middleware vendor, when asked about the poor performance of their security service, replied, "What performance problem?" The vendor's implication that we must sacrifice speed for assurance is widespread and has some truth to it.

We should not compare two dissimilar configurations, one insecure and one secure, and make performance comparisons unless we are certain that there is room for improvement in the latter case. Insisting that security checks be transparent to the user, having no affect on latency, response time, throughput, bandwidth, or processing power is unreasonable.

Security checks also have the habit of appearing at multiple locations on the path between the user and the object being accessed. Security interceptors might have to look up third-party service providers; protocol stacks might need to call cryptographic libraries; syntax validators might need to check arguments; or events might need to be recorded to audit logs. This task is simply impossible to accomplish in an invisible manner.

The first message from this essential conflict is the recognition that we must budget for security in the application's operational profile. We must add suitable delays to prototypes to realistically capture the true hardware and software resources needed to provide quality security service.

Although we believe performance and security to be in conflict, we do not absolve the vendor of any responsibility in writing fast code. Often, performance problems can be fixed by the following measures:

- Profiling the security product to find performance bottlenecks and replacing them with optimized code
- Providing access to optimization parameters

within the security code

- Writing custom solutions for different platforms, each exploiting hardware details such as instruction sets, pipelines, or system cache
- Replacing software library calls with calls to hardware accelerator cards
- Ensuring that we do not have busy waits, deadlocks, or starvation on remote security calls
- Optimizing process synchronization during authentication or authorization checks
- Security response caching
- Fast implementations of cryptographic primitives or protocol stacks

Vendors cannot be miracle workers, but we must require and expect due diligence when it comes to squeezing the best possible effort out of the product.

Portability

We define application portability as the architectural goal of system flexibility. Flexible systems respond well to evolutionary forces that change the fundamental details of hardware, software, or networking of the application—independent of or in conjunction with feature changes. Evolution could force an application to change its database vendor from Sybase to Oracle, its Web server from IIS to Apache, its hardware from Hewlett-Packard to Sun, its disk cabling from SCSI to Fibrechannel, or its networking from 100BaseT to gigabit Ethernet (or in each case, change vice versa). Application portability requires that the same functionality that existed before should be replicated on the new platform.

Note that this definition differs in a slight way from the normal definition of software portability, which takes a product that works on one hardware platform and ports it to another. In the vendor's eyes, the product is central. It is advertised to work on some approved set of hardware, interact with some approved set of databases, or work in conjunction with some approved software. Our definition moves the focus from the vendor product to our application.

Commercial software vendors and Open Source software efforts have disagreements over the meaning of portability, as well.

Commercial software hides the source code, and the responsibility of porting the code falls to the software vendor's development group. Commercial software vendors, despite many protestations otherwise, prefer certain tools and platforms. They have distinct likes and dislikes when it comes to hardware platforms, compilers, partner cryptographic libraries, and operating system versions. They might support combinations outside this comfort zone, but the versions tend to lag in delivery times, or in feature sets, run slower and invariably have more defects than the core platform products because of the relative experience gap.

portability issues to the underlying JVM and core Java libraries. If the vendor for the JVM, libraries, and accessories is not up to par, then critical function calls might be absent or broken, the JVM might have bugs, or its performance might be inferior in some way. Some commentators have called this phenomenon "Write once, debug everywhere." The issue is not one of being compliant to some certification standard; it might just be that the target hardware is incapable of running a fully functional environment (for example, if we port the JVM to a handheld device such as a Palm Pilot or to an operating system that does not support multi-threading in processes, instead perhaps mapping them to a single user thread in the kernel).

Open Source, however, has the powerful advantage that the basic details of how the code works are open for inspection and modification by experts on any target platform. Expertise in the compilation and debugging tools, specific details within hardware instruction sets, and special features of interface development, networking, or performance tricks can all play a part in a successful port of an Open Source product. Open Source code tends to use a combination of two factors that aid portability.

- Hardware abstraction layers (HAL) in the code that contain all the dependencies on the underlying platform
- Sound design decisions behind critical features that have logical parallels on other platforms and are arrived at through some consensus on a design philosophy

Consult [VFTOSM99] for an interesting discussion of what portability means for Open Source, especially the flame fest between Andrew Tanenbaum and Linus Torvalds on portability in OS design and whether Linux is portable.

Our purpose is not to present a preference for one definition of portability over another but to emphasize that you must use the appropriate definition after you pick the application component that you wish to modify.

Security Issues

We believe portability and security are in fundamental conflict, because portability is achieved through abstraction from the underlying hardware, and security is reduced when we lose the ability to reference low-level platform details.

- Security solutions implemented above the HAL are still vulnerable to holes in the HAL implementation and the underlying operating system beneath the HAL. Consider a buggy implementation of the JVM running on a hardware platform. Although we achieve portability through Java, we might run the risk of compromise through failure of the JVM itself or through a poorly secured host, whose configuration we have no knowledge of.
- Security solutions implemented beneath the hardware abstraction layer are closer to the metal and secure the application better but now are not portable. Consider an application that uses a vendor's IPSec library to secure communications between two hosts. If this particular vendor's IPSec solution does not support a

platform type.

Portability issues create a new conflict in the architecture: functional goals now compete with security for resources and priority. Consider the following points:

- Your new database vendor product cannot parse the security solution implemented with stored procedures and functions on your old database. The basic schema and functionality port correctly, but security must be reimplemented.
- Your new hardware platform no longer supports the full-featured, fine-grained access control over resources that you expect. This feature is available if you purchase an expensive third-party solution but carries a performance cost.
- Your new messaging software is not interoperable with clients in secure mode but works fine in insecure mode.
- Your new networking is much faster than the old network but does not support any of your bump-in-the-wire hardware encryption boxes.

When features that the customers want go head to head with security, security will lose every time. We must architect for this eventuality with care, but planning and abstraction cannot conceal the essential conflict between securing a resource well and expecting the solution to run everywhere.

Conclusion

The greatest challenge for an application architect lies in identifying conflicts between goals. Recognizing the problem is half the battle. Once the tension in the design is accepted, we can examine alternatives, plot feature changes, present technical arguments for funding increases, or invest more time in prototyping or analysis. We would not recommend paralysis through analysis, but the current popular alternative of ignoring the problem and wishing it would go away does not work, either. At some later date we will pay, either through a serious security violation, unexpected additional hardware costs, service failures, or software patches that worsen the problem instead of solving it by introducing new holes as fast as we can plug them.

The name of the game in this chapter is conflict management. Even if we successfully recognize conflicts in the architecture, we are confronted with the question, "Who wins?" Deciding on priorities is not easy. It is unreasonable to expect a tidy resolution of all of these tensions. We have three limited resources to accomplish each of these goals: time, money, and people—and the properties of each goal might be unattainable under the realities of schedule deadlines, budget, or personnel.

Applications faced with this conflict abandon security. Applications that choose to request exceptions from security policy enforcement, rather than going back to the drawing board, do their customers a disservice. Architecture reviews can make us better aware of the available options and provide us with the technical arguments to request increases in any of the three constraints. Applications that take the exception

exception of other non-functional requirements. Would the customer be satisfied if your application processed half of the required service requests? What if it had twice the required response time? What if the application refused to support more than half of the user population or broke down whenever and for however long it felt like? If the answer to these questions is "No," why treat security differently?

Each of the architectural goals listed in this chapter has as rich and complex a history as does security. Each rests upon an immense base of research and technology, built and maintained by subject matter experts from academic, commercial research, and development organizations. No single project could adequately address each goal with resources from within the project team. Solving performance problems, building highly available configurations, and designing high-quality human computer interfaces or comprehensive regression test suites require external expertise and consulting.

Representing the conflicts between security, which we have devoted an entire book to, and other goals—each with as much background—within a few pages requires some oversimplification of the relationships, differences, and agreements that an actual application will face. Many applications never face these conflicts head-on, sometimes even deferring the deployment of two conflicting features in separate releases as if the temporal gap will resolve fundamental architectural tensions.

This chapter, more than any other, stresses the role of the architect as a generalist. Architects cannot have knowledge in all the domains we have listed but must have enough experience to understand both the vocabulary and the impact of the recommendations of experts upon the particular world of the application. Architecture reviews are an excellent forum for placing the right mix of people in a room to add specific expertise to general context, enabling the application architect to navigate all available options in an informed manner.

Enterprise Security Architecture

Enterprise security deals with the issues of security architecture and management across the entire corporation. Corporate security groups are normally constrained to the activities of policy definition and strict enforcement across all organizations within the company. Security process owners know policy but might not have the domain expertise to map generic policy statements to specific application requirements. Application architects are intimately familiar with the information assets, business rationale, software process, and architecture surrounding their systems but may have little experience with security. What should an architect do, under business and technical constraints, to be compliant with security policy? This challenge is very difficult—one that calls for individuals with unique, multi-disciplinary skills. Enterprise security architects must understand corporate security policy, think across organizational boundaries, find patterns in business processes, uncover common ground for sharing security infrastructure components, recommend security solutions, understand business impacts of unsecured assets that are at risk, and provide guidance for policy evolution.

A corporation defines security policy to provide guidance and direction to all of its employees on the importance of protecting the company's assets. These assets include intellectual property, employee information, customer data, business applications, networks, locations, physical plants, and equipment. Good security policy defines security requirements and advocates solutions and safeguards to accomplish those requirements in each specific instance within the company. Security policy adoption cannot be by fiat; it must be part of corporate culture to protect the company and its interests against cybercrime.

- Software process improvements such as standards for assessments and audits, reduced development time and cost, shared security test suites, or simplified build environments (where applications can share environments for integration testing of features or performance).
- Business process improvements through security component sharing to lower the total cost of ownership. Applications that share common security architectures are quicker and easier to deploy. Organizations do not reinvent the wheel, and systems are simpler to manage.
- Non-functional improvements such as improved security of customer transactions, reliability, and robustness. Corporations reduce the risk of damaging attacks that can cause loss of revenue or reputation.
- Usability improvements such as SSSO across a wide set of applications.
- Better accountability through shared authentication and authorization mechanisms.

Enterprise security architectures consolidate and unify processes for user management, policy management, application authentication, and access control through standardized APIs to access these services.

Vendor solutions that promise enterprise security accomplish some of these goals. Currently, a small group of vendors provides products for securing a portion of the enterprise at a significant cost in software licenses, development, integration, and testing. These products claim standards compliance and seamless integration with existing legacy applications. They provide security management services by using the components of Chapter 13, "Security Components," such as PKIs, DCE, Kerberos, or other tools, in a subordinate role to some large and expensive central component. Even if we successfully deploy these Enterprise Security Products in our networks, there is no guarantee that we will accomplish the coverage that we desire with the flexibility and evolutionary path that our business goals demand and succeed in matching promise to proven results.

Security policy must be concise and clear enough to be understood and implemented, yet comprehensive enough to address an enormous number of questions from individual system architects on application-specific issues. How can we, as application designers, prevent intrusions? If attacked, how do we detect the intrusion? Once detected, how can we correct damage? What can we do to prevent similar attacks in the future?

We will not discuss issues of physical security but instead focus on security policy definition for application architecture. Although physical security is very important, we consider it outside the scope of our presentation.

Security as a Process

Bruce Schneier [Sch00] calls security a process. This process must provide education and training, accept feedback, actively participate in application development, measure

tion. The key to accomplishing these process goals is good communication and strong relationships between system architects and corporate security.

Applying Security Policy

An architect faced with well-defined security policy guidelines must ask, "How does this apply to my system?" Policy guidelines normally fall into one of the following categories (called the MoSCoW principle based on the auxiliary verbs Must, Should, Could, and Will not in the definition):

- Directives with which the application *must* comply. These cannot be avoided because of the critical risks to exposure and supersede business goals.
- Directives that the application *should* comply with as a priority in line with business goals but that can be shelved if the risks are measured and judged as acceptable. These still address serious security issues.
- Directives that the application *could* comply with if resources are available that do not conflict with business goals. These directives can be shelved without risk measurement, because it is understood that the risks are acceptable.
- Directives with which the application *will not* comply. The application judges these directives inapplicable or below thresholds for feature acceptance, even if funding was available.

One would think that, given a well-defined security policy and a well-architected application, categorizing the directives of the policy would be straightforward. Unfortunately, in most cases this statement is not true. From many application reviews, it seems that the application architect always pegs a directive at one level below where the security policy owner sees it.

Security Data

Our discussion of enterprise security will focus on data. The measures we apply to protect data are commensurate with its value and importance. As the saying goes, some data is information, some information is knowledge, some knowledge is wisdom, and some wisdom is truth. (A footnote: In a curious progression, we have evolved from data processors to information technologists to knowledge workers. What are we next? Wisdom seekers? Soothsayers?)

We are concerned about security data—not just data that describes the things that we wish to protect. Security data answers any questions that we have while securing an application: about security policy ("Why?" questions), assets ("What?" questions), hackers ("Who?" questions), threats ("How?" questions), and vulnerabilities ("Where?" questions).

Applications share many resources, such as the following:

and customers

- Data in corporate databases, corporate records, customer information, and partner databases
- Hardware including host platforms, connectivity, and networking
- Common infrastructure services for domain names, Web hosting, security, mail, storage area networks, and directories

Applications share non-functional requirements for service provision such as reliability, robustness, availability, and performance. Applications also share other resources such as the physical plant and equipment, confinement within geographic boundaries, common legal issues, and intellectual property.

Databases of Record

We secure the assets of the corporation because we attach value to data. This situation creates the concept of a *Database-of-Record* (DBOR) for any information in the enterprise. A DBOR is defined as the single, authoritative, and trustworthy source for information about a particular topic. Payroll might own the DBOR for salaries, human resources might own the DBOR for employee data, operations might own the DBOR for work assignments, a vendor might own a DBOR for cryptographic fingerprints of installed software files, and the CFO might own the financial DBOR.

The DBOR concept is crucial for security, because in the event of an intrusion, our primary response mechanism is to roll back the application state to a point where we trust that it is uncompromised. The quality of data available in backups, in system files, in transaction logs, in partner databases, in billing events generated, and so on critically affects the application's capability to react to, respond, and rectify a problem. If DBOR data is tampered with or modified, there is no unique source to correct the information. We must rely on combinations of all of the information sources, multiple backup data sources, and reconstruction through transaction activity logs (which we hope are clean).

A DBOR can quickly reconstruct other secondary data stores when compromised by replacing all the information within the data store by using some predefined emergency data download and transform. Identifying a DBOR can be hard. Within actual applications, one may or may not even exist as an explicit entity. If no single data source can be certified as authoritative, complete, and correct, we can perhaps combine consistent data from several sources. This task is complex. We must attempt to replay the events on the host from the last-known safe state that we can roll back to, to the most recent state before the machine was compromised. This task is hard, but at least theoretically it is possible. Without authoritative data, it is impossible.

The task of resolving differences, combining information, and updating the application's state often boils down to the question of assignment of ownership. Given a question of data validity, who knows the correct answer?

The impact for security architecture is simple. Ask yourself, is your application a DBOR for some corporate information? If so, DBOR status for the data in your application

The risk assessment must identify all applications that depend on this data and measure the impact of a compromise on either side of each interface on the application.

Enterprise Security as a Data Management Problem

Enterprise infrastructures contain security data. This data can be explicitly stored in some infrastructure component (for example, an X.500 directory associated with a PKI implementation) or can be spread across the enterprise in many individual host databases, router and firewall configuration tables, user desktop configurations, or security components.

Corporations often manage this data through manual procedures and methods of operation that are poorly documented or hard to automate. The details of security management (how do routers get configured, who controls the directory access files on a Web application, who can insert rules on the corporate firewall, who can delete users from the corporate directory, or who can revoke a certificate and publish a new certificate revocation list) are spread across the enterprise.

The problem of building secure enterprise infrastructures reduces to controlling the interactions between several *virtual* databases-of-record for security information. We use the term *virtual* to highlight the fact that principal repositories of security knowledge might not exist. To manage security, we must be able to define the content and meaning of these repositories. We must be able to query them and handle the responses.

The following sections describe repositories that should exist or should be made available to applications in any enterprise. In actuality, the data is available, although it is often strewn through Web sites, application databases, configuration files, subject matter experts, vendors, security advisories, knowledge bases, or other IT assets.

The Security Policy Repository

This repository stores all security policy requirements and recommendations. Architects use this data store for directives and guidelines that are specific to their application. Architects that query this repository can ask, "How critical is a particular requirement? How does it apply to my application? What procedure should I follow for exception handling when the requirement is not met? What technologies should I consider to fulfill my security needs? What infrastructure dependencies do these technologies add to my architecture?"

The Security Policy database is used for more than the extraction of applicable rules. The Security Policy definition is also the source for the following:

- Education and training within the enterprise
- Publication of security requirements and recommendations on the Web or in paper form

- Certification documents attesting that the corporation is compliant with industry standards, or is best in class for security

The policy database is also the target for modifications requested by applications as security needs to evolve.

Every corporation has many recipients of Security Policy directives, each with a different perspective on security. The Security Policy Rules database must be multi-dimensional so that process owners can customize policy to business domains; architects can extract common security principles for reuse or service definition; and vendors can target technology domains for providing services.

The User Repository

Every application has users. The User Repository stores user, user group, and role information. Every entity in the organization that has an associated identity and can access the application should be included, such as partners, interfaces with other systems, business objects that access the application's data, or administrative personnel. Anything with a name and access privileges must be stored.

The User Repository also stores operational profiles for users that describe functional roles; that is, they describe what a user can do within a certain context. Profiles describe the boundaries of normal activity.

User repositories are critical components of many security infrastructure components because they represent a single place to track and audit the corporate user population. Registration authorities look up users before cutting certificates, SSO servers maintain user to application mappings, desktops use directory lookups to authenticate access to the domain, and remote dial-in servers match user IDs to token serial numbers before generating queries to token authentication servers. User data can be replicated across the enterprise to ensure that information is highly available for user authentication and queries.

Security is easier in environments where user management is unified, possibly through an enterprise-wide corporate directory. X.500 directories supporting LDAP are currently a popular choice for centralizing user identity, profile, and role data. Centralized user management always introduces issues of trust because the application must now relinquish control to an external service provider, the security directory.

The Security Configuration Repository

The Security Configuration Repository is the vendor's view of Corporate Security Policy. This repository stores configuration and platform information for any vendor asset. A considerable proportion of security vulnerabilities arise from misconfiguration of vendor products. Examples include incorrect or misconfigured rule bases in firewalls, insecure entries in /etc/passwd files, default administrative passwords, incorrect ordering of rules, or broken master-to-slave configuration mappings that open vulnerabilities within replicated services.

- Applications that switch from one vendor to another must migrate components to new platforms with different features, yet maintain the same security configuration.
- Solutions using multiple vendors might have interoperability issues.
- Vendors might not be compliant with corporate guidelines for product categories and industry standards.

Vendors normally provide a custom interface to their product that allows the definition of users, objects, and access control rules. It can be as simple as editing a default configuration file in an editor or as complex as using a custom GUI that accesses multiple directories or other subordinate hosts. GUIs cause problems for security management. Each vendor has his or her own rule definition syntax and file format. Rules have to be entered strictly through the GUI, and the ordering of rules cannot be changed easily. Using the tool requires training, and each new vendor product adds to the administrator's confusion with juggling multiple incompatible tools on the screen. Manual administration, switching from screen to screen, holds a tremendous potential for error.

Enterprise security architecture requires automation, which requires scripted configuration to all security components that permit bulk uploads of configuration information from text files, or swaps of paranoid configurations for standard ones in the event of an intrusion. Configuration files should be in plain text with well-defined syntax that can be parsed and loaded into an object model of the product. It should be possible to add comments to the configuration to make the human-readable rules more understandable, and it should be possible to transform a single, generic policy into specific configurations for an entire family of appliances in a reasonably mechanical form. Similarly, there has to be a mechanism to extract the vendor product configuration and examine it for completeness and consistency with other instances of the appliance and for correctness with respect to security policy.

Bulk configuration enables us to deploy standard images of security components across the enterprise and enables us to validate the policy enforced by the component by verification of the configuration through some automated test script. This procedure is critical for incidence response in the event of an emergency such as a work stoppage, a physical intrusion, a network intrusion, or an e-mail virus so that we can apply enterprise-wide rules to hosts, firewalls, routers, applications, and databases. We might want to selectively apply rules to contain damage to certain parts of the network or to take systems offline to guarantee that mission-critical resources are not compromised.

The Application Asset Repository

Application assets are identified at the security assessment for the application. The application should adequately secure all or most of its assets or approve a risk assessment for the assets still unprotected. The assessment must identify the assets with database-of-record status. The Application Asset Repository stores all the things that have value and that need to be protected. Each asset at risk within an application is linked to a security control that ensures that the asset is protected adequately in a manner compliant with policy.

ogy all play a part in defining the application's assets. We must match these properties against vulnerability databases to discover potential holes in our products or against threat databases to identify potential modes of attack. We must ask whether the application can support graceful degradation of performance and services in the face of an intrusion or estimate the outcome of catastrophic failure.

Application assets, unlike vendor products, are always part of the architecture. They are essential building blocks, with custom design using the knowledge domain of the application.

Identifying and securing assets can lead to difficult questions. How should we architect security for legacy systems? What strategies can we use to secure systems that are too valuable to turn off and too old to touch? Many of our architecture assumptions might be invalid, or the cost for adding security might be prohibitive. If you do not know how something works, it can be risky to modify it in any manner. Applications normally wrap legacy systems and over time migrate data and features to newer platforms when possible.

The Threat Repository

Threat repositories store information about all known attacks. Architects can refer to this repository for a list of all attacks that are applicable to the application. Threats can be chosen based on hardware models, database versions, software, or other parameters.

Virus scanners and intrusion detection systems are examples of software components that carry threat databases. Virus scanners carry the definitions of tens of thousands of viruses along with information about how to detect, clean, or disable each. Virus scanners have to regularly update this database to add newly discovered viruses or delete ones that have been deprecated because they are no longer effective.

Intrusion detection systems watch network traffic and detect patterns of commands or data that could signify an intrusion or system compromise. IDS sensor boxes support a much smaller database of signatures, normally in the hundreds. The huge volumes of network data, along with the complexities of correctly deploying sensors in the corporate intranet, make complicated configurations impractical. Unlike virus scanners that never have false positives (unless the virus definitions are buggy), IDS can generate alarms from valid traffic if set to be too sensitive.

Vendors and security experts must manage these threat databases, because clearly this information is too specialized for any application. Applications, however, must still be able to track threat database versions (to ensure that installations are up-to-date), must be able to query the database (to extract statistical and summary reports of events), or push updates of threat definitions automatically to client or server hosts.

The Vulnerability Repository

Vulnerabilities complement threats. The vulnerability repository stores a catalog of weaknesses in hardware and software products. The Bugtraq database of security vul-

databases. A large community of security experts maintains these databases along with the associated information for handling vulnerabilities: advisories, analysis, recommended patches, and mitigation strategies. Software vendors also maintain lists of security advisories and required patches for their own products. All of this information is loosely tied together through e-mail lists, Web sites, cross-references, downloadable sanity scripts, and patches.

Matching threats to vulnerabilities for each application is a hard problem. Application architects must be able to reference this complex collection of information to keep up with all security alerts and patches that apply to their system. Corporate security must help with this task, because many applications are overwhelmed by the effort of keeping up with all the security patches thrown their way.

Host and database scanners represent another source of vulnerability information. Scanners (discussed in Chapter 11, "Application and OS Security") can check password strength, user and group definitions, file and directory permissions, network configurations, services, SUID programs, and so on. These scanners create reports of all known weaknesses in the system. The application's system administrators, using security policy and vendor patches, must address each of these identified vulnerabilities—closing them one by one until the system is judged compliant.

The interconnection and dependencies between threats and vulnerabilities is one reason why it is hard to keep up with this flood of information. Every threat that succeeds opens new vulnerabilities; every security hole that is sealed blocks threats that depend upon it. An interesting idea for describing these dependencies in a goal-oriented manner is the notion of attack trees [Sch00]. Attack trees characterize preconditions to a successful attack. The root of an attack tree represents some compromised system state. Its nodes consist of either AND or OR gates. The predicates attached to the tree's leaves represent smaller intrusions. These events, when combined according to the rules of the tree, describe all the scenarios that can result in an attacker reaching the root of the tree. Attack trees depend on the existence of detailed threat and vulnerability repositories, which might not always be the case. Attack trees mix all the possible combinations of security concerns including personnel, physical security, and network and system security. Attack trees are almost the converse of fault trees. Fault trees start at a root component in a system, assume that the component fails, and then trace the domino effect of the failure through the system. Fault trees are a common technique of operations risk assessment in environments such as nuclear stations or complex command and control systems [Hai98].

Tools for Data Management

Why have we taken so much time to delineate security data into classes? We do not subscribe to a utopian ideal where machines will take security policy in English, scan an application's architecture, apply filters to each of the knowledge bases to extract only applicable rules, automatically map requirements to solutions, download software, and

Impossible Goals for Security Management

Before we consider tools for security data management, we wish to firmly dispel any misconceptions about what is possible and what is impossible.

- **It is impossible to automate security from end to end.**
- **It is impossible to expect all vendor products to interoperate.**
- **It is impossible to remove human intervention in any of the data management tasks at this moment. (This task is possible in simplistic scenarios like automated virus definition file updates, but not in the general case).**
- **It is impossible to implement any notion of enterprise security architecture without a trust infrastructure.**

then install, configure, test, and deploy a security solution. This situation is never going to happen. Well, we are left with the question, "What can we accomplish?"

Automation of Security Expertise

The primary goal for security data management lies in the automation of security management functions. What we can accomplish through data management is efficiencies in execution. Security data management is about the presentation and transformation of data that we already possess into target formats that we know are correct. We know the mapping is correct not by magic, but through common sense, experience, testing, and analysis.

Although security architecture requires expertise, many of the tasks can be amenable to automation. We can generate sanity scripts, validate the syntax of configuration files, confirm that several network elements have identical configurations, identify the status of software patches on a host, extract a database of MD5 signatures for all standard executables and directories in the startup configuration, or verify that all our users are running the correct version of their virus software. We write shell and Perl scripts all the time to automate these and many other tasks, and within each we touch a small part of the world of security data relevant to the application. We acquire this data and parse it, process it, and spit out rules or configuration information for our needs.

Our goals are as follows:

- Adopt a data definition standard that enables us to leave existing security objects untouched but that enables us to wrap these objects to create interoperable interfaces for data extraction or insertion.
- Capture security expertise in application-specific domains by using transformations and rules.

and transform it into information that can be inserted into another data repository. This transformation can be complex and depends on our ability to capture security expertise.

- Automate as many aspects of configuration validation, automated testing, installation, and monitoring as is possible.

We can partition the world of security management tasks into buckets that range from tasks that can be completely automated (update a virus definition file) to those that must be manually accomplished (analyze a cryptographic protocol for weaknesses). We want to take grunge work out of the picture.

Viewing enterprise security management as a data management issue can also have positive consequences for performance, analysis, and reporting because these properties are well understood in the database community.

Directions for Security Data Management

In the following sections, we will describe an exciting new area of security data management, still in its infancy but with tremendous potential. We will discuss the use of XML and its related standards to define grammars for security information exchange, code generation, identity validation, privilege assertion, and security service requests.

Before we introduce this technology, we will describe some of its goals. The basic goals include policy management, distribution, and enforcement; authentication and authorization; and application administration, configuration, and user management. The standards start with the management of credentials and access control assertions using XML schemas and request/response protocols (similar to HTTP) that allow these activities:

- Clients can present tokens that establish authenticated identities independent of the means of authentication (for example, passwords, tokens, Smartcards, or certificates).
- Clients with minimal abilities can request complex key management services from cryptographic service providers to execute security protocols.
- Clients can assert access privileges in a tamperproof manner.
- Applications can pass digitally signed messages that assert security properties over arbitrary protocols by using any middleware product and platform.
- Applications can encrypt messages for delivery to an entity at any location, where the message carries within it all the information needed by a recipient with the correct privileges to extract the information (possibly using cryptographic service providers).

over the years, each with sound technical architectures for the goals outlined earlier and all using reliable, standards-based solutions. Unfortunately, these solutions have either used proprietary technologies or interface definitions, have not been of production quality, or are not ported to certain platforms. These problems have prevented widespread adoption.

In contrast, the current efforts from the *World Wide Web Consortium* (W3C) and the *Internet Engineering Task Force* (IETF) are more attractive because of an emphasis on open standards, protocol independence, and the use of an immense base of existing work supporting XML. Although e-commerce and business-to-business communications are presented as the primary reasons for their creation, it is easy to see that these standards have wider applicability.

The proposed standards do not attack the problem from the common single vendor solution viewpoint, solving all issues of encryption, signatures, key management, or assertion definition at one blow. The proposals selectively choose smaller arenas to define data formats. The design shows attention to detail and leaves unspecified many divisive issues, such as the definition of underlying protocols, methods for secure communications, or preferences for messaging. Although many of the current definitions show interdependency on other Working Group standards (and are in fact vaporware until someone starts putting compliant products out), the direction is clear: Security management is about data management.

Before we leap into our synopsis of the acronym fest that is XML and Security Services, we will describe one of the architectural forces driving our goal of representing security-related data for all of the repositories that we have defined; namely, the networking philosophy of the Internet.

David Isenberg and the "Stupid Network"

David Isenberg's influential critique of big telecommunications companies, "Rise of the Stupid Network" [Isen97], contrasted the networking philosophy of the *Public Switched Telephone Network* (PSTN) to that of the Internet. He expanded on the theme in another article: "The Dawn of the Stupid Network" [Isen98].

Isenberg described the Internet as a Stupid Network, expanding on George Gilder's observation, "In a world of dumb terminals and telephones, networks had to be smart. But in a world of smart terminals, networks have to be dumb." IP, the basic routing protocol that defines the Internet, uses simple, local decision making to route packets through self-organized and cooperating networks from one intelligent endpoint to another. The Internet has none of the intelligence of the circuit-switching PSTN, which was built and conceived when computing was expensive, endpoints were dumb, and voice transmission—performed reliably and without delay—was the primary goal. The Internet flipped this model inside out, and as computing became cheap, terminals became immensely powerful—and users clamored for data services. The Internet gives users the ability to write arbitrary, complex applications completely independent of the semantic content of the packets that it routes. It is all just bits to the Internet.

Our dependence on the Internet has raised our non-functional requirements for reliability, security, quality of service, maximal throughput, and minimal delay. The non-functional requirement that is the focus of our book, security, was not initially guaranteed in the old PSTN network either, but the architecture evolved to support a separate *Common Signaling Services Network* (CSSN) that carried network traffic management information (which made securing telephone calls easier). In contrast, the Internet does not manage signaling traffic out-of-band; control of traffic is intimately mixed into each packet, each router, each protocol, and each application.

Security on the Internet is a huge problem because it is in basic conflict with the trust implicit in the design philosophy behind IP. The fields within an IP datagram defining the protocol, flags, source, or destination address can be modified. DNS mappings can be spoofed. Router tables can be altered. Packets can be lost, viewed in transit, modified, and sent on. The list is endless. In addition, hundreds of agents can collude to attack a single host in a distributed denial-of-service attack. It is impossible to distinguish good traffic from bad traffic in some attacks.

Can we change the Internet so that it becomes more intelligent? Isenberg is clear; we can only move forward. There is no putting the genie back into the bottle. We have to make advances in data management and definition, in datagram protection, in intelligent filtering, and application protection to ensure security.

- Our application traffic must move from IPv4 to IPv6. We must increasingly use IPSec or like protocols for communications.
- Our services, from DNS to LDAP directories to mail, have to be more reliable, available, and tamperproof.
- We must exploit cheap computing power and cryptographic coprocessors to make strong cryptography universally available. Every solution to improve security on the Internet uses cryptography.
- Our routers must become less trusting. They must filter packets that are recognizable as forged, dynamically add rules to throttle bad packets, detect the signatures of compromised hosts participating in attacks, and much more. New router based innovations such as "pushback" promise good heuristic defenses against DDOS attacks.
- We must make our endpoints even more intelligent. Our applications must be more aware of security and policy enforcement and must implement authentication and access control. The communications protocols used must be even more independent of the IP protocols underneath. We must create standards for security layers between our applications and the underlying Internet protocols.
- Our data formats have to be flexible, self-describing, and supporting of confidentiality and integrity. We must be able to carry security information with our data that can be verified by a recipient with the possible help of a service provider.

issue of flexible, self-describing data has seen explosive growth in the past few years with the rise of XML.

Extensible Markup Language

XML is a vast effort to create a data exchange and management framework for the Internet. XML is an open standard supported by a consortium of open-source organizations and corporations that require a data definition infrastructure with rich, expressive powers. XML enables people and applications to share information without interoperability issues caused by competing standards. XML documents are self-describing. Developers use the familiar tagged syntax of HTML along with request/response protocols to share self-describing information that can be parsed and understood dynamically without prior knowledge of formats or the use of custom tools. XML promises data transformation through standards that enable data in one format to be rendered in other formats without loss of information.

At its core, XML is a toolkit for creating markup languages. XHTML, for example, is an XML standard for creating well-formed HTML documents, MathML is a markup language for mathematical formulas, and ebXML is a markup language to enable e-business. In addition, developers can use the *Simple API for XML* (SAX) or the *Document Object Model* (DOM) to access XML data programmatically.

We generate, transform, and communicate data in many ways. To do so, we must accomplish all or part of these goals:

Decide what the data looks like. Document definition for XML is through *Document Type Definitions* (DTD) and XML schemas. These enable applications to define new elements, define new attributes, create syntax rules, and define complex data types. XML allows references to other document definitions through includes and namespaces.

Create the data and format it. Users can create well-formed XML documents by using XML editors and authoring environments.

Validate the data format. XML editors can test whether documents are well formed. XML validators can apply semantic rules beyond well-formed syntax guidelines to enforce context-specific compliance.

Create associations with other content. XML documents can link external resources by using the XLink standard, a formal extension of simple HTML hyperlinks, or include other XML fragments using XInclude.

Query data in documents. Applications can reference parts of XML documents through XPointer and XPath or query the document by using *XML Query Language* (XQL).

Manipulate documents. Applications can transform XML documents to other formats for consumption by other applications by using Extensible Stylesheet

specify document presentation styles by using *Cascading Style Sheets* (CSS).

Other standards that support XML can accomplish even more.

XML and Data Security

XML answers the question, "How do we communicate with diverse and complex components without creating a Tower of Babel of point-to-point information exchange formats?" XML enables applications that do not have foreknowledge of each other to communicate by using messages with complex data formats. The self-describing nature of XML enables the recipient to parse and understand the data after possibly transforming it in various ways. Applications that understand XML may be able to intelligently secure information and manage trust in their enterprise security architectures.

The standards are also independent of the platforms used, the messaging paradigm, or transport layer used in the actual communication. Information that conforms to any XML security standard is just a blob of bits that can be added to headers, placed inside messages, referenced by *Uniform Resource Identifiers* (URI), or stored in a directory for lookup. In some models, no negotiation is allowed. In this circumstance, trust must exist and must be established by using some other protocol or mechanism.

It is important to note what XML security standards do not do. They do not introduce new cryptographic algorithms or protocols, and they do not define new models of security or new forms of role-based access control or authentication. They do not mandate the use of certain protocols or messaging systems or means of secure communication. They all hew to Open Source principles.

The new XML standards propose methods for the following functions:

- Encrypting XML documents
- Creating and embedding digital signatures of all or part of an XML document
- Managing the cryptographic keys associated with encryption and digital signatures using service providers
- Adding assertions of authenticated identity to XML data
- Adding assertions of authorized access to XML data to execute privileged operations on a server
- Creating assertions of other security properties within the context of an XML document

The XML Security Services Signaling Layer

We can use these methods, schemas, and protocols to define a link language between the needs of policy definition, publication, education, and enforcement on one hand and the consistent and correct implementation on a target application on the other

rely on transformations from the data to create agents of execution of that intent. This situation is analogous to a declarative, pure SQL statement that describes some relational subset of data from a DBMS and the execution of the query by the database engine to produce the actual data so represented.

This function enables us to create a security services layer analogous to the separate CSSN of the circuit-switched PSTN world. The architecture of XML-based security assertions forms the basis for the implementation of an *XML Security Services Signaling* (XS3) layer across all our applications.

XML and Security Standards

Figure 15.1 shows a schematic of the dependencies between XML digital signatures, XML Encryption, and XKMS with respect to the platform of XML 1.0 and associated standards. We must emphasize that, as of 2001, none of these standards have progressed out of the Working Group stage of development, but standards bodies and industry partners alike are aggressively developing applications and products to these standards.

We present short descriptions of S2ML, SAML, XML-DSig, XML-Enc, XKMS, and J2EE security specifications using XML.

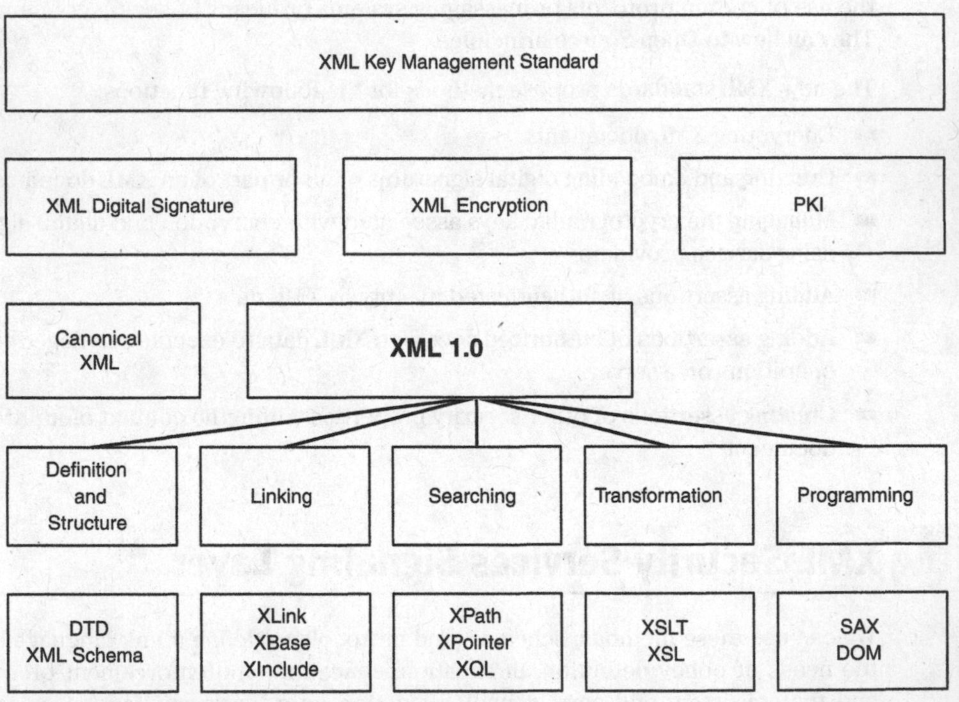

Figure 15.1 XML Security and related standards.

J2EE Servlet Security Specification

In Chapter 10, "Web Security," we introduced Java Servlets and the Java Servlet Security Specification. The JSSS enables Web applications to create role-based access control definitions by using an XML syntax for defining applications, resources, roles, role references, context holders, Web collections, and actual rules mapping roles to collections of Web resources.

For more information, please refer to the security links on http://java.sun.com.

XML Signatures

The *XML Digital Signatures Standard* (XML-DSig) is a draft specification proposed by the W3C and the IETF for signing arbitrary objects for e-commerce applications. XML-DSig can sign any content, whether XML or otherwise, as long as it is addressable by using a *Uniform Resource Identifier* (URI). It is backed by many prominent players in the security services industry and will see many applications.

For more information, please refer to www.w3.org/Signature/.

An important dependency within XML-DSig is the specification of Canonical XML 1.0. XML documents can contain white space or can use tags from included namespaces. Without a well-defined way of handling these elements, we cannot reduce an arbitrary XML document to a canonical form that can be used as the target of the message digest and encryption process that produces the digital signature. Changing a single bit in the canonical form will break the signature. Two communicating identities that cannot agree on canonical XML formatting cannot verify digital signatures unless each maintains a transform that produces the canonicalization desired by the other entity. Multiple semantically equivalent versions of the same document must all reduce to the same exact canonical form. Otherwise, signature verification will become rapidly unmanageable. Considerable effort is underway to solve this technical challenge.

The XML-DSig standard does not specify cryptographic primitives required for generating signatures, platforms, transport protocols, or messaging formats. It also does not specify the legal consequences of the use of digital signatures for e-commerce; the standard considers legal aspects of signatures out of scope.

XML-DSig signatures can be applied to an entire document or to portions specified through XPath or XPointer references. The actual signature can be detached from the document, stored in a network directory, and referenced when verification is required. Signatures can be layered to permit applications such as co-signing, notarization, countersigning, or hierarchical approvals by supervisors. Signatures on a document can include related presentation material such as style sheets. Similarly, we can exclude portions of the document from coverage by the signature in a manner that leaves the signature valid and verifiable despite changes to the elements outside the signed block.

An application verifying the signature can filter out elements from the document that are not covered by the signature or remove enveloping signature blocks. Applications can apply transforms on the transmitted and stored XML document to restore it to the

nature involves several steps:

- The data must be transformed before the digest can be computed.
- Once the digest is computed (for example, using the current default message-hashing algorithm, SHA-1), the application creates a Reference element that contains the digest value, the transforms applied, an ID, a URI reference, and type of the manifest (which is the list of objects we wish to sign).
- The application now generates a SignedInfo element that includes the Reference element, the method of canonicalization, signature algorithm, ID, and other processing directives.
- The application encrypts the digest by using a public-key algorithm such as DSA or RSA and places the resulting signature value in a Signature element along with SignedInfo, signing key information within a KeyInfo element, ID, and other optional property fields.
- The KeyInfo field (which is used by the XKMS specification, described next) holds the KeyName, KeyValue, and RetrievalMethod for obtaining certificates or certificate paths and chains and additional cryptographic directives specific to the public-key technology used. Additional properties are specified by using Object elements.

XML Encryption

The XML Encryption Standard is also a draft specification proposed by the W3C and the IETF for encrypting arbitrary objects for e-commerce applications. XML-Encrypt can encrypt any content, whether XML or otherwise, as long as it is addressable by using a URI. It is also backed by many prominent players in the security services industry, but is in a more nascent state than the XML-DSig specification. The canonicalization issues with digital signatures do not affect encryption as much because the block of encrypted data can be transmitted by using a standard base 64 encoding for raw objects. Once decrypted, the application can apply transforms to modify the content in any manner. For more information, please refer to www.w3.org/Encryption/2001/.

S2ML

The *Security Services Markup Language* (S2ML) is an XML dialect championed by many companies (including Netegrity Inc., Sun Microsystems, and VeriSign) for enabling e-commerce security services. S2ML defines XML tokens for describing authentication, authorization, and user profile information. The token can be used as a delegation credential by a recipient to request further access or service provision on the originator's behalf.

S2ML defines two XML Schemas called Name Assertion and Entitlement. An S2ML Name Assertion proclaims that an entity with a stated identity (using the <ID> tag) has

(<Issuer>). The assertion has a validity period (<Validity>) and is digitally signed. An S2ML Entitlement is an assertion of privileges and proclaims that a stated identity (<ID>) can use specific modes to access an object (<AzData>). Entitlements are also digitally signed.

S2ML supports two request and response services for authentication and access control. Any method of authentication (login/password, certificates, Kerberos, DCE, and so on) or access control (JAAS, access control lists, and so on) can be supported. A client can pass credentials to an S2ML-enabled server by using an AuthRequest element. The server responds with an AuthResponse element containing a Name Assertion (and possibly one or more entitlements). A client can pass the Name Assertion in an AzRequest to a server. The AzResponse returned can contain additional Entitlements.

For more information, please refer to www.s2ml.org.

SAML

SAML is another XML dialect for of security information exchange from Netegrity (which also co-wrote S2ML). SAML, like *Security Services Markup Language* (S2ML), supports authentication and authorization and shares the architecture and security design principles of S2ML. There are some differences in the target scenarios, but for the most part, the two standards overlap.

Both target B2B and B2C interactions and are Open Source initiatives for the interoperable exchange of authentication and authorization information. The basic SAML objects are Authentication and Attribute. An assertion that a name entity has successfully authenticated can also contain a description of the authentication event. Authorization attributes can capture user, group, role, and context information. Both SAML and S2ML assume an existing trust model and do not perform any trust negotiations.

SAML is a component of Netegrity's access control service product, SiteMinder, a central policy service that along with proprietary Web Server plug-ins replaces the default Web security services of multiple Web applications. Integration with an actual product might be a distinction between the two standards.

For more information, please refer to www.netegrity.com.

XML Key Management Service

PKIs, discussed in Chapter 13, have had reasonable but limited success in enterprise infrastructure deployments and are, by their very nature, complex. A group of companies including VeriSign, Microsoft, and webMethods have proposed the *XML Key Management Service* (XKMS) as a means of hiding some of the complexities of PKI from thin Web-based clients with limited capabilities. These capabilities include parsing XML, generating service requests, and handling responses. A PKI enables trust. XKMS enables the actual processing of primitives for enabling this trust to happen on servers

for XML digital signatures or XML encryption.

PKIs manage digital certificates for Web access, content signing, secure e-mail, IPSec, and so on. They perform certificate registration, issuance, distribution, and management. Actions for trust management that would be easy within a conventional PKI such as certificate parsing, validation, certificate status lookup, or challenge-response protocols such as SSL might not be available to thin clients. XKMS enables a client who receives an XML document that references a public key (in the case of an XML digital signature, using the <ds:KeyInfo> tag) to look up the key and to associate context attributes and other information with the owner of the key. An XKMS server can test for the possession of the corresponding private key by verifying successful key registration by the owner. Thus, the XKMS server can validate the owner. Although the XKMS specification is independent of the particular public-key cryptographic infrastructure behind the scenes (for example, supporting SPKI or PGP), it is likely that the majority of applications that use this standard will front an X.509v3 certificate infrastructure.

The XKMS standard contains two service specifications.

- *The XML Key Information Service Specification*, which enables clients to query an XKMS server for key information and attributes bound to the key.
- *The XML Key Registration Service Specification*, which enables possessors of key pairs to declare the public key and associated attributes to the XKMS server. Later, an owner can revoke a certificate—or, if the server maintains the private key, request key recovery.

For more information, please refer to www.verisign.com.

XML and Other Cryptographic Primitives

The current XML security standards do not address other security properties, such as non-repudiation, or describe uniform methods for defining delegation or asserting safety.

The protocols in these standards are based on the paradigm of Web interaction matching one request to one response. More complex challenge-response protocols or methods to bundle multiple request/response pairs into transactions, and multiple transactions into sessions, are not defined.

XML assertions can express dependencies on other assertions with the help of third-party service providers. Once we have created these XML blobs of information, we can decide where we bind the information in our communications. We can bind the elements within new application messages, store them in directories, insert references in headers, or add the data to a variable-length field of an existing object message. In each case, we must develop the means to extract the blob, call procedures to validate the information, and then parse and extract the values within.

We have not yet linked these two elements.

- Our coverage of XML Security standards.
- The problem of managing the data repositories for security information, which we presented earlier.

This problem is difficult—one that we will address after we have expanded on the theme of describing security information with XML.

Recall our security pattern catalog of Chapter 4, "Architecture Patterns in Security," where we introduced the basic recurring elements of most security architecture solutions. We have already seen XML notations for expressing some of these elements. *Principals* can be identified through distinguished names, certificates, or through URIs to directory entries for user information. Hosts can be specified through IP address or domain name. Distributed business objects can be named by using object references or through fixed application-specific naming strings. All of these values can appear in the <Name> field of an assertion. Name assertions capture authenticated names. Other fields of a name assertion capture context information such as the issuer, date and time issued, or the validity period.

We can similarly define new markup elements to capture *context holders*, *session objects*, and *cookies*. The encrypted and digitally signed blobs of XML assertions capture mobile *tokens* that can specify credentials, delegation chains, shared access, or proof of authentication or privilege.

The Entitlement and Authorization XML schemas define *access control rules* that are generic enough to capture most applications, and the gap can filled through application-specific XML schema definitions. Applications can present cipher suite specifications and publish allowed modes of access to databases, directories, or other network repositories. We can be endlessly inventive in our efforts to pass these XML assertions back and forth; inside messages, inside headers of existing protocols, piggybacked over underlying protocols, or communicated through a separate message stream.

We can specify the content and use of XML descriptions for our other patterns, for example, by specifying formats for the rule bases within *wrappers*, *filters*, *interceptors*, or *proxies*. We can describe the access control policy enforced by a *sandbox* or specify the access modes published by a *layer*. We can describe the context for construction of a secure *tunnel* in terms of the properties of the communications and cryptographic endpoints, the protocols secured, acceptable cipher suites, or other technologies.

The core of the problem of enterprise security management when viewed as a data management issue is the conflict between the disparate elements that we wish to protect and the sources of information on how to protect them. This information might be incomplete, inconsistent, presented in incompatible formats, may or may not be trustworthy, might have to be accessed across untrusted WANs, and could describe anything from the highest levels of business process definition to the lowest levels of data link security.

tual security management network. XML transformations enable us to encode security knowledge and business rules into processes that can take policy recommendations and produce application configurations. It is not accomplished through magic (in the pattern sense described in Chapter 4) but through careful analysis and design—but once accomplished, the transform can be repeated again and again, reusing the knowledge to add efficiency to security administration.

XML-Enabled Security Data

Having introduced these standards and projected a vision for the future with new security pattern definitions in XML, what can we accomplish with these tools? The goal is not to accomplish new things but to accomplish reuse of all our current tools for managing security data out there by using XML data definition. We do not propose that XML can work miracles, but do think we can become more efficient through XML usage.

Consider the following scenarios where applications and entities exchange XML data:

- The corporation publishes a new release of the Corporate Security Policy Document in DocBook format, an XML Schema for book definition. The document is mapped into a user-friendly Web site by one transform, is converted into a cross-indexed PDF file by another transform, and is converted into an application-specific set of guidelines by a third transform. A fourth transform takes the old and new policy specifications and publishes a helpful "What's New" security newsletter.
- An application using Solaris exports its configuration to an XML file and sends it to Sun Microsystems, Inc. Sun responds with an XML fingerprint database of all the system files and executables for that configuration. The application applies a transform to this script that generates a sanity script that automatically computes MD5 signatures for all the system files and executables and compares them to the authoritative fingerprint database. Finally, the script presents the results as a vulnerability report.
- A network security manager wishes to examine router and firewall rules for source address spoofing prevention. He sends a query to all network appliances over a secure channel. Each appliance verifies the signature on the query and responds with an encrypted XML configuration file of the rule definitions on each interface. The security manager queries a topology database for network topology information and uses a tool that applies the interface definitions of each device to the network map. The application validates the rule definitions to verify that all appliances correctly drop packets with recognizably forged addresses.
- An application that is upgrading to a new OS sends its configuration to a patch database that returns a list of required security patches as an XML file. A transform converts the file into a shell script that automates the download and installation of the patches.

security, using XML assertions. A transform uses the specification along with a document tree and an LDAP-enabled directory to correctly define all the *htaccess* files within all subdirectories.

- An application automatically downloads a new virus database and uses it to scan all the files on the file system. Wait, we can do that one right now.

Are these scenarios far-fetched? Are the required transformations too application-, host-, OS-, or vendor-specific? Is there a missing link where human intervention is required to verify that the output of the transforms is meaningful? Must we review every communication to assure that we do not misconfigure an application or network element?

The answer to all of these questions is unfortunately a resounding "Maybe." The scope and size of the problem should not stop us from attacking it, however. Consider the efforts behind another formidable task of data management, the *Human Genome Project* (HGP). The HGP is about data management, and its goals and challenges dwarf the ones before us. Read on, and trust me that this topic connects.

HGP: A Case Study in Data Management

Creating security information databases and coordinating their management seems like a daunting task. The fact that we have so much data in so many different formats and so little to go by in terms of patterns makes progress seem impossible.

As an example of the scale and complexity of data management, consider the HGP (www.ornl.gov/hgmis/), a federally sponsored plan with academic and industrial support to map the entire human genome. The HGP goals are to identify all of the approximate 30,000 genes in human DNA, determine the sequences of the three billion chemical base pairs that make up human DNA, store this information in databases, improve tools for data analysis, transfer related technologies to the private sector, and address the ethical, legal, and social issues that might arise from the project.

An initial milestone of the mapping goal, a working draft of the entire human genome sequence, has been accomplished ahead of schedule and was published in February 2001. In the process, we have seen tremendous advances in genetics, bioinfomatics, and medicine. Why did this project succeed? Here are some reasons why it worked:

Idealism. Watson and Crick's discovery of the molecule of life, DNA, is the seminal event in biology in the last century. The HGP claims to extend that discovery into the knowledge of who we are as biological mechanisms and how our genes work.

Economic benefit. The benefits of a better understanding of the human genome range over all aspects of medicine: gene therapy, better diagnostic techniques, drug discovery, and development. Someone will make money from all of this knowledge.

Government support. The HGP is sponsored by the Department of Energy and has support for funding at a very high level.

to tiny, nimble bioinfomatics startups, see the HGP as a business opportunity.

Scientific prestige. Don Knuth famously stated, "Biology has five hundred years of interesting problems." Many academic and industrial research scientists are basing their careers on solving these problems.

The past decade has seen an explosive growth in an innovative, interdisciplinary approach between information and biology: bioinfomatics. Biologists who started out on this problem a quarter of a century ago looked like ants setting out to prove Fermat's Last Theorem. Consider the volume of data, the fuzziness of defining pattern matches, the difficulty in comparing strings with arbitrary breaks, stops, and starts—all with a very complex and hard to visualize goal: mapping an entire human genome.

There has been tremendous progress because of these reasons, however.

Open sources. The HGP community, for the most part, shares all of the information discovered and analyzed, collectively accomplishing what would be impossible by any one organization alone. Bioinfomatics researchers focus on the problems of pattern matching (and when it comes to pattern matching, biologists might already be the world's best Perl programmers).

Data management. The huge volume of data associated with the HGP, along with its explosive daily growth and highly interconnected nature, has lead to the definition, creation, and maintenance of a handful of huge text databases that store all that is known so far. Standard ways of adding to this data pool, querying it, formatting responses, and manipulation have been built around common languages and formats. Interoperability, through standards and data definition, has always been a goal.

Better tools. Kary B. Mullis invented the *polymerase chain reaction* (PCR) procedure as a means of rapidly producing many copies of a DNA molecule without cloning it. PCR alternates between two phases, one to break apart a two-stranded DNA molecule and the other to add nucleotides complementary to the ones in the two templates until each strand forms a normal, double-strand DNA molecule. There is an exponential growth in the number of molecules as the number of iterations increases. There is a striking correlation with the strategy used in the design of block ciphers in cryptography. A block cipher algorithm consists of a number of rounds, each round consisting of two phases. One phase mixes the partially encrypted cipher block built at this stage by using diffusion techniques, and the other phase combines the result with material from the key schedule generated from the original encryption key. As the number of rounds increases, there is an exponential growth in the strength of the block cipher.

Building a Single Framework for Managing Security

There are good reasons why we can succeed in building a single framework for managing security.

the biologists, we have a clear opponent—namely, the hacker attempting to break into our systems.

We have a finite number of target platforms. Unlike the 30,000 genes that biologists have to track, we have a small number of hardware platforms, a small number of operating systems, and a small number of patterns to model.

We have better tools. Public-key cryptography is the greatest advance in security that the field has seen. We have also seen advances in secret key technology through the development of improved, high-performance, portable, and multi-use block encryption algorithms with proven strength against all known forms of cryptanalysis, using bigger block sizes, and longer keys. We have other tools, such as legal recourse along with the well-defined security strategies, tools, and techniques discussed in chapters past.

We understand the power of open-source development for solving enterprise level problems. We have a very active standards community creating new models of secure interaction. Many use cryptography as a fundamental element in the implementation of higher protocols and services.

Vendors will recognize the economic benefits of interoperability, simplified administration, and reusability afforded by an XML-based standard for security administration and data exchange. Many vendors are already champions of standards-based interoperability and will support collaboration for efforts to which they have already devoted considerable resources.

Could we accomplish the task of creating well-defined, general XML schemas for all the data repositories we have described? Can we get buy-in from our vendors to provide text-based interfaces to interact with their software for security management? Can we download and upload configuration information in XML format? Can we communicate policy by using XML? Can we create open-source tools that enable us to transform declarations of policy into programs for executing that policy?

And once we have a basic, dumb communications bus that spans the entire Internet carrying security information, can we build upon it?

Conclusion

In this chapter, we have focused on enterprise security architecture as a data management problem and have chalked out some of the advances we can expect to make this task easier. Data management cannot be automated by any means, however. Human intervention, analysis, cross checking, and validation is still the only method we know for mapping policy on paper to code executing in the field. Implementing these security practices and properties across the corporation is a minimal requirement.

technical expertise, technology evaluation, and security assessment.

- Security programs should address security infrastructure efforts and strongly back and fund security solutions whose costs can be amortized over many applications.
- Corporate security must have teeth; production applications that have vulnerabilities should either address these issues or risk being turned off—possibly affecting business goals and customer satisfaction.
- Assessors should clearly articulate the risk to the corporation to upper management if the project's process owner is unresponsive.
- Applications must know whom to contact in the event of an intrusion and must have clear guidelines on immediate preventive action to contain damage. This aspect of a security program requires 24 by 7 responsiveness and high levels of technical ability. Companies lacking the ability to do so can outsource this work to any of the many security services companies that have risen to respond to this demand.

As each of the diverse application components discussed in chapters past gains some degree of enterprise security maturity, we will see a convergence of security management methods.

The separate security management interfaces, the diverse definitions of the details of role-based access control, variations on security context information, and information ownership will and must come to some common agreement so that the time will come when we can use the phrase "seamlessly integrate" without wincing. When that happens, we can expect to manage our hosts, networks, users, middleware servers, Web sites, databases, and partners in a uniform manner. Until then, well, we can dream, can't we?

Business Cases and Security

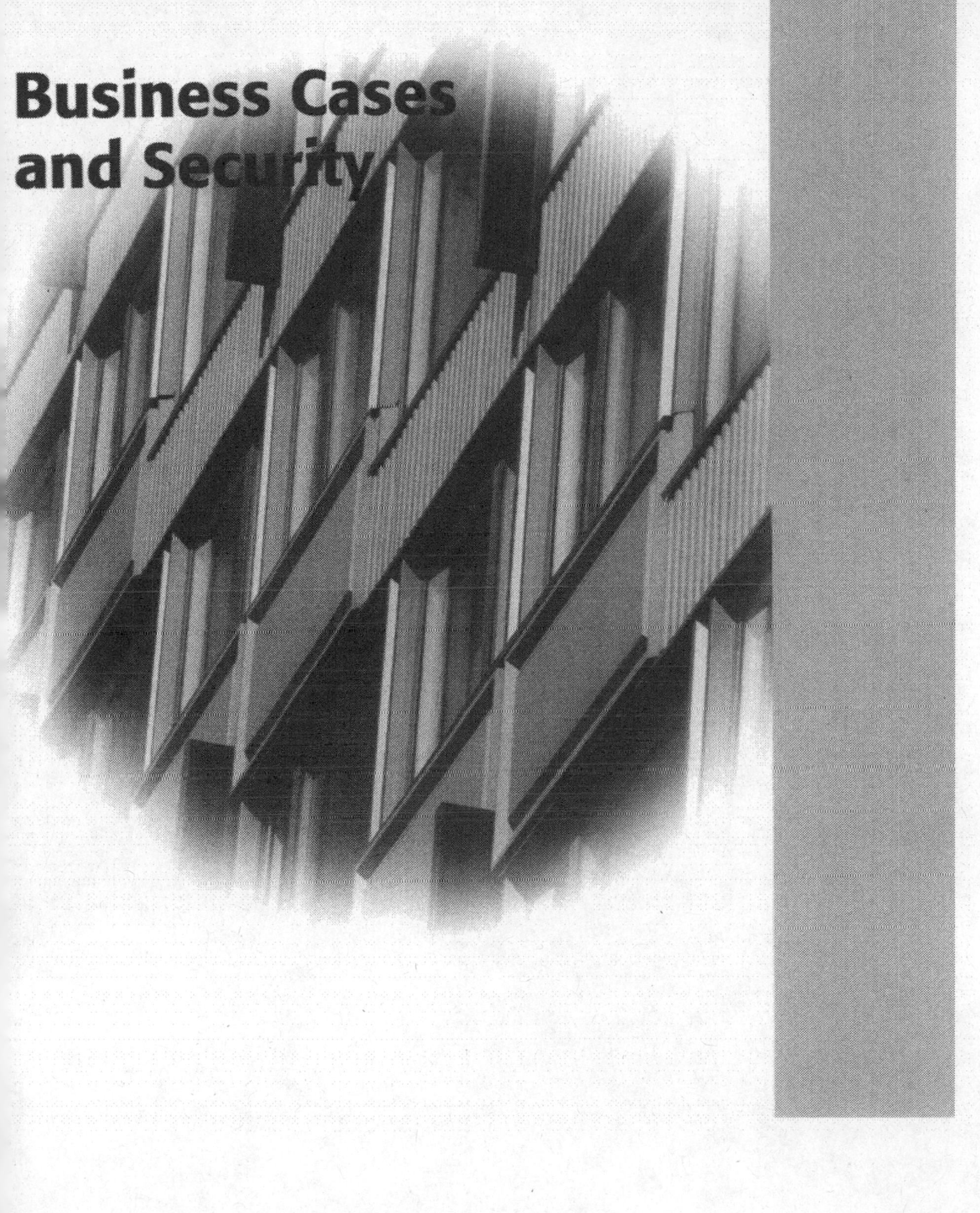

Building Business Cases for Security

A security business case must match accurate estimates of development and operational costs against good estimates of the costs of intrusion over the life of the project. Why is it hard to build business cases for security? The former costs are well understood because we have experience writing and deploying software, but the latter costs are problematic. When a system is partially or completely disabled through an attack, what does its down time cost us? What do we lose when attacked or compromised? How do we measure the loss of revenue and reputation? How do we budget for legal expenses for prosecuting attackers or defending against irate customers? Can we insure ourselves against liability? How much will incident response cost us, over and above the expense to repair our application?

The literature on computer security extensively covers the technical aspects of computer risk, but studies on the financial impacts of information security are rare. To build solid business cases for any particular business sector, we need hard evidence measuring losses from computer intrusions and fraud and the costs of defending against such computer crime. This knowledge is essential for a quantitative analysis of computer risk before we can choose countermeasures such as building security architectures, buying software and services, or paying insurance premiums.

Our objectives for this chapter are as follows:

- We will present data on the financial aspects of computer crime to the computer industry, with some emphasis on telecommunication companies.
- We will describe the AT&T network disruption of January 1990 as an example of catastrophic loss. This disruption was not through computer crime, but through defective software in a single switch that propagated like a virus through the network. At the time, there was even speculation that the disruption was due to hackers, but this fact was later proven incorrect. A malicious attack on any company's network could have the same catastrophic impact.

Invita Securities Corp. The business case will present a cost-benefit analysis for a proposed Security Operations Center. Our business case will use simple financial concepts of interest rate formulas, net present value, payback period, and internal rate of return.

- We will present a critique of the assumptions of the business case to highlight the difficulties of quantifying computer risk.
- We will ask what have we learned from this experience to help build actual business cases.
- Finally, we will examine buying insurance as an alternative to securing assets. We will ask the following questions: "Are systems insurable against security violations?" "Can we buy hacker insurance that works like life insurance or fire insurance?" "What properties make something insurable?"

Building Business Cases for Security

Systems architects are key participants in building security business cases because the probability that an exploit succeeds depends on the underlying architecture. Architects are also experts on the system's operational profile and the interfaces to other systems that could be compromised. Many risk assessment methodologies such as fault tree analysis or attack tree analysis depend on the architect's domain expertise.

Architects cannot disclaim this role merely because they lack knowledge of the financial impacts of intrusions. Without their participation, we run the risk of introducing technical flaws into the business case.

On the contrary, participation in business analysis is an opportunity for system architects to give a business purpose to the architectural guidelines presented in the previous chapters by asking these questions:

- What are the financial aspects of security systems development?
- What attacks are feasible? What is our response if an attack succeeds?
- What losses do we face, and what are the costs of defending against them?
- What data is relevant to support a business case for a security solution?
- How can we get buy-in from upper management?
- Why is computer security a good investment?
- How can we avoid security solutions that represent poor cost-to-benefit choices?

Considerable concrete data exists on the costs of computer crime to companies through computer viruses, intrusions from external entities, violations by internal entities such as employees, and the expense of each action taken by companies to prevent such occurrences. Applying this data to a specific environment is a challenge, however.

nesses and the security industry rarely reveal detailed financial information concerning costs or losses. This information is hidden because we fear negative publicity and possibly losing customers. Imagine Bugtraq with financial information. We could assign vendor products that have security problems a *security cost of ownership* that reflects the savings (or lack thereof) from integrating the product into our architecture solutions. We could quote this cost when we negotiate pricing with vendors.

Losses to computer crime can be classified as follows:

Measurable losses. These include damage to assets, replacement costs, down time costs, disrupted customer services, stolen services, intellectual property loss such as software piracy, and productivity losses from disruptive computer intrusions such as e-mail viruses.

Intangible losses. Security violations also have indirect consequences. They can cause a loss of morale, market share, and reputation and fuel negative advertising by competitors. We will list several indirect costs but will not attempt to estimate them.

In the next section, we will describe some financial data on computer risk.

Financial Losses to Computer Theft and Fraud

Hacking imposes the threat of theft, fraud, extortion, defamation, harassment, exploitation, denial of service, destruction, or eavesdropping. We will not go into a detailed analysis of computer fraud, but the data is interesting in setting a context for the importance of investing in security solutions as a means of containing costs.

Companies depend on telecommunications networks to share information with geographically dispersed domestic and international sites. The Internet has become a vital part of the economic infrastructure of the United States, and the information that it carries must be protected. There is growing evidence of the use of electronic intrusion techniques by industrial spies, often from outside U.S. borders.

We can estimate the costs associated with network intrusions and natural disasters by analyzing previous incidents reported by companies and federal sources. These incidents illustrate the costs associated with network service disruption and give a feel for the intangibles associated with information security, showing that financial losses can happen in many ways.

The following factoids describe some of the financial impacts of computer security:

- The Code Red worm caused an estimated $2.6 billion in cleanup costs on Internet-linked computers after outbreaks in July and August 2001.
- The Federal Bureau of Investigation's National Computer Crimes Squad estimates that fewer than 15 percent of all computer crimes are even detected, and only 10 percent of those are reported.

conducts an annual survey of several hundred companies that have consistently revealed heavy financial losses due to computer crime. Of the more than 500 companies surveyed, one-third were able to quantify the loss, which totaled $377 million over 186 respondents. In contrast, 249 respondents reported only $266 million in losses in 2000, which in turn was a big jump from the $120 million dollar average for the three years before that.

- The CSI survey also reported that theft of proprietary information ($151 million) and financial fraud ($93 million) were the most serious categories.
- Other heavy-hitters from the CSI survey include virus attacks ($45 million), insider abuse of Internet access ($35 million), and attacks by intruders from the outside the company ($19 million).
- In 1996, Peter McLaughlin of Deloitte & Touche's Fraud and Forensic Accounting Practice noted that companies that invest as little as 2 percent to 5 percent of their budget on information security could eliminate fraud before it occurs. Several current consultant reports recommend spending at least 5 percent of the total IT budget on security.
- According to the FBI, 80 percent of victims are unaware that their computers have been violated. In a broad trend over the years, attacks from outside the company are on the rise compared to attacks by insiders.
- Recent cases of cyber crime have involved interception of e-mail, vandalism of Web sites, e-mail viruses, stolen credit cards, customer records, and privacy violations. One of the major problems with hacker attacks is that break-ins are often not characterized as a crime, although cyber fraud losses cost organizations millions of dollars a year. Companies fear a loss of reputation and often do not report violations. This situation is improving somewhat, however.
- Data from the 1993 Federal Uniform Crime Reports showed that for every 100,000 citizens, 306 were crooks working in the fields of fraud, forgery, vandalism, embezzlement, and receiving stolen goods. Extrapolating to today, of the 300 million people using the World Wide Web by the end of 2002, one million will be crooks. Given culture surrounding cyber crime, this figure is probably an underestimate.
- A series of *Distributed Denial of Service* (DDOS) attacks in February 2000 knocked out Yahoo!, CNN, eBay, buy.com, Amazon, and ETRADE. Each attack lasted from two to four hours, during which each Web site was completely unavailable. Losses were estimated at $100 million.
- The annual *Information Week*/Ernst & Young Information Security Survey consistently finds that information security at many organizations is still woefully lacking. Measurable financial losses related to information security, and averaging a million dollars, are found in almost every organization.
- The American Society for Industrial Security reports that computer crime accounts for estimated losses of more than $10 billion per year, factoring in losses in corporate intellectual property such as trade secrets, research, software, price

companies.

- Many sources, including the National Center for Computer Crime Data, Ernst & Young, and the Yankee Group, estimate the market for security-related hardware, software, and services to be $8 to $10 billion in 2002.

We now proceed to describe a major network service disruption at AT&T to illustrate some of the costs associated with network failure. The disruption of January 1990 was due to a software failure. Although hacking did not cause this failure, the method by which the failure started at one switching element and propagated across the network along the eastern seaboard was much like a virus attack. Network intrusions of a catastrophic nature could result in a similar pattern of failure.

Case Study: AT&T's 1990 Service Disruption

On Monday, January 15, 1990, AT&T experienced a 9½-hour shutdown of its public switched network, an incident that then Chairman and CEO Bob Allen called "the most far-reaching service problem we've ever experienced." Faulty software caused the problem, but the symptoms initially lead to fears of a computer virus. Only 58 million calls got through out of 148 million attempts.

The following report is extracted from AT&T's news releases to the media.

"CERTAINLY THE MOST FAR-REACHING SERVICE PROBLEM WE'VE EVER EXPERIENCED."

> On Tuesday, January 16, 1990, AT&T restored its public switched network to normalcy after a suspected signaling system problem cut call completion rates across the country to slightly more than 50 percent yesterday. AT&T Chairman Bob Allen and Network Services Division Senior Vice President Ken Garrett held a press conference from the Network Operations Center in Bedminster, N.J., to explain the situation.
>
> A post mortem indicated that a software problem developed in a processor connected to a 4ESS switch in New York City, which was part of a new Signaling System 7 network carrying call completion data separate from the call itself. The problem spread rapidly through the network, affecting the regular long-distance network, 800 services, and the Software Defined Network (SDN). However, private lines and special government networks were not affected.

After eliminating a number of suspected causes, software overrides applied after eight hours finally restored normal network capabilities. Researchers at AT&T Bell Laboratories and in the Network Engineering organization studied the data accumulated and reported, contrary to initial reports, that no computer virus was involved. AT&T reported that software loaded in signaling processors located at each of its 4ESS digital switching systems throughout the country was buggy. The bug, triggered in a New York

work with control messages. These messages were of such character that they triggered the fault in the other processors, setting off a cascade of alarms that quickly brought the network to its knees. Note that the ability to detect and report a problem added to the disruptive effect, because no one had tested the signaling system's operational profile under such a large volume of alarm messages.

The event launched an intense round of advertising wars between AT&T and its competitors and drew scrutiny from the FCC. AT&T (reported by *The Wall Street Journal*) called this incident its "Maalox moment of 1990." AT&T offered special calling discounts following the service disruption in order to ensure customer loyalty, incurring a considerable loss in revenue. The total cost of the disaster was estimated at anywhere between $100 to $200 million.

Structure of the Invita Case Study

We will use standard techniques from cost-benefit analysis to justify the expense of running the Security Operations Center at Invita Securities Corp. Some models for cost-benefit analysis in the context of information security do exist—for example, [EOO95]—but exhibit gaps between theory and practice. In our toy example, we will attempt to reach an outcome where we show actual financial payoffs from saved losses through security.

This business case is based on material on the financial aspects of computer security, obtained through searches on the Web and in libraries. The bibliography contains references to supporting material to justify the assumptions of the *Saved Losses Model* of the business case worksheet. We have also interviewed people within the security community with backgrounds in this area. We will use some financial concepts, summarized with formulas in the section ahead, to compute the *cash flow*, *net present value*, *payback period*, *uniform payment*, and *internal rate of return* for our project. We used an Excel spreadsheet to automate the calculation of all financial formulae used. We recommend that the reader who is interested in modifying our assumptions do the same by using our tables as a template.

The cash flow from the project matches the future saved losses to crime against the initial development and continuing operations cost of the new work center. The case study values this cash flow in today's dollars and computes a rate of return for the project.

A conventional business case for a project compares the investment cost of a project, funded by some means, against the potential revenues generated by the goods and services of the completed project. The weighted average cost of capital within Invita is the rate of return that must be earned to justify an investment. WACC can be viewed as an interest rate charged internally for investment expenses. The project creates a cash flow that, over an interval called the payback period, is large enough to justify the original expense. We can construct a consolidated cash flow by combining expenses and revenue for each year and can compute the internal rate of return represented by the consolidated cash flow.

The costs of the SOC project are conventional investment expenditures. There is a development cost for building the system and operations, administration, and maintenance

Caveat

The Saved Losses Model matches the development and maintenance costs of the new application and its operations center against expected savings from improved security. We cannot capture the intangible savings that are often important. We must warn against extending the case study analogy too far. The business case is not a blueprint for building your own, because our purpose is exposition (not recommendation). We are attempting to quantify the value of computer security, which is obviously a very difficult task where the actual benefit of building secure systems is reflected indirectly through intangibles, such as improved quality of service. We therefore must make assumptions about the operational profile of the application, and the company that owns it, to boldly give dollar values to quantities that are inexact in reality. This procedure enables us to reach the final conclusion of the toy study: "The Security Operations Center has a net present value of $1 million dollars and an internal rate of return of 22% compared to Invita's 10% weighted average cost of capital. We conclude that the project will pay for itself in the fourth year of its five-year life cycle." This statement would be impressive except for the fudge factor within our assumptions.

costs for running the SOC work center. Security does not earn revenue, however; instead, it prevents the loss of revenue from accidental or deliberate and malicious acts. We must measure these *saved losses* by using an operational model that is specific to Invita and Invita's industry profile by using the so-called *stationary assumption* that our past history is a guide to future trends in losses. This assumption is inexact and depends on unreliable estimates of the probability of risks. We will model these risks, as suggested in Chapter 2, "Security Assessments," by using three levels of cost and probability shown in Figure 16.1.

Of the nine combinations, we will pick only two: high cost/low probability and low cost/ high probability. We do not try to categorize the other combinations of cost and probability because if we can justify the project by estimating saved losses from these two categories alone, then any savings in the remaining cases are just icing on the cake.

High cost/low probability. We call these *catastrophic losses* because they seriously jeopardize the corporation, create high negative visibility in the media, cause widespread customer dissatisfaction, and require responses by corporate officers to shareholders and analysts on the possible business impacts. Distributed DOS attacks, loss of private customer data, loss of assets through large-scale theft or fraud, or otherwise extreme loss of services all qualify as catastrophic losses.

Low cost/high probability. We call these *steady state losses* because they occur frequently with very high probability but do not disrupt services for all employees or customers. Virus attacks that disrupt productivity, isolated DOS attacks that degrade performance, scribbling on noncritical Web sites, or intrusions that do not involve tampering but require corrective action qualify as steady state losses.

Consider the remaining combinations.

Cost	High	Medium	low
High	High/High Military installation High profile company Security service	High/Medium Not estimated or included	**High cost Low probability Included in Business Case**
Medium	Medium/High Not estimated or included	Medium cost Medium probability Excluded from Business Case, but is critical in reality	Medium/Low Not estimated or included
Low	**Low cost High probability Included in Business Case**	Low/Medium Not estimated or included	Low/Low Not worth the effort

Figure 16.1 Matrix of possible exploits.

Medium cost/medium probability. The heart of the problem, and the most interesting one, is the class of medium cost/medium probability attacks. This class includes, for example, attacks by insiders over extended periods on small portions of the corporate assets, stealing enough to make crime profitable but not enough to make the company advertise the theft when discovered. We do not include these in our analysis because it is hard to estimate these values. In a real cost-benefit analysis, we recommend using internal historical data of actual intrusions in this category to justify security expenses in this important category.

The remaining six categories. A low cost/low probability attack is not worth worrying about. At the other end, unless you run a military site or are part of a high-profile security organization, high cost/high probability attacks probably do not apply. Four of the remaining buckets fall in a gray area: medium/high, high/medium, medium/low, and low/medium. Classifying an attack in any of these is a subjective matter. We will ignore these, but they might contain important samples for your company.

Security at Invita Securities Corp.

We present a case study of an imaginary company, Invita Securities Corp. Invita provides Web-based financial services to business customers for online trading. Invita has

year 2001, Invita had profits of $84 million on revenues of $1.2 billion, managing $6 billion in assets.

Invita customers pay monthly subscriptions with a *service level agreement* (SLA) that provides guarantees against disruption of services through refunds of a percentage of monthly fees. Invita has multiple locations with private TCP/IP networking at each site, along with customer premise equipment for telecommunications services. Invita uses a large ISP for remote access and interconnection of corporate networks at each site to the Internet and to each other. The company has also engaged a large telecommunications service provider for local and business telephony, wireless services, and satellite conferencing.

Martha, Invita's CIO, has charged George, who is vice-president of Security and Privacy, to examine the current state of corporate security infrastructure and propose a remedy for protecting the mission-critical, Web-based business application that brings in most of the company's profits in subscription and trading fees each year.

George analyzes the current state of security at Invita and arrives at the conclusion that the security on the perimeter of the network, the current authentication schemes, and access control mechanisms all need improvement. George proposes a new *Security Operations Center* (SOC), an application hosted in a corporate work center for monitoring the security of Invita Securities network and customer applications. Technicians at the new work center will manage access to the mission-critical, Web-based financial services application. This application consists of a complex collection of distributed Web servers, directories, legacy hosts, and connections to partners—none of which is compliant with security policy.

In addition to protecting this key application, the SOC application will monitor the internal network and its perimeters, collect and analyze security logs, and administer security. The benefits of an SOC, in addition to creating savings in all of these areas, will include improved QoS, better accountability, and improved security management.

Martha wants a business case for the project.

The Pieces of the Business Case

Invita's Network Systems Engineering department has evaluated the SOC project and has estimated development costs. Invita's operations and IT management has evaluated the requirements and has information on operational costs. Martha and George call in John, an Invita systems architect, and Abigail, a financial consultant, to validate the information, build a business case, and provide supporting evidence for the commitment agreement. The team agrees that once the architecture is reviewed, they can commit to the project and allocate funding for the 2002 business cycle.

Development Costs

George decides to aim for a 15-month development cycle from January 1, 2002, to April 1, 2003. He adds incentives to complete development one quarter ahead of schedule.

James, a systems engineer, to discuss the development costs of the project. After reviewing the high-level requirements and speaking to vendors, they decide on implementing the project in two phases—the first to lay down a basic framework with management interfaces to all Invita systems involved and the second to integrate all of the vendor components involved. The project schedule is sketched out to the last five quarters, with time included for extensive system and customer acceptance testing. Thomas and James have a lot of experience with Invita's systems and operations, and they are confident that their cost estimates are accurate to within 5 percent of the final costs. George also describes that there will be financial incentives for deploying the system ahead of schedule.

The development costs are divided into two broad components: general costs and application development costs. The costs include estimates for development and production interaction after delivery into the year 2001. The capital budget of $350,000 covers the purchase of development, configuration management, and system test servers and developer workstations. Some details have been omitted for conciseness. Although it is expected that the SOC will have major releases every three to four years, no estimates of development cost can be made because no feature specifications exist.

After several weeks of intensive analysis with vendors and systems engineers, the team decides that the application will need $3.5 million in funding (see Figure 16.2).

All figures (000)	2002				2003			
Year and Quarter	Q1	Q2	Q3	Q4	Q1	Q2	Q3	Q4
General								
Hardware Capital Budget	350	0	0	0	0	0	0	0
Hardware Contracts	0	0	0	0	50	0	0	0
Project Management	48	144	48	48	24	0	0	0
Systems Engineering	72	72	0	0	0	0	0	0
Documentation	0	48	12	12	0	0	0	0
Administative support	0	120	48	24	24	12	12	12
Partner/vendor tech support	0	72	72	24	24	24	24	24
Development licenses	105	0	0	0	16	0	0	0
Project								
Architecture definition	12	0	0	0	0	0	0	0
Product Selection: Hardware	12	0	0	0	0	0	0	0
Product Selection: Software	54	0	0	0	0	0	0	0
Lab Environment	46	0	0	0	0	0	0	0
Design/Develop/Unit Test	107	732	180	0	0	0	0	0
Integration Testing	0	72	144	0	0	0	0	0
System Testing	0	0	48	144	72	0	0	0
Performance testing	0	0	0	36	0	0	0	0
Load testing	0	0	0	36	36	0	0	0
Regression test suite	0	0	0	18	18	0	0	0
Configuration management	72	24	12	12	12	12	12	12
Training costs	46	0	0	0	0	0	0	0
TOTAL	**$924**	**$1,284**	**$564**	**$354**	**$276**	**$48**	**$48**	**$48**
Total by year				**$3,126**				**$420**

Figure 16.2 Development costs.

George visits Dolley, Invita's COO. Dolley has heard about SOC from Martha already and loves the idea, but she is concerned about the operational needs for a new security center. Although the application will be hosted on-site, Invita has no expertise in security management. They agree to hire a security services company to oversee the technical outputs of the application and coordinate incident response activities with managers. The company charges $1,000 a week to be on call, with additional charges based on professional consulting rates. Martha agrees with Dolley that expenses in the event of an intrusion should not be assigned to day-to-day operations costs. With this reassurance, Dolley agrees to assign four of Invita's union technicians for the 24 × 7 operation of SOC. She asks George to contact Elizabeth, head of work center operation, for cost information. George discovers that the four technicians cost $1,000 a week each and would need remote access service, laptops, beepers, and printers. They also need yearly training and have union-mandated contract increases every three years. The next increase is slated for 2005. Departmental fixed costs are separately accounted and budgeted for and removed from the analysis. Elizabeth adds a 40 percent per technician overhead for floor space, utilities, environmental regulations, and human resources administrative support. She also assigns two resources from the common administration pool for production support and systems administration and adds a fractional cost per year to release these resources to work on the SOC (Figure 16.3).

Dolley reviews the final totals and expresses her confidence that the numbers have an error margin of 25 percent but are close enough to actual operational costs for her to sign off on the business plan.

All figures (000)

Year	2002	2003	2004	2005	2006	2007
Personnel						
Operations Support Mgmt	0	140	140	140	140	140
Communications Technicians	0	291	291	311	311	311
Production support	0	21	21	22	22	22
Systems administration	0	21	21	22	22	22
Training	0	20	20	20	20	20
Operations Documention	0	0	16	0	0	0
Security services	0	52	52	52	52	52
Facility/Capital Budget						
Hardware Capital Budget	0	400	0	0	0	0
Remote Access	0	10	0	0	10	0
Environmental/ Utilities	0	0	0	0	0	0
Floor space	0	0	0	0	0	0
Administrative support	0	0	0	0	0	0
Total	**$0**	**$955**	**$561**	**$567**	**$577**	**$567**

Figure 16.3 Operational costs.

Time-Out 1: Financial Formulas

We use the following financial functions from Microsoft Excel in an interactive worksheet. The following definitions can be reviewed from any financial analysis text (for example, [WBB96]).

Interest Rate Functions

We use the following list of five interest rate functions. Here are their definitions. The formula for these functions varies depending on whether the rate argument is greater than, less than, or equal to zero.

- The *FV()* function returns the future value of an investment.
- The *NPER()* function returns the number of periods for an investment.
- The *PMT()* function returns the periodic payment for an annuity.
- The *PV()* function returns the present value of an investment.
- The *RATE()* function returns the interest rate per period of an investment.

All of these functions share a relationship through a general formula for interest rate functions. The formula links a present value and a series of payments under a discount rate of interest to an equivalent future value. The following formulas apply to all of the five functions defined previously. The formula is as follows:

$$PV(1 + r)^n + PMT \times (1 + r \times t)\left(\frac{(1 + r)^n - 1}{r}\right) + FV = 0$$

r is the discount rate, n is the number of periods, t is 0 when the payment is due at the end of the period, and t is 1 when the payment is due at the beginning of the period. The rate r is greater or less than 0.

Net Present Value

NPV() returns the net present value of an investment based on a series of periodic cash flows and a discount rate. The formula is as follows:

$$NPV = \sum_{1}^{n}\left(\frac{\text{values}_i}{(1 + \text{rate})^i}\right)$$

rate is the discount rate, n is the number of regular time intervals, and $values_i$ is the cash flow in time period i, which ranges from *1* to n.

Internal Rate of Ret

IRR() returns the internal rate of return for a series of cash flows, with NPV set to 0. The formula is as follows:

$$NPV = \sum_{1}^{n} \left(\frac{\text{values}_i}{(1 + \text{rate})^i} \right)$$

rate is the discount rate, n is the number of regular time intervals, and *values*$_i$ is the cash flow in time period i (which ranges from *1* to n).

Payback Period

The payback period is the number of years until the initial investments plus returns yield a positive net present value and is calculated as the first year when the discounted cash flow from the initial investment has a positive NPV. In our worksheet, we calculated NPV of all prefixes of our final cash flow values for years 1 through 5 and report the payback period as the first period where the NPV changes sign from negative to positive.

Uniform Payment

The uniform payment converts a series of unequal payments over n periods into an equivalent uniform series of payments under a discount rate.

Now, we return to our show.

Break-Even Analysis

George turns over all the information collected so far to Abigail and John. Abigail has some reservations about the development and operational numbers but agrees to hold off until the business case is complete for review. The costs represent a negative cash flow as the company invests in a new system. She creates a worksheet to estimate the constant cash flow required from saved losses from reduced security intrusions to justify the project. To do so, she first estimates the *net present value* of all costs at the beginning of 2002, which is when Martha must approve and release funding, at Invita's 10 percent rate for the cost of capital. She then computes the *future value* of the project after a year, because there will be no savings in 2002. Finally, she estimates the *uniform payment* necessary over each of the next five years to offset this negative cash flow (the quantity marked x in the saved losses row in Figure 16.4). This estimate implies that the project's internal rate of return is exactly the 10 percent investment rate. She explains to George why uniform payment is independent of the actual saved losses, because it just tells us how much we must save to justify going forward with SOC. George finds this information useful. Now, he must find $1.6 million in savings each year over the next five years from the security architecture. If he can, he has his business case.

All figures (000)

Year	2002	2003	2004	2005	2006	2007
Activity						
Development	($3,126)	($420)	$0	$0	$0	$0
Operations	$0	($955)	($561)	($567)	($577)	($567)
Cost Cash Flow	($3,126)	($1,375)	($561)	($567)	($577)	($567)
Saved losses	**$0**	*x*	*x*	*x*	*x*	*x*

Quantity	**Amount**
Weighted Average Cost of Capital	10.0%
Net Present Value of All Costs	($5,465.27)
Required Internal Rate of Return	10.0%
Number of periods where savings is zero	1
Future Value after 1 year of 2002 NPV of Costs	($6,011.79)
Number of periods	5
Uniform Payment	**$1,585.90**

Figure 16.4 Uniform payment.

Breaking Even is Not Good Enough

George now needs an estimate of actual savings and is stumped. He has no idea where to begin assessing the losses that the system targets. The feature requirements provide technical detail, describing firewalls deployed, auditing software installed, e-mail virus scanning services, strong authentication, and centralized access control management but say nothing about the current losses from operations without these security features. He therefore calls for help.

George schedules a lockup meeting for the team. He also invites a small group of Invita's technical leaders, business process owners for the systems involved, a security guru from the managed services firm hired to assist SOC, and representatives from each organization that could potentially save money. Abigail pulls together any data she can find on the financial aspects of computer risk.

The team meets in a week.

Time-Out 2: Assumptions in the Saved Losses Model

Before we jump into the details of what we can save by building this system, we must first outline some of the assumptions behind the model. Consider the following sources of losses and the capability of the SOC system to prevent them.

Candidates for saved losses. DOS attacks, system penetration by outsiders, access through network spoofing, telecommunications fraud, theft of proprietary business

intellectual property, e-mail virus attacks, some losses from network sniffing of traffic, intrusion-related financial fraud, intrusion-related payouts of cash guaranteed by SLAs, legal expenditures, and the cost of incident response are all included as candidates for saved losses.

Candidates for unprotected losses. Theft of physical property, abuse of access by authorized personnel, nonintrusion-related financial fraud, loss of reputation, morale loss among employees, advertising expenditures for damage control, and losses from network sniffing of unencrypted traffic are all included in this category.

Assumptions in the Saved Losses Model

We will assume that Invita's operational track record in adhering to corporate security policy and closing security holes is not stellar. This situation would mean that they are like most middle-sized companies. Invita's high availability solutions are efficient in restoring the network and services, but they depend on certain assumptions about the behavior of the systems themselves. If a malicious agent causes a widespread failure on the systems themselves, service restoration might not be possible.

Estimating the cost of insecurity is difficult. We will make some assumptions based on industry and internal data to create a final numeric result. If the reader is interested in doing so, however, it is straightforward to reproduce the values and formulas in the worksheets within the sections ahead in the form of a Microsoft Excel worksheet. Because the worksheet is completely interactive, any assumption that you feel like challenging can be modified, and you can see the impact on the Net Present Value, Internal Rate of Return, and Payback Period for the new values immediately. In addition, you can add or remove sources of losses and change development, operations, or schedule details.

We have not described the feature set within SOC, because for the purpose of the business case, this detail would be too much. We will just say that SOC implements strong authentication, does user and role management, does virus scans, manages policy for existing perimeter hosts such as firewalls and secure gateways, deploys a number of security monitors and sensors, collects and logs event, does log analysis, and forwards security alerts to technicians who can respond to the alarm or call in the cavalry.

Steady State Losses

The model estimates these sources of losses and attaches dollar figures, as well.

Each year SOC will save losses in these categories:

- Theft of intellectual property and proprietary information, including market analysis data and customer data. Total losses: $800,000.
- Financial fraud using stolen customer credentials and payouts from violation of service level agreements due to security violations. Total losses: $500,000.

- Denial-of-service attacks. Total losses: $250,000.
- Productivity losses through e-mail viruses. Total losses: $250,000.
- Unauthorized insider access. Total losses: $30,000.
- Telecommunications fraud. Total losses: $50,000.

SOC will *not* save losses in the following categories:

- Sabotage of networks through physical acts. Total losses: $50,000.
- Theft of equipment such as laptops, PDAs, or cell phones. Total losses: $100,000.
- Insider abuse of network access. Total losses: $250,000.
- Some of the losses to unreliable service caused by theft or disruption of network services. Total losses: $50,000.

Losses from a Catastrophic Network Disruption

Another major benefit from the SOC project is the timely response and resolution of a catastrophic security intrusion before it can cause widespread disruption. The first question is, of course, "How likely is a catastrophic disruption that would have been preventable by SOC?"

To gain a picture of the costs associated with such widespread catastrophic failure, please review the AT&T network disruption we presented earlier. Software failures played a major role in the disruption, but a hacker could conceivably do the same to Invita.

We have conservatively estimated that a catastrophic incident will occur once in SOC's five-year operational life with 0.5 percent probability. Please refer to the references in the bibliography on telecommunications fraud to see why that might even be an underestimate.

Although we assumed that Invita would pay penalties if a customer SLA were violated, it must be admitted that if the cost is too great that Invita might default on service guarantees due to the extraordinary nature of any catastrophic event. If Invita refuses to refund customers, we might incur other costs such as loss of market share and reduced customer confidence with even more expensive long-term consequences.

We now return to our story already in progress.

The Agenda for the Lockup

The team must categorize the losses that SOC will potentially save for Invita and for each of the two classes of losses, namely steady state and catastrophic, assign dollar values to losses.

and payment of refunds because of service guarantees and could also require discounts to promote loyalty in dissatisfied customers. In addition, an intrusion might result in any or all of the following: network disruption, advertising costs, legal counsel, productivity losses, morale loss, replacement of equipment, theft of customer records, loss of market share, and financial liability. John describes all of the features of the SOC project and how the architecture will improve security practice at Invita.

Elizabeth from Legal Services immediately removes the cost of legal counsel from the list. She contends that it is inappropriate for an engineering team to justify savings in that area. Nobody argues with her.

Louisa from Advertising states that intrusion response requires advertising to combat the negative advertising of competitors, along with other public relations activities for damage control. She reviews examples of negative advertising launched by rivals against other companies in the sector that have suffered intrusions. The team agrees that charges for countering negative advertising at a cost of $5 million should be included. Louisa estimates that other damage control will cost $2 million in the event of a catastrophe. The team decides that this savings is intangible and excludes it from the model.

The team then considers steady state losses from e-mail viruses, Web site defacement, passive network scans, minor access violations, and loss of data from disrupted communications. The team is certain that productivity losses are an obvious savings, except for the external security guru, Andrew, who believes that the correlation between e-mail viruses and productivity losses is weak. In fact, he asserts, the correlation might be negative because although some people legitimately find their work environment disrupted, others find that not being able to send mail implies not being able to receive mail, either. Andrew says that the resulting phone and face-to-face interaction, along with time away from the network, might actually boost productivity. John remarks that the costs of the Love Bug and the Melissa virus ran into the billions. Andrew, in turn, notes that while everyone reports losses, no one reports time saved or productivity gains from doing creative work away from the computer. No one knows what to make of this situation, so after an uncomfortable pause, they ignore this recommendation.

Rachel from telecommunications services adds a new feature request. The current customer premise equipment enables sales employees with a password to use an 800 number to access the PBX and then dial out. One of the security components included in the architecture has an interface that will protect the local phone equipment at no additional cost. The team agrees to amend the feature requirements, include Rachel's estimate of a $25,000 loss on average to a $100,000 loss at most from a single violation, to the saved losses.

The team quickly decides to remove loss of reputation, morale, and other intangibles from the measurable saved losses list. Martin, from operations, has surprising numbers from several industry surveys, including Ernst & Young, the Department of Defense, and the Computer Services Institute. Considering Invita's share of the overall financial services industry, the average cost from computer fraud, financial fraud, eavesdropping, and laptop theft could be as high as $5 million a year. George is elated to hear this fact until he realizes that although this situation is good for his business case, the company was probably losing money as they spoke.

financial analysis reports that Invita provides as part of its subscription service and the sophisticated Web-based financial analysis and modeling tools that its customers use. The security guru noted that company did nothing to protect the reports once they were in the hands of a subscriber but could protect them on the document server or in transit. The application could also restrict access by password-protecting the electronic documents themselves. This feature was not part of the original SOC feature set, and the team agrees that digital rights management is out of scope for the project. There are some savings from protecting the Web and document servers themselves, however, and from managing subscriptions securely.

Then, Hannah from customer services and William from the CFO organization describe Invita's guarantee program. Invita's customers fall into two categories: individuals and businesses. Each category has its own subscription rate and service level agreement. In addition, Invita promises high availability and good response time for its trading services. Violations of either promise could result in refunds corresponding to free trades or a month's subscription fee, depending on the customer's service request. Hannah and William have data on the success of the guarantee program over the past few years, including some surprises. Not all customers who experience service disruptions asked to invoke the guarantees. Not all those who did invoke the guarantee remembered doing so. For customers who remember invoking guarantees, higher satisfaction scores did not seem related to higher credit awards. In fact, the satisfaction rating was higher for small awards (less than $30) as compared to large awards (awards of more than $250) for problem resolutions. Hannah explained that part of the decrease in satisfaction might be because of the possibility that after a certain point, as credit size increases, so does the magnitude or severity of the problem encountered and the initial relative dissatisfaction of the customer. When the team wished to compare the new security features to the causes of service disruption to see how much would be saved, however, the data was just not there.

Fortunately, Anna, from Invita operations could correlate the times of the disruptions with a service outage database. The team discovers that 2 percent of all the service disruptions can be conservatively attributed to security-related issues.

Finally, the team visits catastrophic costs. Andrew presents the story of a business rival whose customer database was stolen and released on the Internet, causing 20 percent of all customers to leave and triggering losses exceeding $100 million. The team agrees that if SOC prevents a single catastrophic event over its five-year lifespan, then it would have justified its cost many times over. The probability of such an event is unknown, however. The team decides that a catastrophic event could cost Invita at least a year's profit, $80 million, but the probability of such an event is very small (less than one-half of 1 percent). The team agrees that both numbers are somewhat arbitrary. The figure 0.5 percent was chosen because only one of the 40 largest companies on Martin's list of financial services corporations experienced a catastrophic loss in the past five years. Andrew cautioned the team that fewer than 15 percent of computer crimes are detected and perhaps as few as 10 percent of those are reported. He also added that the causality between implementing SOC and preventing a catastrophe was weak, saying, "We could

security coverage. George disagrees, saying, "It is clear that SOC's architecture is sound and valuable, and at the very least SOC makes Invita a less attractive target."

The team decides to use all of the data collected so far to arrive at some conclusions.

Steady-State Losses

The team reviews and revises the estimates, removing some elements. Abigail adds up all of the estimates for high-probability losses to get $1.9 million a year. (Note: This amount is less than what we assumed during the last time-out.) Almost $1.3 million of that total is from theft of intellectual property, financial fraud, and service guarantee payouts.

Catastrophic Losses

Abigail then computes Invita's expected losses over the next five years as follows:

(Cost of catastrophe) × (Probability of catastrophe in five years)

This equation gives us $80 million multiplied by 0.005, which comes out to $400,000. The team does not expect such a small number (and that, too, for a five-year period). Abigail then expresses the present value of $400,000 at the beginning of 2003 as a series of five uniform payments, at Invita's investment rate of 10 percent, to arrive at $100,000 a year in savings. She explains to the team why she assigned the total dollar cost arbitrarily to the year 2003 to be on the safe side. The payment represents the estimated cost each year spread out over five years. The cost is discounted at the rate of 10 percent to represent the decreased cost to Invita over time (Figure 16.5).

George is aghast. He was expecting much more in savings. The team increases the probability of a catastrophe to 10 percent in five years. The savings jumps from $106,000 to $2,110,000 (Figure 16.6).

Event	Cost
Steady state costs	$1,900,000
Catastrophic Disruption Cost	$80,000,000
Probability	0.50%
Probable cost (% probability)	$400,000
WACC	10.00%
Number of years (2003-2007)	5
Estimated annual cost	$106,000
Yearly savings from SOC	**$2,006,000**

Figure 16.5 First estimate of yearly savings from SOC.

Event	Cost
Steady state costs	$1,900,000
Catastrophic Disruption Cost	$80,000,000
Probability	10.00%
Probable cost (% probability)	$8,000,000
WACC	10.00%
Number of years (2003-2007)	5
Estimated annual cost	$2,110,000
Yearly savings from SOC	**$4,010,000**

Figure 16.6 Second estimate of yearly savings from SOC.

Event	Cost
Steady state costs	$1,900,000
Catastrophic Disruption Cost	$80,000,000
Probability	1.00%
Probable cost (% probability)	$800,000
WACC	10.00%
Number of years (2003-2007)	5
Estimated annual cost	$211,000
Yearly savings from SOC	**$2,111,000**

Figure 16.7 Third estimate of yearly savings from SOC.

The team lowers the probability to 1 percent. The savings from catastrophic losses falls to $211,000 (Figure 16.7).

Abigail raises an issue with assuming a 10 percent probability of catastrophic losses. That would imply that 20 of the 40 companies experienced a catastrophic loss over the five-year period from Martin's data. This situation is clearly not the case.

The team decides to call in Martha for the business case readout. They stick with the low probability of a catastrophe figure of 0.5 percent to produce the following cost-benefit analysis (Figure 16.8). The team estimates that the project has an internal rate of return of 26 percent, and the project has a five-year payback period (four years after deployment).

The Readout

Martha is more than a little surprised. She listens to the team explain that many potential savings were blocked out because of inexact numbers or unknown probabilities.

Year	2002	2003	2004	2005	2006	2007
Activity						
Development	($3,126)	($420)	$0	$0	$0	$0
Operations	$0	($955)	($561)	($567)	($577)	($567)
Saved losses	$0	$2,006	$2,006	$2,006	$2,006	$2,006
Total Cash Flow	**($3,126)**	**$631**	**$1,445**	**$1,439**	**$1,429**	**$1,439**

Quantity	Amount
Weighted Average Cost of Capital	10.0%
Net Present Value	**$1,447.75**
Internal Rate of Return	**26%**
Net present value after 1 year	($2,841.82)
Net present value after 2 years	($2,320.33)
Net present value after 3 years	($1,234.68)
Net present value after 4 years	($251.82)
Net present value after 5 years	$635.47
Net present value after 6 years	$1,447.75
Payback Period (years)	**5**

Figure 16.8 First Consolidated Cost-Benefit Analysis.

Martha tries some changes. The first modification that she requests is the removal of the savings from catastrophic losses, reasoning that if a number is that sensitive to changes in a single probability value, it should be discarded as unreliable.

Andrew objects to this vociferously. His company gets the majority of their sales of security monitoring services to corporations based on the fear of the worst-case scenario. He argues that the sensitivity to probability should be disregarded, that the loss from a catastrophe cannot be ignored, and that SOC is a no-brainer. Anna notes that Andrew has a financial stake in seeing SOC implemented, because his company will respond to intrusions. This statement leaves Andrew speechless, and Abigail takes over. Abigail reports that the modification results in the IRR falling to 22 percent, although the payback period stays the same (Figure 16.9).

Martha asks the team to consider an alternative.

Insuring Against Attacks

Martha introduces Sarah and Zachary, who have been listening silently so far. Sarah is from Invita's corporate insurance division, and Zachary is a representative from a large insurance company that sells insurance policies for computer security. Zachary's company will insure Invita's assets at a 10 percent premium.

The team examines this alternative. Zachary will charge $8,000,000 a year for securing Invita against catastrophic losses. Andrew dismisses the premium. "It is like the extended service warranties that electronic stores offer when you buy stuff," he said. "They charge you 20 percent of the purchase price for a year's coverage. Unless one in

Year	2002	2003	2004	2005	2006	2007
Activity						
Development	($3,126)	($420)	$0	$0	$0	$0
Operations	$0	($955)	($561)	($567)	($577)	($567)
Saved losses	$0	$1,900	$1,900	$1,900	$1,900	$1,900
Total Cash Flow	**($3,126)**	**$525**	**$1,339**	**$1,333**	**$1,323**	**$1,333**

Quantity	Amount
Weighted Average Cost of Capital	10.0%
Net Present Value	**$1,082.46**
Internal Rate of Return	**22%**
Net present value after 1 year	($2,841.82)
Net present value after 2 years	($2,407.93)
Net present value after 3 years	($1,401.92)
Net present value after 4 years	($491.47)
Net present value after 5 years	$330.01
Net present value after 6 years	$1,082.46
Payback Period (years)	**5**

Figure 16.9 Second Consolidated Cost-Benefit Analysis.

five of the devices is failing, it's stealing!" Zachary strongly objects to this characterization. When the team asks whether Zachary will charge $200,000 each year, to prevent the steady state losses that Invita incurs, he is more evasive. "Since the losses are guaranteed, they can't be insured for one tenth the value," he explains. "We'd be paying you $1.8 million every year."

The team ends the meeting with no resolution to the business case.

Business Case Conclusion

Martha calls William from the CFO organization to ask whether a project with a 22 percent rate of return is normally given the green signal. William is reluctant to commit to an answer but says that a five-year payback period would be unacceptable for most financial services, which must be profitable in quarters (not years). He also recommends against the $8,000,000 premium because of the unusual nature of insuring against computer risk. It would be unfortunate to have a claim rejected because of some minor clause in the agreement.

Martha calls in George and tells him the bad news. Invita will not build SOC but will instead assign some resources to the individual systems to improve security. She privately wishes that George had found more savings but decides not to re-examine the business case, fearing that the team will tell her what they think she wants to hear rather than the truth.

Eighteen months later, Invita is hacked and loses 25 percent of its customer base. Martha and George resign. What did you expect, a happy ending?

A Critique of the Business Case

Some of our readers might have found our method of presentation unusual. Our apologies if this situation confused more than clarified the issues involved. Analyzing security risk is mainly about reconciling incompatible opinions on the relative value, importance, and cost of alternatives, however, to arrive at estimates of the impact and consequences of decision-making. We thought it easier to assign these viewpoints to separate voices rather than spend twice the space writing conditional or conflicting statements. If you had concerns about the analysis and the outcome, they are probably well founded. Here is why.

Our business case has two central flaws. Both flaws are common in risk assessment analysis, and neither of them is easily fixed. Yacov Haimes' text on risk assessment [Haimes98] extensively discusses the effect of these two factors on risk modeling, assessment, and management.

Money can measure everything. All system properties are reduced to being commensurate with one measure: money. Many risk analysis experts reject this method of cost-benefit analysis because money is inadequate as the sole measure of criteria for project excellence. The interconnected nature of systems leads to the loss of other properties—not all of which can be measured accurately and adequately or can even be characterized by a dollar figure.

Catastrophic risk is undervalued. The mathematical expected value of risk multiplies the consequence of each event (its cost) with its probability of occurrence (its likelihood) and sums or integrates all of these products over the entire universe of events. Using the expected value of risk as an aid for decision-making blurs the relative weight of two events of vastly differing costs by multiplying these costs with the vastly differing probabilities of occurrence of these events. Event A with probability 0.1 and cost $1,000 contributes the same amount of $100 to the expected value of risk as event B with probability 0.0001 and cost $1,000,000. In the real world, where we are remembered by our worst failures, no manager would characterize the two losses as being equivalent if they actually occurred. We cannot discard elements of the analysis that are very sensitive to perturbation because these elements might be the most important.

Risk theory provides other models for assessing extreme risk that categorize all events into ranges of probability and measure conditional risk in each category. These models simultaneously target multiple objectives to prevent the smoothing effect of the expected value of risk measurement in our business case. We can choose to emphasize the effects of some ranges of probability that would otherwise be subsumed by the noise from other categories. These models also assume that the analyst has objective and high-quality evidence to support the probability of occurrence assigned to each event, however, which is rarely the case. Our estimates for the likelihood of most events are fuzzy. In such a case, categorizing fuzziness is not an improvement.

In addition to the real dangers of under-representing catastrophic risk, our business case also shows some other simplifications that could affect our analysis because we have ignored other risk factors.

security exploits. While this assumption might indeed be true for many known exploits, we will fail on some novel attacks. Even if the architecture is sound, it cannot be complete. The probability that the solution will fail against new and unknown exploits has not been made explicit.

- We have omitted the most significant saved losses component; namely, savings gained by defending against medium-sized losses with a medium probability of occurrence. Companies do not wish to advertise exposures from this category in many cases or have insurance against what they perceive as an evil cost of being in operations. We lack detailed facts on the monetary impact of risk in this category, but there are signs that this situation is improving.
- We have ignored project management risks, including cost overruns, schedule delays, personnel changes, project scope creep, or budget revisions.
- We have probably underestimated the level of maintenance, testing, and training required to operate the security center. These costs tend break business cases because they reduce projected savings year over year.
- We have ignored failure of the security operations center itself. If the center is engineered to be highly available, this situation might indeed be acceptable. Nevertheless, it is unlikely that there will be no impact to business operations if a large and central security service falls over either through malicious tampering or through human error or accidental failure of hardware, software, or processes.
- We have ignored how decision-making works in real life. Decision trees, first introduced by Howard Raiffa [Rai68], use graphical and analytic methods to describe the consequences of our choices when assessing risk. We have posited a simple management outcome from the business case: accept or deny the project. In an actual situation, we must do more—including analysis and decomposition of the project into stages corresponding to the architectural options and alternatives available, only one of which corresponds to SOC.
- Our analysis might be fragile. Our systems might be sensitive to fluctuations in assumptions. Some decisions are irreversible while others are not. Any risk model must present rollback opportunities if decisions can be revoked.
- The model might be unstable because of new requirements or other evolutionary design forces. Its ability to perform as advertised in the event that we cut technicians, increase data volumes, add new components, or merge with other security services is unknown.

Insurance and Computer Security

Risk management, modeling, and assessment use many techniques to capture the quantitative risk associated with any venture, the conditional expected value of losses if the venture goes awry, and the ranking and filtering rules required to classify the collection of extreme events that threaten the system.

rity architecture, design, and engineering principles. Another alternative to protecting a venture from risk is through insurance. When we buy insurance, we trade a large and potentially disastrous outcome that is unlikely with a small but guaranteed loss: the premium for insurance. Statistically, the premium loss outweighs the expected value of losses to fires, personal injury, or death. We consider these outcomes unacceptable, however, and therefore prefer a small loss to a potentially devastating consequence.

The principles of insurance define risk as uncertainty concerning loss. Risk makes insurance both desirable and possible. Without uncertainty, no insurer will cover a guaranteed loss at economically reasonable rates. Risk depends on the probability distribution of loss, not on the expected value alone. The more predictable the loss, the less the degree of risk. As the variance in the loss distribution rises, so does the degree of risk.

Insurance protects against peril, the cause of risk. Peril from an accident, for example, could depend on many factors: the age of the driver, the prior driving record, the driving conditions, and the competence of other drivers. Each condition (whether physical, moral, or morale) that can cause the probability of loss to increase or decrease is called a hazard. Physical hazard is an objective property; for example, the condition of the vehicle's tires. Moral hazards capture our subjective estimation of the character of the insured, which could increase the chance of loss. Insurance fraud results from moral hazards. In addition, morale hazards (as opposed to moral hazards) are caused by the existence of the insurance policy itself, because the insured is now indifferent to protecting the asset. Insurance combines the risk of many individual policies together to build a profitable and more predictable model of losses, where the premiums charged clearly exceed the likely losses.

Peter L. Bernstein, in his bestseller *Against the Gods* on the history of risk [Ber98], describes the work of economists such as Kenneth J. Arrow on the forces behind insurable risk. He describes how the lack of complete or correct information about the circumstances around us causes us to overestimate the accuracy and the value of what we do know. In his description of Arrow's complete market, a model where all risk is insurable, he describes the basic quality that makes insurance practical. Insurance works when the *Law of Large Numbers* applies. The law of large numbers requires that the risks insured should be large in number and independent in nature.

Credit card companies already forgive fraud on Internet charges, because although we lack infrastructure for secure transactions beyond SSL to a secure Web server, the sheer volume of business is too valuable to ignore. Companies swallow the losses to keep the customers happy and reissue cards whenever Internet vendors report the theft of a credit card database.

An unfortunate consequence of this line of thinking is the response by governments and corporations to identity theft. Although at a personal level this situation can be devastating, with victims reeling from the effects for years, very little is done at the infrastructure level (because hey, the Law of Large Numbers has not caught up). There are relatively few incidents, and despite the moral and legal dimensions, corporations and legislators alike have decided that paying for a huge and expensive security infrastructure to prevent this situation is not yet worth the trouble. Some improvements have

example, the United States Post Office no longer allows anyone to redirect another person's mail by just dropping off a "Moving to a New Address" card. (This method was the most common route for attackers to gain access to the victim's profile and personal data.) Identity theft is terrible on the individual scale, but attacks are not yet at levels where the costs to our economy justify widespread policy changes.

Hacker Insurance

Purchasing insurance against hackers is complicated because, in our current imperfect environment, the law of large numbers is not applicable. Insurers will offer hacker insurance in two scenarios.

The domain of insurance applicability is extremely restricted. The insurance company adds so many qualifiers to the description of what constitutes a security violation covered by insurance that the project might be unable to file a claim. The value of the policy might be affordable, but it is so exclusive as to be useless outside a tight boundary.

The premium is extraordinarily high. The insurance company sets premium levels so high that policies are guaranteed to be profitable even when the types of insured events is quite large.

Firstly, we lack a rational means of estimating the odds of losses or the actual loss itself. There are no actuarial tables for hacking that correspond to the insurer's statistical tables of mortality, automobile accidents, fire damage, or luggage loss.

Secondly, it might be impossible to take an example of an attack at one company and extrapolate the consequences of a similar attack at another. Even when the insurer has statistical information on the costs of an attack, simple differences in infrastructure, business models, industries, or services can make extrapolation invalid. Our business case of the previous sections illustrates the difficulty of this task. Before we can ask for a quantitative expected value of insurable risk, we must classify and categorize the vast number of security exploits each as a potential hazard. Although the collection of exploits is very large, creating a taxonomy based on system properties can bound the risks. The insurer has the harder problem of policy definition for each of the combinations in our taxonomy. What does it cost to insure a particular hardware platform, with several major configuration details, running one of dozens of versions of operating systems, running some subset of thousands of vendor products, and supporting millions of customers?

Thirdly, even if we succeed in breaking down our many exploits into individual categories, it is hard to describe the impact of a particular exploit on our system. Other metrics (such as cumulative down time, rate of revenue loss in dollars an hour, counts of dropped connection requests, or customer attrition numbers following the attack) are all unrelated to the actual nature of the exploit from the perspective of the insurance company. Some exploits might have limited success; others can be devastating—accounting for the vast majority of all the attacks that succeed. If the insurance com-

out of luck.

Fourthly, there is also the risk of moral hazard. Insurance encourages risk-taking, which is essential for economic progress. Insurance can also result in fraud, however. Auto insurance companies in many states complain that the primary cause of rising auto insurance rates is fraud. Medical insurers similarly blame a portion of the rise in health care costs on excessive, fraudulent claims filed by organized gangs that collude with medical service providers to swindle the company out of enormous amounts of money. Companies that buy computer hacker insurance policies must not be able to exploit that insurance policy to defraud the insurer. This task is extremely difficult. Security forensics is hard enough in genuine cases of intrusion, let alone cases where the insured is an accomplice of the hacker and to the intrusion act.

Finally, insurance works when the individual claims filed are probabilistically independent events. The likelihood of my house burning down at the same instant that your house burns down is small if we live in different cities but much larger if we are neighbors. The Internet and all of the networks we build that connect to it break down the boundaries between systems. The networks we depend on for services also link us together across geographic boundaries to make us neighbors when attacked. One e-mail virus spawns 50, each of which spawn 50 more—affecting all the mail users in a corporation, all their friends on mailing lists, all their corporate partners, and all customers.

We depend on critical services. If a hacker launches a distributed DOS attack at something universally needed such as a DNS, can all the affected systems file claims or only the owners of the DNS server? If Yahoo! goes down, who can file a claim? Is it only the company, Yahoo! Incorporated? Can Yahoo! users file claims? Can Yahoo! advertisers file claims for all the lost eyeballs while the site was down? Insurance companies have a poor way of dealing with dependencies, ranging from denying all claims or paying all claims and declaring bankruptcy (as was witnessed in Florida in the aftermath of Hurricane Andrew).

Insurance Pricing Methods

By law, insurance companies are required to price premiums in a manner that is reasonable, adequate, and non-discriminatory. Many states carry laws prohibiting approval of a policy that charges unreasonable premiums in relation to the benefits provided.

Insurance is also regulated. Not everyone can offer it, and those that do must go through a certification process. In the past, telecommunications companies have worked around this issue by providing different classes of service with guaranteed levels of protection. For example, a small business with a *Public Branch Exchange* (PBX) switch on its premises might pay extra for a plan that absolves them of liability in case of toll fraud. The telecommunications provider might even add stipulations of make and model of the switch and configuration options, and recommend additional hardware as part of the service. If it looks like insurance and it smells like insurance, however, it's probably insurance.

Toll fraud, which stands around $4 billion in annual losses, is hard to quantify. There are many forms of theft of service from long-distance call theft, trunk group theft, cellular

calling card fraud.

Insurance companies socialize risk. They charge higher premiums to young drivers, but not high enough to justify the payouts, instead transferring some of the burden to older drivers. They also spread the costs of fraud across all customers. Pricing models can target individuals where the premium quoted is based on specific details of the one system under evaluation. Pricing can be on based on class rating, where the system is categorized into a class and then a standard pricing model for the class is invoked. An organization that buys comprehensive coverage might be offered bulk discounts, or the premiums across several systems could be averaged in some manner. Pricing is heavily affected by experience and retrospective analysis, normally in annual cycles. The payouts for the past year and fixed profit targets for the next year determine the schedule for insurance rates.

Health insurance companies sometimes insert clauses in policies to deny coverage of certain pre-existing conditions, although this might cause considerable hardship to a newly insured individual. The reasoning is that the probability of a claim being filed has now hit one. This certainty therefore guarantees losses. Hacker insurance companies may invert this logic on its head. They may refuse to insure *post-emergent* conditions, where new bugs are discovered after the policy is written that result in unexpected intrusions and deny claims for the corresponding losses. Again, until the bug is patched, your application is vulnerable, and in the event that you did not apply the patch although it is not certain that you will be compromised, the insurance company may decide that the intrusion falls outside your policy as an undocumented risk.

Feedback for accurate pricing is another aspect where computer security insurance falls short. There is really no correlation between payouts from one year to another. Old bugs are fixed, new ones appear, and the exact losses from an attack vary from event to event. Consider what the discovery of the elixir of life would do to life insurance premiums, or the invention of the crash proof car to automobile insurance, or an outbreak of an extremely contagious virus requiring intensive care to medical premiums. The inability to map past events to future earnings and payouts results in wild guesses. For this reason, when asked what a reasonable premium would be, we always say 10 percent of the application cost. There is no justification for this number, but it seems to make people happier.

Conclusion

In this chapter, we discussed the role of the practicing software architect in justifying the need for security and the dangers that go with insouciance. After the initial glow of release 1.0, where all the stakeholders are in agreement that they need the system and support its deployment, the architect and project manager are left with the difficult technical challenge of managing the project's evolution as new feature requests and architectural challenges appear. Security, which is often paid lip service but rarely dealt with adequately at release 1.0, becomes a larger concern after the inevitable secu-

interfaces.

Nothing works like a good old-fashioned hack attack to wake up upper management to the risks of e-business. There is a thriving industry of white-hat hackers who for a fee will attack and expose vulnerabilities in production systems under the assumptions that their services represent a complete set of attack scenarios and that the risks to the application can be fixed. The architect is placed in the position of adding security to a production system while at the same time justifying all of the expenses associated with the laundry list of countermeasures proposed by the intrusion team.

In this chapter, our goal was to walk a mile in the shoes of an architect who has been charged with building a business case for computer security. This subject, which would clearly need a book of its own, sits at the confluence of many streams that bring together the academic theories of risk assessment and modeling, the practical knowledge of systems architecture, the tools and techniques of the diverse computer security community, the requirements of software process for building large enterprise systems, and the practical, mundane, but vital activity of writing code to actually do stuff on a machine.

We now conclude the book with some advice on security architecture in the next chapter, along with pointers to further resources for architects.

Conclusion

Computers will always be insecure. There are limits to what we can accomplish through technology. However well we partition the problem, strengthen defenses, force traffic through network choke points, create layer upon layer of security, or keep our designs secret, we are still vulnerable. We must face the fact that we live in a world where products have defects, users are sometimes naïve, administrators make mistakes, software has bugs, and our antagonists are sophisticated.

We have tried to be optimistic in our presentation, sticking largely to the facts and to the available options and staying away from other factors affecting software development. Organizations are political beasts. Vendors sometimes wield unusual influence within a company. Funding comes and goes with the ebb and flow of internecine battles at management levels above us. Choices are made without reference to technical merits. Time pressures change priorities. Human beings make mistakes.

We have mentioned other perspectives of security that emphasize that security is a continual process, and the bibliography provides references to many excellent books that share this viewpoint. This dominant perspective of this process rightly portrays information security as a struggle between defenders and attackers. It should be, because information security is indeed a conflict between you (your business, assets, customers, and way of life) and hackers who have no moral or ethical qualms about destroying what you value. They might not like you, might compete with you, or might be indifferent to you. They might claim to be only curious. You are left to manage risk in the event of an intrusion.

The language of war and crime is popular in discourses on computer security. Laws that apply to munitions protect cryptographic algorithms. We defend ourselves against attack. We detect intrusions, conduct intrusion forensics, analyze intrusion evidence,

lant. We institute countermeasures against attack and compromise. We might even counterattack. We fight viruses, rid ourselves of worms, detect Trojan horses, and are the targets of logic bombs. I once heard a security services firm refer to their team of consultants as Information Security Forces.

In this book, we have tried to ask and answer the question, "How does security look from another perspective?" We have described the goals of security at a high level as seen by the members of another busy tribe, system architects. Systems architects cannot by definition be security experts because their domain of expertise is the system at hand. They know about another domain, perhaps the command and control systems on a nuclear submarine, transport service provisioning on a telecommunications network, power management at a large energy plant, launch sequence software for the space shuttle, consolidated billing for a financial services company, testing for a suite of personal productivity tools, critical path analysis for project management software, voice print storage for a speech synthesis engine, graphical rendering for the next dinosaur movie, or satellite communications for television broadcasts. Security experts are producers of information security. Systems architects are consumers of information security.

Is this alternative perspective more important than the attacker-defender dichotomy? Not in general. In specific instances when we are charged with securing our system, however, this perspective is the only one that matters. We see the world through our own eyes. What choice do we have?

We believe that software architecture is a valuable organizing principle for the construction of large systems. We conclude the book with some elements of security architecture style, a series of general abstract principles collected from many sources. In this chapter, we have collected a long list of observations, recommendations, ideas, and some commandments on building security into systems.

Random Advice

Good security architecture is sound. Soundness is an intangible quality that matches the logic of the application's security with the inner logic of the application itself. The system does something to justify its existence and probably does it very well. The security architecture should run along the grain of the system to prevent breaking it in subtle and hard-to-diagnose ways.

At a high level, protect the perimeter first. List interfaces and the direction of data flow in and out of the system. Do not suffocate communication while you are figuring out how to secure it. Keep the design supple enough to bend in the face of change. Check the combined architecture for leaks at every stage of evolution.

Give full architectural attention to the design of incidental security details, especially setting aside time at the security assessment to discuss physical security or social engineering opportunities that might be ignored otherwise. These are not architectural in nature, and we therefore have not spent much time in this book discussing these issues. There is a wealth of material in the references about these issues, however. Balance the

spend one dollar to protect one cent of data.

Consult ancestors. Every project has a history, and someone in the company—no doubt promoted to another level—knows this history. It is important to understand legacy systems to prevent process from degenerating into ritual.

Eliminate unnecessary security artifacts. Avoid over-ornamentation in the security architecture. Vendor products often have ornaments for flexibility in a wider range of applications. Ornaments inhibit growth and have hidden security costs. They hide unnecessary code, link unwanted libraries, add unused files and directories, and can cause undetected vulnerabilities. If a piece of code does not execute a function in the field, it is a hole waiting to be exploited.

Good security components have a modular design. They have a central core orbited by satellite modules, and at installation enable you to load only the modules required for implementing security policy. For an example of good modular design in other arenas, examine the code base of the Linux kernel, which enables dynamic loading and unloading of kernel modules, or the Apache Web server, which enables integration with several hundred modules that support a wide range of server enhancements. Each product defines an event loop or exception/response architecture for providing checkpoints for module insertion. (Modularity in design is, however, a double-edged sword. Hackers have written Linux rootkit exploits that are loadable kernel modules. These compromise the kernel's response to system calls.)

Good security components do one thing well, do it fast, and stay out of the way. They can be dropped in or lifted out of the architecture with minimal impact. Good security software components are as easy to uninstall as they are to install. Security through obscurity in a vendor product is not a good idea, but it helps to keep the details of your system security solution concealed. Do not put them up on the Web site for the application.

End-to-end security is best. It is also usually impossible. Enable transitive trust with care. You are in effect handing over the security of your system to a partner with unknown practices and vulnerabilities each time you perform this action. Transitive trust is a simplifier, but choose carefully from the range of trust relationships (from none to complete) between any two systems communicating over a chain of intermediaries. Realize that the systems you trust might tomorrow extend that trust to others in ways you disagree with.

Avoid capricious redefinition of familiar architectural concepts, especially if you are a vendor. Vocabulary is important; shared vocabulary more so. Words should mean things, and hopefully the same things to all participants.

When you use encryption, compression, or abbreviated codes in messages, the capability of an IDS or firewall to reason intelligently about the contents is lost. This situation is not bad. This statement should reinforce the notion that depending solely on IDS or firewall instances for systems security architecture is a flaw.

Do not implement your own cryptographic protocols or primitives. Start with a single cryptographic family of primitives and use it everywhere until someone complains for performance or security reasons. Consider the risk of implementation errors, and buy a

case flaws are discovered. List the assumptions of the protocols that you plan to use, and ensure that each holds true. Are your secrets concealed? Encoding is not the same as encryption.

Eavesdroppers listen to communications at other places than the midpoint. The endpoints are very popular, too. Minimize the number of different flavors of communication in your application. Do not clutter the security handshake between communicating processes.

If the application architecture has more than two layers, pick a layer and restrict security functionality to that layer if possible. You will have less to change when the application changes. Periodically edit access control lists and update resource lists with the same attention you would give to editing a user list.

Do not clutter the background process space of the application architecture. Link performance levels with some objective metric. Link the labels "fast," "adequate," and "slow" to actual processing rates in your application so as to use these terms consistently. If you wish to avoid performance penalties associated with security measures, you might have no choice but to use insecure solutions. Consider performance gains from using lighter security. It might be worth it.

Bring the interfaces into the heart of the security design. Your system interfaces are how the world views your application. If you alter an interface specification to add security extensions, spend some time documenting your reasons. The system on the other side will need to know why. Wrap all insecure legacy code. Re-examine objects with multiple wrappers. Look for opportunities for reuse.

Think in other dimensions when you are enumerating the interfaces with your system. Did you remember the automated tape backup system? How about hardware access to data when swapping disks? Do the security procedures at a secondary disaster recovery site protect it as well as the primary? Do you have any extra administrative interfaces, undocumented debug modes, universally known administrative passwords, or a special back-door admin tool? Ask the vendor about undocumented keystrokes for its tools.

Automate security administration, and try to make changes consistently. Make sure to synchronize the security state in a distributed application and propagate state securely.

Do not let security audit logs yoyo in size. Offload logs regularly, and clean up logs incrementally. Never wipe the last weeks' worth of logs, even if backed up. You never know when you might need them. Avoid ambiguity in your log files. Add enough detail to each entry to specifically link the entry to some transaction without referring to too much context from the surrounding text. Logs can be (and are) hacked. Avoid breaking logs at strange places. Look for logical places that enable you to break the log file into meaningful sets of transactions. Avoid distributing security logs over too many machines. Interleaving multiple logs for analysis is much harder. Look into tools for analysis of merged logs.

Your wallet is a good place to keep passwords. Your screen is not. It is unlikely that you will be hacked and mugged by the same person on the same day, but it is exceedingly

all variants of a theme, cracking one will reveal the rest.

Always authenticate on opening a session and budget for performance hits when sessions start or end. Within a session, maintain and verify the validity of the session for all transactions. Invalidate a session whenever credentials expire.

If you plan to use patterns, spend some time with someone who has actually implemented the ones in which you are interested. Do not stretch a design pattern until it breaks. Consider the assumptions under which the pattern was originally developed. Call the design pattern by its proper name if you can.

When testing, change one parameter at a time. Budget for training. Budget some more. Join the team at testing and deployment. Spend some time in the field to see the application running. Hire a tiger team to attack the system. Do not use inertia as a reason to promote insecurity. Remember that evolution is about the survival of the fittest, and when you see the need for special measures, recognize the fact and act on it. Improvise (or else die).

Implement security policy and guidelines uniformly and consistently or not at all. If examined close enough, all analogies fail. Beware of special effects. Do not ask for an exception unless you really need one.

Volunteer as a reviewer to help another team. You never know when you might need the favor returned. It is challenging and enjoyable work, and you might learn something new.

Finally, abandon any rules and guidelines of security architecture that clearly fail to serve the actual needs of your system's security. If your knowledge of the problem, its constraints, and its unique architectural needs contradict any guideline, assume that you have found a specific instance where the general rule fails to apply to you. As with all decisions in life, common sense comes first.

Glossary of Acronyms

ABI	Application Binary Interface
ACE	Access Control Entry
ACL	Access Control List
ACM	Association of Computing Machinery
AES	Advanced Encryption Standard
AIX	IBM Unix flavor
ANSI	American National Standards Institute
API	Application Programming Interface
ARP	Address Resolution Protocol
ASN1	Abstract Syntax Notation 1
ASP	Active Server Pages
BER	Basic Encoding Rules
CBC	Cipher Block Chaining
CDPD	Cellular Digital Packet Data
CDS	Cell Directory Service
CFB	Cipher Feedback Block
CFF	Cumulative Failure Function
CGI	Common Gateway Interface
CIFS	Common Internet File System

COM+	Common Object Model Plus
CORBA	Common Object Request Broker Architecture
COTS	Common (or Commercial) Off the Shelf
CPS	Certificate Practices Statement
CPU	Central Processing Unit
CRC	Cyclic Redundancy Check
CRL	Certificate Revocation List
CSF	Critical Success Factors
CSI	CORBA Security Interoperability
CSI	Computer Security Institute
DAP	Directory Access Protocol
DBA	Database Administrator
DBMS	Database Management System
DBOR	Database-of-Record
DCE	Distributed Computing Environment
DDL	Data Definition Language
DDOS	Distributed Denial of Service
DES	Data Encryption Standard
DFS	Distributed File Service
DHCP	Dynamic Host Configuration Protocol
DIB	Directory Information Base
DIT	Directory Information Tree
DML	Data Manipulation Language
DMZ	Demilitarized Zone
DNS	Domain Name Service
DNSSEC	Domain Name Service Security
DOI	Domain of Interpretation
DOM	Document Object Model
DRM	Digital Rights Management
DSA	Digital Signature Algorithm
DSA	Directory Service Agent
DSL	Digital Subscriber Line
DSS	Digital Signature Standard
DTD	Document Type Definition

DUA	Directory User Agents
ebXML	XML Standard for E-Business
ECB	Electronic Code Book
ECC	Elliptic Curve Cryptography
ECDH	Elliptic Curve Diffie-Hellman
ECDSA	Elliptic Curve Digital Signature Algorithm
EFF	Electronic Frontier Foundation
EJB	Enterprise Java Beans
ESP	Encapsulating Security Payload
FDDI	Fiber Distributed Data Interface
FIPS	Federal Information Processing Standards
FMS	Fault Management System
FRF	Failure Rate Function
FSM	Finite State Machine
FTP	File Transfer Protocol
GAAP	Generally Accepted Accounting Principles
GID	Group ID
GIGO	Garbage In Garbage Out
GIOP	General Inter-ORB Operability Protocol
GPS	Global Positioning System
GSS-API	Generic Security Services API
GUI	Graphical User Interface
HFS	HPUX File System
HGP	Human Genome Project
HMAC	Keyed Hash Message Authentication Code
HPP	Homogeneous Poisson Processes
HTML	Hypertext Markup Language
HTTP	Hypertext Transfer Protocol
HTTPS	Hypertext Transfer Protocol over SSL
ICMP	Internet Control Message Protocol
IDL	Interface Definition Language
IDS	Intrusion Detection System
IETF	Internet Engineering Task Force
IFS	Input Field Separator

IIS	Microsoft Internet Information Server
IKE	Internet Key Exchange
IOR	Interoperable Object Reference
IP	Internet Protocol
IPC	Inter-process Communication
IPSec	Internet Protocol Security Standard
IRC	Internet Relay Chat
IRR	Internal Rate of Return
ISO	International Organization for Standardization
ISP	Internet Service Provider
ITUT	International Telecommunications Union
JAAS	Java Authentication and Authorization Service
JCE	Java Cryptography Extension
JDBC	Java Database Connectivity
JFS	Journaling File System
JSP	Java Server Pages
JSSE	Java Secure Socket Extension
JVM	Java Virtual Machine
KDC	Kerberos Key Distribution Center
LAN	Local Area Network
LDAP	Lightweight Directory Access Protocol
LSA	Local Services Authority
MAC	Message Authentication Codes
MIME	Multipurpose Internet Mail Extensions
MTBF	Mean Time Between Failures
MTTR	Mean Time to Recover
NAT	Network Address Translation
NFS	Network File Systems
NIC	Network Interface Card
NID	Network Intrusion Detection
NIS	Network Information Service
NIS+	Network Information Service Plus
NIST	National Institute of Standards and Technology
NNTP	Network News Transfer Protocol

NOS	Network Operating System
NPER	Number of Periods
NPV	Net Present Value
NSA	National Security Agency
NTLM	NT LAN Manager
NTP	Network Time Protocol
OCSP	Online Certificate Status Protocol
OFB	Output feedback mode
OMG	Object Management Group
ORB	Object Request Broker
OSF	Open Software Foundation
OSI	Open Systems Interconnection
PAC	Privilege Access Certificate
PAM	Pluggable Authentication Modules
PBX	Public Branch Exchange
PDA	Personal Digital Assistant
PDC	Primary Domain Controller
PGP	Pretty Good Privacy
PHP	Hypertext Preprocessor
PKCS	Public Key Cryptographic Standard
PKI	Public Key Infrastructure
PKIX	Public Key Infrastructure (X.509)
PRN	Pseudo-Random Number
PROM	Programmable Read Only Memory
PTGT	Privilege Ticket Granting Ticket
PTSN	Public Telephone Switched Network
QOS	Quality of Service
RACF	Resource Access Control Facility
RADIUS	Remote Authentication Dial-In User Service
RAID	Redundant Array of Inexpensive Disks
RBAC	Role-Based Access Control
RDN	Relative Distinguished Name
RFC	Request for Comments
RM-ODP	Reference Model for Open Distributed Processing

RSA	Rivest Shamir Adleman
S/MIME	Secure MIME
SADB	Security Associations Database
SAF	System Authorization Facility
SAM	System Accounts Manager
SAML	Security Assertions Markup Language
SANS	System Administration, Networking, and Security Institute
SAX	Simple API for XML
SCSI	Small Computer Systems Interface
SDN	Software Defined Network
SEAM	Solaris Enterprise Authentication Mechanism
SECIOP	Secure Inter-ORB Protocol
SEI	Software Engineering Institute
SET	Secure Electronic Transactions
SETI	Search for Extraterrestrial Intelligence
SHA-1	Secure Hash Algorithm
SLA	Service Level Agreement
SMB	Server Message Block
SMTP	Simple Mail Transfer Protocol
SOC	Security Operations Center
SPD	Security Policy Database
SPI	Security Parameter Index
SQL	Structured Query Language
SRE	Software Reliability Engineering
SSH	Secure Shell
SSL	Secure Sockets Layer
SSO	Single Sign-on
SSSO	Secure Single Sign-on
TCP	Transmission Control Protocol
TGT	Ticket Granting Ticket
TLA	Three-Letter Acronym
TLS	Transport Layer Security
TMN	Telecommunications Management Network
TOCTTOU	Time of Check to Time of Use attacks

UDP	Uniform Datagram Protocol
UML	Unified Modeling Language
URI	Uniform Resource Identifier
URL	Uniform Resource Locator
UTC	Coordinated Universal Time
VPD	Virtual Private Database
VPN	Virtual Private Network
VVOS	Virtual Vault Operating System
WACC	Weighted Average Cost of Capital
WAN	Wide Area Network
WAP	Wireless Application Protocol
WEP	Wired Equivalent Privacy
WTLS	Wireless TLS
WWW	World Wide Web
XHTML	XML standard for HTML
XKMS	XML Key Management Service
XML	Extensible Markup Language
XML-DSig	XML Standard for Digital Signatures
XML-Enc	XML Standard for Encryption
XOR	Exclusive OR
XQL	XML Query Language
XSL	Extensible Stylesheet Language
XSLT	Extensible Style Language for Transformations

Bibliography

[Ale95] AlephOne. *Smashing the Stack for Fun and Profit*, Phrack Online, Volume 7, Issue 49, File 14 of 16, www.fc.net/phrack, November 1996.

[Alex96] Alexander, S. "The long arm of the law." *Computerworld*, v30 n19, pp. 99–100, May 6, 1996.

[AN94] Abadi, M. and Needham, R. *Prudent Engineering Practice for Cryptographic Protocols*, Proceedings of the 1994 Computer Society Symposium on Research in Security and Privacy, pp. 122–136, 1994.

[AN95] Anderson, R. J. and Needham, R. M. *Robustness Principles for Public Key Protocols*, Crypto 95, pp. 236–247, 1995.

[AN96a] Abadi, M. and Needham, R. *Prudent Engineering Practice for Cryptographic Protocols*, IEEE Transactions on Software Engineering, v22 n1, pp. 6–15, January 1996.

[AN96b] Anderson, R. J. and Needham, R. M. "Programming Satan's Computer." Computer Science Today—Recent Trends and Developments, Springer LNCS v1000, pp. 426–441, 1995.

[And01] Anderson, R. J. *Security Engineering: A Guide to Building Dependable Distributed Systems*, John Wiley & Sons, ISBN 0471389226, January 2001.

[Ant96a] Anthes, G. H. "Firms seek legal weapons against info thieves." *Computerworld*, v30 n22, pp. 72(1), May 27, 1996.

[Ant96b] Anthes, G. H. "Hack attack: cyber-thieves siphon millions from U.S. firms." *Computerworld*, v30 n16, pp. 81, April 15, 1996.

0070025606, February 1993.

[BBB00] Bachman, F., Bass, L., Buhman, C., Comella-Dorda, S., Long, F., Robert, J., Seacord, R., and Wallnau, K. *Volume II: Technical Concepts of Component-Based Software Engineering*, Software Engineering Institute Technical Report, CMU/SEI–2000-TR-008, May 2000.

[BBC00] Bachman, F., Bass, L., Carriere, J., Clements, P., Garlan, D., Ivers, J., Nord, R., and Little, R. *Software Architecture Documentation in Practice: Documenting Architectural Layers*, Software Engineering Institute Special Report, CMU/SEI–2000-SR-004, March 2000.

[BC00] Bovet, D. P. and Cesati, M. *Understanding the LINUX Kernel: From I/O Ports to Process Management*, O'Reilly & Associates, ISBN 0596000022 , November 2000.

[BCK96] Bellare, M., Canetti, R., and Krawczyk, H. *Keying Hash Functions for Message Authentication*, Advances in Cryptology, Crypto '96 Proceedings, LNCS Vol. 1109, Springer-Verlag, 1996.

[BCK98] Bass, L., Clements, P., and Kazman, R. *Software Architecture in Practice (The SEI Series)*, Addison-Wesley Publishing Co., ISBN 0201199300, January 1998.

[BCR97] BCR Editors, "Worried about security? Yes. Taken action? No." *Business Communications Review*, v27 n1, p. 60, January 1997.

[Bel96] Bellovin, S. *Problem Areas for the IP Security Protocols*, Proceedings of the Sixth USENIX Unix Security Symposium, July 1996.

[Ber98] Bernstein, P. L. *Against the Gods: The Remarkable Story of Risk*, John Wiley & Sons, ISBN 0471295639, August 1998.

[Berg97] Berg, A. "Survey reveals users' firewall concerns." National Computer Security Association study, *LAN Times*, v14 n10, p. 33(2), May 12, 1997.

[Bish87] Bishop, M. "How to Write a SUID Program." *;login* (USENIX newsletter), January 1987.

[BPP69] Beard, R. E., Pentikainen, T., and Pesonen, E. *Risk theory*, Methuen's Monographs on Applied Probability and Statistics, Willmer Brothers Ltd., ASIN: 0416128505, 1969.

[BS01] Barrett, J. and Silverman, R. *SSH, The Secure Shell: The Definitive Guide*, O'Reilly & Associates, ISBN 0596000111, February 15, 2001.

[BST00] Baratloo, A., Singh, N., and Tsai, T. *Transparent Run-Time Defense Against Stack Smashing Attacks*, Proceedings of the 9th USENIX Security Conference, 2000.

[CB94] Cheswick, W. R. and Bellovin, S. M. *Firewalls and Internet Security: Repelling the Wily Hacker (The Addison-Wesley Professional Computing Series)*, Addison-Wesley Publishing Co., ISBN 0201633574, January 1994.

Riders, ISBN 0735700456, 1999.

[CFMS94] Castano, S., Fugini, M., Martella, G., and Samarati, P. *Database Security*, Addison-Wesley Publishing Co., ISBN 0201593750, 1994.

[Com95] Comer, D. E. *Internetworking with TCP/IP Vol. I: Principles, Protocols, and Architecture*, Prentice Hall, ISBN 0132169878, March 1995.

[Con01] Conry-Murray, A. "Kerberos, Computer Security's Hellhound," *Network Magazine*, 16(7), pp. 40–45, July 2001.

[Cop95] Coplien, J. O. "The Column without a Name: Software Development as a Science," *Art and Engineering*, C++ Report, pp. 14–19, July/August 1995.

[Cop97] Coplien, J. O. *Idioms and Patterns as Architectural Literature*, IEEE Software, pp. 36–42, January 1997.

[CPM98] Cowan, C., Pu, C., Maier, D., Hinton, H., Walpole, J., Bakke, P., Beattie, S., Grier, A., Wagle, P., and Zhang, Q. *StackGuard: Automatic Adaptive Detection and Prevention of Buffer-Overflow Attacks*, Proceedings of the 7th USENIX Security Conference, 1998.

[Cur96] Curry, D. A. *Unix Systems Programming for SVR4*, O'Reilly and Associates, ISBN 156592–163–1, July 1996.

[Dee96] Deering, A. "Protecting against cyberfraud," *Risk Management*, v43 n2, pp.12, December 1996.

[Den82] Denning, D. E. R. *Cryptography and Data Security*, Addison-Wesley Publishing Co., ISBN 0201101505, June 1982.

[Den98] Denning, D. E. *Information Warfare and Security*, Addison-Wesley Publishing Co., ISBN 0201433036, December 1998.

[Denn90] Denning, P. J. (ed.), *Computers under Attack: Intruders, Worms, and Viruses*, ACM Press, ISBN 0201530678, 1990.

[DH99] Doraswamy, N. and Harkins, D. *IPSec: The New Security Standard for the Internet, Intranets, and Virtual Private Networks*, Prentice Hall PTR, ISBN 0130118982, August 1999.

[DKW00] Dikel, D. M., Kane, D., and Wilson, J. R. *Software Architecture: Organizational Principles and Patterns*, Prentice Hall PTR, ISBN 0130290327, December 2000.

[DL96] Dam, K. W. and Lin, H. S. (Eds.). *Cryptography's Role in Securing the Information Society*, National Academy Press, ISBN 0309054753, October 1996.

[EDM98] Emam, K. E., Drouin, J., and Melo, W. (Eds.). *SPICE: The Theory and Practice of Software Process Improvement*, IEEE Computer Society Press, ISBN 0818677988, January 1998.

information security hazards." *Computers & Security*, v14 n8, pp. 707–717, 1995.

[FFW98] Feghhi, J., Feghhi, J., and Williams, P. *Digital Certificates: Applied Internet Security*, Addison-Wesley Publishing Co., ISBN 0201309807, October 1998.

[FK92] Ferraiolo, D. and Kuhn, R. " Role-Based Access Control." 15th National Computer Security Conference, pp. 554–563, 1992.

[FMS01] Fluhrer, S., Mantin, I., and Shamir, A. *Weaknesses in the Key Scheduling Algorithm of RC4*, to be presented at the Eighth Annual Workshop on Selected Areas in Cryptography (August 2001).

[FMS97] *FM3000 class notes, Mini MBA in Finance*, AT&T School of Business and Wharton, May-June 1997.

[Fry00] Frykholm, N. *Countermeasures against Buffer Overflow Attacks*, RSA Labs Technical Note, www.rsa.com/rsalabs/technotes/buffer/buffer_overflow.html, November 2000.

[GACB95] Gacek, C., Abd-Allah, A., Clark, B., and Boehm, B. *On the Definition of Software System Architecture (Center for Software Engineering, USC)*, ICSE 17 Software Architecture Workshop, April 1995.

[Gan97] Gantz, J. "A city of felons at T1 speeds." *Computerworld*, v31 n7, pp. 33, February 17, 1997.

[GAO95] Garlan, D., Allen, R., and Ockerbloom, J. *Architectural Mismatch*, Proceedings of the 17th International Conference on Software Engineering, April 1995.

[GHJV95] Gamma, E., Helm, R., Johnson, R., and Vlissides, J. *Design Patterns*, Addison-Wesley Publishing Co., ISBN 0201633612, January 1995.

[GO98] Ghosh, A. K. and O'Connor, T. *Analyzing Programs for Vulnerabilities to Buffer Overrun Attacks*, www.rstcorp.com, proceedings of the National Information Systems Security Conference, October 6–9, 1998.

[Gol01] Goldreich, O. *Foundations of Cryptography: Basic Tools*, Cambridge University Press, ISBN 0521791723, August 2001.

[GR01] Garfinkel, S. and Russell, D. *Database Nation: The Death of Privacy in the 21st Century*, O'Reilly & Associates, ISBN 0596001053, January 2001.

[GS96] Shaw, M. and Garlan, D. *Software Architecture: Perspectives on an Emerging Discipline*, Prentice Hall, ISBN 0131829572, April 1996.

[GS96a] Garfinkel, S. and Spafford, E. *Practical Unix and Internet Security*, O'Reilly & Associates, ISBN 1565921488, April 1996.

[GS97] Garfinkel, S. and Spafford, E. *Web Security & Commerce (O'Reilly Nutshell)*, O'Reilly & Associates, ISBN 1565922697, June 1997.

Environment for Untrusted Helper Applications, 6th USENIX Security Conference, pp. 1–13, 1996.

[Hai98] Haimes, Y. Y. *Risk Modeling, Assessment, and Management (Wiley Series in Systems Engineering)*, Wiley-InterScience, ISBN 0471240052, August 1998.

[Hal00] Hall, M. *Core Java Servlets and JavaServer Pages*, Sun Microsystems Press, Prentice Hall PTR, ISBN 013089340, May 2000.

[Hal94] Haller, N. *The S/KEY One-Time Password System*, Proceedings of the First Symposium on Network and Distributed System Security, 1994.

[HBH95] Hutt, A. E., Bosworth, S., and Hoyt, D. B. (Eds.). *Computer Security Handbook*, 3rd Edition. Published by John Wiley & Sons, ISBN 0471118540, August 1995.

[HNS99] Hofmeister, C., Nord, R., and Soni, D. *Applied Software Architecture, The Addison-Wesley Object Technology Series)*, Addison-Wesley Publishing Co., ISBN 0201325713, October 1999.

[How95] Howes, T. A. *The Lightweight Directory Access Protocol: X.500 Lite*, University of Michigan, CITI Technical Report 95–8, July 1995.

[HP01] *Hewlett-Packard Technical Documentation*, http://docs.hp.com.

[Hun92] Hunt, T. F. (Ed.). *Research Directions in Database Security*, Springer-Verlag, ISBN 0387977368, May 1992.

[IBM00a] IBM International Technical Support, *OS/390 Security Server Documentation*, IBM Corporation, www.ibm.com, August 2000.

[IBM00b] Best, S. *Journaling File System Overview*, IBM Open Source Developer Works, Linux Technology Center, www–106.ibm.com/developerworks/, January 2000.

[Ico97] Icove, D. J. *Collaring the cybercrook: An investigator's view*, IEEE Spectrum, v34 n6, pp. 31–36, June 1997.

[Isen97] Isenberg, D. "Rise of the Stupid Network." *Computer Telephony*, pp. 16–26, August 1997.

[Isen98] Isenberg, D. "The Dawn of the Stupid Network." *ACM Networker 2.1*, pp. 24–31, February/March 1998.

[ISO96] International Standards Organization, *Reference Model for Open Distributed Processing*, IS 10746–1, ITUT Recommendation X.901, 1996.

[IWEY01] Information Week/Ernst & Young, *Security Survey 2001*, www.ey.com.

[IWEY96] Information Week/Ernst & Young *Security Survey IV*, www.ey.com.

[Jac00] Jacobson, I. and Bylund, S. *The Road to the Unified Software Development Process (Sigs Reference Library)*, Cambridge Univ Pr (Trd), ISBN 0521787742, August 2000.

Development Process (The Addison-Wesley Object Technology Series), Addison-Wesley Publishing Co., ISBN 0201571692, January 1999.

[Jon94] Jones, E. B. *Finance for the non-financial manager*, Pitman, ISBN 0273360507, 1994.

[JRvL98] Jazayeri, M., Ran, A., Van Der Linden, F., and Van Der Linden, P. *Software Architecture for Product Families: Principles and Practice*, Addison-Wesley Publishing Co., ISBN 0201699672, January 2000.

[Kahn96] Kahn, D. *The Codebreakers; The Comprehensive History of Secret Communication from Ancient Times to the Internet*, Revised edition, Scriber, New York, ISBN 0684831309, December 1996.

[Knu92] Knuth, D. E. *Literate Programming (Center for the Study of Language and Information - Lecture Notes, No 27)*, CSLI Publications, ISBN 0521073806, May 1992.

[Kob94] Koblitz, N. I. *A Course in Number Theory and Cryptography*, 2nd Edition, Graduate Texts in Mathematics, No 114, Springer-Verlag, ISBN 0387942939, September 1994.

[KP99] Kernighan, B. W. and Pike, R. *The Practice of Programming (Addison-Wesley Professional Computing Series)*, Addison-Wesley Publishing Co., ISBN 020161586X, February 1999.

[KPS95] Kaufman, C., Perlman, R., and Speciner, M. *Network Security: Private Communication in a Public World*, Prentice Hall PTR, ISBN 0130614661, March 1995.

[Kru95] Kruchten, P. *Architectural Blueprints—The "4+1" View Model of Software Architecture*, IEEE Software 12(6), pp. 42–50, November 1995.

[Lam73] Lampson, B. *A Note on the Confinement Problem*, CACM, v16 n10, pp. 613–615, October 1973.

[Lam81] Lamport, L. *Password Authentication with Insecure Communication*, Communications of the ACM, 24(11), pp. 770–771, November 1981.

[Lav83] Lavenberg, S. S. *Computer Performance Modeling Handbook*, Academic Press, 1983.

[Liv97] Livingstone, J. L. (Ed.). *The Portable MBA in Finance and Accounting*, 2nd Edition, John Wiley & Sons, ISBN 047118425X, August 1997.

[Los99] Loshin, P. *Big Book of IPSec RFCs*, Morgan Kaufman, ISBN 0124558399, November 1999.

[Lyu96] Lyu, M. *Handbook of Software Reliability Engineering*, McGraw-Hill, ISBN 0070394008, 1996.

Security Conference, 1999.

[MC76] Mehr, R. I. and Cammack, E. *Principles of Insurance*, Sixth Edition, Richard Irwin Inc., ASIN: 0256018332, 1976.

[McCa96] McCarthy, J. L. "Cyberswindle!" *Chief Executive*, n113, pp. 38–41, May 1996.

[McF97] McGraw, G. and Felten, E. *Java Security: Hostile Applets, Holes & Antidotes*, John Wiley & Sons, ISBN 047117842X, 1997.

[McL00] McLaughlin, B. *Java and XML*, O'Reilly and Associates, ISBN 0596000162, June 2000.

[MFS90] Miller, B. P., Fredrikson, L., and So, B. *An Empirical Study of the Reliability of Unix Utilities*, CACM 33 (12), pp. 32–44, December 1990.

[MHAC01] Mishra, P., Hallam-Baker, P., and Ahmed, Z. et. al. *Security Services Markup Language, Draft Version 0.8a*, www.netegrity.com, January 2001.

[Mic01] Microsoft Technical Documentation, *What's New in Security for Windows XP Professional and Windows XP Home Edition*, Microsoft Corporation, www.microsoft.com/technet, July 2001.

[Mill00] Miller, B. P., Koski, D., Lee, C. P., Maganty, V., Murthy, R., Natarajan, A., and Steidl, J. *Fuzz Revisited: A Re-examination of the Reliability of Unix Utilities and Services*, CSD Technical Report, University of Wisconsin, www.cs.wisc.edu/~bart/ fuzz/fuzz.html, 1995.

[MM00] Malveau, R. C. and Mowbray, T. *Software Architect Bootcamp*, Prentice Hall PTR, ISBN 0130274070, October 2000.

[MOV96] Menezes, A. J., Van Oorschot, P. C., and Vanstone, S. A. (Ed.). *Handbook of Applied Cryptography (CRC Press Series on Discrete Mathematics and Its Applications)*, CRC Press, ISBN 0849385237, October 1996.

[MOV96] Menezes, A. J., Van Oorschot, P. C., and Vanstone, S. *Handbook of Applied Cryptography*, CRC Press Series on Discrete Mathematics and Its Applications, ISBN 0849385237, October 1, 1996.

[MS00] Marcus, E. and Stern, H. *Blueprints for High Availability: Designing Resilient Distributed Systems*, John Wiley & Sons, ISBN 0471356018, January 2000.

[MS01] *Sun Microsystems Technical Documentation*, www.microsoft.com .technet/.

[Nas99] Nash, A. *Public Key Infrastructures*, RSA Data Security Conference, 1999.

[Nee01] Needham, P. *Oracle Label Security—Controlling Access to Data*, Oracle White Paper, http://otn.oracle.com, January 2001.

Sharing Security Services on the Internet, Netegrity Corporation, www.netegrity.com, November 2000.

[Net01] Netegrity White Paper, *Security Assertions Markup Language (SAML)*, Netegrity Corporation, www.netegrity.com, May 2001.

[News90] News releases on the AT&T Network Service Disruption of January 15, 1990.

[News91] News releases on the AT&T Network Service Disruption of September 21, 1991.

[NIST00] NIST CIO Council report, www.nist.gov, *Federal Information Technology Security Assessment Framework*, National Institute of Standards and Technology, Computer Security Division, Systems and Network Security Group, November 2000.

[NN00] Northcutt, S. and Novak, J. *Network Intrusion Detection: An Analyst's Handbook*, 2nd Edition, New Riders Publishing, ISBN 0735710082, September 2000.

[Noo00] Noordergraaf, A. *Solaris Operating Environment Minimization for Security*, Sun Microsystems Enterprise Engineering, www.sun.com /blueprints, November 2000.

[Nor01] Norberg, S. *Securing Windows NT/2000 Servers*, O'Reilly and Associates, ISBN 1565927680, January 2001.

[NW00] Noordergraaf, A. and Watson, K. *Solaris Operating Environment Security*, Sun Microsystems Enterprise Engineering, www.sun.com/blueprints, April 2001.

[Oaks01] Oaks, S. *Java Security*, 2nd Edition, O'Reilly & Associates, ISBN 0596001576, June 2001.

[Oaks98] Oaks, S. *Java Security*, O'Reilly & Associates, ISBN 1565924037, 1998.

[OMG01a] Object Management Group, *CORBA Security Specification, version 1.7*, www.omg.org, March 2001.

[OMG01b] Object Management Group, *Resource Access Decision Facility Specification*, version 1.0, www.omg.org, April 2001.

[Orb01] *OrbixSSL C++ Programmer's and Administrator's Guide*, www.iona.com/docs/, Iona Technologies, 2001.

[OTN01] Oracle Technical Network Resources, *Oracle Label Security*, http://technet.oracle.com/deploy/security/ols/listing.htm, 2001.

[OTN99] Oracle Technical Network Resources, *The Virtual Private Database in Oracle8i*, Oracle Technical White Paper, http://otn.oracle.com, November 1999.

[PC00] Perrone, P. J. and Chaganti, V. S. R. R. *Building Java Enterprise Systems with J2EE*, SAMS Publishing, 2000.

Maturity Model, Version 1.1, IEEE Software, Vol. 10, No. 4, pp.18–27, July 1993.

[Per00] Perens, B. *Are buffer-overflow security exploits really Intel and OS makers fault?*, message posting, www.technocrat.net, July 2000.

[Perl99] Perlman, R. *Interconnections: Bridges, Routers, Switches, and Internetworking Protocols*, Second Edition, Addison Wesley Professional Computing Series, Addison-Wesley Publishing Co., ISBN 0201634481, October 1999.

[PLOP3] Martin, R. C., Riehle, D., and Buschmann, F. (Eds.). *Pattern Languages of Program Design 3*, Addison-Wesley Publishers, ISBN 0201310112, October 1997.

[POSA1] Buschmann, F., Meunier, R., Rohnert, H., Sommerlad, P., and Stal, M. *Pattern Oriented Software Architecture—A System of Patterns*, John Wiley & Sons, 1996.

[POSA2] Schmidt, D., Stal, M., Rohnert, H., and Buschmann, F. *Pattern-Oriented Software Architecture, Volume 2, Patterns for Concurrent and Networked Objects*, John Wiley & Sons, ISBN 0471606952, September 2000.

[PW92] Perry, D. E. and Wolf, A. L. *Foundations for the Study of Software Architecture*, Software Engineering Notes, SIGSOFT, 17(4), pp. 40–52, 1992.

[Rai68] Raiffa, H. *Decision Analysis: Introductory Letters on Choices under Uncertainty*, Addison-Wesley Publishers, Menlo Park, CA, 1968.

[Ray01] Ray, E. T. *Learning XML*, O'Reilly & Associates, ISBN 0596000464, February 2001.

[Ray95] Raymond, E. S. *The Cathedral and the Bazaar*, www.tuxedo.org/~esr/writings/cathedral-bazaar/, Revision 1.51, 2000.

[RFC1309] Reynolds, J. and Heker, S. *RFC 1309: Technical Overview of Directory Services Using the X.500 Protocol*, March 1992.

[RFC1320] Rivest, R. *RFC 1320 The MD4 Message-Digest Algorithm*, www.ietf.org/rfc/rfc1320.txt, April 1992.

[RFC1321] Rivest, R. *RFC 1321 The MD5 Message-Digest Algorithm*, www.ietf.org/rfc/rfc1321.txt, April 1992.

[RFC1828] Metzger, P. and Simpson, W. *RFC 1828 IP Authentication using Keyed MD5*, www.ietf.org/rfc/rfc1828.txt, August 1995.

[RFC1829] Karn, P., Metzger, P., and Simpson, W. *RFC 1829 The ESP DES-CBC Transform*, www.ietf.org/rfc/rfc1829.txt, August 1995.

[RFC2040] Baldwin, R. and Rivest, R. *RFC 2040 The RC5, RC5-CBC, RC5-CBC-Pad, and RC5-CTS Algorithms*, www.ietf.org/rfc/rfc2040.txt, October 1996.

with Replay Prevention, www.ietf.org/rfc/rfc2085.txt, February 1997.

[RFC2104] Krawczyk, H., Bellare, M., and Canetti, R. *RFC 2104 HMAC: Keyed-Hashing for Message Authentication*, www.ietf.org/rfc/ rfc2104.txt, February 1997.

[RFC2144] Adams, C. *RFC 2144 The CAST–128 Encryption Algorithm*, www.ietf.org/rfc/rfc2144.txt, May 1997.

[RFC2251] Wahl, M., Howes, T., and Kille, S. *RFC 2251 Lightweight Directory Access Protocol (v3)*, www.ietf.org/rfc/rfc2251.txt, December 1997.

[RFC2401] Kent, S. and Atkinson, R. *RFC 2401 Security Architecture for the Internet Protocol*, www.ietf.org/rfc/rfc2401.txt, November 1998.

[RFC2402] Kent, S. and Atkinson, R. *RFC 2402 IP Authentication Header*, www.ietf.org/rfc/rfc2402.txt, November 1998.

[RFC2403] Madson, C. and Glenn, R. *RFC 2403 The Use of HMAC-MD5–96 within ESP and AH*, www.ietf.org/rfc/rfc2403.txt, November 1998.

[RFC2404] Madson, C. and Glenn, R. *RFC 2404 The Use of HMAC-SHA–1–96 within ESP and AH*, www.ietf.org/rfc/rfc2404.txt, November 1998.

[RFC2405] Madson, C. and Doraswamy, N. *RFC 2405 The ESP DES-CBC Cipher Algorithm With Explicit IV*, www.ietf.org/rfc/rfc2405.txt, November 1998.

[RFC2406] Kent, S. and Atkinson, R. *RFC 2406 IP Encapsulating Security Payload (ESP)*, www.ietf.org/rfc/rfc2406.txt, November 1998.

[RFC2407] Piper, D. *RFC 2407 The Internet IP Security Domain of Interpretation for ISAKMP*, www.ietf.org/rfc/rfc2407.txt, November 1998.

[RFC2408] Maughan, D., Schertler, M., Schneider, M., and Turner, J. *RFC 2408 Internet Security Association and Key Management Protocol (ISAKMP)*, www.ietf.org/rfc/rfc2408.txt, November 1998.

[RFC2409] Harkins, D. and Carrel, D. *RFC 2409 The Internet Key Exchange (IKE)*, www.ietf.org/rfc/rfc2409.txt, November 1998.

[RFC2411] Thayer, R., Doraswamy, N., and Glenn, R. *RFC 2411 IP Security Document Roadmap*, www.ietf.org/rfc/rfc2411.txt, November 1998.

[RFC2412] Orman, H. *RFC 2412 The OAKLEY Key Determination Protocol*, www.ietf.org/rfc/rfc2412.txt, November 1998.

[RFC2451] Pereira, R. and Adams, R. *RFC 2451 The ESP CBC-Mode Cipher Algorithms*, www.ietf.org/rfc/rfc2451.txt, November 1998.

[RFC2807] Reagle, J. *RFC 2807 XML Signature Requirements*, www.ietf.org /rfc/rfc2807.txt, July 2000.

[RGR97] Rubin, A., Geer, D., and Ranum, M. *Web Security Sourcebook*, John Wiley & Sons, ISBN 047118148X, 1997.

Institute Technical Report, CMU/SEI–98-TR-017, November 1998.

[Rub01] Rubin, A. V. *White-Hat Security Arsenal: Tackling the Threats*, Addison-Wesley Publishers, ISBN 0201711141, June 2001.

[Sal96] Salomaa, A. *Public-Key Cryptography*, 2nd Edition, Texts in Theoretical Computer Science, Springer-Verlag ISBN 3540613560, December 1996.

[SC97] Schwartz, R. and Christiansen, T. *Learning Perl*, O'Reilly & Associates, ISBN 1565922840, July 1997.

[Sch00] Schneier, B. *Secrets and Lies: Digital Security in a Networked World*, John Wiley & Sons, ISBN 0471253111, August 2000.

[Sch95] Schneier, B. *Applied Cryptography: Protocols, Algorithms, and Source Code in C*, 2nd Edition, John Wiley & Sons, ISBN 0471117099, October 1995.

[Sch95] Schneier, B. *Applied Cryptography: Protocols, Algorithms, and Source Code in C*, 2nd Edition, John Wiley & Sons, ISBN 0471117099, 1995.

[SFK00] Sandhu, R., Ferraiolo, D., and Kuhn, R. "The NIST Model for Role-Based Access Control: Towards a Unified Standard," in Proceedings of the 5th ACM Workshop on Role-Based Access Control, pp. 47–63, July 2000.

[SG98] Silberschatz, A. and Galvin, P. *Operating System Concepts*, 5th Edition, John Wiley & Sons, ISBN 0471364142, January 1998.

[Sha48] Shannon, C.E. "A Mathematical Theory of Communication," in Bell Systems Technical Journal, v 27, pp. 379–423, 623–656, July and October, 1948.

[Sha49] Shannon, C.E. "Communication Theory of Secrecy Systems," in Bell Systems Technical Journal, v 28, pp. 656–715, 1949.

[Sibl97] Sibley, K. "The big theft scare: how safe is your site," *Computing Canada*, v23 n6, pp. 14, March 17, 1997.

[Sin99] Singh, S. *The Code Book: The Evolution of Secrecy from Mary, Queen of Scots to Quantum Cryptography*, Doubleday, ISBN 0385495315, September 1999.

[Sin99] Singh, S. *The Code Book*, Doubleday, Random House Inc., ISBN 0385495315, 1999.

[SIR01] Stubblefield, A., Ioannidis, J., and Rubin, A. D. *Using the Fluhrer, Mantin, and Shamir Attack to Break WEP*, AT&T Labs Technical Report TD–4ZCPZZ , August 6, 2001.

[SL96] Samar, V. and Lai, C. *Making Login Services Independent of Authentication Technologies*, 3rd ACM Conference on Computer and Communications Security, March 1996.

Edition, McGraw-Hill Professional Publishing, ISBN 0072127481, October 2000.

[Sol96] Van Solms, B. *Information Security—The Next Decade*, Chapman & Hall, ISBN 0412640201, December 1996.

[Sri98] Srinivasan, S. *Advanced Perl Programming*, O'Reilly & Associates, ISBN 1565922204, August 1997.

[SSL96] *SSL 3.0 Specification*, www.home.jp.netscape.com/eng/ssl3.

[Sta00] Stallings, W. *Operating Systems: Internals and Design Principles*, Prentice Hall, ISBN 0130319996, December 2000.

[Sun00] Sun Microsystems, *Java Servlet 2.3 Specification, Proposed Final Draft*, http://java.sun.com, October 2000.

[Sun01] *Sun Microsystems Technical Documentation*, http://docs.sun.com.

[Thom84] Thompson, K. *Reflections on Trusting Trust*, CACM, 27(8), pp.761–763, August 1984.

[TNSR94a] *Telecom and Network Security Reviews*, February 1994.

[TNSR94b] *Telecom and Network Security Reviews*, December 1994.

[TNSR95a] *Telecom and Network Security Reviews*, March 1995.

[TNSR95b] *Telecom and Network Security Reviews*, April 1995.

[TNSR96a] *Telecom and Network Security Reviews*, March 1996.

[TNSR96b] *Telecom and Network Security Reviews*, June 1996.

[TNSR97] *Telecom and Network Security Reviews*, April 1997.

[Ubo95] Ubois, J. *Auditing for security's sake*. Midrange Systems, v8 n14, p27, July 28, 1995.

[Uls95] Ulsch, M. *Cracking the security market*. Marketing Computers, v15n1, p20(2). January 1995.

[VFTOSM99] Dibona, C. (Ed.), Stone, M. (Ed.), and Ockman, S. (Ed.). *Open Sources: Voices from the Open Source Revolution (O'Reilly Open Source)*, O'Reilly & Associates, ISBN 1565925823, January 1999.

[Vio96] Violino, B. "The security facade." *Informationweek*, *n*602, pp. 36–48, October 21, 1996.

[Visi01] *Visibroker SSL Pack 3.3 Programmer's Guide*, Inprise Corporation, 2001.

[VMW01] Hallam-Baker, P. *XML Key Management Specification (XKMS)*, Versign, Microsoft, and webMethods Draft Version 1.1, www.verisign.com, January 2001.

[WBB96] Weston, J. F., Besley, S., and Brigham, E. F. *Essentials of Managerial Finance*, 11th Edition, Dryden Press, ISBN 0030101999, January 1996.

Edition, O'Reilly & Associates, ISBN 0596000278, July 2000.

[WCS96] Wall, L., Christiansen, T., and Schwartz, R. *Programming Perl*, 2nd Edition, O'Reilly & Associates, ISBN 1565921496, September 1996.

[Wil97] Williams, K. *Safeguarding companies from computer/software fraud*, Management Accounting, v78 n8, p.18, February 1997.

[WN00] Watson, K. and Noordergraaf, A. *Solaris Operating Environment Network Settings for Security*, Sun Microsystems Enterprise Engineering, www.sun.com/blueprints, December 2000.

[WV95] Wilder, C. and Violino, B. "Online theft." *InformationWeek*, n542, p30, August 28, 1995.

[You96] Young, J. "Spies like us." *Forbes*, ASAP Supplement, pp. 70–92, June 3, 1996.

[Zal96] Zalud, B. "Industrial security: Access, theft; but spying grows." *Security*, v33 n10, pp. 30–31, October 1996.

[Zal97] Zalud, B. "More spending, bigger budgets mark security-sensitive business." *Security*, v34 n1, pp. 9–18, January 1997.

[ZCC00] Zwicky, E. D., Cooper, S., and Chapman, D. B. *Building Internet Firewalls*, 2nd Edition, O'Reilly & Associates, ISBN 1565928717, January 2000.

Index

B

C

D

E

F

G

H

I

J

K

L

M

T

U

V

X

Y

Z